SENECA

Seneca stands apart from other philosophers of Greece and Rome not only for his interest in practical ethics but also for the beauty and liveliness of his writing. These twelve interrelated studies give detailed treatment to Seneca's philosophy and to his ambitions as a philosophical author. Part I concerns his position on the philosophical life and his Stoic-inspired analyses of action, emotion, voluntariness, and acts of kindness; Part II, his relation to Epicurean and Peripatetic thought; Part III, his views on the nature and management of anger, grief, and joy. Recalling Socrates's critique of philosophical writing in Plato's *Phaedrus*, Part IV treats Seneca's handling of the written word for the purposes of ethical therapy, as well as his use of humor, his ideas on prose style, and his claims for reading and writing as mechanisms of self-creation. Clear explanations and careful translations make the volume accessible to a wide range of readers.

MARGARET GRAVER is the Aaron Lawrence Professor of Classics at Dartmouth College. Her previous publications include *Stoicism and Emotion*; *Cicero on the Emotions: Tusculan Disputations 3 and 4*; and, with A. A. Long, a complete translation of Seneca's *Letters on Ethics*.

SENECA
The Literary Philosopher

MARGARET GRAVER

Dartmouth College

CAMBRIDGE
UNIVERSITY PRESS

Shaftesbury Road, Cambridge CB2 8EA, United Kingdom

One Liberty Plaza, 20th Floor, New York, NY 10006, USA

477 Williamstown Road, Port Melbourne, VIC 3207, Australia

314–321, 3rd Floor, Plot 3, Splendor Forum, Jasola District Centre, New Delhi – 110025, India

103 Penang Road, #05-06/07, Visioncrest Commercial, Singapore 238467

Cambridge University Press is part of Cambridge University Press & Assessment, a department of the University of Cambridge.

We share the University's mission to contribute to society through the pursuit of education, learning and research at the highest international levels of excellence.

www.cambridge.org
Information on this title: www.cambridge.org/9781107164048

DOI: 10.1017/9781316683125

© Margaret Graver 2023

This publication is in copyright. Subject to statutory exception and to the provisions of relevant collective licensing agreements, no reproduction of any part may take place without the written permission of Cambridge University Press & Assessment.

First published 2023

A catalogue record for this publication is available from the British Library.

A Cataloging-in-Publication data record for this book is available from the Library of Congress

ISBN 978-1-107-16404-8 Hardback

Cambridge University Press & Assessment has no responsibility for the persistence or accuracy of URLs for external or third-party internet websites referred to in this publication and does not guarantee that any content on such websites is, or will remain, accurate or appropriate.

Contents

List of Figures	*page* viii
Preface	ix
List of Texts, Translations, and Abbreviations	xi
Introduction: Seneca's Philosophical Literature	1

PART I RECREATING THE STOIC PAST

1 The Life of the Mind: Seneca and the *Contemplatio Veri*   17
    The Arguments of *On Leisure*   18
    On Leisure and the Stoic Tradition   21
    Tensions within the Argument   25
    Letters on Ethics: The Rule of Genre   27
    Representing the Philosophical Life   32

2 Action and Emotion: Seneca and the Stoic Tradition   40
    Thought, Belief, and Action   42
    Emotion and Eupathic Response   44
    The Theory of Action in Seneca   47
    Seneca on Emotion and Eupathic Response   51

3 The Treatise *On Benefits*: Real Kindness and Real Agency   57
    Defining a Benefit   59
    Enactment   62
    Persistence   65
    Intersubjectivity and Independence   68
    Specificity of Aim   73
    Autonomy and Freedom   75

PART II RIVAL TRADITIONS IN PHILOSOPHY

4 Seneca and Epicurus   87
   Extent and Provenance of Seneca's Knowledge   88
   Physics and Theology   91
   Ethics   93
   Leisure and Contemplation   97
   Maxims and Meditation   98
   Human Nature and the Tactics of the Therapist   102

5 Refuting the Peripatetics: Seneca and the School of Aristotle 109
   Explicit Citations   111
   Implicit References   115
   Letter 92 and Stobaean Doxography "C"   120
   Seneca's Version of the Tripartite Mind   124
   Distinctive Features of Seneca's Peripatetics   127

PART III MODELS OF EMOTIONAL EXPERIENCE

6 Seneca's Therapy for Anger   135
   Anger Theory in Book 1   136
   Book 2: The Causal History of Anger   140
   The Predicted Therapy   145
   The Therapies of Book 2   147
   The Preface to Book 3   150
   The Therapeutic Program of Book 3   153

7 The Weeping Wise: Stoic and Epicurean Consolations
   in Seneca's 99th Letter   160
   Mourning without Grief   161
   "A Necessity of Nature"   164
   Eupathic Tears?   167
   An Epicurean Expedient   172

8 Anatomies of Joy: Seneca and the *Gaudium* Tradition   176
   The Convergent Stoic Account   177
   Seneca and the Convergent Account   179
   Kinetic versus Static Joy   181
   Mutual Joys   184
   Joys as "Primary Goods"   186
   Seven Senecan Joys   188

PART IV THE SELF WITHIN THE TEXT

9   The Challenge of the *Phaedrus*: Therapeutic Writing and
    the *Letters on Ethics*   195
        Deficiencies of the Written Word   199
        Speaking across Time and Space   203
        Finding the Right Audience   207
        One Half of a Conversation   210
        Reader Emotions and Moral Progress   214

10 The Mouse, the Moneybox, and the Six-Footed
    Scurrying Solecism: Satire and Riddles in Seneca's
    Philosophy   222
        Seneca's Comic Style   223
        Tambourines and Riddle-Syllogisms   227
        The Pilferer in the Garden   231
        "Greek Shoes and Cloaks"   234

11 The Manhandling of Maecenas: Senecan Abstractions
    of Masculinity   239
        The Color of the *Ingenium*   241
        The Nature of the Masculine   246
        The Psychology of *Virtus*   252
        Peculiar Results   255
        Epilogue: Seneca and the *Malagma Moecharum*   259

12 Honeybee Reading and Self-Scripting   262
        Reading Like a Honeybee   263
        Techniques of Selfhood   265
        The Meaning of Study   269
        Nourishing a Talent, Creating a Self   274
        Postmortem Survival   277
        The Rule of Reason   280

Bibliography   284
Passages Treated   300
Index   303

Figures

1.1 The arguments of *On Leisure* — page 21
8.1 The joys of the wise — 189
9.1 Modes of discourse in Plato, *Phaedrus* 274b–277c and in Seneca, letter 38 — 212

Preface

Twenty-seven years of thinking and writing about Seneca have convinced me, finally, that I have something to say about this author that is best said in a book: that my smaller investigations have all along tended in the same direction, and that Seneca himself offers one version, not many, of a life devoted to philosophical reading, writing, and teaching. Hence this volume, which brings together twelve studies that were written at different times, but with a single objective: to see how this unquestionably literary talent perceived, reimagined, shaped, and was shaped by the philosophy of his time. Ten of the twelve have been published before:

- Chapter 1 under the title "Seneca and the *Contemplatio Veri*: *De Otio* and *Epistulae Morales*," in *Theoria, Praxis, and the Contemplative Life after Plato and Aristotle*, ed. Thomas Bénatouïl and Mauro Bonazzi (Brill, 2012), 73–98
- Chapter 2 in *Brill's Companion to Seneca*, ed. Gregor Damschen and Andreas Heil (Brill, 2014), 257–75
- Chapter 4 in the *Oxford Handbook of Epicureanism*, ed. Phillip Mitsis (Oxford University Press, 2020), 487–506
- Chapter 5 in a longer version titled "Seneca's Peripatetics: *Epistulae Morales* 92 and Stobaean Doxography 'C,'" in *Arius Didymus on Peripatetic Ethics: Text, Translation and Discussion*, ed. William Fortenbaugh (Routledge, 2018), 309–42
- Chapter 6 in French under the title "La Maîtrise de la Colère: Théorie et pratique stoïcienne," in *Lectures plurielles du "De ira" de Sénèque: Interprétations, contextes, enjeux*, ed. Valéry Laurand, Ermanno Malaspina, and François Prost (Walter de Gruyter, 2021), 150–72
- Chapter 7 in *Tears in the Graeco-Roman World*, ed. Thorsten Fögen (Walter de Gruyter, 2009), 235–52
- Chapter 8 in *Hope, Joy and Affection in the Classical World*, ed. Ruth R. Caston and Robert A. Kaster (Oxford University Press, 2016), 123–42
- Chapter 10 in *Laughter, Humor, and Comedy in Ancient Philosophy*, ed. Pierre Destrée and Franco V. Trivigno (Oxford University Press, 2019), 245–62

- Chapter 11 in *American Journal of Philology* 119.4 (1998), 607–32 (Johns Hopkins University Press)
- Chapter 12 under the title "Honeybee Reading and Self-Scripting: Seneca's Epistle 84," in *Seneca Philosophus*, ed. Jula Wildberger and Marcia Colish (Walter de Gruyter, 2014), 269–93

A portion of Chapter 3 was also published, under the title "Interiority and Freedom in Seneca's *De Beneficiis*," in *Self, Self-Fashioning and Individuality in Late Antiquity*, ed. Maren R. Niehoff and Joshua Levinson (Mohr Siebeck, 2020), 69–86. All the previously published studies have been revised for inclusion here, and I have done my best to incorporate at least some of the insights from much excellent work that has appeared in print since my earlier versions were written. I wish to thank the respective publishers for permission to reproduce these pieces in their current form, with particular thanks to the volume editors, anonymous peer reviewers, and copyeditors who lavished their expertise on my efforts.

In addition, I am very grateful to Dartmouth College, to the Sorbonne University in Paris, and to the University of Bordeaux–Montaigne for institutional support. Thanks are due to the following individuals, who provided comments and suggestions at various points either orally or in writing: Thomas Bénatouïl, Susanne Bobzien, Thorsten Fögen, Christopher Gill, William Fortenbaugh, Allison Glasscock, Brad Inwood, Bob Kaster, David Konstan, Valéry Laurand, Carlos Lévy, Tony Long, Ermanno Malaspina, Camille Marrou, Stefano Maso, Phillip Mitsis, Scott Smith, Jan Szaif, James Tatum, Franco Trivigno, and Jula Wildberger. Thanks are due also to several of my former students at Dartmouth College, in particular to Leah Alpert and Aaron Pellowski, each of whom discussed Seneca's philosophy with me for a period of several months, and Gabriela Sommer and Lynette Long, who aided me with the bibliographical work. Many others have contributed to this project at the various seminars, lectures, and conferences where ideas for these essays were first developed. Although I cannot name them all, I am very conscious of how much I owe to their patient attention and thoughtful questioning.

As always, my deepest gratitude belongs to Bruce Graver for his never-failing love and support. The dedication is to my children, Sarah Margaret Graver and Nicolas Robson Graver, who have grown to maturity along with this book.

nemo non olivetum alteri ponit

Texts, Translations, and Abbreviations

For the works of Seneca, I use the following abbreviations and English titles:

Anger	*On Anger* (*De ira*)
Ben.	*On Benefits* (*De beneficiis*)
Brevity	*On the Brevity of Life* (*De brevitate vitae*)
Clemency	*On Clemency* (*De clementia*)
Cons. Helv.	*Consolation to Helvia* (*De consolatione ad Helviam Matrem*)
Cons. Marc.	*Consolation to Marcia* (*De consolatione ad Marciam*)
Cons. Polyb.	*Consolation to Polybius* (*De consolatione ad Polybium*)
Constancy	*On the Constancy of the Wise* (*De constantia sapientis*)
Happiness	*On Happiness* (*De vita beata*)
Leisure	*On Leisure* (*De otio*)
Letters	*Letters on Ethics* (*Epistulae morales ad Lucilium*)
NQ	*Natural Questions* (*Quaestiones naturales*)
Prov.	*On Providence* (*De providentia*)
Tranq.	*On Tranquility of Mind* (*De tranquillitate animi*)

For the Latin texts of the letters and dialogues, I rely on Reynolds (1965) and (1977), respectively, except that I use *v* to represent consonantal *u*. For the *De Beneficiis*, I use Hosius (1914). Translations from the *Letters on Ethics* match those in Graver and Long (2015), with minor adjustments for clarity in a handful of places. Other translations of Greek and Latin are my own unless otherwise indicated.

Note also the following:

LS	A. A. Long and D. N. Sedley (eds.) (1987) *The Hellenistic Philosophers*
LSJ⁹	H. J. Liddell, R. Scott, and H. S. Jones (eds.) (1940) *A Greek–English Lexicon*
OLD	P. G. W. Glare and C. Stray (eds.) (2012) *Oxford Latin Dictionary*
SVF	H. von Arnim (ed.) (1921–24) *Stoicorum Veterum Fragmenta*

Introduction
Seneca's Philosophical Literature

In Seneca, we encounter a serious reader of philosophy who was at the same time a talented and ambitious writer. Thanks to his excellent collection of books on Stoicism, Epicureanism, and other philosophical systems, Seneca has played a major role in the transmission of Greek thought. But he is much more than a reporter. Deeply invested in his reading on theoretical subjects, he also has much to contribute to the conversation, in his spirited and sometimes satirical interpretations of philosophical arguments and in his active resistance to earlier positions of even his favorite authors. Though he describes himself as merely a student of philosophy, he is now universally recognized as a philosopher in his own right. Yet the word "philosopher" is inadequate to describe what he was, for as a Roman senator well connected within a burgeoning equestrian elite, thoroughly trained in rhetoric, and steeped in poetry, narrative history, and drama, Seneca brings rich cultural resources to the service of philosophical reflection.[1] In his way of thinking, the work of philosophy is not done if it cannot also engage the imagination through illustrative analogies, through vivid descriptions of scenes from his own experience, and through the manipulation of literary form. What he produced is not only a literary sort of philosophy; it is philosophy *as* literature: a distinctively Roman answer to the intellectual artistry of Plato.

In this book I offer twelve studies that approach Seneca's major works in a coordinated though not entirely linear fashion. While most of the chapters have been previously published and each can be read on its own, they work together here to give a more nuanced account of the Roman philosopher's achievement than any one of them could do individually. For if we are to understand Seneca at all, we need to come at him

---

[1] Would the man we refer to as "Seneca *philosophus*" have called himself a *philosophus*? Hine (2015: 19–21) argues persuasively that he would not, on grounds that the Latin term denoted a professional teacher of philosophy, who would in that period have been a person of inferior social status.

from more than one direction. It is, in my view, absolutely essential to look closely at how he engaged with the philosophical tradition: what he actually knew about Stoicism and about other philosophical approaches that were on offer in first-century Rome, what aspects of those philosophies he chose to emphasize or deemphasize, and where he thought elements from competing traditions might be compatible – for while it is not accurate to characterize Seneca as an eclectic philosopher in the old sense of the term, he is certainly an open-minded one. At a deeper level, we must come to grips with his attitude to philosophical argument itself: where he is careful and exact in reproducing terminology and steps in argumentation, where he seems unconcerned about inconsistencies in his own presentation, why he sometimes dismisses a serious argument as silly and unproductive. But beyond all that, we need to recognize Seneca's philosophical effusions as his attempt to make a career as a writer. Our perception is incomplete if we fail to attend to his self-conscious reflections on genre, style, and imagery; his numerous directives on approaches to reading; and his constant critique of other writers. These obviously literary features belong to one and the same project with his studies in ethics, psychology, and natural science, for in Seneca's conception, *studia* or "studies" are not a set of different disciplines. They are a single discipline whose aim is the creation of an aesthetic and intellectual self.

The facts of Seneca's life come into this book just insofar as they have a bearing on the ideas we find in his writings. In order to assess his project as a philosophical writer, one needs to know that he had the education and the resources to pursue whatever studies he wanted and also that he had been trained in the techniques of rhetoric, for his father, Seneca the Elder, was an authority in that area. It matters, too, that he had friends who shared his interest in books: people like Marcia, the historian's daughter to whom he addressed his first consolatory essay, Annaeus Serenus, for whom he wrote *On Tranquility of Mind* and *On the Constancy of the Wise*, and Gaius Lucilius Junior, the civilian governor of Sicily and an author in his own right, to whom he addressed the *Letters on Ethics* as well as the *Natural Questions* and the essay *On Providence*. In order to understand his attitude toward the philosophical life, traditionally viewed as an alternative to the life of political activity, one needs also to know that he had a political career of his own, was well acquainted with the imperial court, and was cognizant of the dangers that attended political influence during the difficult years of the Julio-Claudian dynasty. He could write about wealth and privilege from the standpoint of one who had possessed them, but both he and his friends had reason to think that a more obscure life might be more desirable in the end.[2]

In this vein, it is interesting to consider the conversation imagined by the historian Tacitus between a Seneca eager to withdraw from his position in the court and a suitably reluctant Nero (*Ann.* 14.53–56). The tension depicted there between administrative work and the time required for meaningful study was a real part of Seneca's life, one to which the philosopher himself often refers. With his usual subtle wit, Tacitus had Seneca compare himself first to Marcus Agrippa and then to Gaius Cilnius Maecenas, both client-friends of the emperor Augustus who were allowed eventually to retire from public service. Now, Agrippa was a military man, which Seneca emphatically was not. The more telling comparison is to Maecenas, like Seneca a personal rather than a military companion of the princeps, whose importance to the regime was chiefly at the cultural level. That the real Seneca is sharply critical of Maecenas both for his demeanor and for his prose style only adds force to the comparison. In his financial circumstances and social standing, both obtained through imperial favor, he indeed resembled Maecenas; in his character and writings – his *ingenium*, to use his own term – he meant to be quite different. In studying Seneca's books, we gain privileged access to that *ingenium*. Not, indeed, to Seneca's actions in life, for actions are hard to judge even in proximity, but to the aspect of Seneca that still exists and matters.

***

If Seneca's life story has sometimes been seen as a troubling frame for his works, it is largely because of the directness with which he offers to tell other people how to live. Nearly all his works are formally therapeutic in nature, which is to say, they present themselves as seeking to improve the persons addressed by ridding them of troubling emotions like anger, fear, and grief; by teaching them how to endure hardship and to live in community; and in general by leading them toward the most fulfilling form of human life, termed variously as "wisdom," "virtue," or "happiness." The position of the moral teacher is always a bit problematic. We expect the teacher to be adept

---

[2] The best overall treatment of Seneca's life is still Griffin (1976), which also offers extensive comments on many issues in his philosophical writings. In that work, see especially 67–103, which review Seneca's career as an *amicus principis*, giving special consideration to the reliability of Tacitus's narrative and to the circumstances of Seneca's retirement. Among other broad-based studies of Seneca's career and achievement, see especially Vogt (2020), Bartsch and Schiesaro (2015), Maurach (2000), Grimal (1978). I provide an annotated bibliography in Graver (2016).

at the subject taught, but Seneca does not seem to have led an exemplary life and does not claim to have done so. At the time he was writing, though, the therapeutic stance was sanctioned by a long tradition in philosophical writing. The philosophers of the Hellenistic world had sometimes set themselves up in relation to the medical writers, as healers for the mind rather than the body. For Seneca, a notable precedent might have been the fourth book of Chrysippus's treatise *On Emotions*, called the *Therapeutic Book*, which claimed specifically to treat the "diseased" mind as a doctor would, with "item-by-item theory and therapy."[3] It is in keeping with that metaphor that Seneca often speaks of writings on ethics as efficacious "remedies"; or, as he puts it in the *Letters on Ethics*, "healthful admonitions, like the recipes for useful salves" (*Letters* 8.2). Such statements imply an assumption about the power of reading: that effective instruction is not limited to the lecture hall or to live discussion but can also take place through the written word.

There is good reason to accept Seneca's statements of therapeutic purpose as crucial to the interpretation of his works. Just as in a defense speech every utterance, every inflection of the voice, every gesture of the hands works to exonerate the defendant, so in a work of therapeutic philosophy it should be possible to understand every authorial decision regarding subject matter, style, and design as an effort to improve the reader's moral state. Further, the intention to address readers' moral or spiritual ills, and in particular to rid them of disturbing emotions, necessitates reflection on the causes of mental events and the ways that certain therapeutic approaches may or may not counteract them. Seneca often addresses such points, and one can productively inquire whether his remarks are consistent with one another and with his practice.

At the same time, our sensitivity to Seneca's therapeutic aims must be balanced with recognition of his freestanding theoretical interests and of his ambitions as a literary artist in a more conventional sense. He does not limit himself to those basic lessons that he regards as essential to curing the passions and vices. Especially in his longest works, *On Benefits*, *Natural Questions*, and *Letters on Ethics*, he takes on more ambitious topics, in physics and theology, in ethical theory, even in metaphysics.[4] One could

---

[3] Chrysippus in Galen, *PHP* 5.2.22 (*SVF* 3.471). For this aspect of Hellenistic philosophy, see especially I. Hadot (1969, 2014); Nussbaum (1994).

[4] Thus, Brad Inwood writes (in Inwood (2007a: xvii)), "[I]n approaching Seneca's letters philosophically, it is surely a mistake to take it for granted that the author's central motivation is to play the role of moral or 'spiritual' guide for his readers." This remark garnered a vehement response in I. Hadot (2014: 9, 30). Others who have seen the therapeutic premise as the central

undoubtedly make the case that these topics, too, might be included for the sake of advancing us toward the perfection of our rational nature. In a sense, all philosophy is therapeutic, because all disciplined thinking and study works to improve our thought processes. But Seneca does not make that case. On the contrary, he sometimes scolds himself or his interlocutor for venturing into topics that go beyond his purview as a moralist, thus signaling a divergence between his theoretical inquiries and his therapeutic aims. For this reason, I have found it helpful at some points to think of Seneca's therapeutic premise as a *rule of genre*. It explains the existence of the work, makes a claim as to its nature, and sets the terms of interaction between author and reader, "I" and "you," in something like the way that the invocation to the Muse explains the existence of an epic, identifies its theme, and creates a role for the poet. Yet even so, it need not make manifest the entire purpose for which the book was written. There may be further objectives, formally subordinate and yet real enough, that we can discern in the author's relationship to the material, to the addressee, or to the reading public.

A useful way to think about this issue is to relate Seneca's use of the therapeutic premise to a debate that had been carried on intermittently since the time of Plato about the value of intellectual activity itself. In a world full of practical problems to be solved, how does one justify spending time on philosophical study, or on any kind of study that has no immediate application? In the Hellenistic period, the issue was typically presented as a decision among three modes of life: the life of active service, that of pleasure, and that of study. Stoic ethics had always given the priority to active service, yet Seneca in his writings appears exclusively as a man of leisure, devoting his time to reading and writing projects in retirement from the world. In Chapter 1 ("The Life of the Mind"), I review the arguments he puts forward in the fragmentary treatise *On Leisure* to support the life of study. Of particular interest among these is a claim that the secluded activity of the philosopher is justified because of the discoveries it may record for future generations. This is exactly the argument that Seneca makes on his own behalf in the much longer *Letters on Ethics*. However, this justification is both limited and limiting in that it applies only to the ethical part of philosophy. Accordingly, Seneca in this major work makes use of a series of rhetorical devices to expand the

explanatory principle of Seneca's project include Hachmann (1995), Schafer (2009), and Dietsche (2018).

therapeutic frame he has established, creating openings for more adventurous philosophical questions without violating generic decorum.

***

Looking now more closely at the nature of Seneca's engagement with Hellenistic philosophy, we find ourselves enmeshed in a number of interrelated questions. Conspicuously in his works the word *nostri* ("our people") refers to the Stoics, meaning in the first instance Zeno of Citium, Cleanthes, and Chrysippus, the third-century originators of that system of thought, but also later figures like Posidonius and Hecaton of Rhodes. But there are many questions to be asked about Seneca's philosophical stance. What parts of Stoicism does he consider to be essential, and how closely do the views he expresses resemble what we know about Stoicism from other sources? What is the nature of his interest in the hedonist philosophy of Epicurus? How does he respond to the Aristotelianism of his day? Further, there are questions to be asked about his relation to philosophy itself. To what extent does he demand consistency of view from himself and others? When he claims the right to develop and change the tradition he inherited, is he signaling that he has in fact created his own versions of Stoic doctrine, or is he only making a general point about intellectual independence?

The first order of business is to work out what Seneca knew of the Stoic tradition. The remaining chapters of Part I both deal directly with Seneca's understanding of Stoicism, but from different angles. In Chapter 2 ("Action and Emotion"), I compare his views on the mechanisms of judgment, voluntary action, and emotion with what is known of the Stoic tradition on those subjects. Here abundant, though fragmentary, information about earlier Stoic thought makes it possible to verify the extent of Seneca's adherence and to discern some of his distinctive emphases. For the subject matter of Chapter 3 ("The Treatise *On Benefits*"), the situation is quite different, for while Seneca tells us that he is drawing on earlier works on the *beneficium* or deed of kindness, we have very little outside information about those sources. Thus, his treatise becomes our sole window onto a topic that has deep implications for Stoic understandings of action, autonomy, and friendship. The work is revealing, too, for Seneca's priorities as a philosopher: his interest in social relations, his deep engagement with issues of agency and volition, and his love of close reasoning and fine distinctions.

Another way to probe Seneca's relation to Stoicism is to look in some detail at what he says about its major competitors. The two chapters of

Part II take up that challenge as concerns first Epicureanism and then the Peripatetics, Hellenistic admirers of Aristotle. There is no question that Seneca has good access to Epicurean texts; indeed, his information on some points is superior to what we have from any other source. His engagement with the school has been found puzzling, however, for while his overall attitude toward the central tenets of Epicureanism is unremittingly hostile, he is at times strikingly appreciative, even to the point of restating recognizably Epicurean claims in his own voice. To make sense of his position, Chapter 4 ("Seneca and Epicurus") draws a distinction between Epicurus's core philosophical views and his tactics as a writer and a therapist. In matters of pedagogy and of the psychology of the pupil, Seneca finds much in Epicurus that he can adapt to his own purposes; on such doctrines as the pleasure principle, the idleness of the divine, and the conventional basis for justice, he makes no compromise at all. When he enters Epicurean terrain, he does so "not as a deserter, but as a spy," ready to take whatever he can use, but not in the least inclined to alter his philosophical allegiance.

Though less well known to the Romans than Epicureanism was, the doctrines of the Peripatetic philosophers seem to have been even more important for Seneca as he honed his positions in ethics and psychology. For Peripatetic thought was closely akin to Stoicism on some points, especially as concerns the centrality of virtue to human happiness. However, there were also significant differences, notably in the system of value and in the treatment of the emotions. In contesting these points, Seneca indicates the depth of his Stoic commitments. In Chapter 5 ("Refuting the Peripatetics"), I juxtapose a series of passages in the *Letters on Ethics* with the encyclopedia-style text usually referred to as Doxography "C," which offers a résumé of Peripatetic ethics dating probably to the principate of Augustus. In particular, I show that certain features of letter 92 are best explained on the assumption that Seneca is responding point by point to a summary account of Peripatetic ethics that was similar in style to "C," but was not "C" itself. Recognition of this fact can give insight into Seneca's motivations, including his motivations for positing a tripartite division of mind in the opening paragraph of that letter.

***

The three chapters of Part III concentrate on that part of Stoic philosophy that sought to analyze the various phenomena of emotional experience and to provide therapies for the most problematic emotions. Here, too, we want to ask not only about Seneca's positions but also about his method. In Chapter 6 ("Seneca's Therapy for Anger"), I confront some of the difficulties he seems to have had in imposing order on his material. The earliest of the multi-book treatises, *On Anger*, brings great energy both to the exposition of Stoic doctrine and to the crafting of therapeutic recommendations. There is some lack of fit, though, between the temporal structure of anger that he lays out, quite correctly from a Stoic perspective, in the first half of the treatise and the program of anger management that he outlines in the second. One cannot say, then, that the philosophical analysis has been fully integrated. I make the case, however, that the structure of book 3 gives signals of Seneca's own discomfort with this aspect of his work, and that these can be read as promising for his further philosophical development.

From this perspective it is interesting to compare a work on grief that Seneca wrote near the end of his life, in his *consolatio* to Marullus. This short piece, presented as an enclosure in the 99th of the *Letters on Ethics*, is the subject of Chapter 7 ("The Weeping Wise"). Ordinarily a *consolatio* is a conventional type of essay for comforting the bereaved. In this case, however, the content of the essay is anything but conventional, for, as Seneca explains to Lucilius, the treatment of Marullus's grief is intended to be entirely on Stoic principles. Although modern sensibilities are likely to be offended by Seneca's endeavor to argue down Marullus's grief at the loss of a young child, his disciplined handling of the task proves to be instructive for its close look at the phenomenology of both involuntary and voluntary emotional reactions. There are implications, too, for the emotions related to friendship.

In Chapter 8 ("Anatomies of Joy"), I show how Seneca's several accounts of eupathic joy can give insight into his working methods as a philosopher. Seneca is clearly invested in the idea that the fulfillment of our rational nature would result in a life filled with joy, the virtuous counterpart to the problematic pleasure or delight of ordinary agents. Yet there are interesting differences in his explanations of how wise joy relates to objects of value. In fact, there are no fewer than seven philosophically distinct accounts to be found in his works, reflecting different views of the phenomenology of joy, the nature of its objects, and its dependence on social interactions. I argue that these discrepancies reflect a tendency to preserve ideas found in his various reading materials without attempting to impose a system. We can surmise that the Stoic tradition itself had room for divergence of view concerning some specifics of moral psychology, as long as the core principles of Stoic ethics were maintained.

In working with Seneca's treatments of the emotions and other issues in Stoic thought, I am careful not to assume that the philosophical works of Cicero were his immediate authority. While Cicero's *De Finibus* and *Tusculan Disputations* are important sources for us, we cannot be sure that they are similarly important to Seneca, or even that Seneca was familiar with those particular Ciceronian works. Seneca does regard Cicero as a precedent for philosophical writing in Latin; indeed he comments that Cicero's books on philosophy are "almost as numerous as those of Fabianus" *(Letters* 100.9). But the works that he quotes or mentions by title are only the *Letters to Atticus* and *On the Republic*.[5] For such points as the special importance of joy in Stoicism, it is safest to assume that similarities have arisen because both Roman philosophers have consulted the foundational writings of Greek Stoicism.[6]

***

While I work with a number of Seneca's essays and at length with the treatises *On Benefits* and *On Anger*, the centerpiece of this book is the *Epistulae Morales ad Lucilium*, or *Letters on Ethics to Lucilius*.[7] Concerning this work, I share the view of the late Miriam Griffin, that the *Letters* were never in reality a private correspondence but were destined for a wide audience from the time of their composition.[8] For all their verisimilitude, they are fictive epistles, like those that make up an epistolary novel, with the real Gaius Lucilius Junior named as the recipient in roughly the same way as Gaius Memmius is named as the recipient of Lucretius's *De Rerum Natura* or Marcus Terentius Varro as the recipient of Cicero's *Academica*. Although this reading of the work is now widely held among specialists, it

---

[5] For the quoted material, see *Brevity* 5.2, *Letters* 97.3–5, 108.30–34, 118.1–2, and fragment 1 (Aulus Gellius, *Attic Nights* 12.2).

[6] In an author who likes to cite his sources, Seneca's silence about the philosophical series Cicero completed in 45–43 BCE seems to me significant. I have also been struck by the way that in treating specific points from the Greek tradition Seneca sometimes includes information that he could not have found in Cicero, while showing no awareness of highly relevant points that Cicero treats at length, such as the alternative Epicurean accounts of friendship and the ethical position of Antiochus of Ascalon. Further to the topic see Graver (2021); Graver and Long (2015: 18); Setaioli (2003); Gambet (1970); and on page 111.

[7] I write *Letters on Ethics*, rather than (e.g.) *Moral Letters*, on grounds that Seneca's term *moralis philosophia* is closer to our word "ethics" (a branch of inquiry) than it is to our word "morals" (good conduct). See *Letters* 88.24, 89.9, 106.2, and especially 121.1 *non quidquid morale est mores bonos facit* ("what pertains to ethics does not necessarily make for ethical conduct").

[8] See Griffin (1976: 349–53, 416–19, 519).

remains controversial for some, and so it will be useful at this point to say a word about the argument that seems to me conclusive in its favor.[9]

The key point, in my view, is the stance assumed by the epistolographer relative to the knowledge base of his expected reader. In a letter intended for a specific individual, the content will normally be tailored to that person's point of view: it will provide just the information that person does not have and offer just the advice that person needs in their particular situation. As a point of reference, consider Cicero's letters to his close friend Atticus. Valuable as those letters are to the historian, they also leave us in the dark at many points, for Cicero constantly refers to people and events whose significance must have been obvious to Atticus but is unknown to us now and would have been almost equally opaque to the vast majority of Cicero's contemporaries. By contrast, the *Letters on Ethics* are fully comprehensible to anyone who is even minimally familiar with the contemporary culture. There are no private jokes, nothing really cryptic; indeed, when Seneca mentions an individual of his and Lucilius's acquaintance, he takes care to supply the words of identification that are needed for understanding, and when he mentions a letter Lucilius is supposed to have written, he gives indications of what that letter is supposed to have said. In a word, the letters are not written *for* Lucilius at all, but aim instead to entertain and inform a wider public. Similarly, the moral teaching within the letters is for general use; it is not calculated to match the intellectual and personal needs of the historical Lucilius. For example, as Seneca concludes an exhortation not to fear poverty, he adds, "This material applies to others, for *you* [that is, Lucilius] are more nearly among the wealthy" (*Letters* 17.10). Likewise, his disquisition on the evils of slavery, though cast in the second person, is not meant as admonishment to Lucilius, who has "no need of encouragement" on this point (*Letters* 47.21). The true role of the historical Lucilius is indicated in letter 21, where Seneca writes, "Your studies will make you famous," and compares Lucilius to Idomeneus and Atticus, made famous by the letters of Epicurus and Cicero respectively (*Letters* 21.2–5).[10] Lucilius's name is made known just insofar as the letters addressed to him are in fact

---

[9] Among those who have insisted on the historicity of the correspondence are Grimal (1978: 441–56), Mazzoli (1989: 1846–50), and to a large extent Setaioli (2014a: 193–94). Those who have seen it as intended for a wide audience from the time of composition include Cancik (1967), Maurach (1970), Abel (1981), Lana (1991: 269–74), Wilson (1988, 2001), Richardson-Hay (2006), Inwood (2005: 346–47 and 2007b); Conradie (2010: 60–87), Wilcox (2012), Wildberger (2014), Williams (2014), Gunderson (2015: 6–7), and Dietsche (2014: 35–38). I discuss the issue at more length in Graver (1996: 8–41).

[10] *Letters* 21.2–5.

meant for a wide audience: his presence is honorific, rather than functional. Accustomed to rhetorical stands, open letters, and literary fronts of various kinds, a Roman readership would have had no difficulty understanding the dynamics.

This observation opens onto a broader reflection on Seneca's use of literary form. The claim of the *Letters on Ethics* – one might almost call it a generic manifesto – is that Seneca's life of intellectual leisure is justified precisely because the writing he produces conveys moral benefits to a wide community of readers present and to come. This claim presupposes that written works of philosophy can sometimes provide such benefits. But in Greco-Roman philosophical culture, the therapeutic potential of arguments presented only in written form could not be taken for granted. Socrates, famously, had taken a position against writing in Plato's *Phaedrus*, arguing that written works cannot improve the character of the reader because they lack the immediacy, the adaptability, and the interactive possibilities of spoken discourse. In Chapter 9 ("The Challenge of the *Phaedrus*"), I show how the format and rhetorical technique of the *Letters on Ethics* gives Seneca a point-for-point response to the arguments of Socrates. Crucial elements of that response are the verisimilitude of Seneca's authorial presence, the training provided to the reader in methods of application, and the reader's quasi-dialogic engagement with a text presented as an epistolary conversation. Also important, though perhaps surprising for an author of Seneca's Stoic commitments, is the reader's emotional experience. Unlike the involuntary aesthetic reactions Seneca sometimes describes, reader emotions in the *Letters on Ethics* are full-scale affective responses that can be compared on the one hand to the *pathē* of the nonwise and on the other to the eupathic responses of the Stoic sage. While Seneca does not claim Stoic wisdom either for himself or for his readers, he offers a means of access to the sage's joy that can be motivational for those still in the realm of moral progress.

***

The remaining chapters of Part IV examine the relationship between Seneca's literary achievement and his concerns as a philosopher. The theme is the creation of a literary self, which is equally the creation of an effective philosophical voice. That Seneca was constantly aware of the Roman literary tradition and sought to establish his own place in it is not to be doubted.[11]

---

[11] For recent work on this aspect of Seneca's endeavors, see the essays in Garani, Michalopoulos, and Papaioannou (2020), in particular the opening essays by Wilcox (2020) and Smith (2020).

In these three pieces, I go on from there to consider how his strong interest in questions of genre, style, and rhetoric interacts with his specifically philosophical concerns.

Chapter 10 ("The Mouse, the Moneybox, and the Six-Footed Scurrying Solecism") deals with his use of satire and humor. Fond of wordplay, riddles, and the incongruous, Seneca deploys humor not only to entertain but also to enforce certain rules of generic decorum. With its capacity to stain and degrade, humor is well suited to delegitimize modes of philosophical speech and writing that Seneca deems unproductive for the therapeutic project, whether it be an Epicurean maxim, a trick syllogism, or a riff on Stoic metaphysics. But the ridicule of opponents may sometimes turn into self-ridicule, when he as an author has ventured into areas of inquiry that are forbidden by the therapeutic rule of genre. In these contexts, the Senecan self that we meet within the text is marked as transgressive, prone to violate the boundaries he himself has established for philosophical literature.

While gender dynamics often play a role in Seneca's humor, there is also a serious role for the language of gender in his discussions of prose style. The figure of Gaius Cilnius Maecenas, the cultural minister of Augustus, emblematizes the old claim that style mirrors conduct (*talis oratio qualis vita*), with the laxness that Seneca discerns in Maecenas's writing a direct reflection of character flaws that he, as a heterosexual Roman male, attributes to defective masculinity. In Chapter 11 ("The Manhandling of Maecenas"), I bring out the philosophical ideas that undergird this remarkable assertion. In keeping with Stoic thought, the Seneca of the *Letters* attaches great importance to integrity and coherence in one's thought. But thought, or "internal speech," is hardly to be distinguished from what he calls the *ingenium* – that is, the linguistic ability of an individual that is manifested in speech and writing. Thus it is with philosophical intent that he creates a notion of a masculine style of writing (*compositio virilis*), consisting, it seems, in a highly structured, hypotactic style that traces connections between all elements of the thought. Whether this is a good description of Seneca's own Latin prose must remain an open question.[12]

The final chapter ("Honeybee Reading and Self-Scripting") turns at last directly to the idea of self that is situated at the intersection of Seneca's literary ambitions and his lifelong interest in Stoic moral psychology.

---

[12] Richardson-Hay (2006: 75–126) gives examples of the main stylistic features of Seneca's writing. For a sensitive and suitably minute reading of the inner workings of that style within the Letters, see Henderson (2004).

Instructive at the outset are the reflections of Michel Foucault, in the year before his death, on the metaphor of the honeybee in *Letters on Ethics* 84. Although Foucault's understanding was deficient in some points, he captured an essential idea about writing as an act of self-constitution. With a philologically informed reading, we can recover yet more. Seneca in letter 84 lays claim to self-constitutive writing not in terms of the subliterary activities that Foucault envisioned, but via a consciously aesthetic practice of creation for the reading public. Study (*studium*), as invoked in the letter, depends on reading but then comes to fruition in the crafting of what Seneca calls the *ingenium*, the literary talent that is to be recognized by future generations. Yet study is simultaneously and without contradiction the training of one's character, fitting it for moral action. Seneca thus shows himself to be very much attuned to Roman canons of literary achievement even as he reflects ever more deeply on a Stoic conception of the rational directive faculty of the human. In the metaphoric progression of the letter, we watch him develop a notion of a scripted and exteriorized self more tightly integrated, through art, than the biological self and capable of surviving the death of the body.[13]

***

Before closing this introduction, I should make clear that my remarks about literary achievement are made in reference to Seneca's prose works, independently of the extant Senecan tragedies. Concerning the plays, I admit to a certain methodological conservatism. While the philosophical Seneca was certainly a poet, I have been inclined to doubt whether the "Seneca" who is said by Quintilian to have written the tragedy *Medea* was the same person as Lucius Annaeus Seneca the Younger.[14] The context in Quintilian tells us nothing, and there is no other external evidence from the early centuries CE that can settle the issue.[15] Attributions in late-

---

[13] For better or worse, we cannot say that Seneca was mistaken in believing he could insert himself into the canon of influential Roman authors. For a thoughtful treatment of Seneca's extensive literary reputation in antiquity, see Habinek (2000).

[14] Quintilian, *Inst.* 9.2.9; the reference may be to Seneca the Elder as in *Inst.* 9.2.42–44. Quintilian attests at *Inst.* 10.1.129 that the philosopher Seneca wrote *poemata*, Tacitus in *Annales* 14.52 speaks of *carmina*.

[15] Kohn (2003) reviews an impressive list of considerations against identifying the playwright Seneca with the philosopher. The prevailing tendency, however, has been to regard the question as settled, as if some conclusive evidence had surfaced in the modern era – which is simply not the case. Among those who have tried with varying degrees of success to pull the plays into a single interpretive frame with the treatises and letters are Wray (2009), Ker (2006), Schiesaro (2003: 20–25), T. G. Rosenmeyer (1989).

medieval manuscripts are of little to no value, and the internal evidence that has been offered in terms of similarity of phrasing and outlook does not strike me as compelling for the determination of authorship.[16] At no point do we find connections between the prose works and the plays of the kind that exist among the prose works themselves: exact correspondences of theme and assertion, topical references to the same set of people, places, and political circumstances, and even explicit cross-references.[17] Methodologically it is cleanest to come to grips with the cohesive prose corpus on its own. Results of that work may then be of use in interpreting the tragedies, which whether or not they were written by the philosopher Seneca were certainly Stoic-influenced works of the same generation.

---

[16] For example, in Fischer (2014).

[17] Among the more obvious connections are that Annaeus Serenus appears both in the treatise *On Tranquility of Mind* and in the *Letters*; Gaius Lucilius Junior is the dedicatee of *On Providence*, *Letters on Ethics*, and the *Natural Questions*, and the treatise *On Benefits* is referred to by title in *Letters* 81.3. Traina (1974) documents with precision the characteristic turns of phrase that tie the philosophical works together as a single corpus. Even more significant are the echoes of thought; for example, when *Letters* 8.1 echoes precisely *Leisure* 1.4, or when *Letters* 84.13 repeats the peculiar idea about "level ground" from *Anger* 2.13.2. Williams (2014) identifies four such close connections between the *Letters* and the *Natural Questions*.

PART I

Recreating the Stoic Past

CHAPTER I

The Life of the Mind
Seneca and the *Contemplatio Veri*

Seneca makes a formal case for the contemplative life in the fragmentary treatise titled *De Otio*, or *On Leisure*.¹ *Otium*, a term with multiple connotations in Latin, here refers to the leisure needed for philosophical study, in the sense of the Greek *scholē* (σχολή); similarly, Seneca's word *contemplatio* ("contemplation") is his equivalent for *theōria* (θεωρία), the word used by Greek philosophers to refer to their own activity of study and reflection.² Though incomplete, *On Leisure* is of interest for the way it combines themes from Stoic ethics with elements of the Platonist and Aristotelian tradition, setting these over against Epicurean quietism. Working from familiar Stoic axioms concerning the mutual responsibility of all rational beings and the naturalness of intelligent inquiry, Seneca presents a series of arguments in favor of a retired life devoted to philosophical pursuits. As later in the *Natural Questions*, the study of cosmological and theological topics is both satisfying and uplifting, for it raises the mind above mundane concerns and brings it closer to the divine.³ Yet even so, legitimate concerns may be raised about the demands philosophical study imposes on a limited lifespan. The sheer expenditure of time required by philosophy demands some justification, and this Seneca seeks to provide through a medley of arguments appealing to the nature of the individual, the demands of circumstances, the need for personal moral improvement, and the ethical benefits conferred through teaching.

---

[1] Text in Reynolds (1977); critical editions with commentary Dionigi (1983); Williams (2003). The title is known from the contents list of the Codex Ambrosianus; see Williams (2003: 63–64).
[2] For the moral and political implications of *otium* in Roman culture, see Grilli (1953) and André (1966, 1962a). Seneca treats the topic also in *On the Brevity of Life* and *On Tranquility of Mind* 3.1–6.3; for a broad-based study, see now Dross (2022). Discussions of *theōria* in Greek philosophy go back to Plato, *Republic* 486a, 517d; Aristotle, *Nic. Eth.* 10.7; see Bénatouïl and Bonazzi (2012).
[3] See especially *NQ* 3 *praef.* 10–18; 1 *praef.* 1–17, as well as Barnes (1997a: 21–23); Williams (2012: 22–37).

The result is a rather puzzling treatment that leaves us with no clear conception of what specific activities make up the contemplative life (astronomy? spiritual exercises? writing books?) and which of those endeavors is supposed to impart value to the enterprise as a whole. The treatise takes on new meaning, however, when read in conjunction with Seneca's most comprehensive work, the *Letters on Ethics*. Close to *On Leisure* in date, the longer work shares many of its themes and arguments and develops on a much larger scale its concern with the role of specifically philosophical activities in a virtuous life.[4] Moreover, the *Letters on Ethics* makes explicit a tension that is present without acknowledgment in *On Leisure*: the difference between philosophical study for the sake of personal moral development, to tame the passions and prepare oneself for courageous action, and theoretical activity for its own sake, simply to increase one's understanding of the world. Although Seneca advocates for philosophical retirement on grounds that all one's time is needed for self-improvement, he also makes a show of pursuing some entirely abstract investigations, at odds with himself. To resolve the tension, he resorts to a series of rhetorical strategies calculated to win favor for the inclusion of technical material without sacrificing the epistolary decorum he has established.

In addition, the *Letters on Ethics* does a good deal to flesh out the sparse indications given in *On Leisure* as to what specific pursuits make up the life of a philosopher. Although we cannot treat the letters as straightforwardly autobiographical, we can learn much from them about how Seneca envisions philosophical activity. In particular, the figure of Claranus in letter 66 provides us with our best Neronian portrait of a contemplative philosopher. Through that portrait, as well as through the epistolographer's reports of his own activities and those of his addressee Lucilius, we glimpse a distinctively Senecan understanding of the contemplative life: a life of self-cultivation but also of abstract thought, filled with solitary reading and writing but also with long philosophical conversations.

The Arguments of *On Leisure*

Although the opening of *On Leisure* is truncated, not much can have been lost there, for as the extant portion begins, Seneca is still making an initial

---

[4] If *On Leisure* is dedicated to Annaeus Serenus, then it must have been composed in or near 62, around the time the *Letters on Ethics* were begun. Unfortunately, the dedication is attested only by a "virtually illegible" notation in the Codex Ambrosianus. See Griffin (1976: 316–17, 399); Williams (2003: 12–13).

statement of his view that it is morally beneficial to retire by oneself for philosophical study. A nameless interlocutor objects: How is this recommendation consistent with Seneca's professed commitment to Stoicism? For Stoics urge active public service up to the very moment of death (1.4). To defend his claim, Seneca could have appealed to the founders' own practice of philosophy as against their precepts. His preference, though, is to make the case that the Stoic call to action is fully consistent with devoting all of one's time to contemplation, whether that be throughout one's working life or only for the years following a career in public service (2.1–2). As it turns out, only the arguments concerning the whole of one's working life are presented in the portion of the treatise we have, but since this is the stronger position, the apparent loss of arguments for the fallback position is of no great moment.[5]

In contrast to the Epicurean recommendation to live unknown, not engaging in politics unless there is compelling reason to do so (*nisi si quid intervenerit*), the Stoic doctrine reported by Seneca is that one should choose civic engagement unless there is some hindrance (*nisi si quid inpedierit*) (3.2). In other words, the Epicureans favor retirement as a life-plan (*ex proposito*), the Stoics only under the pressure of circumstances (*ex causa*). But in fact there is a wide range of circumstances that may make the civic life unsupportable. First of all, the state may be too corrupt to benefit from one's services; second, one may not have sufficient power and influence to change the course of events; third, one may be hampered by ill health. If any of these conditions obtains, one may legitimately devote one's entire life to the "good arts"; that is, to philosophical studies (3.4).[6]

But these arguments for exemption from public service would hardly be convincing if Seneca did not also provide reasons for thinking that philosophical activity does some good. That is, he needs to show that one who chooses the contemplative life can still fulfill the Stoics' moral requirement to benefit as many others as possible – in effect, that philosophy is an alternative form of public service. He takes up this challenge at first by saying that cultivating the inner life will make one more fit to serve others at some time in the future (3.5). Then, from a different perspective, he appeals to a broader understanding of the polity to which one belongs. Each of us is a member of two communities: the specific city into which we are born,

---

[5] On the fragmentary nature of the work, I am in agreement with Griffin (1976: 328) and Smith (2014a: 147–49). Williams (2003: 16–18) argues for completeness.
[6] For *bonae artes* in this sense, compare *NQ* 6.32.1: *non enim aliunde animo venit robur quam a bonis artibus, quam a contemplatione naturae.*

such as Athens or Carthage, and the universe as a whole, which encompasses all human beings and also the gods. The studies we pursue in solitude are in effect a service to this second and larger community, for in them we benefit god by providing a witness to his activities (4.1–2). Finally, our studies provide a very great benefit to future generations whenever philosophical discoveries are recorded and transmitted. In this sense, Zeno and Chrysippus can be credited with public service not merely to a single city but to all humanity. "They did greater things than if they had led armies, held magistracies, enacted laws – but they did enact laws, not for a single community but for the whole human race. . . . They found a way for their retirement to aid human beings more than other people's busyness and sweat" (6.4–5).

Moreover, Seneca claims that philosophical study is required of us by the widely held principle that one should live in accordance with nature. For certain innate human tendencies can serve as evidence that contemplation is natural to us, just as action is. The universal love of narrative, of travel, and of solving puzzles and mysteries demonstrates that we are by nature a curious race, designed to study the universe in all its beauty and complexity (5.1–4). Even the very structure of our bodies, with our upright stature and flexible neck, is well adapted to observe the pageantry of the constellations, indicating that nature means us also to proceed to more abstract objects of contemplation: the generation and workings of the cosmos, the origin of souls, the continuous or particulate nature of matter, the intermingling of elements. Since the time that could productively be devoted to such studies exceeds the human life span, even an entire life devoted to them will be a life in accordance with nature (5.5–7).

Such studies bring pleasure, but one is not authorized to pursue them merely for that reason (6.1–2). The familiar debate about the lives of pleasure, of action, and of contemplation fails to recognize that each of these lives involves both of the others as concomitants. Just as contemplation is accompanied by pleasure, so also the lives devoted to pleasure and to moral action are not without some form of reflection (7.1–2). Thus, proponents of all three lives turn out to favor a very similar mix of activities, although it still matters whether one chooses contemplation as a life-plan (*propositum*) or as an adjunct (*accessio*). For Stoics, the life-plan is action, whereas contemplation is merely a "harborage" (*statio*); that is, a respite on life's journey but not a destination in itself (7.3–4).

Now concluding his argument in favor of lifelong contemplation, Seneca returns to the first of the reasons listed earlier to remain aloof from ordinary political action, namely that one's community may be too corrupt to benefit

ARGUMENTS AGAINST POLITICAL ENGAGEMENT		ARGUMENTS JUSTIFYING THEORETICAL PURSUITS	
Corruption	The state may be too corrupt to receive service.	Self-amelioration	Others benefit from improvements in the philosopher's character.
Weakness	The philosopher may lack power and influence.	Wider Polity	The world benefits when there is a witness to god's activities.
Chronic Illness	The philosopher may be in poor health.	Naturalness	Both philosophy and action are natural to human beings.
Universal Corruption	All states may be too corrupt to receive service.	Legacy	Future generations benefit from what philosophers leave behind, e.g., their writings.

Figure 1.1   The arguments of *On Leisure*

from one's services. In fact, he says, this justification can be extended to cover all cases, for if one's standards are high enough, no state is ever such as to merit the philosopher's efforts at civic service, or to welcome them (8.1). Hence a life of leisure is always permissible, provided one's leisure is made to serve the public interest in some larger sense. Indeed the Chrysippan mandate can be understood to say that we should not only tolerate a life in retreat, but even choose that life. The supposed requirement to engage in the political life of existing cities turns out to be a kind of self-cancelling instruction, like recommending the sailing life but saying one should not embark on the kind of sea that includes shipwrecks and contrary winds (8.3).

In sum, *On Leisure* offers four arguments whose aim is to show that the requirement to engage in public service cannot be universal, and four arguments that seek to justify theoretical pursuits as an alternative form of service. These are summarized in Figure 1.1. It will be helpful to refer back to these arguments as we look more closely at the problems presented by the treatise.

On Leisure and the Stoic Tradition

Seneca's professed commitment in *On Leisure* is to Stoicism, and his report of this portion of Stoic doctrine is in fact corroborated at key points. Crucially, his call to action "unless there is hindrance" is matched in the doxography of Diogenes Laertius, which cites Chrysippus's view that "the wise person will engage in politics if nothing prevents him."[7] The Wider Polity argument likewise draws on a familiar Chrysippan conception of the universal city to which all rational beings belong.[8] The existence of that

---

[7] Diog. Laert. 7.121 (*SVF* 3.697).
[8] The cosmos meets the definition of a city because it is "a number of persons dwelling in one place governed by law" (Dio Chrysostom 36.20 [LS 67J]); see further Schofield (1991: 57–92).

wider polity enables activities pursued in retreat from one's immediate community to be construed as an alternative form of service. The moral requirement then applies equally to both forms of service, and the selection between them can be made on the basis of circumstances.[9] Also characteristically Stoic is Seneca's effort to establish the naturalness of the theoretical urge via an appeal to our innate curiosity. Arguments derived from supposed innate tendencies of the human species were used by more than one school, but the appeal in *On Leisure* 5.2 to a universal love of problem-solving strongly resembles that of Cato, Cicero's Stoic spokesman, in Book 3 of *De Finibus*.[10]

An especially subtle feature of Seneca's discussion concerns the pleasure scholars experience in pursuing their favorite subjects. It is implied throughout the treatise that such pleasure could become the very motivation for the life of study, in which case one would no longer be acting in accordance with Stoic principles. A fragment from Book 4 of Chrysippus's *On Lives* gives evidence of the classic Stoic attitude on this point:

> Those who suppose that the life of leisure is best suited to philosophers seem to me to make the fundamental error of assuming that one should do this for the sake of some sort of amusement or something like that, and that one should somehow spend one's entire life that way – that is, pleasurably, if one examines it clearly. For we should not mistake their assumption: many of them say this clearly; others more covertly.[11]

In speaking of philosophers who "say this clearly" and of others who say it "more covertly," Chrysippus is presumably attacking first the Epicureans and then the Peripatetics.[12] But he is not necessarily seeking to eliminate pleasure from the philosopher's experience. His general position on pleasure is not that it is wrong in itself but that it should not be regarded as a

---

[9] *Leisure* 8.1: *e lege Chrysippi vivere otiose licet: non dico ut otium patiatur, sed ut eligat*. For selection (ἐκλογή) and selective value elsewhere in Stoicism see Stobaeus 2.7.7g, 84–85 Wachsmuth (LS 58E, SVF 3.128); Cicero, *Fin.* 3.20; Diog. Laert. 7.88.

[10] Cicero, *Fin.* 3.17–18. Compare the specific points made in *Leisure* 5.2 with Cicero's appeal to young children being delighted when they find something out even when it brings no further reward. Seneca's argument is closer to *Fin.* 3.17 than it is to the Peripatetic argument from innate tendencies in *Fin.* 4.18. Also relevant are Hierocles's treatment of social *oikeiōsis* (col. 11 [LS 57D]) and Diog. Laert. 7.130: "the rational animal is begotten by nature suited for both contemplation and action."

[11] The passage is quoted in Plutarch, *Stoic Self-Contradictions* 1033d (*SVF* 3.702). For discussion, see Bénatouïl (2007: 1–13); Griffin (1976: 340).

[12] The *locus classicus* for the pleasures of contemplation is Aristotle, *Nic. Eth.* 10.7, where one reason *theōria* is the ultimate good is that it yields exceptionally pure and stable pleasures. Cicero in *Lucullus* 127 makes the pleasures of contemplation an Antiochean or "Old Academic" trademark. See Dionigi (1983: 92–95); Bénatouïl (2007: 13–21) and (2009: 9–20).

primary motivator: it is merely a concomitant (ἐπιγέννημα) of virtuous activity.[13] Seneca is thus in accord with Chrysippus when he says at *On Leisure* 6.1 that what matters is whether one chooses a contemplative life *voluptatis causa*, for the sake of the pleasure it entails; and again in 7.2, where he refers to the pleasure of study as an "adjunct" (*accessio*) to its main purpose.[14]

The tendency toward doctrinalism is not mitigated in the least by Seneca's talk of how all three lives favor some combination of action, study, and pleasure. He will derive a rhetorical advantage where he can find one, but the fact is that his admission in 7.2 about the great distinction between a life-plan and a concomitant undermines the coalition he offers to build. And his overtures to the rival schools are not very convincing. His report on the role of reflection in Epicureanism, though well grounded in Epicurus's own statements, does not credit the school with any real scientific interests, and the wording is tinged with contempt: the school is a "voluptuary sect" and its motive for rational thought is "to make pleasure secure for itself" (7.2).[15] Of the third party to the discussion, those who advocate contemplation for its own sake, the paragraph says nothing specific, only that some people do this (*alii petunt eam*, 7.2). One gets the impression that these scarcely identifiable "some people" have no arguments to offer in support of their view and are included merely for the sake of symmetry. What emerges from the paragraph is the distinctiveness of the Stoic view, the one that is committed to moral action for its own sake.

All the same, there are some features of Seneca's own professedly Stoic argument that look to be of Platonist derivation. The strongest of the Stoics' exemption claims, that there is no government which can tolerate a philosopher or which a philosopher can tolerate (the Corruption argument), would seem to derive from the sixth book of Plato's *Republic*. There Socrates answers the charge that philosophers are useless to their cities by pointing out that existing cities are invariably hostile to philosophers' efforts

---

[13] Diog. Laert. 7.86.
[14] Seneca assigns supervenient status to both joy and pleasure also in *On Happiness*: see page 183.
[15] Dionigi (1983: 242–43), Williams (2003: 95), and Scott (2014a: 151) have all noted a resemblance between Seneca's description of how the study of nature "bursts through the barriers of heaven" (*caeli munimenta perrumpit*, *Leisure* 5.6) and Lucretius 1.70–73, where Epicurus wishes "to break out of the tight enclosures of nature's gates" (*effringere ut arta / naturae primus portarum claustra*), and his mind advances "far beyond the flaming bulwarks of the sky" (*extra ... longe flammantia moenia mundi*). Seneca had read Lucretius (note esp. *Letters* 95.11), but even if the echo here is deliberate, it should not be read as indicating any receptivity to Epicurean ethics or to the reasons Epicureans would give for preferring a retired life. See further pages 97–98.

to improve them (487cd). In general, human communities are so much given over to lawlessness that philosophers will reasonably prefer to keep to themselves (496cd). So also with the exemption for those with chronic illness. The same portion of the *Republic* has Socrates remark that the only people who will be able to remain free of corruption are those philosophical natures who are exempt from public service by reason of exile, provincial origin, or what he calls the "bridle of our friend Theages" – that is, chronic bodily illness (496c). Seneca's remarks about viewing the constellations in *On Leisure* 5.4 also have a Platonic cast, reminding one of the released cave dweller of *Republic* 7.516a–b, who progresses to more and more exalted sights, and of the chariot-souls of *Phaedrus* 247c–e, who mount to the upper realms in order to view the exterior Forms. Even the observations about our upright stature and flexible necks recall the analysis of the human body in *Timaeus* 47a–b and 90a–d.

Given these Platonic associations, it is very striking that Seneca treats these lines of argument as part of the Stoic position rather than ceding them to the absolute devotee of the contemplative life (*ille qui contemplationi inservit*, 7.1). To explain this, either we must accept that Seneca deliberately conflates his Stoic view with those of its rivals in this area or we must posit that the features we associate with Plato had already been taken up by Seneca's Stoic predecessors, so that he does not regard them as belonging to the opposition. Considering the strong doctrinal bias of some portions of the treatise, the second option is preferable. The intervening history is very long, with many Stoic authors working through the same issues in dialogue with Academics and Peripatetics of various kinds.[16] Plato's works were the shared heritage of all these philosophers, and points made in support of one position could easily be co-opted and reinterpreted to favor an opposite view. Seneca appears to have studied a work by Panaetius on the contemplative and active parts of philosophy, and he also knows some works of Posidonius, who took *theōria* in the sense of "observing the order of the

---

[16] A minor but interesting indication of the prior history of the discussion may be gleaned from the two references to Carthage, alongside Athens, as a city in which philosophers might live (4.1, 8.2). This has been thought puzzling: if a Neronian author is casting about for examples of Mediterranean cities, long-destroyed Carthage ought not to be the second example that comes to mind. (Williams (2003: 14–15) rightly contests the suggestion by Dionigi (1983: 103–4, 275–76) that Rome is meant.) Carthage does, however, have a profile in the Hellenistic Academy as the home city of Clitomachus, also known as Hasdrubal, a pupil of Carneades and later head of the Academy (Diog. Laert. 4.67; Cicero, *De or.* 1.45; *Tusc.* 3.54). If the arguments Seneca presents have their prior history in dialectical exchange between Stoics and Academics in the third and second centuries, Carthage might indeed be a natural example to mention of cities not conducive to public service by philosophers.

cosmos" into his definition of the ethical end.¹⁷ We also know from *On Tranquility of Mind* that Seneca was familiar with a work by Athenodorus of Tarsus that argued in favor of philosophical retirement on the basis of a Platonic-sounding claim about the corruption of all governments.¹⁸ Rather than crediting what look like Platonist elements in his own view to some unannounced program of eclecticism, we should accept his framing of the work as containing Stoic arguments to defend his own contemplative activity and that of his Stoic forebears – even if the real provenance of those arguments is considerably more complicated.¹⁹

Tensions within the Argument

With that said, serious questions remain about the nature and content of the theoretical activity Seneca has in mind. If contemplation is permissible on Stoic principles, then what is it that one is permitted to contemplate, and how does one go about contemplating it? Does contemplation need to reach any conclusions, and if it does, must these be conveyed to anyone besides the philosopher himself? How, if at all, do the specifically moral benefits that accrue to the philosopher extend to others? On these points *On Leisure* yields confusing and contradictory answers.

At first, it appears as if the retirement Seneca recommends has only one purpose: to improve one's functioning as a moral agent. Retreat will be beneficial (*proderit*) and conducive to psychic health (*salutare*) because it will make us better people, enabling us to live in a single-minded and consistent way (*aequali et uno tenore*). This language in *On Leisure* 1.1 precedes the introduction of Stoic material, but it is continued later at 3.5, where it also grounds the Self-Amelioration argument, that improving one's own character counts as a form of service to one's community. If the treatise went no further than this, we might be inclined to conclude that typical "contemplative" activities would be reading treatises on morals and performing spiritual exercises based on them, no doubt coupled with

---

[17] For Panaetius, compare *Letters* 94.45 with Diog. Laert. 7.92 and Cicero, *Off.* 1.15–17; and see Griffin (1976: 340). For Posidonius, see fragment 186.13–15 Edelstein and Kidd: τὸ ζῆν θεωροῦντα τὴν τῶν ὅλων ἀλήθειαν καὶ τάξιν καὶ συγκατασκευάζοντα αὐτὴν κατὰ τὸ δυνατόν. See further Kidd (1988: vol. 2, 672–73), with Bénatouïl (2009: 7–8).
[18] Seneca quotes Athenodorus and discusses his position in *Tranquility* 3.1–8. The consistency of Seneca's position between the two works is argued in Griffin (1976: 324–27, 331–34).
[19] For an assessment of the problematic notion of eclecticism in ancient philosophy, with a helpful perspective on Seneca in particular, see Donini (2011) and page 87.

the same kinds of self-examination and self-admonishment Seneca usually recommends for those seeking moral progress.[20]

With the introduction of the wider polity, however, the scope of contemplation broadens. Ethics is still at the fore, but the concern now seems to be about ethical theory rather than about one's own disposition to ethical behavior. In *On Leisure* 4.2, the topics listed for contemplation begin with "what virtue is, whether there is one virtue or many, whether it is nature or craft that makes men good." And the same passage also mentions additional objects of study: whether there is one physical world or many, whether matter is continuous or interspersed with void; where god dwells and whether he manages the world or only observes its workings, whether the world is eternal. The contemplative procedure seems to be different here as well. Rather than addressing only one's own moral shortcomings, contemplation is now a matter of pondering and seeking to understand so as to provide god with a witness for his works. Similarly, in 5.5–6, one is to observe the things Nature has designed us to observe, the list of which begins with the parade of constellations and then proceeds to more abstract topics in physics and cosmology: the origin and structure of the universe and the human soul, the elements, and the like. In this second list, there is no mention even of ethical theory.

Yet in the following paragraph, the role of practical ethics is again central. Turning "from things human to things divine" involves both "the love of the virtues" and "the cultivation of the intellect" (6.2). The relation between *otium* and political engagement is that between virtue as a capacity ("thinking what one ought to do") and virtue in action ("bringing what one has practiced to fruition"). The language here suggests that the operative procedures for contemplation are deliberation concerning prospective actions and spiritual exercises that provide the resolve to carry them out. Seneca even goes so far as to say that a virtuous life spent entirely in contemplation would be an "incomplete and listless good." To give point to the exercise, one must give evidence of what one has learned.

This "showing" might consist in someday acting upon what one has learned; this again would be justification by self-amelioration. Or, as Seneca goes on to suggest, it might consist in leaving something for posterity, presumably either through oral transmission or through the medium of writing (the Legacy argument). Such is his defense of Zeno and Chrysippus

---

[20] Reading is indicated by the expression *secedere ad optimos viros* in 1.1. The expression is correctly interpreted by Williams (2003: 64) from parallels in *On the Brevity of Life*; but the theme is a favorite one in Seneca, in such passages as *Letters* 39.2.

in 6.4–5. But again, the actual content of the requisite legacy is not specified. Is one's leisure defensible if one has discovered a new planet? A new sort of syllogism? Or would it be necessary to have discovered what virtue is – and in that case, can more than one person leave such a legacy? We can see that the work of the theoretical philosopher ought to be other-directed in some sense, but without further specification, it remains quite unclear how the justification is supposed to work.

Especially puzzling is the relation between contemplative philosophy and improvement in one's own moral character. Much is made of this in *On Leisure*; in fact, at some points it seems as if the argument from self-amelioration is the primary justification for the life of study. But we can hardly suppose that the contribution made by Zeno and Chrysippus consists only in their personal moral improvement. To render the dialogue coherent, we would need to assume at least that discoveries in ethical theory improve the character of anyone who learns of them. Theology and physics could perhaps be got on board by similar means, on grounds that they alter our disposition as agents by putting trivial objects of pursuit into a larger perspective. The tenor of *On Leisure* 4–5, however, is surely against Seneca's putting those studies merely in a supporting role.

Letters on Ethics: The Rule of Genre

Would the continuation of *On Leisure* have resolved these problems for us if it had survived? I doubt it, for the work we have never even acknowledges that such difficulties exist. Matters are quite different, though, when we track the subsequent career of these same arguments within the *Letters on Ethics*. In that work, which is itself much concerned with the question of philosophical retirement, Seneca often revisits the themes and even the specific phrases of *On Leisure*, adapting them to suit the new context.[21] But he also regularly shows awareness of the lack of fit between the justification via self-amelioration and some of the most characteristic pursuits of the contemplative philosopher. Although he does not refrain from purely theoretical inquiries and expresses some enthusiasm for them, his premise throughout the *Letters* is that philosophy aims strictly at moral progress and the eventual attainment of the *vita beata*. The challenge for

---

[21] In addition to *Letters* 8.1–2, themes from *On Leisure* are addressed in letters 1, 19, 22, and 68. Enthusiasm for theoretical study comes through strongly in *Letters* 78.26, 89.1, 93.8–9, and 95.10–11. Further to the connections between the two works, see André (1962b); Griffin (1976: 334–39); Dionigi (1983: 51–52).

him is to use his rhetorical talent to find ways of mitigating the tension between *sui causa* reflection and the ethical objectives he has established for the work.[22]

A general similarity of situation links book 1 of the *Letters* with *On Leisure*. As the work opens, we find Seneca urging his correspondent Lucilius to follow his own example and withdraw from public service in order to devote all his time to philosophical studies. Lucilius is to read the moralists and to select a model of life from their writings, just as the addressee of *On Leisure* was urged to do.[23] Seneca's own life, as represented within his work, will serve as his exemplum of a philosophic retirement during old age; the somewhat younger Lucilius will be the point of identification for any reader who is considering a whole-life retirement. In letter 8, especially, Seneca echoes the language of *On Leisure* 1.4 in speaking of his own writing project. Like the nameless interlocutor of the fragmentary treatise, Lucilius challenges Seneca with the Stoic precept that one should continue "in action" (*in actu*) right up to the moment of death. Again, Seneca responds that the life that he recommends, which is also the life he himself leads, counts as an alternative form of moral action:

> "Are you, then, telling me to avoid the crowd, retire, and content myself with my private thoughts? What about those instructions of your school that bid us die in action?" Well, do you think this is inaction that I am urging upon you? Here is the reason I have hidden myself away and closed the doors: to benefit the greater number. Not one of my days is spent in leisure, and I claim a part of the nights for study. I have no time for sleep, until it overcomes me; my eyes are exhausted and drooping with late hours, but I keep them to the task. . . . I have withdrawn not only from society but from business, and especially from my own business. The work that I am doing is for posterity: it is they who can benefit from what I write. I am committing to the page some healthful admonitions, like the recipes for useful salves. I have found these effective on my own sores, which, even if not completely healed, have ceased to spread. (*Letters* 8.1–2)

Like Zeno and Chrysippus in *On Leisure* 6.4–5, Seneca as a philosophical author does more for humanity than he could by legal advocacy and other forms of public service. "Believe me, those who appear to be doing nothing are doing greater things – they are dealing with matters both human and divine" (*Letters* 8.6).

---

[22] For a thoughtful reading of the tension between Seneca's therapeutic stance in the *Letters* and his broader philosophical interests, see Inwood (2007a: xvi–xviii).

[23] *Letters* 2.2, 6.4–5, 11.8–10; and see note 20.

Yet these "matters human and divine" are not as wide-ranging as they sound. In contrast to the miscellany of topics recommended for study and contemplation in *On Leisure*, the suggestion of eighth letter seems to be that one should devote oneself exclusively to ethics – and not ethical theory, either, but a steady diet of self-amelioration. Seneca himself has withdrawn from business only so that he can deliver "healthful admonitions" that will enable his readers to amend their lives. These admonitions will be like recipes for medicaments that he has tried out on his own "sores"; that is, they are methods of promoting healthy agency in oneself, written out by one who has found them to be effective. Seneca even provides a sample of the kind of discourse his *otium* produces: a straightforward sermon on the dangers of vice, the advantages of asceticism, and the superfluity of wealth. What we have, then, is not a recap of the Legacy justification of *On Leisure* 6.4–5 but rather a combination of that argument with the Self-Amelioration argument of *On Leisure* 3.5.[24] Seneca now claims both that he is making himself a better moral agent and that he is leaving behind a written legacy, passing on the benefits of philosophy to future moral agents. Both parts of the argument are strengthened by being combined, for an elderly philosopher might not have much opportunity to act again in the world, and a philosophical legacy that consisted only of unjustified studies would not become justified merely by transmission. At the same time, this is a very limited form of justification. It does nothing to support spending one's time on abstract topics in physics and cosmology. Even the finer points of ethical theory might not be a defensible topic of study.

Indeed, the first sequence of letters would seem to make matters rather worse for anyone who wishes to devote long stretches of time to the study of philosophy in abstraction from the business of ethical living. With his emphasis on using one's time productively to improve one's own character, the Seneca of the *Letters on Ethics* establishes a general policy of concentrating on the practicalities of life. Adhering to this policy, the epistolographer makes a point of restricting his topics to such practical matters as whether to attend sporting events (letter 7), how to exercise the body (letter 15), and how to behave during holidays (letter 18), eschewing any very sophisticated discussion. It is not that more technical material is excluded altogether, for the letters also venture into such topics as Platonic ontology (letter 58), the

---

[24] Compare the view attributed to Athenodorus in *Tranquility* 3.3, which likewise insists that a life of retirement benefits others by speech or writing (*prodesse velit singulis universaque ingenio, voce, consilio*). Again, the implication is that the content of the speech and writing is moral instruction.

classification of causes (65), moral theory (71, 76, 94–95), and even Stoic metaphysics (106, 117). But such material is present on sufferance, as it were. The epistolographer allows himself to include it, but in most cases he also draws attention to his own breach of decorum. In so doing, he preserves the justification he has established for the project as a whole but leaves his more technical discussions outside the umbrella.

A favorite device for mitigating the tension between Seneca's stated objectives for the *Letters* and his forays into more sophisticated philosophy is what Brad Inwood calls the "pragmatic break."[25] Some more abstruse reflection will be cut short with an apology, as if the epistolographer had merely digressed from some intended disquisition on practical ethics. In the 58th letter, for instance, a fascinating discussion of Platonic ontology is interrupted after only six pages, at which point Seneca verbally smacks his brow:

> "What have I to gain," you say, "from these fine distinctions (*subtilitates*) of yours?" Nothing, if you ask me. But just as the engraver, tired from a long period of close work, turns his eyes away to rest and, as we say, to "pasture" them, so should we sometimes relax our minds and refresh them with some amusement.[26]

As a rule, the pragmatic break is followed immediately by a return to therapeutic ethics, often by drawing some unanticipated and quite tangential moral out of what has been said. Here, as in the similar passage in 65.17–18, Seneca apologizes for his truancy with the claim that theoretical studies provide relaxation and refreshment for the mind, as if to strengthen it for the more difficult work of practical ethics. But the excuse is unconvincing – and is not intended to be convincing, for the pragmatic break is not really an admission of regret. If anything, there is a touch of ostentation, not unlike the orator's *praeteritio* or the *recusatio* of the Augustan poets. Despite the show of disciplining himself to spend time on practicalities, the author of the *Letters* does not want anyone to miss the fact that his real philosophical retreat is an intellectually sophisticated one.[27]

---

[25] Inwood (2007a: 131); for additional examples see pages 236–37.
[26] *Letters* 58.25. The imagery is strikingly similar to that of *NQ* 1 *praef.* 2 and 3 *praef.* 11. Additional examples in the *Letters* include 106.11–12; 113.21–22. For the metaphor, compare Antiochus in Cicero, *Lucullus* 127 *animorum ingeniorumque naturale quoddam quasi pabulum*.
[27] Inwood (2007a: 263): "We should perhaps see Seneca's apologetic introduction of technicality not as a betrayal of his own principles but rather as an attempt to extend technical philosophy into an otherwise inhospitable genre; that is, far from indicating his distaste for technicality it would be a mark of his enthusiasm for it."

The Life of the Mind

Another convenient ploy is to assign responsibility for some abstruse bit of philosophy to someone other than the author. This happens, for instance, in letters 45, 48, and 49, where Seneca's objections to the excessive subtlety of Stoic logicians do not hinder him from quoting their favorite conundrums in full.[28] With greater tolerance, some letters late in the extant collection represent the theoretical question as an inquiry submitted by Lucilius in one of the intervening letters, one potentially related to Seneca's own separate project in moral philosophy.[29] Seneca will answer his correspondent's question, but, reluctantly, with a certain amount of preliminary scolding:

> You want me to send you my opinion on the question our school has bandied about, as to whether justice, courage, prudence, and the other virtues are animate creatures. It is by such sophistry (*subtilitate*), dearest Lucilius, that we have made people think that we train our minds on trivialities and waste our free time on discussions that will do us no good. (*Letters* 113.1)

The ambiguous term *subtilitas* links these latter devices to 58.25 and related passages. *Subtilitas*, "subtlety, precision," can refer either to a quality of discussions or to an argument itself. Seneca uses it with disapprobation, even scorn, when his point is that more time has been spent on an inquiry than is morally justifiable: it is "your fancy syllogism" (*subtilissima collectio*, *Letters* 45.8); "those splitters of hairs" (*istis subtilibus*, *Letters* 48.4); "pointless scholarly sophistication" (*subtilitatem inutilem*, *Letters* 65.16). But the word is neutral in itself, and its connotations can be reversed. In the midst of his treatment of Platonic ontology in letter 58, Seneca comments that the difficulty of the subject is Plato's fault, but then adds, *nulla est autem sine difficultate subtilitas* ("without difficulty, however, there is no fineness of distinction") – as if *subtilitas* were a desirable quality well worth the effort needed to achieve it.[30] In all cases, the term picks out the technical studies of the committed philosopher, whether in logic or in other theoretical studies, and in all cases it makes the point that these studies demand both time and energy. If there is a shift of valence, it is because that expenditure of time is sometimes regarded as justified and sometimes not.

---

[28] See pages 228–29.
[29] Questions from Lucilius are mentioned in *Letters* 67.2–3, 102.3, 106.1, 108.1; 109.17, 113.1, and 124.1. References to a separate work on moral philosophy are at 106.1–3, 108.1, 109.17. Given the questions that are said to belong to it, that project seems to be conceived as a systematic venture in ethical theory. See further Leeman (1953); Lana (1991: 275–78); Inwood (2007a: 262–64); fragments in Vottero (1998: 206–9).
[30] *Letters* 58.20; compare 65.14, 91.17, 95.61. The comments of Scarpat (1965: 157–89) are apposite here.

Representing the Philosophical Life

Perhaps the most telling indications of Seneca's attitude toward theoretical philosophy are to be found in the representational elements of the *Letters on Ethics*: literary portraits, snatches of conversation, and bits of narrative that reveal how the epistolographer and his associates spend their time in retreat. For although these elements must have been modeled on Seneca's real experience (so that the picture could be recognizable and believable in its own time), they are still fictive elements, selected and shaped to display to the reading public the image that Seneca as author wants them to see. The bits of self-portraiture are more akin to the carefully crafted self-representation of Cicero in his philosophical dialogues than they are to the topical details included in Cicero's private correspondence. Similarly, the impression that is given of Lucilius and the cameo roles for others of Seneca's acquaintance are on the same level as Cicero's literary portraits of Lucius Licinius Crassus, Marcus Antonius, and other historical figures who appear in his dialogues.

Because Seneca's widely disseminated letters could potentially incur political repercussions for himself and his friends, it was in his interest to craft his representations of the lives of philosophers in such a way as to avoid anything that might draw hostile attention. While he certainly presents himself as one who has withdrawn from political life for the sake of study and urges his friend to do the same, he also speaks pointedly of the gratitude of philosophers toward their rulers (letter 73), and he does not mention again the possibility that corruption in the existing state might constitute a reason for retirement.[31] Even if he believes in the Corruption argument from *On Leisure*, it would hardly be expedient to press that case in a work with strong autobiographical elements. Chronic illness, even feigned illness, was a safer form of exemption in Nero's Rome.

Even beyond the political concern, however, the manner in which Seneca chooses to represent himself and others is worth attending to for what it reveals about his conception of the theoretical life. Relevant material could be supplied from many points in the collection, but the most interesting examples are to be found in a consecutive series of letters in book 7, comprising letters 64, 65, 66, 67, and 68. In these letters,

---

[31] The point has been well treated in Griffin (1976: 360–66). Griffin holds that the statement of this very view in *Leisure* 8.1 is not endorsed by Seneca. I disagree, but her case is still very persuasive as concerns the *Letters on Ethics*. The recent work by Carey Seal is especially helpful in framing the complexities of Seneca's attitude to political participation (2021: 138–76).

Seneca shows himself to be very much attracted to the contemplative life on Platonist-Aristotelian lines, but also constantly retrenching to the programmatic justification for the correspondence as a written legacy promoting self-amelioration in others. We can read this movement in the narrative material that frames each of these letters; that is, in the brief notice of a day's events that sets the scene and in his interactions with Lucilius and other interlocutors.

In the 64th letter, Seneca recounts an evening visit from friends. After dinner and a wide-ranging conversation, everyone listens to a reading from the moralist Quintus Sextius. Seneca describes the effect of the reading on him. He has been fired with enthusiasm for moral action and is eager for opportunities to act courageously, but he is also struck with wonder at the achievements of philosophy itself.

> For me, at least, the very thought of wisdom absorbs much of my time. I am no less astonished when I gaze at it than I am sometimes by the heavens themselves, which I often see as if for the first time. For that reason I hold in awe both the discoveries of philosophy and those who have made those discoveries; and I thrill to claim what is, as it were, an inheritance from many predecessors. Everything they collected, everything they labored over, was for me! (*Letters* 64.6–7)

The language and exalted tone recall image of the philosopher as the *admirator naturae* from *On Leisure* 5.8, one who studies the cosmos and especially the movements of the stars. It seems, though, that merely gazing in wonder does not suffice, for Seneca immediately promises to augment the philosophical heritage with discoveries of his own, in a renewed version of the Legacy justification:

> But let us do what a good head of household does: let us add to our endowment. May it be a larger inheritance when it passes from me to posterity. (*Letters* 64.7)

Proceeding, he again combines the idea of making philosophical discoveries with that of philosophy as a remedy for moral failings. The achievements of his predecessors now become medications for the cure of various ailments, and the intellectual work of the present day consists in determining the means of application: "selecting the time and method of administration that is right for the individual" (64.8). This, too, is an achievement, but a distinctly secondary one.

The 65th letter continues and develops the imagery even as it offers a rather different form of justification. Seneca is ill for an entire morning, but in the afternoon is able to read for a while and then, progressing, to do some unusually intense writing. He is then interrupted by friends who strike up a conversation on the classification of causes, a report of which occupies the bulk of the letter. Challenged eventually by Lucilius to explain the attraction of "frittering away your time on these matters which do not eliminate any of your passions nor drive out any desires" (65.15), Seneca explains in unmistakably Platonic language that discussions of this kind are beneficial to the spirit. As long as they are not carried to extremes, they uplift the mind, which is otherwise always longing to escape the shackles and weight of the body and return to its place of origin. He continues with a more original analogy:

> Just as craftsmen, when they are engaged in some intricate task that strains the eyes and the light is indirect and poor, come out into the open and visit some place devoted to public recreation, there to refresh their eyes with the free light of day; even so does the mind, shut away in this somber, dark apartment, emerge whenever it can into the open and relax in the contemplation of the universe. The wise person, and likewise the seeker after wisdom, abides indeed within his body, yet with his better part is absent, turning his thoughts to things above. (*Letters* 65.17–18)

This beautiful image calls to mind Plato's Cave analogy from the *Republic*, yet takes it in a different direction in keeping with Seneca's own objectives.[32] Here, theoretical philosophy is essentially a respite, a means of refreshment for the mind when it is exhausted with more productive but less enjoyable endeavors. The body in the analogy is the poorly lit room in which the mind is constrained to work. But the "intricate task" itself can only be the productive work Lucilius has just complained Seneca is neglecting – that is, the schooling of emotion and desire, the usual business of the *Letters on Ethics*. Rather than representing personal moral development as itself a form of contemplation, Seneca here treats the therapeutic endeavor as a necessary but fatiguing task and theoretical philosophy as something quite different, an abstract and essentially impractical pastime that assists ethical therapy mainly by providing an occasional relief from it.

Bodily illness figures prominently also in Seneca's portrait of Claranus at the beginning of letter 66. Claranus is introduced as an old schoolmate of Seneca's and hence must be of about the same age. But Claranus has not had Seneca's opportunities to purse a life of advocacy in the courts and to work his way up the *cursus honorum*. Instead, his circumstances have

---

[32] The Platonic resonance is noted by Lowenstam (1998: 70–71). For Seneca's management of Platonism in the passage, see Sedley (2005: 137–38); Inwood (2005: 314–18).

The Life of the Mind 35

imposed a life of seclusion, for Claranus, we learn, is physically misshapen and severely stooped (*deformi humilique corpusculo*, 66.3), and this condition is not merely in consequence of his age but has been with him since birth. The portrait is of one with some very noticeable congenital defect, perhaps involving spasticity or paralysis, since Claranus is not only misshapen but also hampered in his movements (*impeditos*, 66.3). Yet his mind is unimpaired: it shows through the body as a demonstration of the independence of ethical and intellectual characteristics from the physical.[33]

To this physically debilitated but intellectually powerful Claranus is assigned the philosophical content of one of Seneca's most ambitious letters. Seneca and Claranus have spent several days together and have had multiple conversations; these are to be recorded and sent to Lucilius. The present letter treats a technical point in Stoic axiology: how a certain classification of goods can be reconciled with the Stoic postulate on the equality of values.[34] This, we are told, was "the topic investigated on the first day" (66.5) – as if Seneca and Claranus had been the discussants in the first book of some Ciceronian treatise. And it has indeed been a lengthy conversation, for the letter itself extends without apology to thirteen pages, longer by far than any letter Seneca has yet written and the third longest in the collection.[35] We are here in the realm of dedicated, unhurried philosophical discussion, more meticulous and sustained than the quick summaries of Platonic and Aristotelian doctrine offered in letters 58 and 65. Claranus and Seneca will work together to solve a particular problem in ethical theory, and they will devote whatever time that discussion requires.

There can be no doubt that the character Seneca gives to his interlocutor is connected to the unusually rarefied content of letter 66. Claranus's illness provides the excuse for developing that content via the Chronic Illness exemption: with his physical impairment, he cannot be faulted for devoting his time to philosophical studies. More important, though, is the transformation this extended practice of thinking and discussion has worked upon his character, and at the same time on Seneca's way of perceiving his character:

---

[33] The thought is more in accordance with Plato, *Phaedo* 66d–67e, than with Stoic ideas of beauty – if we are to give any weight to the texts on Stoic physiognomics; for example, Diog. Laert. 7.173.
[34] The main argument of the letter is analyzed in Inwood (2005) 259–70; a more detailed treatment is given in Inwood (2007a: 155–81).
[35] Only the 94th and 95th letters exceed it in length. Compare Seneca's apologies for length in much shorter letters: *Letters* 30.18 *tam longas epistulas*, 45.13 *ne epistulae modum excedam*, 58.37 *in longum exeo*. Lana (1991) provides statistics on the lengths of the individual letters.

> Certainly I have begun to see our friend Claranus in a new way. He seems quite handsome to me, and as upright in stature as he is in spirit. A great man may come out of a hovel; a great and handsome mind from a lowly and misshapen body. (*Letters* 66.2–3)

It is not only that Claranus is brave in enduring his physical impairments, although that is true of him. It is actually that he is beautiful, *formosus* rather than *deformis*. What is intimated here is that the intellectual activity represented by the letter is somehow ennobling in itself, even without any subsidiary payoff in conduct. There is a distinct resemblance between Claranus as the contemplative philosopher and the iconic *sapiens* described within the letter, the "spirit that gazes at what is real, that knows what to pursue and to avoid, that assigns value to things in accordance with nature and not by opinion – the spirit that injects itself into the cosmos as a whole and casts its contemplation over every action of the universe" (66.6). Claranus is admired for depth of thought that produces moral action, but his bearing witness to god's activities is equally important.

Now Claranus himself is soon to be forgotten as the epistolary narrative moves on its intermittent way. His influence continues, though, in that he helps us to understand the significance of Seneca's own age and ill health within the correspondence. In the 67th letter, as in the 65th, Seneca draws attention to his chronic illness.[36]

> I am grateful to old age for keeping me to my bed. And why not be grateful on that account? Things that all along I should not have wanted to do, I now cannot do. (*Letters* 67.2)

The parallel between himself and Claranus can hardly be missed, especially when the remainder of letter 67 investigates a question closely related to that of letter 66 and presupposes knowledge of it.[37] As the previous discussion was presented as a report of what was discussed "on the first day" (66.5), we are perhaps meant to think that this is the second day's discussion, and to read the two letters together as an extended project in moral theory. But Claranus no longer appears as interlocutor; instead, the material is presented entirely as an epistolary exchange between Seneca and Lucilius. "Let's take up the subject you are asking about," he says to Lucilius, "and scrutinize its

---

[36] Not much developed in *On Leisure*; the sickness justification operates throughout the *Letters on Ethics*. Tacitus reports a rumor that the illness was feigned (*Ann.* 15.45.3), but this is not the point; see Griffin (1976: 362). Courtil (2015: 130–40) argues convincingly that Seneca suffered for much of his life from both tuberculosis and consumption.

[37] The backward references are obvious even on a casual reading, especially in *Letters* 67.3–4 and 67.15 (*re* Epicurus). Maurach (1970: 145) traces additional connections.

nature as we would in conversation" (67.2). For readers of the *Letters on Ethics*, this means that instead of learning about philosophy at two removes, through a written report to of an earlier conversation, they are positioned to observe it directly, as Seneca thinks on paper how he will respond to Lucilius.

Following letter 67, the framing narrative of the *Letters* takes a new turn. Lucilius has at last determined to devote himself to the recommended life of leisure, abandoning his career in public service, and Seneca advises in letter 68 that part of his commitment to seclusion should be to conceal the very fact that he is secluded (*et ipsum otium absconde*, 68.1). After this rather cryptic remark, he launches into the Wider Polity justification. One who retires will be "following the example of the Stoics, even if not their instructions"; but the example is in fact consistent with the instructions, for the Stoics do not enjoin service to every state, and neither do they hold that one should serve at all times or without ending (68.2). Moreover, the wise person has a larger state which is worthy of his services. Because his true community is the entire world, he does not cease to serve even in retirement. All this is repeated from *On Leisure* 3, although the imagery is expanded:

> Indeed, it may be that in abandoning this one little corner he is moving into a greater and more spacious realm – that he is taking up a seat in heaven, and realizes now what a lowly position he held when he used to mount to the tribunal or preside from the curule chair. Bank this away in your mind: the wise person is never more active than when things divine and human come into his view. (*Letters* 68.2)

Also reminiscent of *On Leisure* is the challenge voiced by the interlocutor in 68.10: "So, Seneca, are you recommending leisure to me? Are you lowering yourself to Epicurean maxims?" The reply is that the leisure Seneca recommends will enable greater and also more beautiful actions than the affairs of the forum. He wishes heartily that Lucilius had settled on this plan (*propositum*) much earlier in life; even at his more advanced age, though, the retreat will yield good results.

For all its resemblance to *On Leisure*, however, letter 68 also differs from that work in two very noticeable ways. First, the content Lucilius is told to study in his retirement is restricted in the same way as in letter 8: he is to spend time speaking truth to himself, identifying his personal failings and treating them severely. This will be an unsavory business, comparable to the least pleasant procedures of medicine: the treatment of wounds and infections, the administration of emetics and purges, the clearing of bronchial suppurations. Second, and not unrelated, is the emphasis on concealment, a theme also present in the opening of letter 8 ("I have hidden myself away and closed the doors"). The reason offered to Lucilius for secretive behavior is a trivial one, that only if people do not know about his studies will they leave him alone to pursue them. But the point is novel, and odd, especially when Seneca goes so far as to suggest that Lucilius should name ill health or weakness or laziness as a pretext (68.3). Coming from one who has himself put forward illness repeatedly to justify all kinds of studies – and who is now publishing that fact abroad in written works meant for posterity – the remark can only be sharply ironical.

***

Seneca's thoughts on the life of study turn out to be exceptionally rich and varied. While he thinks of himself as a Stoic, he does not allow himself to be limited by the stereotypical notion of Stoics as active rather than contemplative. Indeed he lays considerable emphasis on the value of contemplation as we know it from Plato and Aristotle; that is, as *sui causa* reflection on a variety of issues in physics, theology, metaphysics, and ethical theory. In attempting to justify the philosophical retreat in *On Leisure*, he works primarily from well-established principles of Stoic ethics; in the *Letters on Ethics*, he brings in many of the same arguments, but deploys them in more flexible and creative ways.

His most frequent strategy for justifying the time given to study is to insist upon its moral benefits, how it improves one's own character for future conduct or that of others through written or oral teaching. This approach works well as long as the content of one's reflection is restricted to questions of value and techniques of self-therapy. When the topic is metaphysics or logic, however, or even some points in moral theory, the justification is more difficult. In the *Letters on Ethics*, Seneca shows himself aware of the issue and accordingly devises various rhetorical strategies to preserve the decorum of his larger project even as he allows the more technical topics to encroach upon it. Readers are expected to savor the ironies that result.

The dramatic frame of the *Letters on Ethics* provides Seneca with rich opportunities to explore these ideas, but also with a particular need for tact in addressing them. Because the letters offer Rome a lifelike representation of their author and his associates, Seneca must proceed with caution lest he seem to endorse an attitude toward public service which could prove dangerous for his philosophically minded readers. Apparently cognizant of the forces that would eventually lead to the criminalization of Stoic philosophy under imperial law, Seneca tactfully deemphasizes the notion that all existing states are corrupt beyond repair. Instead, he offers chronic ill health, Plato's "bridle of Theages," as a safer form of exemption from the senatorial career. Through his portrait of Claranus, and by implication through his portrait of himself, he endeavors to replace the negative connotations of illness with a more uplifting ideal of the independence of intellectual life from the body.

Bits of narrative in the *Letters* present us with an appealing picture of Seneca's life in retreat. We see a man deeply engaged in reading and composition, pondering the deeper meaning of each event of the day, sharing entire days in conversation with friends on a variety of philosophical issues. This at least is what he envisions of the contemplative life, and it is what he would like his readers to believe is the life he leads. Is it also an accurate description of the historical Seneca's practice of philosophy? There one should be cautious, for just as the author of the *Letters* has a clear motive for representing himself as more of an invalid than he may really have been, so also he might choose to show himself in dialogue with others to make a point about the joys of friendship, even if his real activity was primarily in the library.[38] We saw in letters 66 and 67 how contiguous questions in Stoic axiology, no doubt drawn from the same written source, can be framed as a live conversation in one letter and as an epistolary exchange in the next. "My most abundant conversation is with books," Seneca writes in 67.2, and it may well be that this is the truer picture; that is, that his day to day contemplative activity consisted entirely in reading and writing.

---

[38] This is in response to Inwood (2007c).

CHAPTER 2

Action and Emotion
Seneca and the Stoic Tradition

Therapeutic writing cannot help but delve into theoretical psychology. Any author who seeks to influence a reader's behavioral dispositions must make certain basic assumptions about how the mind works: where motivation comes from and how it interacts with belief, what emotions are and how they can be managed. Such was the case for Chrysippus of Soli and for his predecessor, Zeno of Citium, for the nature of action and the elimination of ordinary emotion were important concerns of early Stoic thought. The same is true for Seneca, writing three centuries later in a very different intellectual context. Probably it was the practical exigencies of devising philosophical treatments for the emotions that first stirred Seneca's interest in psychological questions, for his earliest writings were on grief, in his three consolatory essays; and on anger, in the treatise on that subject written for his brother Novatus. But his interest in the underpinnings of judgment, volition, and emotion remained strong throughout his career as a prose writer.

His assertions in the area of ethical psychology are of two kinds: (1) descriptive claims about how we come to initiate different kinds of behavior, how our actions connect to our beliefs about what is best for us, and why our emotions often seem to override our better judgment, and (2) normative claims about the idealized version of human existence that is the goal of personal development. These two philosophical agendas are linked by an integrated conception of human nature. Like Plato in book 1 of the *Republic* and like Aristotle in the *Nicomachean Ethics*, Seneca assumes that a benevolent Nature has designed the human psyche to function in a rational way.[1] The exercise of our reasoning abilities is our human function, and the best life for us is the one that uses our reason in the best possible way. While it is true that in our present state our rational

---

[1] Plato, *Republic* 1.352d–54a; Aristotle, *Nic. Eth.* 1.7, 1097b24–1098a18. Stoic versions of the function argument are attested in Diog. Laert. 7.86 (LS 57A), in Cicero's criticism of Chrysippus at *Fin.* 4.28, and in Seneca, *Letters* 41.8 and 76.12–16.

nature is imperfect and subject to grave error, we are also capable of self-correction; hence, we can aspire to fulfill our human potential in lives of virtue and wisdom.

In nearly every case, Seneca indicates that his positions are not of his own devising but are those of the Stoic school, *Stoici nostri* or just *nostri*. These statements need to be assessed with care, both to improve our knowledge of the history of the school and to understand Seneca's working methods. If we want to understand his relationship to the ethical psychology of the Hellenistic Stoics, we need to compare what we find in his works with the Stoic positions that were already in existence, views that he might have learned from his teachers in philosophy or studied in treatises available at Rome. Only on the basis of such comparisons can we judge whether he is a knowledgeable and orthodox exponent of early Stoic thought, an independent-minded innovator who molds school doctrine to his own taste, or an eclectic who combines Stoic ideas with elements of other philosophical traditions.

Determining what positions were held by Stoics prior to Seneca is not always easy, for we do not have any of the Hellenistic treatises in anything like its original form. Our primary resources for reconstructing Stoic doctrine are the verbatim fragments quoted by Galen, Plutarch, and other Greek authors, together with doxographical summary quoted by Stobaeus from Arius Didymus and that of Diogenes Laertius, as well as the extensive accounts given by Cicero in his *Academica, De Finibus,* and *Tusculan Disputations*. Fortunately, these accounts converge to a remarkable degree, at least as concerns the main psychological assertions of the founders of Stoicism.[2] Drawing on extensive work that has been done in this area, one can establish a baseline for interpreting Seneca's statements on the same subjects.

That is what I propose to do here. I will first offer a brief summary account of Stoic ethical psychology in the period before Seneca, drawing on the types of material just named and considering first the springs of action and then the emotions and other affective responses. Once that account is in place, I will proceed to examine Seneca's own handling of those same points, again beginning with the theory of non-emotive action and proceeding to his views on anger and other emotions. For it is in observing the way he handles the existing doctrine, his characteristic emphases and manner of

---

[2] For fuller information on these portions of Stoic doctrine, consult Inwood (1985), Long and Sedley (1987), Inwood and Donini (1999), Long (1999), Brennan (2003, 2005), Wildberger (2005), Graver (2007, 2017a). Especially valuable works on Seneca's handling of Stoic thought include Wildberger (2006), Inwood (2005), and Rist (1989). Some issues treated in this chapter have received sustained attention recently in Röttig (2022).

presentation, that we come closest to identifying a specifically Senecan set of views on these important topics.

Thought, Belief, and Action

A minimum requirement for a workable theory of action is that the potential agent should have some way of registering facts or potential facts about that environment, as *that it is day* or *that danger is approaching*. The Stoics, like Aristotle, met this need by positing a capacity for impression (φαντασία) as one essential function of the psyche.[3] The mind's directive faculty (ἡγεμονικόν) is able to think in that it can undergo a modification corresponding to some state of affairs past, present, or future, actual or possible. Since Stoics conceived of the mind as material in nature, made up of the air-fire mixture they called "breath" (πνεῦμα), this modification is at one level a material change, comparable to an imprint in wax. But the material account of psychic function plays only a minor role in Stoicism. What matters about an impression is that it represents some kind of content and that the animate creature is aware of it: in the standard definition, an impression "reveals itself and what made it."[4] In some cases, the impression takes its origin from the senses, as when one registers a certain effect of the visual world upon one's eyes and thinks, *That is a horse*.[5] Other impressions arise from within, by combining and recombining items from the mind's existing stock of concepts.

Wherever it comes from, the impression, by itself, is what one might call a mere thought. It has content of which one is aware, but no belief is formed unless one also comes to think of the relevant proposition as being either true or false. That further step was termed "assent" (συγκατάθεσις). Assent is conditioned on the character of the mind assenting: a strong mind gives strong assent, weak minds give weak assent, with strength and weakness being explicable either at the material level, in terms of the tension that holds the mind-material together, or at the logical level, in terms of the relations among the propositions a person will accept.[6] But the likelihood and suitability of giving assent may also be expressed as a characteristic of the impression itself. Some impressions are said to be not only true but particularly clear or "graspable," and these, when they gain

---

[3] Diog. Laert. 7.49–51 (LS 39A), Origen, *Princ.* 3.1.2–3 (LS 53A).
[4] Aetius (LS 39B); Sextus Empiricus, *Against the Professors* 7.161–3 (LS 70A).
[5] Cicero, *Acad.* 2.21 (LS 39C).
[6] Cicero, *Acad.* 1.41–42 (LS 41B); Sextus Empiricus, *Against the Professors* 7.151–7 (LS 41C). For tension (τόνος) as the explanatory factor at the physical level, see page 252.

assent, become the building blocks of knowledge in the person of perfect understanding.⁷ By contrast, a deranged or hallucinatory person assents to "empty" impressions.⁸

Much of the material on impressions is epistemological in interest, concerned with the nature of representation and the possibility of certain knowledge. But the basic mechanisms of impression and assent are also essential to the Stoic notion of action. In all animals, including humans, behavior is generated in response to impressions. The psychic event that initiates a behavior is termed "impulse" (ὁρμή); it is this, rather than the resulting movement of the limbs, that is of interest to ethics. Naturally the impressions to which we respond are ones we accept as true: even an animal must be assumed to believe certain things about its surroundings if it behaves accordingly.⁹ According to Arius Didymus, "what stimulates impulse is an impulsory impression of what is then and there appropriate."¹⁰ That is, an impulse can always be described as an assent to an impression with the content, *It is appropriate for me to do X right now*. For instance, walking is what happens when one decides that walking is the thing to do just at that moment. One may not always be fully conscious of making such a decision, but if asked, one would say that one meant to walk. It is that fact that differentiates the action of walking from similar movements like sleepwalking or stumbling forward when pushed.

What is it, then, that sets adult human action apart from the instinctive behaviors of animals and young children? As rational beings, adult humans experience rational impressions, ones whose propositional content they can verbalize when needed. And human beings are more reflective than even the most intelligent animals in their manner of giving and withholding assent. Specifically, they possess the concept of "following," that is, of logical consequence.¹¹ While animals can behave in complex ways and must be assumed to perform at least some inferences, only humans recognize the inferences themselves, and hence only humans are capable of evaluating and amending the thought processes that underlie their own behavior. It is for this reason that the actions of rational beings are said to be "up to us," while the behaviors of animals and young children are not.

---

[7] Cicero, *Acad.* 1.40–42 (LS 40B), 2.77–78 (LS 40D).
[8] Chrysippus *apud* Aetius 4.12 (LS 39B). Compare Sextus Empiricus, *Against the Professors* 7.246 (LS 39G).
[9] Chrysippus and Antipater *apud* Plutarch, *Stoic Self-Contradictions* 1057a (LS 53S): "without assent is neither action nor impulse."
[10] Stobaeus 2.7.9, 86 Wachsmuth (LS 53Q); cf. 2.7.9b (LS 33I).
[11] Sextus Empiricus, *Against the Professors* 8.275 (LS 53T).

This account of action was formulated in such a way as to remain consistent with the school's position on universal causal determinism. Each of our actions is determined by identifiable causes, some external to us and some internal. The external causes include impressions arising from our circumstances, while the internal causes are mental characteristics that predispose us to give or withhold assent in various cases.[12] While the Hellenistic Stoics occasionally used the term προαίρεσις ("volition" or "choice"), they did not see any need to posit a special faculty of will (i.e., an indeterminate freewill) to explain why we act in one way rather than another.[13] In their view, we make choices based upon our character, and those choices are quite real even though our character has itself been shaped by heredity and environment. As in Aristotle (*Nic. Eth.* 3.5, 1114b23), we also contribute to the shaping of our own behavioral dispositions through previous decisions that we have made. Moral responsibility remains with the agent even within a determinate world order.

Emotion and Eupathic Response

We come now to the Stoics' extraordinarily thoughtful analysis of the ordinary emotions (πάθη).[14] This is one of the points at which Stoic psychology presents a clear difference from that of Plato in book 4 of the *Republic*. For where Plato puts forward the view that episodes of anger, fear, grief, and other emotions emanate from a different part of the psyche from the part that reasons and makes decisions, the Stoics posit a single directive faculty that determines all our responses to stimuli. In speaking of the causes of the emotions, they refer to the same explanation they give for actions generally, making them an activity of the same unitary psyche.[15] They do not disregard those features that set emotions as a class apart from non-emotive actions like walking across a room, but they insist that those features can be explained without appeal to extra motivation centers or psychic functions.

---

[12] Cicero, *De fato* 39–43 (LS 62C). For discussion, see Bobzien (1998).
[13] Evidence for προαίρεσις in the early period is reviewed in Voelke (1973: 142–43), Dobbin (1991), and Graver (2003); summary in Graver (2007: 233n12).
[14] Source texts are collected in Graver (2002a: 203–23) and Long and Sedley (1987) chapter 65. I study the Stoic position more extensively in Graver (2007), which supplies additional detail on all the account that follows. See in addition Gill (2005), Price (2005), Nussbaum (2004), Sorabji (2000). For the reconstruction of Chrysippus's treatise *On Emotions*, see especially Tieleman (2003).
[15] The doctrine is attested most explicitly in Plutarch, *On Moral Virtue* 441cd (LS 61B) and 446f–447a (LS 65G). For the development of psychic monism as an issue in the ancient debate, see Gill (2005).

From the earliest period of the school, an emotion was defined as an "excessive impulse." It is, in the first instance, an impulse to feel something, for there are certain ways the mind changes in emotion, called by such terms as "expansions," "contractions," and "upliftings," and we are able to feel these changes happening in the chest region when we are excited or upset. But it may at the same time be an impulse to observable action, as when we strike someone in anger. Like every impulse, an emotion has a specifiable propositional content to which one gives assent. Distress, for instance, is caused by a belief that an evil is present, combined with a belief that mental suffering is the appropriate response to such an evil.[16] In assenting to the conjunct of these we accept something in the form of an impulsory impression; for example, that *It is now appropriate for me to feel distress*; that is, to contract the psyche. A similar account was given for the causation of each of the four genus-emotions: fear, desire, delight, and distress. Each genus could then be particularized into a number of specific emotions by listing additional phenomenological or intentional characteristics. Pity is "distress over the misery of another who is suffering unjustly"; terror is "fear that strikes hard."[17]

The inclusion of the term "excessive" in the definition requires additional explanation. Chrysippus is known to have devoted extra attention to this point, seeking to clarify how it is that we sometimes feel carried away by a mental event that is essentially our own impulse.[18] He used an analogy to a person who tries to stop running. Although running is certainly a voluntary action that occurs "through impulse," it is also an inherently vigorous movement. When one tries to stop, one cannot do so instantly: there is a moment in which one has already chosen to stop but is carried forward by momentum. The loss of control in emotion is like this. Once we initiate an emotional response, there is a period of time in which we cannot stop ourselves from feeling, and yet it is still the case that the emotion occurs through a kind of decision. It is of little use, then, to try to reason with someone while their emotion is going on, during the period of "inflammation" or emotional flooding. One may still make the attempt, but some arguments will certainly be ineffective.[19]

---

[16] Stobaeus 2.7.10b, 90 Wachsmuth; Cicero, *Tusc.* 3.25, 61, 79.
[17] Cicero, *Tusc.* 4.18, 4.19. Similar sets of definitions appear in Diog. Laert. 7.111–114 and in Stobaeus 2.7.10b–c, 91–92 Wachsmuth.
[18] Galen, *PHP* 4.2.10–18 (LS 65J, *SVF* 3.462), 4.6.35 (*SVF* 3.475); compare Cicero, *Tusc.* 4.22, 4.41–42, and see Graver (2007: 61–83); Tieleman (2003: 94–102, 170–78).
[19] Chrysippus *apud* Origen, *Cels.* 8.51 (*SVF* 3.474).

Emotions of the ordinary kind were classified as actions taken in error, on grounds that they could not occur without assent to evaluative propositions that are in reality false. As a rule, grief, fear, anger, desire, and similar emotions are directed at indifferents; that is, at circumstances external to one's own sphere of agency. In Stoic ethics, indifferents are neither genuinely good nor genuinely bad, but our emotions have implicit in them the belief that they are; indeed, it is that implicit belief that makes the emotional impulse especially powerful relative to our other impulses. Feelings that arise from false belief should not merely be limited or suppressed: if the belief is false, rational living requires eliminating it altogether. Consequently, the person of perfect understanding is characterized by impassivity (ἀπάθεια) simply as a concomitant of a correct understanding of the world.

Stoic theorists were also interested in how human beings first came to make the erroneous judgments of value that result in the ordinary emotions. Some universal causes of error were traced to earliest childhood, in cultural influences transmitted by parents and teachers, and also, more obscurely, in the "persuasiveness" of certain impressions.[20] There was also a theory of character relating to patterns of emotional behavior in individuals. Such traits as misogyny (i.e. the tendency to experience aversive emotions toward women) or irascibility (the tendency to experience anger in many situations) were explained in terms of erroneous evaluative beliefs that are especially deeply ingrained. That such "diseases" (νοσήματα) develop is at least partly the fault of the agents themselves.[21] For instance, the person who repeatedly desires money is at risk of developing the "disease" of greed and needs to prevent it by exercising the rational being's capacity for self-assessment and correction of view.

Despite their objections to the emotions of common experience, the Stoics did not deny that the capacity for affective response is a natural characteristic of the human species. Indeed, they strongly asserted this, claiming that the ideal human condition would include perfected forms of affective response. For these they used the general term "good emotions" (εὐπάθειαι) and listed three genera: "joy" in present goods, "wishing" (βούλησις) for prospective goods, and "caution" against prospective evils.[22] These eupathic responses are phenomenologically similar to the ordinary emotions, for they involve the same kinds of changes in the mind-material: joy, for instance, is "rational

---

[20] Diog. Laert. 7.89; Galen, *PHP* 5.5.14 (LS 65M, *SVF* 229a). See further Graver (2007: 149–71).
[21] Cicero, *Tusc.* 4.24–25; compare Epictetus, *Discourses* 2.18.8–10, and see Graver (2007: 164–67).
[22] Cicero, *Tusc.* 4.12–15; Diog. Laert. 7.116. Especially helpful discussions of the underlying issue may be found in Striker (1991) and Irwin (1998).

uplift." They differ from the ordinary emotions, however, in that they are directed not at externals but at features of the wise person's own character or conduct. Hence there is no eupathic response directed at present evils: the wise have no occasion for such a response, since by definition no bad activity or trait can be present in them. Conversely, they have abundant occasion for joy, since any exercise of virtue – performing a generous action, for instance – would count as a present good. Stoics also identified various more specific varieties of eupathic response, like "cheerfulness" (εὐφροσύνη, a species of joy) and "goodwill" (εὔνοια, a species of wishing).[23] The wise have occasion for these especially in the context of friendship, another important Stoic theme. Further, the wise can experience erotic love toward young persons who exhibit potential for virtue.[24]

Both emotions and eupathic responses could be contrasted with quasi-emotional reactions that occur even without the mind's assent. Chrysippus was interested in involuntary tears and laughter, which he attributed to impressions and to "the beginnings of the circumstances bringing about the movement."[25] And it is clear from several sources that nonprejudicial terms like "biting" were used by Hellenistic Stoics for low-level affective events that do not have any moral significance; in later Greek texts, the term is "pre-emotions" (προπάθειαι). Cicero writes, reporting Stoic doctrine, that once the "entirely voluntary belief" that grieving is appropriate is removed, distress itself is eliminated; nonetheless, the mind will still experience "a bite and a small contraction from time to time," and this response is natural even in the wise.[26] His inclusion of the word "natural" is of interest: it indicates once again that the capacity to experience certain feelings is accepted as part of human nature.

The Theory of Action in Seneca

Seneca's concern with impressions is primarily as they figure in the account of action. He does not report the standard Stoic definition of an

---

[23] Diog. Laert. 7.116 (LS 65F, *SVF* 3.431); Ps.-Andronicus, *On Emotions* 6 (*SVF* 3.432). For friendship in Stoicism, see Reydams-Schils (2005: 70–82); Graver (2007); on eupathic responses in the context of wise friendship, see Graver (2007: 58–59, 179–80).

[24] Stobaeus 2.7.5b9, 66 Wachsmuth (*SVF* 3.717); Diog. Laert. 7.113, 130.

[25] Galen, *PHP* 4.7.16–17 (LS 65O, *SVF* 3.466). Further to the history of the concept, see Graver (1999a, 2007: 85–108); Tieleman (2021).

[26] Cicero, *Tusc.* 3.83. For the terminology in "bite and small contraction," compare Philo, *Questions on Genesis* 2.57, and Plutarch, *On Moral Virtue* 449a. For *voluntarius* in connection with emotion, note also Cicero, *Acad.* 1.38 (reporting Zeno); *Tusc.* 3.64, 3.66, 3.83, and Origen, *Comm. in Ps.* 4.5 (where the term is προαιρετικός). See Graver (2007: 65–66).

impression, and neither does he enter into the fascinating Hellenistic debates concerning the mind's powers of representation. At most, he shows in passing remarks that he has a basic familiarity with the role of impressions in epistemology. Thus in letter 71 he mentions the old example of straight objects which when seen underwater give the impression of being curved or bent; the fault, he says, is not in the objects themselves but in us.[27] Similarly, in *On Tranquility of Mind* he mentions the "empty" impressions experienced by the insane: "they are instigated by the impression of some circumstance which the afflicted mind is unable to refute as empty."[28] Even in these passages, though, his emphasis falls on the role of the impression as a stimulus to action more than on the epistemological issues that had interested Chrysippus.

Occasional references in Seneca show that he was well aware of the Stoics' physical explanation of impressions as changes in the mind-material. In *On Anger*, for instance, commenting on non-human animals, he appeals to the qualities of the directive faculty and of its impressions to explain why non-human animals do not have emotions like ours:

> Just as they have a voice, but an inarticulate voice, muddled and unable to form words; just as they have a tongue, but a fettered tongue that is not free for various movements, so also their directive faculty itself is not in the least fine-textured or exact. Thus it receives impressions of things by which it is stimulated to impulses, but those impressions are murky and confused. Hence their attacks and agitations, though vehement, are not cases of fear, worry, sadness, and anger but just emotion-like reactions (*his quaedam similia*).[29]

Observations of animal behavior show that they do not persevere in resentment or anxiety the way human beings do: they may be fierce or panicky in one moment and quite calm in the next. This difference in their nature is attributed to the "murky and confused" nature of animal impressions (*visus speciesque rerum ... turbidas et confusas*), which itself is owing to physical characteristics of the animal mind, a directive faculty that is "not in the least fine-textured or exact" (*ipsum principale parum subtile, parum exactum*). In the *Letters*, too, Seneca sometimes draws on Stoic thought to explain psychological processes by reference to the mind-material, notably in letter 50.6, where he argues for malleability of character on grounds that the breath (*spiritus*) of which the mind is composed

---

[27] *Letters* 71.24. For *voluntarius* in connection with emotion, note also Cicero, *Acad.* 1.38 (reporting Zeno); *Tusc.* 3.64, 3.66, 3.83, and see Graver (2007: 65–66).
[28] *Tranq.* 12.5 *proritat illos alicuius rei species, cuius vanitatem capta mens non coarguit.*
[29] *Anger* 1.3.7–8; cf. *Letters* 121.12–13. For emotion analogues in animals, compare Cicero, *Tusc.* 4.31.

Action and Emotion 49

is "suppler and more yielding than any liquid" (*flexibilis et omni umore obsequentior*) and "lighter than any other material."[30]

Seneca is also well acquainted with the Stoic doctrine that action originates in assent to an impression "of what is then and there appropriate."[31] Concerning action in rational agents, he spells out the full sequence of mental events:

> No animate creature endowed with reason does anything unless, first, it has been prompted by the impression of some particular thing; next, it has entertained an impulse (*impetum cepit*); and finally, assent has confirmed this impulse. Let me tell you what assent is. *It is fitting for me to walk*: I walk only after I have told myself this and have approved my judgment. *It is fitting for me to sit*: then only do I sit. (*Letters* 113.18)

Before the rational animal can generate an impulse to act, it must first be stimulated by an impression of some fact (perhaps the availability of a comfortable chair), and then it must conceive an impulse; that is, it must generate a thought in propositional form as to what action might be taken – the Stoics' impulsory impression.[32] Only after that thought is ratified by assent does the person actually sit down.

In another passage, Seneca makes use of the concept of impulsory impressions to explain the Stoic view that perfect knowledge implies inerrancy in action. For him as for earlier Stoics, knowledge is not just one item of true and justified belief but an overall condition of the mind. Such knowledge guarantees the propriety of assent, including any assent to impulsory impressions, with the result that the wise are as free of error in behavior as they are in their theoretical judgments:

> Virtue itself is located in our better part, namely, the rational part. What is this virtue? True and unshakeable judgment, for from this come the impulses of the mind; by this, every impression that stimulates impulse is rendered perfectly clear (*redigetur ad liquidum*). (*Letters* 71.32)

---

[30] See also *Letters* 99.18 (tears spring up when *spiritus ictu doloris inpulsus* presses upon the moisture around the eye); 113.23 (citing Cleanthes: walking is *spiritum a principali usque in pedes permissum*). *Spiritus* is also referred to in explaining the causes of arthritis (*Letters* 78.8).

[31] See note 10.

[32] The expression *impetum capere* has caused some confusion for interpreters who assume that the impulse to act must occur at this point, prior to assent: Zöller (2003: 149); Stevens (2000); Rist (1989); Ioppolo (1987: 460); Inwood (1985: 179–80, 282). In fact it need imply nothing more than the conceiving of an impulse; that is, the entertaining of an impulsory impression. See *OLD* s. v. *capio* 16, and compare *Letters* 78.2, where Seneca conceives an impulse (*impetum cepi*) to end his own life but does not act on it, from concern for his aged father.

In contrast to the murky and confused impressions of animals, the impressions of the wise are crystal clear.[33] From their point of view, it is immediately apparent what the facts of the situation are, and they act accordingly. By the same token, the behavior of those who fall short of wisdom is never completely reliable: "What is imperfect cannot help but stumble" (*Letters* 71.35). Yet moral progress is possible in those who make a consistent effort.

Like Chrysippus before him, Seneca treats assent to the impulsory impression as the criterion for moral responsibility. When he uses the language of volition, it is this that he means: a decision arising from one's own beliefs and preferences, not some additional faculty for generating uncaused mental events.[34] Many however have been struck by passages such as the following, in which willingness (*velle* or *voluntas*) emerges as a key ingredient in moral progress:

> Let us press on, then; let us persevere. The challenges that lie ahead are greater than those we have overcome already. But most of progress consists in being willing to make progress. This I recognize in myself: I am willing – with my entire mind I am willing. (*Letters* 71.36)[35]

> Anything that can make you a good person is already in your possession. What do you need in order to be good? Willingness. (*Letters* 80.3–4)[36]

The language in these and similar passages is emphatic, but still consistent with the Stoic position on causal determinism.[37] Seneca's point is that the attitude one adopts in the present toward moral progress can be expected to make a real difference in one's future behavior. In effect, one can act now to shape those habits of mind that will determine one's actions in the future, for instance by carefully observing the habits of some person one admires.[38]

---

[33] For *liquidus* in connection with the mental experience of the wise, compare *Clemency* 2.6: *Adice, quod sapiens et providet et in expedito consilium habet; numquam autem liquidum sincerumque ex turbido venit.*

[34] The passages quoted here are among those treated in Inwood (2005: 137–42); see also Wildberger (2006: vol. 1, 338–40); Dihle (1982: 134–35), Donini (1982: 202–4) and, among older treatments, Voelke (1973) and Pohlenz (1948–49). The case for Senecan innovation was revived in Zöller (2003); but cf. Smith (2004).

[35] *Letters* 71.36: *Instemus itaque et perseveremus; plus quam profligavimus restat, sed magna pars est profectus velle proficere. Huius rei conscius mihi sum: volo et mente tota volo.*

[36] *Letters* 80.3–4 : *Quidquid facere te potest bonum tecum est. Quid tibi opus est ut sis bonus? velle.*

[37] Seneca's commitment to the Stoic view is most evident in *Letters* 76.23, which speaks of "the divine law by which all events are regulated" (*lege divina qua universa procedunt*). He probes the issue more deeply in *Ben.* 6.20–24, on which see pages 76–81.

[38] Points of comparison for Seneca's use of *voluntas* can be found in Arius's definition of προαίρεσις as "choice before choice" (Stobaeus 2.7.9a, 87 Wachsmuth (*SVF* 3.173)) and later prominently in Epictetus. See note 13. Both Kahn (1988: 255) and Inwood (2005: 21–22) are struck by the

Seneca on Emotion and Eupathic Response

Like other Stoics, Seneca treats the emotions of anger, fear, grief, and delight as a special case of action. Although he does not reproduce the elaborate classification of emotions, with definitions for each, that we find in Cicero and other sources, he does adhere to the Stoic view that every emotion consists in an assent to an impulsory impression.[39] The importance of this position for him is especially in its implication that our emotional dispositions can be altered for the better through a disciplined program of study and reflection. Other relevant doctrines, including the occurrence of involuntary feelings, the overriding force of emotional impulses while they last, and the joy that accompanies the attainment of wisdom, appear in his work as subsidiary to this larger program of intellectual and moral development.

Material on the workings of emotion can be found throughout Seneca's works, much of it concerned with particular emotions such as grief or anxiety. From a theoretical standpoint, however, the most important discussions are in the first half of *On Anger* and in letters 85 and 116. In these works, Seneca resists what he understands to be the position of the Peripatetic school, that emotions are inevitable, that they are sometimes useful, and that they should be moderated rather than eliminated. He does not deny that the capacity for emotion is part of human nature, but he agrees with his Stoic predecessors that the emotions we ordinarily experience are inherently erroneous, via a misuse of our rational capacities. Hence he favors eliminating the ordinary emotions rather than merely limiting them in degree: for him, a moderate amount of emotion is like being only moderately ill.[40] Moreover, he holds that limiting or controlling an emotion that is already in progress is not a workable strategy. Echoing Chrysippus's runner analogy, he argues that emotional impulses are of such a kind as to propel us onward to wherever they are headed. Instead of trying to govern the ungovernable, we should reject the stimulus from the outset, withholding our assent from the impulsory impression.[41]

---

similarity and are inclined to conclude from it, incorrectly in my view, that Seneca is the innovator and has directly influenced Epictetus.

[39] Seneca does occasionally quote a standard definition; see *Anger* 1.2.3 (anger); *Clemency* 2.5 (pity); *Letters* 59.2 (joy).

[40] *Anger* 1.10.4, *Letters* 85.9, 116.1; cf. Cicero, *Tusc.* 3.22.

[41] *Anger* 1.7.4–1.8.1; *Letters* 85.6–13; 116.3–4. In *Letters* 40.7, Seneca uses a downhill runner analogy that matches even more closely with that of Chrysippus but applies it to the orator who lets his eloquence run away with him.

Responsibility for whatever is done in emotion is thus firmly assigned to the reasoning mind itself. We should not make the mistake of thinking that there is some other motive force within a person, some emotive part of us that wrests control of our motivations away from the faculty of judgment. Seneca means to resist any such splitting of the psyche into opposing camps. For him, it is the errors of the directive faculty itself that produce the emotional reaction.[42] What matters to him about the model, however, is not the unitary psyche itself, but the more fundamental claim that action *always* depends on choices made by the reasoning faculty. As long as that essential moral insight can be maintained, he does not hesitate to deploy metaphors suggestive of struggle and combat between oneself and one's emotions.[43] In letter 92, he goes so far as to concede to his Peripatetic opponents that the mind has non-rational as well as rational components and that one of these components is "spirited, ambitious, and wayward, consisting in emotions" (92.8). But he does not concede that a person's behavior is ever determined by something other than the rational faculty. Flawed as it may be, reason is still "the head of all things, subordinate to none of them."[44]

Seneca's endeavor to cure his readers of anger, grief, and other emotions is therefore centrally concerned to alter their beliefs about what objects are good or bad for the self. These beliefs will generally have their origin in cultural influences absorbed in early childhood, for Seneca echoes that part of the Chrysippan account of human development.[45] In many cases, though, there is some more particular error of evaluation at work, in the category of emotive traits of character, what the Stoics call "diseases." In letter 75, Seneca discusses the Stoic doctrine of emotive traits as part of an analysis of moral progress.[46] It is a promising sign, he thinks, if one can get rid of the persistent error of evaluation that is the disease, even if one is still subject to the related emotion on occasion. This is to say that moral teaching can have significant positive effects even if it does not succeed in producing perfection.

In addition to the emotions themselves, Seneca also allows for quasi-emotional reactions that occur in the absence of assent. He speaks in *On Anger* of an involuntary reaction that "follows immediately upon the impression itself," contrasting it with the more complex response that is

---

[42] The point is clearly stated in *Anger* 1.8.2–3, quoted on page 139.
[43] For example, in *Anger* 1.7.2; *Letters* 85.6; 116.3.
[44] *Letters* 92.1 *omnibus praeposita est, ipsa sub nullo est.*
[45] See page 46. Seneca echoes the account especially in *Letters* 115.11–12.
[46] *Letters* 75.11–12; compare the texts cited in note 21.

properly called anger (2.1.3). Someone who conceives a desire for revenge for some slight but then changes his mind and does not take any action has not experienced anger but only a preliminary to anger (2.3.4–5). Like Chrysippus, he speaks of the "beginnings" of the emotional movement (*principia proludentia adfectibus*, 2.2.5), without meaning to imply an involuntary reaction will always lead to a full-scale emotion. Examples of such emotion-like reactions include stage fright, contagious laughter, some responses to literature and the visual arts, a young person's blush when meeting a respected elder, and Seneca's own nervousness when passing through a dark tunnel.[47]

Although Seneca did not originate the discussion of involuntary feelings within Stoicism, he explains the received doctrine at much greater length than any other author, and with greater richness of examples. Indeed his treatment of the theme is so elaborate as to create certain difficulties of interpretation. The most significant concerns the role of the body in affective response. Seneca says several times that the involuntary feelings are movements of the body rather than of the mind.[48] In view of this, one might be tempted to assume that the distinction being drawn is that between a strictly mental event and the corporeal realization of that event. But this cannot be right, for the involuntary feelings are also called by him "movements of the mind," and some of his examples clearly require full conceptualization of the stimulus and even linguistic processing. In calling such events responses of the body, he is merely saying that they occur without exercise of the rational mind's most characteristic function, that of assent.

Thus far I have been concerned with Seneca's treatment of the ordinary emotions only, the ones that he, like earlier Stoics, excludes from the ideal of virtuous wisdom. But Seneca does not think that the ideal condition for human beings must be lacking in all forms of affective response. For one thing, the wise person's inner experience would include the involuntary reactions, since these do not involve any sort of erroneous judgment. Faced with danger, the wise person may tremble or grow pale or change expression; when bereaved, the wise may experience a "biting and contraction" or

---

[47] *Anger* 2.2.1–2.3.3; *Letters* 11.1–7, 57.3–6.
[48] *Anger* 2.4.2, 2.3.3, *Letters* 11.1, 71.29. *Letters* 71.27 explicitly associates the involuntary feelings with the irrational part of the psyche, mentioning physical pain as belonging to the same category of response; see Inwood (2005: 41). For clarification concerning the Stoics' version of body–soul dualism, see Long (1996: 224–49); *pace* Fillion-Lahille (1984) and Rist (1989), one need not think specifically of Posidonius.

even shed tears.⁴⁹ The point is important to Seneca, for he does not believe that Stoic impassivity renders one impervious to stimuli, like "some sort of rock" (*Letters* 71.27). In his view, it is the Cynic school that thinks of wisdom in that way.⁵⁰ His own conception of the moral end is not of an inhuman hardness, but of a triumphant fulfillment of all that is best in human nature.

Seneca does not have any generic Latin term for the Stoic concept of "good emotions" (*eupatheiai*), and neither does he list the three eupathic genera of joy, caution, and wishing.⁵¹ However, he does speak emphatically of joy (*gaudium*) as an affective response that is specific to the Stoic sage. In his several treatments of the theme, he repeatedly mentions such points as that the joy of the wise is frequent or even constant, and that it relates to the wise person's own goods of character rather than to externals. In *On Happiness*, for example, he writes:

> When one has such a foundation, he cannot but be visited, like it or not, by constant exhilaration, by gladness that is deep and comes from the depths. For he is rejoicing in what is his own; he desires nothing more than what he has at home.⁵²

At least where joy is concerned, Seneca has embraced the Stoic notion of eupathic response and made it his own.

While Seneca is familiar with the Stoic claim that the wise person will experience erotic love, this idea is not particularly important to him.⁵³ He is, however, deeply interested in wise friendship and in the imperfect but promising form of friendship that may exist between those who are progressing

---

⁴⁹ *Letters* 71.31; *Cons. Marc.* 7.1; *Letters* 99.18–20. "Biting" (*morsus*) in Seneca refers to either involuntary sensations of mental pain or mental pain as part of ordinary distress. The language of *Cons. Marc.* 7.1 (*necessarius morsus et firmissimorum animorum quoque contractio*) suggests this Stoic doctrine (compare also Cicero, *Tusc.* 3.83) but appears also to invoke Peripatetic ideas: note *quam diu modicum est* just above. (However, the "tiny, meaningless, short-lived movement of the body" of *Happiness* 4.4 refers not to involuntary affect but to bodily pleasure.)

⁵⁰ *Brevity* 14.2; *Letters* 9.1, 9.3. It may be the Cynic impassivity, rather than the Stoic, that Seneca has in mind in *Cons. Marc.* 4.1, *Cons. Helv.* 16.1, *Cons. Polyb.* 18.5–6. Cf. Pohlenz (1948–49: 308).

⁵¹ The word *constantia*, used by Cicero in a sense equivalent to *eupatheia* in *Tusc.* 4.12–15, is used by Seneca only in the broader sense of "consistency" or for the virtue of constancy. Caution (*cautio*) and wish (*voluntas*) are not known to Seneca as affective responses. In *Letters* 85.26, for instance, he uses the word "caution" for an attitude of the wise person as contrasted with the ordinary person's fear but seems to mean only that the wise person can act to avoid danger. This is non-emotive action, called by Stoics "selection," on which see note 9 in Chapter 1.

⁵² *Happiness* 4.2–5; compare *Constancy* 9.4, *Anger* 2.6.2, *Letters* 23.3–4, 27.2–3, 59.1–2.

⁵³ *Amor* in *Letters* 116.5 refers specifically to erotic love. Erotic love in the nonwise condition is regularly classed by Seneca as an activity of vice, in parallel with anger and fear; an interesting example is *Anger* 2.15.3. His affection for Paulina (*Letters* 104.2–3) falls into the category of tender concern for family members generally: *indulgendum est honestis adfectibus*.

toward wisdom.⁵⁴ In *Letters* 9.3–5, for example, he argues that the Stoic wise cherish their friends because they value the opportunity to exercise the virtues for their benefit, for instance by sitting at the bedside of one who is ill. Their affection runs deep: losing a friend is like having a hand cut off or both eyes blinded. Nonetheless, the wise person is self-sufficient (*se contentus*) and impassive (*impatiens*) in the sense of the Stoic *apatheia*. He will not be distressed in times of bereavement and will continue to be happy, taking satisfaction in the life that he still has and confident in his ability to make new friends. He indeed feels the loss, but he bears it with equanimity.

***

Scholarly accounts of Seneca's position relative to the ethical psychology of the older Stoa have sometimes presented him either as an innovator who developed his own significantly changed version of Stoicism or as an eclectic who combined Stoic ideas with elements from other philosophical traditions. My review of the evidence yields a different understanding of Seneca's project. Neither in psychology nor in ethics did he make it his business to alter any essential commitments of the school to which he adhered.⁵⁵ Although he claimed the right to abandon the official line, in fact he was well satisfied with the existing Stoic theory of action and emotion. Rather than innovating, he devotes his efforts to inventing novel rhetorical strategies for putting the most edifying elements of that theory across to his readers. Within that therapeutic program, however, he does have his own distinctive emphases, particularly as concerns involuntary emotive reactions and the eupathic response of joy.

Central for him is the notion that human beings are rational creatures, and that rationality is perfectible: our actions are driven by belief, and beliefs can be corrected. Yet it is no contradiction to say that we are also emotional creatures, equipped by nature to respond affectively to what we perceive as good or evil. The goal of moral progress is not to try to eliminate all affective response, but to understand at a deep level what things really are good or bad for us. If we fail to do this, we set ourselves up for responses that can easily run away with us, with many dangerous consequences. But if we should succeed, we would not become completely

---

⁵⁴ Further to the topic, see Wilcox (2012); Wildberger (2017: 115–56).
⁵⁵ In metaphysics his attitude was different, but metaphysical speculation was rampant in his day; see Sedley (2005). His views on death and the afterlife seem also to have been heterodox; see Rist (1989) and Smith (2014b).

unresponsive to the kinds of objects that stir our emotions in our present flawed condition. We would still feel the same kinds of sensations we have now, but in slight and short-lived versions, while in response to genuine goods, the goods of virtuous action and of loving relationships, we would have new, clear, and strong feelings, and, above all, feelings of joy.

CHAPTER 3

The Treatise On Benefits
Real Kindness and Real Agency

It was during the last decade of his life that Seneca produced his most extensive and ambitious philosophical writings: the massive compilation of *Letters on Ethics*, the lofty *Natural Questions*, and also his longest work on a single theme, the seven-book treatise *On Benefits*.[1] This last takes up a topic that had long been recognized as essential to the study of friendship and of interpersonal relations generally: acts of giving and of disinterested service, with the associated motives of goodwill and of gratitude. The subject held great interest for him. As a member of Rome's privileged class, he was keenly aware of the social mechanism that converted noblesse-oblige gifts and services into political capital; indeed, he saw it as material for satire.[2] But he was also deeply engaged in certain philosophical questions that the topic of benefits brings to the fore: the meaning of public service, the affective dimensions of mutuality and reciprocity, the relation between human nature and the benevolent deity. These issues attract his attention also in the *Letters*, and indeed there are many points of contact between the two works.[3]

While the giving and receiving of favors is analyzed in some detail by Aristotle, it was in the Hellenistic period that it became a regular subject

---

[1] For overview, bibliography, and reception study, see Griffin (2013), as well as Lentano (2009, 2014). Griffin (2013: 91–98) dates the work to between 56 and mid-64 and argues that it cannot be dated more precisely. Grimal (1978: 304) argues that the date cannot be after Seneca retired in 62, on grounds that *Ben.* 2.19.2 would have been offensive to Nero. However, Seneca was quite capable of making remarks in his writings that could have been seen as disloyal to the *princeps*. *Letters* 76.4 is an egregious example, as noted by Griffin (1976: 360).
[2] Such passages as *Ben.* 2.11.1–2, 2.26.1–27.2, 5.15.3–6, and 7.8.2–11.2 fit the pattern of satirical writing in Seneca as treated on page 223 and following.
[3] The argument of letter 9 can easily be connected to that of *Ben.* 4.1–25; *Letters* 19.11–12 matches to *Ben.* 2.24; letter 73 to *Ben.* 4.28.4–6 and 6.18–24; letter 81 to *Ben.* 3.12.4 and 6.4–6 (and *Letters* 81.3 mentions *On Benefits* by title); letter 109 to *Ben.* 7.4–11. Some of these connections are discussed in detail in Griffin (2013: 149–63).

for philosophical treatises.⁴ The Hellenistic works are no longer extant, but relevant titles are attested for the Peripatetic authors Theophrastus and Demetrius of Phalerum; for Epicurus and Metrodorus; and for the early Stoics Cleanthes and Chrysippus.⁵ Seneca himself refers to a treatment of the subject by Hecaton of Rhodes, a pupil of Panaetius, and he seems also to have known Chrysippus's *On Acts of Kindness* and at least one Epicurean work.⁶ The obvious relevance of the work to Seneca's contemporary milieu is no reason to doubt that much of its content was already in existence before him, for, as P. A. Brunt argued in connection with Cicero's *De Officiis*, a Roman author might well choose to reproduce an existing body of thought precisely because he found it congenial to his own ideas and opinions. Such a project might have some elements geared for the contemporary audience, including examples drawn from Rome's own history and culture.⁷

Just as the authors of Peripatetic treatises on gratitude undoubtedly took on many of Aristotle's philosophical commitments, and as Epicurus wrote on the same subject from a hedonist perspective, so Seneca's work is thoroughly infused with Stoic thought. One of his most disciplined intellectual products,

---

⁴ The usual terms in Greek are εὐεργεσία ("good-working"; Seneca's word *beneficium* is an exact translation) and χάρις (either "act of kindness" or "gratitude"). Both were well established in the popular moral lexicon by Plato's time. See, for instance, Plato, *Gorgias* 520e, *Meno* 91c, Xen. *Mem.* 2.2.1–13; and see Griffin (2013: 15–25); Inwood (2005: 66–68); Dover (1974: 201–3). In Aristotle, εὐεργεσία and χάρις are often virtually synonymous, and both are important components of friendship: see *Rhet.* 1.5.9, 2.7.1–6; *Nic. Eth.* 8.1, 8.5, 8.7, 8.13, with Konstan (2006: 156–68).

⁵ The Peripatetic treatises are attested in Diog. Laert. 5.48 and 5.81; Epicurus's work *On Gifts and Gratitude* is in Diog. Laert. 10.28. Metrodorus produced a treatise *On Greatness of Soul* (Diog. Laert. 10.24), a topic that in Aristotle is closely connected with the giving and receiving of benefits (*Nic. Eth.* 4.3, 1124b), so it is probably this work that Seneca refers to in *Letters* 81.11; see further note 6. For the Stoic works, see Diog. Laert. 7.175, Philodemus, *De Pietate* 14 (*SVF* 2.1081).

⁶ Hecaton wrote extensively in ethics, and Seneca mentions him frequently not only in *Ben.* 1.3.8–9 and 2.18.2 but also in other works; see Chaumartin (1985); Setaioli (1988: 308–15); Griffin (2013: 24–25); Veillard (2022). We do not know whether the citations in *On Benefits* refer to an otherwise unattested work Περὶ χάριτος or to a section of the attested Περὶ καθηκόντων; the question is perhaps not very significant. Seneca quotes Cleanthes three times in *On Benefits* (at 5.14.1, 6.11.1, and 6.12.2) and Chrysippus five times (at 1.4.4, 2.17.3, 2.25.3, 3.22.1). The way Chrysippus is spoken of in *Ben.* 1.3.8–9 suggests direct familiarity with the work Περὶ χαρίτων that is attested in Philodemus, *De Pietate* 14 (*SVF* 2.1081), but it is possible that Seneca's knowledge comes via Hecaton: Setaioli (1988: 287–95). Epicurean views are often mentioned in *On Benefits*, and while many of Seneca's remarks about them could represent his own understanding of what an Epicurean might say, *Ben.* 4.16.1 ("they themselves admit that they return a favor not because it is honorable but because it is expedient") seems to refer to Epicurean writing specifically on this topic. Also significant is *Letters* 81.11, which attributes to Epicurus the claim that only the wise person knows how to return a favor, but then changes the attribution to *Metrodorus certe*.

⁷ Compare Brunt's treatment of the role of Panaetius in Cicero's *De Officiis*: Brunt (2013: 180–219). The relevance of *On Benefits* to the practices current in Roman society is treated extensively in Griffin (2013: 30–87); see also Accardi (2015); Wolkenhauer (2014).

the treatise first lays out a careful definition of the concept in question, then proceeds to unpack the implications of that definition through a series of particular cases. The *beneficium*, "benefit" or "act of kindness," is analyzed in the Stoic manner, that is, strictly in terms of intent, and the discussion frequently draws on Stoic doctrine on other relevant issues including the innate tendencies of the human being, the ideal form of friendship, and the aims of divine providence. For this reason, a close study of the treatise can be informative not only for its immediate topic but also for a number of interrelated issues in Stoicism.

Seneca's notion of benevolent action is fascinating in itself, and it is historically significant, for it supplies the precedent not only for studies of gift exchange in anthropology but also for treatments of supererogation, or admirable but non-obligatory action, in contemporary metaethics.[8] Moreover, because of the way it is framed by Seneca's Stoic commitments, the analysis of benefaction in this work also leads us into some important issues in the Stoic understanding of action. Among the points of greatest interest are an especially rich understanding of kindness in terms of the mutual understanding of giver and receiver, as well as an unusually comprehensive understanding of action and a more interesting notion of autonomy – that is, of independent agency in relation to fate or god's will – than the Stoics are usually credited with. If we possessed the treatises of Chrysippus and of Hecaton, we might find that these elements were part of Stoicism all along; as it is, though, we owe them to Seneca.

Defining a Benefit

Early in book 1, Seneca promises to define the word *beneficium*, saying that he will tell its *vis* and *proprietas*, its "force" and "proper signification."[9] He then states quite emphatically that a benefit must not be thought of as consisting in a material gift, such as gold or silver, nor in an outcome, such as a rescue from shipwreck. These things are often referred to as benefits, but that is a misnomer: in reality, they are only the "material of the benefit" (1.5.2). They are visible "signs" or "traces" of the benefit, but the benefit *itself* is a mental activity, consisting in "the very will of the giver" (1.5.6, 1.5.2) Accordingly, if some misfortune happens to do away with the tangible gift or observable outcome,

---

[8] Studies oriented toward anthropology, interpersonal dynamics, and semiotics include Degand (2015); Takaki (2014); Raccanelli (2010: 15–68); Goux (2002). For supererogation, a good starting point is Heyd (2019).
[9] *Ben.* 1.3.2; for the term, compare *Letters* 89.9.

the benefit remains. "So all those things that falsely usurp the name of benefit are just services through which the amicable will unfolds itself" (1.5.5).

From here, Seneca proceeds to give the promised definition:

> *Quid est ergo beneficium? Benevola actio tribuens gaudium capiensque tribuendo in id, quod facit, prona et sponte sua parata. Itaque non, quid fiat aut quid detur, refert, sed qua mente, quia beneficium non in eo, quod fit aut datur, consistit, sed in ipso dantis aut facientis animo.* (Ben. 1.6.1)

> What then is a benefit? It is a benevolent action which confers joy and finds joy in conferring it, aimed at the very thing it does and provided on one's own initiative. Hence what matters is not what is done or given, but with what intention. For the benefit consists not in the thing done or given, but in the very mind of the giver or doer.

So a benefit is a particular kind of action. Action is its genus, and the species is indicated by the addition of "benevolent"; it is, then, an act of goodwill, performed in a spirit of friendship. It is a right action (*recte factum*, 1.5.3), but it is not only that, for right actions include those performed from a sense of legal or moral obligation, whereas benefits are unforced acts of kindness. In addition, it is specified that the benevolent action must be one that "confers joy and finds joy in conferring it." There is an element of *intersubjectivity*. Giving in the right spirit requires thinking about the other person's feelings, and it also means that one gives or serves cheerfully, rejoicing to anticipate the other's pleasure; conversely, the receiver is pleased just insofar as she appreciates the benefactor's goodwill. The Stoic Chrysippus supplies an analogy: in a game of catch, each player must consider both his own throwing and the other's catching, or the ball will land in the middle (2.17.3). Then too, an action will not be a benefit unless it is "aimed at the very thing it does." There must be some *specificity of aim*. The benefactor is not acting for some ulterior motive, and neither is the supposed gift or service an unintended consequence of some other act.[10] Finally, a benefit has to be "provided on one's own initiative." In speaking of this requisite *autonomy*, a key term of the treatise is "willingness," *voluntas* or *velle*, also translatable as "wishing," "wanting," or simply as "will." A person who aids another without wishing or willing to do so is not credited with a benefit (6.7.1).

---

[10] Seneca clarifies in *Ben.* 6.12.1–2 that the benefit may provide some advantage to the benefactor as well as the beneficiary, but not if the advantage to self is the real purpose of the action. One who feeds war captives amply in order to get a better price for them on the slave market has not done them a service and does not deserve their gratitude.

Clearly this stringent definition of benefits is not intended to be a description of actual social practice at Rome or anywhere else. Instead, it states what a benefit is conceptually, as practiced in a thought-realm of pure motives and correct calculations. It comes as no surprise that for Seneca, the "true and absolute" benefit is given and received only by the person of perfect wisdom, the theorized Stoic sage (7.17.1). The rest of us, in our flawed condition, may aspire to benefit others but currently produce only suboptimal benefits, just as in Stoic theory the nonwise can perform appropriate actions but are not yet capable of fully right actions.[11] This is the same philosophical approach as generates the Stoic paradoxes, and indeed this is one of them: only the wise person is rich, only the wise person is a ruler, only the wise perform benefits or are grateful for them.[12]

Still, even though we fall short of beneficence proper, our everyday experience of gift-giving and gratitude can provide some insight into the nature of beneficent action. In accordance with Stoic axioms, Seneca holds that even imperfect versions of altruistic behavior have a basis in the human being's innate tendency toward sociability.[13] Our intuitions about what kinds of giving and service are pleasing to others and what forms of gratitude are sincere may well be correct; they need, however, to be organized and tested by philosophical reflection. Examples drawn from ordinary experience thus play an important role in *On Benefits* as Seneca works to unpack the theoretical claims made in the Stoic definition.

In examining the remainder of the treatise, we will want to consider several implications of the definition. A point of particular interest is the way Seneca works through the practical implications of defining an action – here, a benefit – entirely in terms of intent. It emerges that a Stoic account can retain this important principle and still give some consideration to whether the action has been put into effect in the world. Even though the benevolent action is not dependent on its enactment, those benefits that have observable effects obligate the recipient differently from those that are not. Another point of interest has to do with the linkage of one person's capacity for action with another's. The expectation that responsibility for

---

[11] For the claim that only the wise person can either give or receive a benefit *stricto sensu*, see *Ben.* 7.17.1 and *Letters* 81.10. Seneca will sometimes speak of the more familiar kind of gifts and services as "quasi-benefits," that resemble benefits proper without fully instantiating them (*Ben.* 5.13.3–4). For the Stoic distinction between appropriate actions and right actions, see Stobaeus 2.7.8, 85 Wachsmuth (LS 59b, *SVF* 3.494); 2.7.11a, 93 Wachsmuth (*SVF* 3.500).

[12] Seneca uses the term *paradoxa* in this connection in *Ben.* 2.31.1 and *Letters* 81.11. For discussion in these terms, see Inwood (2005: 65–94).

[13] See *Ben.* 4.17.1–18.4; and compare *Letters* 9.17; discussion in Inwood (2015), Kühn (2011: 330–64); Graver (2007: 175–78).

action will rest with an individual agent is not abridged by the element of intersubjectivity in the definition; however, it is put to the test by certain types of relationship between agents, including the relation of enslaved persons to their legal owners, of children to their parents, and of humans to their divine creators. Third, and relatedly, Seneca's emphasis on the willingness of the giver raises some interesting points about autonomy in relation to the regular workings of the Stoic cosmos. In a later segment of the treatise, Seneca goes so far as to inquire whether an agent who is incapable of acting otherwise can be considered to act willingly – and answers this question in the affirmative. In fact, for him the actions performed by such an agent are the paradigm case of voluntary action. In what follows, I'll touch on each of these points in turn, seeking to bring out the underlying coherence in Seneca's sometimes scattered presentation of the issues.

Enactment

Seneca's works make it clear that he knows and accepts the classic Stoic analysis of action as consisting in assent to an impulsory impression. Action is, in its very essence, a mental event: it is a movement interior to the psyche in which one tries to bring about some result, regardless of whether the result is ultimately achieved.[14] Letter 113 refers to a disagreement between Cleanthes, the second head of the Stoic school, and Chrysippus, the third. When Cleanthes defined walking as "the vital breath stretching from the directive faculty all the way to the feet," his successor replaced that definition with just "the directive faculty itself," removing any mention of the feet (*Letters* 113.23). Once the mind has sent its signal, the action has occurred.

The account of action in *On Benefits* is very much in accordance with this Stoic position. We have seen already how insistent Seneca is that a benefit be understood in terms of agency, that is, of the volition (*voluntas*) or intention (*mens*) or mind (*animus*) of the giver. It is not just that the benefit consists in an action rather than an item given or service performed; it is also that the action itself consists entirely in "the very will of the giver" (*ipsa tribuentis voluntas*). Like Chrysippus, Seneca holds that even movements of the body are not essential to the action. In book 2,

---

[14] This is to say that action (πρᾶξις) equates to rational impulse (ὁρμὴ λογική), defined as "a movement of the intellect toward something in the realm of action" set in motion by "an impulsory impression of what is appropriate in that moment": Stobaeus 2.7.9, 86–87 Wachsmuth (LS 53Q, *SVF* 3.169). For Seneca's awareness of the Stoic background, see page 49.

speaking of the reciprocal benefit that expresses gratitude for a prior benefit received, he writes,

> For since we [Stoics] bring everything back to the mind, each person acts just insofar as he wills to act; and since piety, loyalty, justice, and every other virtue is complete within itself even if not permitted to lift a finger, it is possible also to be grateful through volition. (*Ben.* 2.31.1)

Hence, "he who willingly receives a benefit has repaid it" – a claim that Seneca designates "the least surprising of the Stoic paradoxes."[15] Similarly, he later remarks that a benefit is "non-embodied" (*incorporale*), with the result that it can never be taken away from the one who receives it (6.2.1–2).

We can see the advantages of this position. For anyone who thinks seriously about moral responsibility, it makes sense that ethically significant action should be entirely within the agent's control. If beneficence is to reflect on the character of the benefactor, then one's capacity to give ought not to be merely a matter of luck. Book 5 makes this consequence explicit: if two people are equal in goodwill, then the benefits they bestow are equal, even if one of them gives or does more than the other in material terms (5.2.2–3). This point must have seemed especially important to Seneca, surrounded as he was by a Roman culture that attached great significance to acts of patronage and munificence. With benefits understood in terms of action, and action in terms of intention, the extent of one's resources for gift-giving and grand gestures ceases to matter. Benefaction ceases to be a province of the elite: even an enslaved person can be a benefactor, while many wealthy and influential people turn out not to be.

Yet even for one who welcomes this conclusion, there is reason to question whether it includes everything that needs to be said. In the vast majority of cases, an endeavor to walk does result in movements of the feet, since that is what the directive faculty commands, and it will sometimes be important to mention whether locomotion-by-foot has in fact occurred. The study of benefits presents us with just the sort of situation where one might need to think not only about the action itself but also about what might be called the *enactment* of the action – how and whether the willing mind puts its intention into effect. For the exchange of benefits involves two people, a benefactor and a recipient, and the circumstances of the latter include the effective actions of the former. Once the initial benefit has been conferred, it imposes certain obligations on the recipient, duties of gratitude and reciprocation, and that

---

[15] *Ben.* 2.31.1. Compare *Letters* 36.5 *ille quod debet sola potest voluntate persolvi*.

obligation will look different if the benefactor's action has achieved some result: assets that were actually transferred, a child that was actually rescued.

Seneca is much engaged with this issue. In book 2, he gives voice to the indignant objections of one who does not agree that gratitude can be expressed in intention alone. "What? Has a person who did nothing returned the favor?" (2.34.1)[16] Picking up on the ball-playing analogy, the objector points out that the game does not consist only in the skill of the players: the movements of the ball are part of it as well.

> But even if the player is in no way deficient in skill, since he did one part and is capable of doing the other; still the playing itself is incomplete, since the fulfillment of it consists in the exchange of throwing and return throwing. (*Ben.* 2.32.3)

Responding to this objection, Seneca repeats the essential Stoic claim. One *can* be grateful empty-handed (*excussis manibus*, 2.31.5), the person who received the gift in the right spirit has in fact repaid it (2.33.3); benefaction is "a transaction between minds" (2.34.1). But he also concedes the point about the ball game:

> Let's agree that that's how it is: the game is deficient, though the player is not. Likewise, in the matter we are discussing, there is a deficiency in the thing given, for which there should be equal recompense, even though there is none as regards the mind. (*Ben.* 2.32.4)

For the enactment of the action, Seneca uses a single term, *res*, also translatable as "the thing" (i.e., the material thing given) or "the outcome" or "the realization" of the benefit. He also speaks of the "putting into effect" of the benefit, as in section 10 of book 6: "[N]aked volition does not put the benefit into effect" (*non efficit*, 6.10.2). And just as he allows his interlocutor to be concerned about whether the ball game is "fulfilled" (*consummatur*), so also he speaks of the "fulfillment" of the benefit (6.11.3–4). It turns out that both *voluntas* and *res*, both the volition and its enactment, are needed in order to fulfill the benefit, and that it is only the fulfilled benefit that imposes an obligation of fulfillment on the recipient. Thus, in a situation where A attempts to provide some gift or service to B but is prevented from doing so by facts beyond her control, B need not worry if her attempt at recompense is likewise unsuccessful. However, if A does manage to put her benefit into effect, then B's response of gratitude needs to achieve its aim as well: in this case, effort alone does *not* suffice. "By our volition we have satisfied the

---

[16] Similarly in *Ben.* 7.14.6, an objector asks, "Suppose there are two recipients, both of whom have the same intent, but only one of whom found a way to reciprocate the benefit: is the person who did not return the benefit in the same position as one who did?"

volition, but for the enactment, we owe an enactment" (*Voluntati voluntate satis fecimus; rei rem debemus*, 2.35.1).

In taking this position, Seneca goes directly to that contested boundary at which the mind of the rational agent interacts with the world around it. Without giving up on volition as the essential element in action, he finds a way to speak as well about the effects of that internal decision, the way that it is embodied in tangible outcomes for other people. These outcomes are the usual, though not indispensable, concomitants to the action that takes place internally.

> It is not that the appropriate action is incomplete and this is the remaining part of it; rather, it is an adjunct to one that is already complete. (*Ben.* 2.33.1)

The point is made also through metaphors. Action and enactment are related as skillful ball-playing is to the movements of the ball (2.32.3), as the artistry of the sculptor is to the sculptures themselves (2.33.2–3), as the lovemaking between two people is to their mutual caresses (7.13). We would not call them different events: they are different aspects of the same event.

Persistence

To say even this much is also to acknowledge some role for contingency, some impact of luck on what we are able to achieve. What action I take depends entirely on me, since in initiating my action, I have already fully acted. But the effect of my action does not depend entirely on me: there are further conditions that have to be met. Walking *is* deciding to walk, but whether the feet move does also matter. My gratitude as the recipient of a benefit is already an action, since it is a wish to give back, but "there is still the use of me (*usus mei*), some advantage issuing from the grateful person" (2.33.1). For there to be that effect, the action has to make its way into the world outside my mind, and if it is to do that, that world has to cooperate.

The impact of contingency is very much mitigated, however, by a further set of reflections on change and what persists through change. In this work, as often elsewhere, Seneca finds reason to remark on the impermanence of everything around us. The world we live in is constantly changing. All things are transitory; our bodies, too, are subject to change, as are our pleasures and the emotions that belong to our disordered state.[17]

---

[17] *Ben.* 1.5.3, 3.3.4; compare *Anger* 1.13.4; *Cons. Marc.* 21.1, *Constancy* 6.6, *Leisure* 4.2, *Brevity* 14.2, *Happiness* 7.3, *Letters* 58.24, 27. See Wildberger (2006: 87–9, 604–10). Inwood (2007a: 129), commenting on letter 58, suggests a prehistory in Stoic-Platonist dialogue on Heraclitean flux, but

But the ability to reason can steady our minds. What is logical does not change, and as we grow into our full potential as rational beings, we begin to be consistent about what we want: we begin to stabilize our will. So, the situation I'm in is bound to change, but my intention to reciprocate the benefit does not have to change. It can remain in place, waiting for an opportunity to take effect. Seneca cites Chrysippus for another analogy drawn from the realm of athletics, saying that the grateful person is like a runner in the starting blocks, poised to dart forward the minute the signal is given.[18] He has already decided to run in the race; all that is lacking is the awareness that *now* the race has begun.

We should assume a certain fungibility in the particulars of fulfillment. Consider a case studied in book 7. Suppose I owe you a benefit, Seneca says, and suppose that I sell my worldly possessions and undertake a dangerous journey to rescue you from where you were captured by pirates, but by the time I get there, you have already been rescued by someone else. At that point, you should consider my obligation to have been discharged; I, however, should not rest content but should look for another opportunity to repay you (7.15.1–16.4). Now, we can hardly think that Seneca means for the would-be rescuer to wait until his benefactor is again captured by pirates. If the wish to repay were formulated in such restrictive terms as *I mean to save you from Cilician pirates, by ship and before the end of this month*, then its chances of realization would be quite limited.[19] But the wish to do good to another person may well be of a more general nature: *I want to do something good for you* or *I want to repay you in a way commensurate with what you did for me*. The specifics can vary, as long as the opportunity that arises is recognized as fulfilling the intention to do good or to repay.[20] Given that flexibility, a firm intention can find its way to realization in virtually every case. The limiting factor is just that human beings have only a short time in the world: we may not live long enough

---

remarks that the appropriation may equally well be Seneca's own. The claim is consistent with Stoic physics in its emphasis on cyclical change; see LS vol 1, 280–89; with Sedley (1999: 387–411).

[18] *Ben.* 2.25.3. Diog. Laert. 7.179 reports that Chrysippus trained as a long-distance runner.

[19] Given the epistemic limitations that go with the human condition, a particularized intention will often come to naught, and a fully rational human agent will take this into account, by incorporating a reservation into the volitional judgment: *if such be Zeus's will*. See *Ben.* 4.34.4, and see further Inwood (1985: 19–26).

[20] A more technical account might treat both goodwill (*benevolentia*, εὔνοια) and gratitude (*gratia*, χάρις) as second-order wishes relating to the future. The summary of Stoic ethics in Stobaeus gives evidence of an account of impulse at this level. Note especially the definition of ὅρμησις as an "impulse toward something in the future" (Stobaeus 2.7.9a, 87 Wachsmuth (*SVF* 3.173)), meaning apparently that one directs oneself to generate an impulse of a certain kind on any future occasion that meets specified criteria. See Inwood (1985: 230–31).

for all of our intentions to come into effect. But provided we live, the stability of intent and the fungibility of suitable enactments mean that every intention we have will eventually come to fruition.

All this is very much dependent on the power of memory. Mireille Armisen-Marchetti has drawn attention to the prominence of memory as a theme in *On Benefits* and to how it serves to enable the exchange of benefits.[21] With the passage of time and the changing content of experience, our awareness of benefits received would inevitably fade away if it were not constantly renewed (7.28.2). Just as tools do not rust if they are in constant use, so gratitude can be kept in force by thinking often about what one has received (3.2.2–4).[22] One's thoughts, at least at this level, are under one's own control, and so the recipient of a benefit has the capacity to maintain the will to reciprocate for as long as might be necessary. Conversely, the giver of a benefit can choose to forget about the obligation laid on the recipient, if the circumstances make reciprocation unusually difficult.[23]

A further question concerns the permanence of the obligation itself, whether, with the passage of time, it might come about that the giver of a benefit ceases to be a person to whom it is appropriate to repay it. What if A, who has done a kind service for B, later shows regret for that action, or even turns around and injures B? Should B still follow through with the reciprocation? After mentioning this issue briefly in book 3, Seneca treats it in some detail in book 6.[24] There he argues that the benefit "remains" – meaning that one still owes reciprocation for it – but that one should *also* retaliate for the injury. The one is weighed against the other, and their relative magnitude determines how one should proceed.

This position is moderated, however, when Seneca returns to the same question in *Letters on Ethics* 81.[25] In that letter he explicitly rejects his handling of the issue in *On Benefits* and suggests instead that even a strict judge might seek mitigating circumstances that would weight the calculation in favor of repaying the benefit. Then he goes even further. A more lenient judge, he says – and the judge he himself would prefer to be – would deliberately forget the wrong; that is, he would forgive it. This lenient judge is not excusing the offense out of softness or indulgence; instead, he does so specifically because this particular malefactor is also the

---

[21] Armisen-Marchetti (2004). [22] Armisen-Marchetti (2004: 13–15).
[23] *Ben.* 1.4.5, 2.10.4. *Ben.* 7.22.2 suggests that the rule is overstated: the benefactor may continue to remember his or her own action but behave as if it were forgotten to save the recipient's feelings.
[24] *Ben.* 3.12.4, 6.4–6. [25] *Letters* 81.3; see further Griffin (2013: 155–61); Inwood (2005: 76–81).

giver of a benefit (*Letters* 81.3–7). The obligation created by the act of giving or service thus persists even through the subsequent injury.

Intersubjectivity and Independence

In stating the definition of benefit in book 1, Seneca specifies that it is a benevolent action "which confers joy and finds joy in conferring it."[26] A genuine act of kindness creates positive feelings both in the intended recipient and in the benefactor, who experiences an anticipatory joy in acting to produce joy in another. The benefit thus links two minds in a single act of goodwill.

The wording of the definition does not make it clear what exactly Seneca means to say about the reaction of the recipient. Does the recipient of the benefit have to be pleased in actuality, or does it suffice if the benefactor acts with the intention of conferring joy and in a way that can reasonably be expected to have that result? Intuition prefers the latter alternative, which allows the act of kindness to be defined with reference to just the one agent. This reading is confirmed by an example given in book 5. Suppose two brothers are at odds, and you save the life of one of them: the other brother might actually feel resentment, but he has been given a benefit nonetheless. What matters, Seneca says, is that the action is of such a kind that the recipient *ought* to rejoice at it.[27] Similarly, a difficult medical intervention or a friend's frank criticism might cause pain in the short run, but can still count as a benefit.

There is some lack of clarity also as to what it means to *confer* joy on another person. Seneca's verb *tribuere* is usually translated "give" or "bestow"; in fact, it is one of the verbs that he uses for the bestowing of a benefit. But glad feelings are internal to the psyche of each person; they are not passed like coins from hand to hand, and neither are they done for one person by another, as a rescue might be. So we cannot think of joy as being itself the good that the benefactor provides to the recipient.[28] That model would not work in any case, for joy or delight is normally thought

---

[26] *Ben.* 1.6.1 *tribuens gaudium capiensque tribuendo*. I take it that the force of the participle *tribuens* is entirely attributive. The expression is slightly awkward in Latin but corresponds exactly to the participle κεχαρισμένος in Greek locutions like κεχαρισμένα τοῖς θεοῖς λέγειν τε καὶ πράττειν in Plato, *Euthyphro* 14b, or κεχαρισμένως ἄρχειν in Isocrates 2.15 (LSJ s.v. χαρίζω III.2). It is likely that Seneca in this passage is translating as exactly as he can from a definition in his Greek source.

[27] *Ben.* 5.20.1–2. The case study is easiest to understand on the assumption that the benefactor is unaware of the feud, or at least of the resentful nature of the surviving brother.

[28] This suggestion is made in Konstan (2014). Further on joy and pleasure in *On Benefits*, see Degand (2015: 279–90).

of as a *reaction* to some present good. If joy were itself the good of the benefit, then what would be the good to which that joy responds? A regress threatens.

A better interpretation is that conferring joy on another person means just that one supplies an occasion for that person to rejoice by providing him with some good. But what sort of good is that? Initially one thinks of external goods, such as silver coins or the life of a child, and of course these are the objects of the ordinary person's delight. But Seneca writes as a Stoic, and elsewhere he is very clear that joy in the Stoic sense of the word relates properly to goods of character.[29] The position we should expect him to take, then, is that while the benefactor does bring about some sort of advantage for the recipient, that advantage is only a preferred indifferent. The good that is present resides in the beneficent action itself, in the goodwill that prompts it and in the correctness of the decision it represents. Similarly, the reaction of the recipient may be a genuine good if it is well judged and expresses a proper sense of gratitude. Thus, there is something to rejoice in on both sides of the equation.

But do the giver and receiver rejoice in one another's goods, or does each respond to his own? Seneca allows for both possibilities. Speaking of proper gratitude in book 3, he says that the grateful person "rejoices to look upon the intention of the giver"; then, within the same paragraph, he goes on to say that this same person "is glad and cheerful, looking forward to an opportunity to return the favor and finding great joy in that very thought."[30] It seems then that gratitude brings with it a double joy, both in the beneficent action of the other and in the anticipation of making an appropriate response. Similarly, he says in book 2 that givers and receivers experience "mutual joy."[31] There is a natural connection to the Stoic notion of wise friendship as a sharing (κοινωνία) of goods.[32] Seneca refers to this doctrine later in the treatise and draws a comparison to the sharing of two children between their two parents: it is not that each parent has one child, but that each has two (7.12.1).

Seneca's account of benefaction thus establishes an element of intersubjectivity between giver and a receiver, as each intuits the thoughts of the other and even responds affectively to the goods inherent in the other's

---

[29] For the exclusion of external goods, see *Ben.* 5.12.3–13.2. For the Stoic sense of joy, see *Letters* 59.2, which defines *gaudium* as "the elevation of a mind that is confident in goods that are real and its own" (*animi elatio suis bonis verisque fidentis*), and pages 178–81.
[30] *Ben.* 3.17.3–4. This second option is similar to what Seneca says in *Letters* 109.1–6.
[31] *Ben.* 2.31.2. See further page 185.
[32] For instance, in Diog. Laert. 7.124. See further Reydams-Schils (2005: 70); Graver (2007: 178–82).

actions. It is important to realize, however, that the action of benefiting another person is still properly an exercise of independent agency, in consideration of the independent interests of the other. In order for benefaction to occur, the giver needs to be able to act independently of the recipient, and the intended recipient needs to be in a position to gain something from that action. If everything A can do is actually caused by B, or if every good A can achieve is already fully possessed by B, then it is simply not possible for A to bestow a benefit on B. It follows immediately that one cannot bestow a benefit on oneself: as Seneca later remarks, a benefit is "a social matter" (*res socialis*, 5.11.5). But even where there are two distinct agents, there are some types of relationship that call into question the ability of one person to benefit another.

In book 3 of *On Benefits*, Seneca takes up one kind of relationship that was common in both Greek and Roman societies, that between enslaved persons and their owners under the law. Although he does not challenge the institution of slavery itself, he does take issue with a previous intellectual tradition that denied the capacity of enslaved persons for independent agency relative to their owners.[33] He cites Hecaton in particular for the view that a benefit is necessarily performed by an *alienus*; that is, by someone who does not in any sense belong to the recipient and therefore is not bound to do anything for the recipient. According to Hecaton, anything done by a family member counts as an obligation rather than a benefit, while the actions of the enslaved are merely "services" (*ministeria*).[34] Not only does everything that belongs to the slave already belong to the owner, but the slave's work throughout the day is also the property of the owner and does not entitle the slave to any recompense.

In arguing against Hecaton's position, Seneca first points out that enslaved people have all the rational capacities that are necessary conditions for beneficence. Slavery is just a misfortune; it does not change a person's nature, and every human being has the potential for virtue (3.18.2–4). His main argument, though, is that slaves can do things for their owners that the owners were not entitled to expect. He cites a number of instances in which slaves choose to help their owners even where there is no penalty for acting otherwise. These mostly consist in heroic actions taken by slaves to protect their owners in extraordinary situations: an owner's misguided attempt at suicide, the sack of a city, confrontations with death squads,

---

[33] See Seal (2021: 108–37); Bradley (2008); Sampino (2008); Griffin (1976: 256–85).

[34] *Ben.* 3.18.1. In Greek, a family member is an οἰκεῖος, someone who belongs to the house; the opposite is an ἀλλότριος, a "non-belonger."

and the like (3.19.1–28.6). But Seneca can also envision an everyday situation in which a slave might buy a gift for the owner out of his or her personal savings, called the *peculium*. Even if legal ownership of the *peculium* resides with the master or mistress, the slave does have possession of it and can make choices about how to use it.[35] The point is that beneficent action is a possibility only insofar as both custom and law establish certain boundaries between the benefactor and the beneficiary. Other relationships in which there is an element of subordination lend themselves to a similar analysis, including that of soldiers to their commanding officer and that of citizens to their king (3.18.3).

The problem presents itself somewhat differently when one considers the relationship between parents and their children, including their grown children.[36] Here, the concern is not that one party is subordinate to the other, but rather that one party owes its very existence to the other. Since it is because of the parents that the child is alive in the first place, how can the child do anything that will not simply redound to the parents' credit? And how could any gift given by the child even begin to measure up to the parent's gift of life? (3.29.3). All the same, Seneca feels that children can indeed benefit their parents. To make his case, he appeals to some basic principles of causation. The parent was a necessary condition for the child's existence, but so too were many other factors, from the milk the child drank to the doctor who long ago cured the parent's life-threatening illness. The parent gives corporeal life and the wet nurse gives nourishment, but the subsequent actions of the child owe much more to the child's own life experiences, abilities, and efforts. In any case, parents are hardly a point of origin, since they themselves result from earlier causes (3.29.6–31.5).

The question about independent agency is thus resolved as concerns one's biological parents. But it comes back in a different form when Seneca begins to speak about the gods – or, equivalently, about Jupiter, Nature, or Fate. Throughout the treatise, Seneca maintains the Stoics' usual view of divine providence. For him there is a supreme creator god who is the ultimate cause of all events, who works constantly to bring about good within the cosmos, and who may respond favorably to prayers. This god is intimately connected to human reason, for divinity is present in every

---

[35] This comes up later, in *Ben.* 7.4.4. See Griffin (2013: 325).
[36] Seneca's discussion of family relationships in book 3 is well treated in Gloyn (2017: 107–34). More broadly on parenthood in Roman Stoicism, see Reydams-Schils (2005: 115–42).

rational being.³⁷ And god, or the gods, provide us with many benefits. The beauties of nature, the food we eat, and our very selves are all gifts from above in just the same way as we humans give gifts to one another – or rather, in a more perfect way, for the gods exhibit true beneficence.³⁸

For our part, just as we respond with gratitude to benefits from other human beings, so also we should be grateful for the divine gifts and should want to give something back.³⁹ But here there is a difficulty, for when it comes to the divine authors of our existence, it is not at all clear that we have the independent agency that is required in order to perform a benefit. One could reason as follows:

> No one can act independently of a person who is the origin of their existence.
> The gods are the origin of existence for every human being.
> Therefore no human being can act independently of the gods.
> But if one cannot act independently of someone, one cannot benefit that person.
> Therefore no human being can benefit the gods.

It seems then that a grateful response to the divine giver is very much called for and yet is impossible.

Seneca is aware of this line of reasoning, for he mentions it several times in passing. However, this is not the position that he takes himself. Instead, he retrenches, reminding his readers yet again that beneficence inheres in volition alone. It is true that we can't bestow any benefits on the gods in actuality, since they have no needs that we could supply. They are perpetually like that friend who has already been rescued from the pirates. But Seneca holds that there is a fully satisfactory response that we can make through volition alone, in "an intention without an enactment" (*animus sine re*).⁴⁰ The gods expect nothing more from us, and like our human benefactors, the answering volition is what they really want.

In taking this position, Seneca commits himself to the view that human beings have some independent agency relative to their divine originators. Our will to act must be distinct from the divine will; otherwise we could not respond to the divine gifts at all. But it is not yet clear what having one's own agency can consist in when a human being is situated within a

---

³⁷ For the multiple names of Seneca's divinity, see *Ben.* 4.7.1–8.3; for his theology in general, Setaioli (2007); Wildberger (2006: 3–48, 453–553); Dragona-Monachou (1994: 4436–43). For the Stoic background, see Collette (2022); Algra (2003); Long and Sedley (1987: vol. 1, 274–79, 323–33); Dragona-Monachou (1976: 177–208).
³⁸ *Ben.* 4.4.2–9.1; 4.25.1–3. See Degand (2015: 361–68).   ³⁹ *Ben.* 1.1.9, 2.29.1–30.2; 7.31.2–4.
⁴⁰ *Ben.* 7.15.4; compare 2.30.2, 4.9.1.

world order that is established and governed by an omnipotent deity. At this point, the concern about independent agency merges into the more general problem of autonomy. We will need to look at that problem separately. First, however, we should consider a subsidiary problem that has to do with the beneficent will of the deities themselves.

Specificity of Aim

As we have seen, Seneca states in book 1 that a benefit is by definition "aimed at the very thing it does" (*in id, quod facit, prona*, 1.6.1). We benefit others just insofar as our actions are meant to do something for them in particular: if I save a child without realizing that she is *your* child, then I did not do anything for *you*, however pleased you might be. Unintended consequences are excluded: your opponent at law who contradicts himself on the stand may have helped you, but has not conferred a benefit on you (6.8.4). And even when one did mean to help, and to help the very person who was helped, the action is not a benefit in Seneca's sense of the word unless one has selected the recipient in the expectation that he or she will recognize one's goodwill and feel gratitude and joy because of it. If someone whom we know to be of an ungrateful temperament is in desperate straits and asks us for water or some other necessity of life, we should grant the request, but in that case the help we give was intended for that person merely as a human being, not as the specific person he or she is. For that very reason, it will not count as a benefit, but only as a "useful activity" (*opera utilis*, 4.29.1–3).

This strict account of the intention that is required for giving a benefit makes it quite challenging to try to think of god as providing benefits to humankind. For many of the things that are conventionally named as gifts from the gods are given to all alike, with no apparent regard for the worthiness of the receiver. As Seneca puts it, "the sun rises also for criminals, and the sea is available to the pirate" (4.26.1).[41] In individual cases, too, it often happens that some exceptional advantage, like a financial windfall or a chance to exercise royal power, befalls a person who is patently unworthy of it. These facts make it seem that the gods must not

---

[41] *Ben.* 4.4.3–6.6 and 6.23.5–8 stress the gifts of the gods toward the human race in general (i.e., as distinct from animals and plants). Seneca refers to these gifts also as *beneficia*, using the word in a broader sense: they are a *commune munus*, like the emperor's gift of citizenship to all the Gauls in 6.19.2–5, and for them we owe *collective* gratitude.

have specific recipients in mind when they distribute their blessings. And without the specific intention, there is no true benefit and no reason for gratitude.

Seneca offers two arguments to defend his view that the gods do confer benefits. First, he points out that rain, wind, and other widespread occurrences are of such a kind that it is not possible to bestow them on some people and not others. With these, it could be that the gods intend them especially for those humans that are fit recipients. Others would get them as well, but as free riders: in their case, the rain is not a gift from god but only a side effect of someone else's gift, an unintended though not unforeseen consequence. He draws an analogy to some purely human cases. Authors of great books may write for the benefit of their readers even if some readers will fail to comprehend their work, and medical researchers may develop new medications for the benefit of future patients even if some of the sick do not deserve to be cured (4.28.1–6). Then, concerning those individual advantages that sometimes befall the unworthy, he points out that the person who appears to have come out ahead is not necessarily the one whom the gods favor. Even human agents sometimes honor one person by providing a gift or service to another, as when a degenerate son is elected to public office because of his illustrious ancestors. The gods might do the same, allowing a Caligula to accede to the principate for the sake of his father Germanicus and his grandfather Augustus Caesar. The apparent gifts to the Caligulas of this world are thus explained away as side effects of the divine plan (4.31.1–2, 32.1).

We may feel at this point that the argument has become sophistical and unconvincing. Is the idea of gods as benefactors really viable in the face of deranged autocracy? But these rather overintellectualized maneuvers are a price Seneca is willing to pay in order to preserve his view that all our lives and fortunes should be understood as benefits from the gods. Some people think they do not owe the gods anything at all; these, Seneca feels, are "poor interpreters of the divine gifts" (1.1.9). By choosing what he regards as the correct interpretation, one adopts a stance of gratitude that sets one apart from those foolish ingrates and makes one a proper recipient of the gods' benefits. In an analogous structure of thought, Seneca argues in letter 73 that philosophers have more reason than others do to be grateful for the peace and security that their rulers provide. All the citizens enjoy the advantages of peace, but only philosophers fully appreciate its value and know how to use it well (*Letters* 73.5–8).

The recognition that the gods give without expectation of return provides the thoughtful person with a motive to exercise a similarly profuse and selfless generosity toward other human beings. A prominent theme in the Platonic tradition, the conscious imitation of the divine plays a role in Stoic thought as well.[42] In *On Benefits*, the abundant and yet discerning generosity of the gods functions as the paradigm for human acts of giving at beginning (*Ben.* 1.1.9), middle (4.25.1–3), and end (7.31.5). Like the divine gifts, one's benefits will sometimes accrue to the undeserving. One is to realize this and be undeterred, while still taking care that one's specific aim in giving is correct. Thus, in the closing apothegm (a riddling turn of phrase Seneca must have been proud of), it is not greatness to bestow one's benefits where they are wasted (*dare et perdere*); it *is* greatness to waste some and yet give (*perdere et dare*, 7.32).

Autonomy and Freedom

Volition, human and divine, is at the heart of Seneca's account of beneficence. We know from the definition in *Ben.* 1.6.1 that a benevolent action is necessarily one that is provided "on one's own initiative" (*sua sponte*). As the work proceeds, Seneca often speaks of *voluntas* ("willingness," also translatable as "wishing," "wanting," or simply as "will"), or the related verb *velle* ("wish" or "want") as a necessary condition for conferring a benefit. Along the same lines, he stresses that one cannot be conferring a benefit if one is acting under compulsion.[43] Conversely, a person who makes proper use of volition is always able to confer a benefit, since one's willingness to confer it is the very essence of the benefit.

In one sense, the language of voluntariness, choice, and freedom is just what one would expect to find in a work on benefits. Benefits are distinguished from appropriate actions generally (*officia* or καθήκοντα) by the fact that they go above and beyond the obligations one has as a family member, a citizen, a subject, or other socially defined role. Seneca's word *arbitrium* ("choice") appears in *On Benefits* only for what is done in the absence of socially imposed obligations or constraints, and *voluntas* is occasionally used in the same way.[44] But we have seen already how his

---

[42] The *locus classicus* for the Platonic tradition is Plato, *Theaetetus* 176b. For the Stoic version, see Epictetus, *Discourses* 2.14.11–13; and compare Seneca, *Letters* 59.18, 92.30, 104.23, 124.23–24; *Prov.* 1.5. For the Stoic handling of the theme, see especially Reydams-Schils (2017, 2019).

[43] *Ben.* 3.19.1, 3.21.1–2, 6.7.2.

[44] For the usage of *arbitrium*, see *Ben.* 2.11.1, 2.18.7, 2.19.2, 3.7.1. The word carries a broader signification in *NQ* 2.38.3: *dicam quemadmodum manente fato aliquid sit in hominis arbitrio*. For the narrower sense of *voluntas*, see *Ben.* 3.21.2 *quidquid est, quod servilis officii formulam excedit, quod non ex imperio, sed ex voluntate praestatur, beneficium est*; also 6.16.1.

work moves into a more psychological realm when it contrasts the observable effects of a benefit with the interior will that *is* the benefit. In combination with Seneca's broader interests in causation and the divine governance of the universe, that emphasis on the interior will moves quite naturally into questions about the nature of volition itself.

In this context it is helpful to remember how Seneca's Stoic predecessors addressed the issue of individual agency within a determinate cosmos.[45] Chrysippus had maintained that all events are determined by prior causes, not excepting those that take place within the human mind; he did not, however, regard the existence of prior causes of an abridgment of our agency. The actions that we initiate are caused in a principal sense by the character each one of us has, that predisposes us to accept or reject our mental impressions of what is to be done, and in an auxiliary way by various external triggers and background conditions. The distinction between principal and auxiliary causes allows moral responsibility to rest with the individual agent, even though the character of the individual has itself been shaped over time by various factors: genetics, environment, education, and one's own previous decisions. As agents we participate in the determination of the world's events without being in any sense exempt from it.

Seneca recognizes the determinist framework of Stoic thought and in general accepts it without much discussion.[46] But he clearly knows that there were other philosophical views in this area. With his extensive knowledge of Epicurean texts including the poem of Lucretius, and perhaps also through his familiarity with Peripatetic thought, he must have encountered claims that determinism is in some way injurious to basic concepts of willingness and choice.[47] In particular, he is aware that for some people, the notion of choice requires alternatives: we cannot say that a person chooses to give unless in that same situation it is also possible for that same person to choose not to give. In book 6 of *On Benefits*, he offers a response to those who think that will and choice require an element of indeterminacy.

---

[45] For determinism and the will in Stoicism, see Long (1971); Voelke (1973); Long and Sedley (1987: vol. 1, 386–94); Salles (2005: 33–89); Bobzien (1998, 2021: 217–52).

[46] See, for instance, *Letters* 19.6, 76.23 (quoted in Chapter 2, note 37), 88.15, 107.11; *NQ* 2.32.4. In view of other passages, the apparent agnosticism of *Letters* 16.4–5 should be read as rhetorical. See Setaioli (2014c); I. Hadot (2014: 299–312); Wildberger (2006: 317–51); Inwood (2005: 132–56).

[47] The indeterminist aspect of Epicurean thought is represented for us mainly in Lucretius 2.251–93, using the phrase "free will" (*libera voluntas*, 2.256–57). The emphasis on a two-sided freedom of decision was primarily Peripatetic; see Bobzien (1998: 396–412), citing passages in Philopator and Alexander of Aphrodisias. Bobzien sees that emphasis as a development of the second century CE, but this is without introducing the Senecan evidence treated here.

The Treatise On Benefits

The issue arises first in reference to the agency of divine beings. Seneca has already stated, in the introduction to book 1, that the gods' beneficence is a constant expression of their nature: they help us "from their abundant and unceasing kindness" (*effusa nec cess<ante benign>itate*), because "they are exercising their nature" (*naturam suam exercent*, 1.1.9). It seems then that the beneficent actions of the gods are inevitable: they express an inherent trait of the divine nature that does not ever change. Sections 20 and 21 of book 6 follow up on that assumption.[48] There, pressing the point about specificity of aim, Seneca remarks that while the divine sun and moon move through the sky for everyone, their movements are indeed benefits, since they also are performed for the sake of each individual human.[49] He realizes, though, that this claim is open to an objection. How can anyone say that the sun and moon act of their own volition? For there seems to be no possibility of their doing anything else.

> I would know that the sun and moon will to help us if they could be unwilling. But they are not allowed *not* to move. In brief, let's see them stand still and stop their work. (*Ben.* 6.21.1)

According to the objector, variability of conduct is actually a requirement in order for us to believe that the conduct is voluntary. For only those things whose movement sometimes changes can be said to have a capacity to act otherwise, and only one who has the capacity to act otherwise can be said to act willingly.

Seneca, however, rejects the premise. For him, the fact that one's conduct is invariable does not necessarily mean that there is no act of volition. On the contrary, he says, not being able to alter one's wish is an indication that one has an especially firm volition.

> A person who cannot be unwilling is not for that reason any less willing. On the contrary: the greatest proof of a firm willingness is that it cannot be altered.[50]

---

[48] For earlier treatments of this passage in connection with these issues, see Zöller (2003: 219–23); Wildberger (2006: 338–41, 925–31).

[49] *Ben.* 6.20.1. The appeal to the heavenly bodies as examples of beneficent deities is standard in a Stoic context: Balbus in Cicero, *Nat. Deor.* 2.46–60, is similarly concerned with astral deities. Compare Seneca *Prov.* 1.2; *Letters* 102.21. The assumption does not extend to all natural features: one does not thank the river that enables shipping (*Ben.* 6.7.3).

[50] *Ben.* 6.21.1. The passage that follows (6.21.2) promises a series of refutations (*hoc vide quot modis refellatur*). In the discussion here, I omit the first of these, which reads as follows: *Vir bonus non potest non facere, quod facit; non enim erit bonus, nisi fecerit; ergo nec bonus vir beneficium dat, quia facit, quod debet, non potest autem non facere, quod debet.* "The good man cannot but do what he does, for otherwise he will not be good. It follows that not even a good man confers a benefit

If someone were compelled to act by some external force, that would indeed mean they did not confer a benefit. But it is different with an internal, psychological necessity, the sort of necessity that arises from one's own mental character.[51] Here, the compulsion comes from oneself.

> It makes a big difference whether you say, "He cannot but do this," because he is forced, or "He cannot but want to." For if it is necessary for him to do it, I do not owe the benefit to him but to the one who compels him; but if it is necessary for him to want to do it (because out of everything he could want, this seems to him to be the best), then he compels himself. In that case, what I would not have owed him as one who benefited me under compulsion, I do owe him as one who compels a benefit toward me. (*Ben.* 6.21.2–3)

Something like this can presumably be said in any instance of rational action. The wish one has in any given moment is a necessary result of one's character in that moment, which sees that action as the thing to do in the given circumstances. Consequently, both the action and the wish itself are, in a sense, compelled. But the mental character that sees this particular action as the thing to do is identifiable with the person herself. As long as we know that the action came about through her wish and not someone else's, we can reasonably assign credit or blame to her.

The crucial instance is behavior that remains invariable over a long period of time. The movements of the heavenly bodies come under this heading, and so too do some forms of human behavior. We might think for instance of a thoroughly compassionate parent who cannot see a child in distress without wanting to help, or of a born teacher who cannot pass up an opportunity to promote learning. Suppose, then, that in fact the sun and moon cannot will to alter their movements, and similarly, that these human agents cannot even wish to refrain from helping the distressed child or teaching the receptive pupil. Must we therefore say that their entirely consistent actions are done mindlessly and not of their own volition? That

---

because he is doing what he should; rather, he cannot but do what he should." (My translation takes the negative in *nec* to apply to *quia*, as does Basore (1935).) On my reading, this initial attempt at refutation refers only to *logical* necessity: since good people are by definition those who do good actions, a good person cannot act otherwise without ceasing to be good. This is distinct from the internal or psychological necessity that features in the subsequent discussion.

[51] A different but related issue arises in *Ben.* 5.9.1–2. Seneca asserts there that the human being's natural instinct for self-preservation and the promotion of one's own interests does not count as a case of self-benefaction, arguing that there one is not performing a voluntary act but rather obeying one's nature (*naturae suae paret*). In the book 6 passage, though, acting in accordance with one's character involves more than being guided by one's instinctual constitution. Subrational animals also obey their constitution (as Seneca explains in letter 121), but they are not capable of judgment or volition in the way that the divine and human agents of *Ben.* 6.21.4 are.

is not Seneca's view of the matter. On the contrary, he holds that these agents who cannot will otherwise have a *better* claim to volition than those who can:

> It would be crazy to say that a wish that isn't at risk of stopping or changing to its opposite isn't really a wish. On the contrary, one ought to think that the most willing person of all is the one whose will is so certain as to be permanent. Given that willingness belongs also to the person who can be unwilling in the next moment, will we not think that the person is willing whose nature doesn't admit of his being unwilling?[52]

On this point there is a clear analogy between human and divine volition. Speaking of divine agents, Seneca says in the following paragraph that "their will is an enduring law for them," and

> it is their own strength that holds them to their plan; they do not remain with it out of weakness, but because they have no inclination to deviate from what is best. (*Ben.* 6.23.1–2)

Concerning human beings whose behavior is entirely consistent, his position is exactly the same: that far from being defective in the rational being's capacity for choice, these people exercise that capacity in its truest form.[53] In terms of agency, there is no difference between them and the gods. The contrast is to be drawn rather with subrational animals, who act from instinct rather than from decision, and with less-sure humans whose decisions may change. The latter have the same capacity for volition as the consistent agent but exercise it differently: they choose to do a thing and then realize shortly after that they do not want to do it, or they choose not to act in a certain way and then decide that they want to after all. Such inconsistency is plausibly related to the logical inconsistencies that abound in the mind of anyone who is not perfectly rational. We decide one way on the basis of prior beliefs that support that decision, but we also hold conflicting beliefs that support the opposite decision. This is very different from the fully rational agent, who "has no inclination to deviate from what is best." Stoic terminology speaks at this point of "strong" assent, as opposed to "hasty" or "weak" assent.[54]

It should be clear by now that Seneca is not at all concerned with free will in the sense that the Epicureans had in mind; that is, a will that operates outside the usual sequence of cause and effect. Such a conception of freedom would

---

[52] *Ben.* 6.21.4. For the gods' inability to harm, see also *Anger* 2.27.1–2; *Letters* 95.49.
[53] Compare *Letters* 35.4.
[54] For the terminology, see for instance Stobaeus 2.7.11m, 112 Wachsmuth (LS 41G, *SVF* 1.54), with Graver (2007: 65).

be incompatible with his position on the world order and on divine providence. But Seneca has his own understanding of freedom. In accordance with Stoic doctrine, he holds that freedom consists essentially in the capacity for self-regulation; or, as he puts it in *Letters* 75.18, "to have the greatest power over oneself."[55] We have no need to worry about whether people are able to act otherwise than they do, for that is not what freedom is. Rather, a person is free just insofar as she is able to act in accordance with her own wishes.

The word "freedom" does not occur in the book 6 passage, but freedom (*libertas*) and being free (*liberum esse*) do appear elsewhere in the treatise as the opposite of external constraint and as a hallmark of choice.[56] Still more pertinent is a brief statement in the *Natural Questions* that neatly summarizes the same position. Writing in the preface to book 1 (originally book 7), Seneca reflects on the satisfactions of abstract study and lists some of the cosmological and theological questions that philosophers are privileged to consider. Among these is the following query about the supreme deity:

> Is it permitted for him to make decisions also today, detracting to some extent from the law of fate, or is that a diminution of his majesty and an admission of error, that he made something that needed to be changed?

Answering his own question, Seneca makes a case for freedom even in an agent whose decisions have been predetermined:

> <But> he who cannot but prefer the best should always have the same preferences. That does not make him any less free and powerful, for he is his own necessity.[57]

In this case, of course, the prior determination is by that agent himself, since the Stoic Zeus is identified with fate. But saying that god "is his own necessity" means more than that. The point here is not that god necessitates all events from the beginning (true as that might be), but that at every moment of time god is able to act exactly as he wishes. He is free and powerful precisely because his will is never thwarted, and that in turn is because his preferences never change, a natural consequence of his perfected rationality: he cannot but prefer the best.

---

[55] The Stoic definition is given in Diog. Laert. 7.121 (*SVF* 3.355) as "the power of self-determination" (ἐξουσία αὐτοπραγίας); cf. *Letters* 75.18 *in se ipsum habere maximam potestatem*. See Long (1971); Botros (1985); Bobzien (1998: 339–41) and (2021: 194–216); for Seneca, Inwood (2005: 302–21); Wildberger (2006: 338–41, 925–31); Setaioli (2014c).

[56] *Ben.* 2.18.7, 3.20.1–2, 4.35.2, 5.6.7.

[57] *NQ* 1 *praef.* 3. Hine (1996) minimizes what has sometimes been treated as a lacuna between the two sentences.

On Seneca's way of thinking, the ability to change one's mind when there is no relevant change in situation is not a token of independence, but actually a limitation on one's freedom. And if I understand his view correctly, that limitation is not only in consequence of theory, but is a matter of inner experience. We actually feel ourselves to be unable to carry out a course of action we have decided upon, or we find we cannot maintain our resolve to refrain from some action. Where strong emotion is involved, the sense of helplessness or loss of control can be attributed to the overwhelming vigor of emotional impulses.[58] But the phenomenon is more general. In the realm of instability and error, there are many different ways for our wishes to be in conflict with one another, and thus many ways for us to act, or fail to act, contrary to our own wishes. By contrast, the perfectly rational agent would always act exactly as she wants to, because her wishes relative to a particular situation do not change. With no internal conflict or hesitation, she would be able to act confidently, wholeheartedly, and swiftly.

This freedom is not well described by accounts that make it sound like merely a matter of submission to fate or to god's will. Scholars sometimes speak as if the Stoic sage were a rather feckless individual who trots along behind his fate like a dog tied to a wagon.[59] This is not the emphasis that we find in *On Benefits*. Here, freedom consists in the perfected agent's acting exactly as she herself wishes, with a clarity of purpose that ordinary agents can only aspire to. The picture is not inconsistent with the other one: the stable will is indeed aligned with the will of Zeus.[60] But freedom as Seneca describes it here would also confer a tremendous sense of power, for it is the ability to do whatever one wants, constrained only by the limits of mortality. This is an ability that we conflicted and emotional beings do not currently have, but that can be attained with maturity and training.

***

---

[58] Further to this issue, see Graver (2007: 66–70, 81–83), with page 138.
[59] Inwood (1985: 110–11) sums up a generation's worth of scholarship when he cites *Ben.* 6.21.2–3 for the idea that internal necessity "must be compatible with the 'freedom' of the wise man, such as it is," and that with all contingency banished, obedience to Zeus "is the only freedom left." Bobzien (1998: 351–57) rightly objects to accounts of Stoicism that give pride of place to the dog and cart analogy from Hippolytus, *Haer.* 1.21.2 – which, she argues, does not originate with early Stoic views and is not consistent with them.
[60] Seneca does certainly hold that wise human beings gladly accept the workings of the divine plan, and he may even lean on the paradox that in the deeper scheme of things, obedience to god is freedom. Thus *Happiness* 15.7: "obedience to god is freedom"; and compare the prayer of the Cynic Demetrius from *Prov.* 5.5–8.

On Benefits is a circuitous and sometimes tedious work, meandering in its argumentation and relentless in its casuistry. Few will find it an appealing read. But for material on intention, agency, and mutual aid in Stoic thought, Seneca's longest treatise proves to be extremely rewarding. Of all his works, *On Benefits* yields the deepest insight into the meaning of agency, both in the divine creator and in the generous human giver. Although its specific concern is with just one kind of human action, the implications of its analysis extend to all areas of Stoic moral psychology. The statements Seneca makes at the philosophical level are all the more significant in that many of them appear to have been drawn from earlier Stoic works that are not otherwise available to us.

In some respects, beneficent actions are quite different from other kinds of action. Because benefits go above and beyond what the intended recipient has a right to expect, they raise many challenging questions about the nature of human relationships, the limits of mutual obligation, and the extent to which one person is able to act independently of another. The interpersonal nature of benefits also adds an interesting dimension of intersubjectivity. Because acts of kindness are by definition intended to please another person, they rely on an agent's ability to anticipate another person's reactions, while at the same time, the appreciation of the recipient responds to assessment of the benefactor's generous intent. In the ideal case, each derives joy from the interaction, and that joy relates on each side to character goods both in the self and in the other. The specific nature of benefits thus contributes to an understanding of the Stoic analysis of friendship and of Seneca's remarks on mutual joy in the *Letters*.

But in some ways benefits are actions like any other. They are open to the same questions about how decisions made within the mind find concrete expression in the world, and they raise the same issue about the meaning of individual choice within a larger world order. I have tried to show here how the study of benefits puts pressure on the Stoic account that defines action strictly in terms of the mental event that initiates it. In order to sort through the obligations of the recipient of a benefit, Stoic philosophers find it necessary to be explicit about the way that actions are fulfilled in observable effects on the lives of others. Beyond this, Seneca's study of unforced acts of kindness provides a natural lead-in to the study of volition. We see in *On Benefits* that Seneca has definite ideas about what it is to act of one's own volition. He specifically rejects the notion that voluntary action depends on one's having the ability to act otherwise. With the perfection of our rational nature comes steadiness of aim, and that is the truest form of volition.

Seneca is fond of saying that the wise person differs from Zeus only in the limitation imposed by mortality.[61] The treatise on benefits gives us some idea of what that extraordinary claim is supposed to mean. The providential activity of the Stoic Zeus finds its human counterpart in the benevolent actions of the perfected will whose sole aim in acting is to bring about good for another rational being. Like Zeus, the virtuous agent is able to realize every one of her intentions, for a properly formed intention can always be fulfilled in time, unless death intervenes. Finally, while the person of perfect wisdom certainly accepts the will of Zeus as representing the best possible plan for the world's events, he or she is also similar to Zeus in having a will that is genuinely free – free because it does not change and cannot be countermanded.

---

[61] *Prov.* 1.5, *Constancy* 8.2, *NQ* 1 *praef.* 11–17, *Letters* 31.8–9, 53.11–12, 66.11–12, 73.13; Russell (2004); Setaioli (2007). Compare Cicero, *Nat. Deor.* 2.153; Plutarch, *On Common Conceptions* 1061f (LS 63I).

PART II

Rival Traditions in Philosophy

CHAPTER 4

Seneca and Epicurus

Seneca occupies a position of interest within the history of Epicurus's reception at Rome. Despite his Stoic commitments, he is deeply engaged with Epicurean thought and Epicurean texts, referring to Epicurus or to his doctrines and members of his community more than eighty times and giving over forty direct quotations from Epicurean works.[1] Yet his overall attitude is by no means easy to characterize. At times painstakingly accurate, he is also capable of what seems like willful misrepresentation of Epicurus's views; often antagonistic, he is also on occasion strikingly appreciative of what Epicurus has to offer. On some points he even takes over ideas that he knows to be Epicurean in origin, stating them as his own opinion. More than that, he will sometimes modify and develop those ideas in ways that make him a fascinating case of Epicurean influence outside the Garden.

The complexity of Seneca's response at one time made him the central exhibit for that older view of Roman philosophy that spoke of "eclecticism." Indeed, Pierluigi Donini has argued that the very notion of eclecticism as formulated by Eduard Zeller and Karl Praechter was devised in part as a way of accounting for Seneca's extraordinary attitude toward the rival school.[2] More recent scholarship has in general resisted the implication that Seneca lacked a clear sense of doctrinal commitment. Following a seminal article by John Rist in 1989, numerous careful studies have demonstrated the depth of Seneca's familiarity with the Stoic system and the thoroughness of his adherence to it.[3] Yet this reassessment of the

---

[1] A full list of references is provided in Ferguson (1990: 2280–82); most can also be found, grouped by topic, in Motto (1970). Lana (1991: 263–68) compares the citations from Epicurus with those from other authors.
[2] Donini (2011: 204).
[3] Seneca's orthodoxy on the main outlines of Stoic doctrine was established in Rist (1989); the argument has been extended in Cooper (2004: 339–34); Cooper (2006); Inwood (2005: 23–64, 132–57); Wildberger (2006); Graver (2007: 125–32).

Roman philosopher's main doctrinal adherence has not as yet been followed by any comprehensive re-examination of the role of Epicureanism in his works.[4]

In what follows, I collect and study most of the relevant passages, grouping them loosely by topic. In so doing I hope to bring out the thinking behind Seneca's response, which is more consistent and principled than has usually been recognized. Toward the core commitments of Epicurean philosophy – its anti-teleological physics and cosmology, its hedonist ethics, and its utilitarian approach to other-concern and friendship – Seneca is consistently hostile, as befits one whose instincts are those of a Stoic. He is careful, though, to identify some de facto common ground between the two schools on the question of whether philosophers should participate in politics or withdraw into a life of study and contemplation. Meanwhile, he willingly endorses a number of points made by Epicurus concerning the psychology of the individual and the therapeutic strategies that are most likely to assist moral progress. However, this agreement does not ever carry with it any general approval of the a priori commitments of Epicureanism. It is rather a practical appreciation for Epicurus's sensitivity to the nuances of human behavior.

Extent and Provenance of Seneca's Knowledge

Seneca's familiarity with the Epicurean school and its doctrine was extensive and detailed. Although the nature of the evidence does not permit definitive identification of his specific sources, there is reason to think that his information was often better than our own and reliable enough to yield the basis for a sophisticated response.

Concerning Epicurus himself, Seneca knows that he lived in Athens and that his personal habits were abstemious (*Happiness* 12.4; *Letters* 18.9). He is able to quote from Epicurus's letters concerning the character of his friends Metrodorus, Polyaenus, Idomeneus, Pythocles, and Hermarchus, and can give a date for at least one such letter.[5] He knows, too, that these friends were philosophers in their own right, but he believes that their views were so close to those of Epicurus as to justify some casualness in

---

[4] Earlier overviews include Mutschmann (1915); Schottländer (1955); André (1970); Setaioli (1988: 172–248); Mazzoli (1989: 1872–73); Hachmann (1995: 220–37); Maso (1999: 83–105); Dietsche (2014: 157–254). Some aspects are usefully explored also in Inwood (2007b); Wildberger (2014); and Schiesaro (2015). Graver (2015) overlaps in part with this chapter but is more specific to the *Letters on Ethics*.

[5] *Letters* 18.9, 21.3–5, 21.7, 22.5, 52.3–4, 79.15–16. The date given in *Letters* 18.9 to "the magistracy [*i.e., archonship*] of Charinus" was probably copied from the superscription in his source.

attribution.[6] On the basis of a letter exchange with Metrodorus, he infers that Epicurus was little known during his lifetime (*Letters* 79.15–16). He knows of Epicurus's deathbed suffering from urinary blockage and dysentery and can quote his dying words (*Letters* 66.47, 92.25).

In matters of doctrine, he shows a broad understanding of Epicurean ethics in particular and refers often to such key elements as freedom from pain and anxiety, the classification of desires, the basis of friendship, the preference for a retired life, and the interentailment of virtue and pleasure. He can also state accurately many points from throughout the Epicurean system, among them the intermingling of atoms and void, the downward movement of atoms, arguments against the fear of death, the elimination of logic from the curriculum, the effort to eliminate ambiguous terms, and the use of the term "rule" (*kanōn*) for philosophical methodology.[7]

It is possible that some of this information came to him by oral transmission, for he has some Epicurean friends, among them his kinsman Annaeus Serenus and the elderly Aufidius Bassus of letter 30.[8] But he also speaks of reading Epicurean books, and although he does not mention the titles of these books, we can be confident that most of his knowledge has a textual basis. Determining what specific works he had on hand is more difficult, since many points of doctrine were stated in exactly the same words in more than one Epicurean text or were quoted or paraphrased in handbooks and in works by opponents of the school. In some cases the best we can do is to identify the works with which Seneca *appears* to be familiar when the doctrines he reports are compared with Epicurus's extant writings. On this basis we can say that he appears to know the *Letter to Menoeceus*, because he quotes a phrase from it in one of his letters and in another states Epicurus's formula for the highest good in exactly the form that appears there.[9] He also quotes the exact words that we know as the first, fourth, and fifth of the *Key Doctrines* – although, again, the *Key Doctrines* may themselves have been excerpted from other Epicurean works, in which case Seneca may be quoting the originals.[10]

---

[6] *Letters* 14.17, 33.4, 81.11–12, 98.9.
[7] On downward movement, see *Letters* 72.9 (as a satiric comparison); on logic, ambiguity, and the *kanōn*, *Letters* 89.11, and see Atherton (2009: 212). The other points are all treated in what follows.
[8] Serenus's allegiance seems clear in *Constancy* 3.2 and 15.4, but in *Tranq.* 1.10 he has abandoned the school in favor of Stoicism: Griffin (1976: 316).
[9] *Letters* 14.17 (cf. *Menoeceus* 130) 66.45 (cf. *Menoeceus* 131). Note, however, that in *Letters* 14.17, he claims not to know whether the words he quotes are by Epicurus or by another of his school; evidence perhaps that his knowledge of the *Letter to Menoeceus* comes only through a *gnomologion*. See Setaioli (1988: 184–88).
[10] What look like exact quotations from the *Key Doctrines* are found at *Apoc.* 8 (*KD* 1), *Letters* 30.14 (*KD* 4), and *Happiness* 7.1 (*KD* 5).

Sometimes, too, Seneca quotes from Epicurean texts with which we are not otherwise familiar. In the *Letters on Ethics*, especially, he is fond of quoting brief maxims from Epicurus's correspondence with friends, and many of these are from letters otherwise unknown to us. Five of Epicurus's letters are described at some length: the letter summarized in letter 9, criticizing Stilpo's view on friendship; the dated letter to Polyaenus cited in *Letters* 18.9; the letter to Idomeneus on political participation quoted in letters 21 and 22; the one on moral progress quoted in 52.3–4; and the one described in 79.15 concerning his friendship with Metrodorus.[11] Seneca also knows at least three letters by Metrodorus, one of which he quotes at some length in Greek.[12] Since he also describes what it is like to select Epicurean maxims out of their original contexts (letter 33), it is likely that he possesses complete texts for other letters as well, and that at least some of the other short sayings quoted in the *Letters on Ethics* derive from this source. But he must also have access to some sort of gnomologion or maxim collection, for at one point he indicates that he is quoting from "the less well-known, uncirculated sayings of Epicurus" (*secretior nec inter vulgata Epicuri dicta*, *Letters* 13.17).

Could the wealthy Seneca have possessed a large collection of Epicurean writings? His description of a work authored by his friend Lucilius seems relevant in this regard, where he says "it seemed light to me, though its bulk would seem at first glance to be that of Livy or Epicurus, not of your writings or mine" (*Letters* 46.1). This remark suggests that he at least knows Epicurus's corpus to be of substantial length, comparable to Livy's multi-volume histories and certainly more extensive than Seneca's own writings. If he did have access to some substantial work – a long epitome or perhaps even *On Nature* itself, then we have an explanation for an unexpected citation of Epicurus in his meteorological treatise, the *Natural Questions*. Explaining various theories for the causes of earthquakes, Seneca quotes a long series of explanations in what he says are Epicurus's own words, explanations similar but by no means identical to the ones we find in *Letter to Pythocles* 105.[13] In addition, we might ask ourselves how he knows

---

[11] Setaioli (1988: 171–82) effectively counters Usener's assumption that Seneca knew only a *gnomologion*; see Usener (1887: iv–vii).

[12] *Letters* 79.16, 81.11–12, 98.9, 99.25–26. In *Letters* 81, Seneca does not say that the remarks of Metrodorus he refers to were made in a letter, but it seems likely in view of the other passages. The material in letters 98 and 99 is likely to be all from the same letter of Metrodorus. For the format of the citation in *Letters* 99.25, compare the citation of Cicero in 97.3–4, and see, for all these matters, Setaioli (1988: 249–56).

[13] *NQ* 6.20.5–7; the passage is given in Usener (1887) as fragment 151. In this context it is worth noting that Seneca in the *Natural Questions* sometimes follows the principle of multiple explanations, which we know as Epicurean; see further Inwood (2005: 183). I am not convinced,

that the Epicurean gods inhabit the spaces between the worlds, a view not to be found in Epicurus's writings as we know them, although Cicero, too, associates it with the school.[14] Such information could perhaps have come from *On Nature* (if the view was indeed Epicurus's own), but alternative explanations are certainly available, including that Seneca sometimes repeats Epicurean doctrines or even entire quotations that he found in intervening works. For the citation in *Natural Questions*, for instance, he may have drawn on criticisms of Epicurus contained in the meteorological compendium by Posidonius.[15]

Well informed as Seneca may be on some points, there are also some aspects of Epicureanism that he gives no indication of having studied. We find no mention in his works of the conservation of matter, atomic shapes, or the atomic "swerve"; no specifics on the composition of the soul; nothing on εἴδωλα, sense perception, or the validity of the senses; nothing on the origin of species, the development of civilization, or social contracts. Yet his failure to mention these points does not necessarily indicate ignorance. All of them are treated by Lucretius, whom he seems to know well, since he quotes him eight or nine times from widely scattered contexts. Perhaps Seneca regarded these more abstract and theoretical dimensions of Epicureanism as too far distant from his own concerns to be worth explaining to his readers.

Physics and Theology

Although his works contain no systematic treatment of Epicurean physics, Seneca does state a definitive position on atomism in *Natural Questions* 2.6–7, speaking about the physical properties of air. Before giving his own explanation of the causes of lightning and thunder, he finds it necessary to establish that air is a unitary body, and in order to do that, he must first dismiss the rival claim that air is composed "from discrete little bodies" or "particles" mingled with void. Those who defend this claim believe that it is proven by the ease with which motion occurs in air. But this is incorrect: motion in air, like motion in water, is enabled by the retrograde flow

---

however, that this principle must have been derived solely from Epicurus. The meteorological tradition has its own conventions, and Seneca's use of it is rather different from what we find in Epicurus; see, for instance, *NQ* 5.5.1, and see Graver (1999b); Hine (2010: 3–7).

[14] Seneca mentions the point a number of times: *Ben.* 4.19.1–2, 7.31.3; *Letters* 90.35. For Cicero, see *Nat. Deor.* 1.18, but that passage is too oblique to have been Seneca's source. Concerning Seneca's sources for *On Benefits*, see Griffin (2013: 15–25), as well as Griffin's notes on particular passages.

[15] Inwood (2005: 163–64).

(ἀντιπερίστασις) that closes in behind a moving object.[16] In fact, observation tells us that air must be a unified substance, since without unity and coherence it could not exhibit the "tension" (*intentio*) that is manifested in the various phenomena of air pressure: inflated balls, windstorms, trumpets, and the hydraulic organ. The operation of "breath in tension" (*intenti spiritus*) explains a vast range of phenomena, from stone walls broken up by roots to the cohesion and movement of the human body, and even the movements of the mind. Without it, Seneca insists, there could be nothing strong, and its own strength surpasses everything else.

Although Seneca does not name Epicurus specifically in the passage, the attitude he takes toward particulate air is significant for his reception of Epicurean thought. His own understanding of the world depends on there being a unified nexus of causality effected through the medium of *pneuma* – for his "breath in tension" is manifestly the same as the all-pervasive pneumatic tension (πνευματικὸς τόνος) that effects all causation in standard Stoic physics. A view that dissolves physical nature into particles interspersed with void is irreconcilably at odds with his and must be resisted at every turn. In a similar vein, he consistently expresses strong objections to the Epicurean theology that denies god or the gods any causal involvement with the world. For him as for other Stoics, god or Zeus is identical with the causal principle: he is "the intellect of the universe ... everything you see, and everything you do not see," who "maintains his creation both from within and from without" (*NQ* 1 *praef.* 13). To place the gods outside the world makes them lazy rather than blessed (*Ben.* 7.31.3, cf. 4.4.1), and leaves the world without a controlling intelligence. Events in it will come about "by some kind of random impulse or by a nature that has no awareness of its own actions" (*NQ* 1 *praef.* 15).

Seneca recognizes that Epicurean theology is meant to remove the fear of divinities; in fact he agrees with Epicurus that an important function of natural science is to rid oneself of superstition (*NQ* 6.3). But he feels that freedom of anxiety comes at too high a price when god's beneficence is eliminated along the way.[17] In *On Benefits* 4.19, he satirizes the Epicurean position on the divine nature:

---

[16] Compare Lucretius 1.370–97, but the debate is older than Epicurus; see Plato, *Timaeus* 79a–80c.
[17] Also of interest here is the argument of *On Benefits* 4.4, which sets the Epicureans' denial of divine beneficence against their own argument from the agreement of all peoples (*consensus omnium*). For the role of this argument in Epicurean theology, see Obbink (1989: 190–94); Konstan (2011: 61–69).

> For your part, Epicurus, you make god weaponless. You have taken away all his thunderbolts, all his power, and to make sure that no one needs to fear him, you have thrown him out of the world entirely. Hence you have no reason to fear this deity, given that he is shut out by a huge and insuperable wall and barred from mortal contact and mortal sight. He does not have the wherewithal to bless or to harm us. Stranded in that space between this and another sky, with no living being, no humans, no possessions, he is dodging the debris of worlds collapsing above and all around him, and does not hear our prayers or care for us at all.[18]

Because this powerless Epicurean god has not conferred any benefits on human beings, who according to Epicurus are only "a fortuitous conglomeration of atoms and those motes you speak of" there is no reason for anyone to feel gratitude or reverence toward the divine (*Ben.* 4.19.3). Seneca knows that Epicureans recommend such attitudes, mentioning god's "surpassing majesty and unique nature" (*Ben.* 4.19.4). But he argues that such non-utilitarian worship would only make sense if it came from philosophers who hold that honorable conduct is choiceworthy in its own right.

Ethics

Seneca's response to the core positions of Epicurean ethics is of a piece with the cosmological and theological postulates just described. In book 4 of *On Benefits* and also in the essay *On Happiness*, he distinguishes sharply between his own views and those of Epicurus, stating as usual his adherence to the Stoic position that virtue alone is the human good. To the hedonist's essential postulate that pleasure is the goal of all rational behavior he is unremittingly hostile: it is "putting the highest good in the belly," "coupling things that are opposites," that is, virtue and pleasure, and "making virtue the handmaid of pleasure" (*Happiness* 7.1, 7.3, 13.5). On this point his tone tends to be sharply polemical:

> Here we have a quarrel with the Epicureans, a pampered, shade-dwelling crowd of party-time philosophers. For them, virtue is the instrument of their pleasures: it obeys them, is their slave, is subject to them. (*Ben.* 4.2.1)

Likewise, he complains, playing on the gender stereotypes of the Roman elite, that the Epicurean notion of the highest good is "effeminate" and Epicurean sayings typically unmanly (*Ben.* 4.2.4, *Const.* 14.5). All the

---

[18] *Ben.* 4.19.1–3, reading *extra mundum*; compare 7.31.3, and see the parallels in Usener (1887: 242–43), section 364.

same, he understands quite well that Epicurus is not a mere devotee of pleasure as commonly understood. Although his criticisms are sometimes aggressively phrased, he credits Epicurus with a serious position in ethics, and his objections are properly philosophical ones. When he grants that the "pleasure of Epicurus" is in reality "sober and austere," he is referring in part to the personal habits of Epicurus himself, but also more generally to the style of life recommended by Epicurean teaching, which is "chaste, upright, and if you look closely, severe."[19]

The problem he sees is that even if serious adherents of Epicurus's teachings do maintain an austere style of life, there are many who will be led astray by their talk of pleasure to believe that philosophy sometimes gives license to indiscriminate pleasure-seeking. Concern over this perception motivates him to polemicize in spite of what he knows of the actual style of living within the Garden. His real target is the licentiousness that results from a mistaken impression of Epicurean ethics – an impression that he faults the Epicureans themselves for creating. "This is why it is harmful to praise pleasure in the way that you do," he writes. "What is honorable in your teaching is kept hidden; what corrupts is in plain sight" (*Happiness* 12.5). He has strong language for the philosopher who would attract converts in that way:

> What then? Any fellow who holds that happiness consists in idleness and in gluttony and lust by turns seeks an authority for his misdeeds, and when he has been led there by the alluring language, he follows not the pleasure he was told about but the pleasure that attracted him, and when he begins to think his faults are just like their precepts, he no longer indulges them fearfully or in the dark, but in baldfaced riotousness. (*Happiness* 13.2)

Elsewhere he imagines the discomfiture of one who enters the Garden after being attracted by the sign above the door: "Here, Guest, will you be well entertained: here pleasure is the highest good" – only to be received with "a plate of porridge and a generous goblet of water" (*Letters* 21.10). The situation is more than a little comical; nonetheless, the sign ought to be changed.[20]

At the theoretical level, Seneca is familiar with the basis of Epicurean asceticism in the hedonic calculus and in *Key Doctrine* 5, of which he gives a Latin version:

---

[19] *Happiness* 12.4, 13.1; and for Epicurus's personal habits, see *Letters* 18.9 and 33.2.
[20] For the humor, see further page 227 and following.

> It is not possible for pleasure to be separated from virtue ... no one lives honorably without living pleasurably, nor pleasurably without also living honorably. (*Happiness* 7.1)

He recognizes that this doctrine makes virtue a necessary condition for pleasure and can cite at least two Epicurean arguments in support of this claim: that intelligent management is needed if one is to maximize one's pleasure over time, and that those who devote themselves unreservedly to the pleasures of the flesh necessarily suffer mental turmoil (*Happiness* 10.2, 12.1). Elsewhere he admits, again apparently on the basis of *Key Doctrine* 5, that for Epicurus, anyone who is virtuous will also have pleasure (*Letters* 85.18).[21] He knows, too, that Epicureans emphasize mental pleasures, specifically those of memory and expectation (*Happiness* 6.1, 10.2).

But from a Stoic perspective, none of this is enough. Virtue cannot play an instrumental role, for the meaning of virtuous conduct changes if one behaves prudently or temperately in order to gain some further reward. Nor is it satisfactory to say that virtue is both necessary and sufficient for a pleasurable life. For the Stoic, virtue, not pleasure, must be the very thing that makes life good. This is not to say that a life of virtue needs to be disagreeable, since Seneca and his Epicurean interlocutor both hold that engaging in virtuous conduct brings pleasure to oneself. For Seneca, however, as for the early Stoics, such pleasure is not what motivates the virtuous person; instead, it is a by-product (*accessio*), like the poppies that grow around the edges of a cultivated field.[22] The true reward for virtuous conduct is the fact that one is behaving virtuously. "The highest good is in the capacity for judgment and in the character of the optimal mind" (*Happiness* 9.3). As for the Epicurean emphasis on mental pleasures, it is not specific enough to identify the form of pleasure that a virtuous person can legitimately experience. For mental pleasures can also consist in such discreditable feelings as "the thrill of being superior to others" or "arrogance that delights in insults."[23]

Seneca takes a similarly strong position on Epicurus's general approach to justice and other-concern. He does not accept the claim of *Key Doctrine* 31 that the justice of nature is nothing other than the pledge of reciprocal

---

[21] From what Seneca says in *Letters* 85.18, it seems that Epicurus (who may use a different criterion for sufficiency; see Inwood (2007a: 229–30)) holds that virtue always yields a pleasurable life and yet denies that it is *sufficient* for a pleasurable life. But Seneca himself thinks Epicurus is committed to the sufficiency thesis.

[22] *Happiness* 9.1–2; compare Diog. Laert. 7.86.

[23] *Happiness* 10.2. Except in *Letters* 66.45 (for which see note 25), Seneca does not seem to recognize the Epicurean distinction emphasized by Cicero in books 1 and 2 of *De Finibus* between pleasures of activity (kinetic or "in movement") and pleasures of state (katastematic). *Happiness* 7.4 treats *all* pleasures as kinetic.

utility. As he understands it, Epicurus is merely denying that there is any such thing as what is just by nature (*Letters* 97.15). He is aware that Epicureans give consequentialist arguments to support some forms of service to others, but he does not believe that a genuinely virtuous agent would be motivated in this way. Just as the gods cannot truly confer benefits unless beneficence is choiceworthy in itself, so human beings are not really behaving virtuously when they have ulterior motives (*Ben.* 4.3).

He complains also about the Epicurean position on friendship. Unlike Cicero in *De Finibus* 1.69, Seneca does not recognize any basis in Epicureanism for disinterested friendship. In his most extensive treatment of the subject in letter 9, he speaks only of amicable behavior that promotes the agent's material interests via reciprocity. On his understanding, the Epicurean values having friends merely "to have someone to sit beside him in illness, or to assist him in imprisonment or in need" (*Letters* 9.8). By contrast, the Stoic wise person cherishes friends as a means of exercising the virtues:

> "Why make a friend?" To have someone I can die for, someone I can accompany into exile, someone whose life I can save, even by laying down my own. What you describe is a business deal, not a friendship, for it looks to its own advantage; it thinks in terms of results. (*Letters* 9.10)

Seneca would be "talking like an Epicurean" if he were to say that the interests of two friends could ever be fundamentally at odds (*Letters* 48.2). His own view is exactly the opposite: friendship requires each of the friends to live for the other in everything, in a commonalty (*consortium rerum omnium*) that is grounded in the bond shared among all human beings. "For he who has much in common with a fellow human will have everything in common with his friend" (*Letters* 48.3).

On all these doctrinal points Seneca expresses sharp disagreement with Epicurean views, and with good reason, for the theoretical commitments he adopts in calling himself a Stoic are indeed fundamentally opposed to the main assumptions of Epicurean ethics. On those few occasions when he finds himself in agreement with Epicurus on a philosophical doctrine with this kind of centrality, he draws attention to the point as an a fortiori argument for the rightness of the Stoic view. If even Epicurus, who "indulged the body the most," believes that the blessedness of the wise is unimpaired by bodily pain, then the Stoics are all the more likely to be correct on that point.[24] In a more intricate example, Epicurus is invoked in letter 66 to support a difficult Stoic case for the equality of all goods. The

---

[24] *Constancy* 16.1; cf. *Letters* 66.47–48 and 92.25–6.

Stoic position is that all goods must be of equal magnitude because only virtues and virtuous activities are good, and virtue does not vary in degree. The claim is counterintuitive, but it turns out that Epicurus too is committed to it, since Epicurus's "highest and happiest good" consists in freedom from pain in the body and freedom from disturbance in the mind, and these conditions, once fulfilled, cannot be increased in degree any more than the Stoic goods can.[25] Evidently Seneca has in mind *Key Doctrines* 18–20, concerning the limits of pleasure, as well as the famous deathbed letter, which he goes on to discuss. But while he has reflected on these Epicurean texts, his way of using them runs exactly counter to Epicurean hedonism.

Leisure and Contemplation

The value the Stoic finds in service to others can be expressed as an admonition to political involvement, in opposition to the Epicurean maxim "live unknown." Seneca regards quietism as a hallmark of the school ("to rest with Epicurus," *Brevity* 14.2), and in some contexts he expresses strong objections to it. In his view, Epicureans' idea of pleasure is "to give the body to sloth" and "hide out in the shade"; a typical Epicurean "praises civic repose while living amid songs and parties"; living in retirement is "lowering yourself to Epicurean maxims."[26] There is nothing inherently valuable in repose:

> I will never call freedom from pain a good: a cicada has that, and so does a flea. I will not even say that a quiet, untroubled existence is a good: what is more leisurely than a worm? (*Letters* 87.19)

The issue of leisure is not straightforward, however, for Stoic philosophers, too, abandon the rigors of political action in order to pursue the activities they like best, namely study, discussion, and writing. Indeed it is not easy to see how one can be a philosopher at all without secluding oneself from the demands of public service, and Seneca, being a veteran of the imperial administration, fully appreciates what the contemplative life has to offer him.

---

[25] *Letters* 66.45–46. Seneca's argument is interesting not only for its opportunism but because it suggests an awareness on Seneca's part of a difference in structure between kinetic and katastematic pleasure. Epicurus does not maintain the equality of *all* goods; that is, of all pleasures: kinetic pleasures differ in magnitude. Seneca's point, however, is that some Epicurean pleasures are defined by privation (*kata sterēsin*; cf. *Letters* 87.39), and that privation is a non-scalar property in the same way as consistency is.

[26] *Ben.* 4.13.1; *Letters* 88.5; *Letters* 68.10.

In his essay *On Leisure*, he does what he can to resolve the tension in his own position. He admits right away that advocating a life of study seems like "preaching the doctrines of Epicureanism" (*Leisure* 1.4). But while Stoics favor a life of action, they can also supply various justifications for a philosophical retreat. For instance, one may have some chronic illness, or one may live in a state that is too corrupt to benefit from one's endeavors. Essentially, the Stoic is obligated to serve the public "unless there is some obstacle," while the Epicurean is encouraged to refrain "unless some need arises."[27] The kinds of needs that would impel an Epicurean into the public sphere would presumably be utilitarian ones, for Seneca comments lower down that Epicurus's hedonic calculus commits him to action in some instances (*Leisure* 7.2–4). He thus claims to find some common ground between the schools. But this is without minimizing the differences between them. Epicureanism is still subject to "the implacable hatred we have decreed toward those whose ends differ from ours" (*Leisure* 7.1). If the positions overlap, it is only because each side allows for exceptions to its injunction.

We find a deeper exploration of the tensions concerning leisure and contemplation in the *Letters on Ethics*. From the very beginning of the collection, Seneca repeatedly urges his friend to retire from his career in public service, withdraw from all society, and devote himself to a life of study and reflection. In brief, Lucilius should imitate Seneca himself and "spend life in obscurity" (*Letters* 19.3). Such advice is admittedly at odds with the Stoic injunction to remain active throughout life (*Letters* 8.1, 68.2), and Seneca actually draws attention to the parallel with the Epicurean retreat (*Letters* 22.5–6). Yet he also insists that a philosophical retirement is in accordance with Stoic ethics as a whole – provided one's leisure is put to good use. In justification he invokes an argument mentioned only briefly in *On Leisure*: that writing and study may itself be a form of public service if it enables others to improve themselves. In such cases, one is denying one's services to the local community in order to provide them to the greater community of humankind. Again, his view coincides only superficially with that of Epicurus.

Maxims and Meditation

I turn now to a remarkable instance of Seneca's creative engagement with Epicurean texts that takes place throughout the first three books of the

---

[27] *Leisure* 3.2–3 *nisi si quid impedierit . . . nisi si quid intervenerit*. See page 19.

Letters on Ethics. Very near the beginning of the correspondence, Seneca instructs Lucilius in the manner of reading that will best promote his progress toward wisdom. One should not range widely through large numbers of books, he says, but instead concentrate on just a few, extracting from them every day some useful precept to memorize and ponder at length. To illustrate, he offers an extract from his own reading in an unspecified text by Epicurus:

> Today it is this, which I found in Epicurus – for it is my custom to cross even into the other camp, not as a deserter but as a spy: "Cheerful poverty is an honorable thing." Indeed, it is not poverty if it is cheerful. (*Letters* 2.5–6)

Several sentences of reflection follow, as Seneca ponders the implications of the phrase "happy poverty" and the advantages of restricting one's desires. Thus begins a regular practice of closing each letter with an excerpt "from today's reading" (4.10), taken usually from the works of Epicurus, although Metrodorus is also mentioned as a source (14.17, 15.9), and other philosophers and poets occasionally play that role as well.

In giving Epicurus pride of place among his sources of memorable maxims, Seneca is not declaring any new philosophical allegiance. On the contrary, he seems to savor the irony of a Stoic author's finding something of value in this unlikely source, crossing "into the other camp" (*in aliena castra*).[28] When he cites Epicurus, he is taking "another's material" (*aliena*), and if anyone should challenge his right to use that material, he can reply that the utterances are "public property" (*publicae*).[29] And indeed the extracts he chooses are never very distinctive in terms of their philosophical content. Similar to the example from letter 2, they represent the blandest sort of admonition to restrict desire, avoid the crowd, and overcome the fear of death. At no point does Seneca feel compelled to seek the Epicurean author's original intent. On the contrary, he will sometimes carry the thought in a new direction, as in letter 20, which argues *against* Epicurus's emphasis on literal poverty.[30]

Nor can the preponderance of Epicurean authors be ascribed to Epicurean leanings on the part of Lucilius, as has sometimes been inferred.[31] Lucilius is never represented in the *Letters on Ethics* or elsewhere as holding

---

[28] *Letters* 2.5. Although many of the early letters are only general exhortations to practice philosophy, letters 8, 9, 23, 24, and 29 all clearly adopt a Stoic perspective.
[29] *Letters* 14.17, 21.9; cf. 12.11.
[30] *Letters* 20.10–11. A more puzzling case is 22.13–16, where Schmid (1984) has argued that Seneca deliberately misconstrues *Vatican Sentence* 60.
[31] This suggestion by Schottländer (1955: 136–37), rightly resisted by Mazzoli (1972–73 and 1989), has been defended especially by Miriam Griffin: see Griffin (1976: 351), (2007: 90–95), (2013:

any Epicurean beliefs; his commitments are rather to his career in government, to his literary projects, and, increasingly as the letters proceed, to Stoicism. The entire evidence for his supposed allegiance to Epicurus consists in two remarks relating to the excerpted maxims: "you may complain" (*invideas licet*) in *Letters* 20.9 and "a saying of your dear Epicurus" (*vocem Epicuri tui*) in *Letters* 23.9. These assign Lucilius a proprietary interest, but not a doctrinal allegiance. Rather, they should be recognized as part of a pattern of playful utterance that spans the entirety of books 1–3. Seneca begins early on to speak of the quotations from Epicurus and others as a kind of commodity, a "payment" or "little gift" enclosed with each letter, a "present from Greece."[32] Lucilius is soon co-opted into the game, represented reaching out his hand for the "daily dole" or demanding, "Pay what you owe!"[33] To pay him, Seneca must "get a loan from Epicurus."[34] Hence whatever Seneca might find in Epicurus's writings is already by implication owed to Lucilius: "you know whose money-box I use" (26.8). When Seneca speaks of "your Epicurus," then he is referring to his adherent's expected "gift," not to his supposed philosophical adherence.[35]

The role given to Epicurus in the early books of the *Letters* probably has something to do with Seneca's literary ambitions for his work, for the collected letters of Epicurus were by this time a classic of philosophical writing.[36] In letter 21, he draws a striking parallel between his own admonitions to Lucilius and those of Epicurus to Idomeneus: in both cases, the addressee is to be made famous not by his achievements in politics but by his role as addressee of a work of philosophical literature. Comparisons are also made to the letters of Cicero and to Vergil's *Aeneid* – names that speak volumes about Seneca's perception of Epicurus's status as a writer. As Brad Inwood has noted, the Epicurean letters known to Seneca

---

146–47), as well as I. Hadot (2014: 116, 188); Setaioli (2014b: 245). Griffin relies primarily on *invideas licet* in *Letters* 20.9 and *Epicuri tui* in 23.9 but also on *Epicure* in 20.11. There she recognizes that the reading *Epicuree* ("follower of Epicurus") is corrupt but insists that Lucilius "is clearly represented as speaking for Epicurus." On the humor, see pages 231–33; further to Griffin's argument, note 30 in Chapter 10.

[32] *Letters* 12.10 (*peculium*); 10.5 and 16.7 (*munusculum*); 15.9 (*munus Graecum*, accepting Haase's emendation).

[33] *Letters* 15.17, 18.14.   [34] *Letters* 17.11.

[35] Chrysippus *apud* Origen, *Cels.* 8.51 (*SVF* 3.474), cited by Setaioli (2014b: 245) in this connection, does not have any bearing on the question of Lucilius's philosophical adherence. It does show an openness on the part of Chrysippus to using arguments from a rival philosophical school in a therapeutic context, but only in addressing persons in the immediate grip of strong emotions. See further Graver (2007: 196–201).

[36] Articles by Inwood (2007b: 141–46) and Wildberger (2014) develop in more detail the suggestions of Lana (1991:)268–74 and Rosati (1981). On letter 21 in particular, see Seal (2021: 91–100).

may have been different in style from the three letters we have extant today: more personal in tone, less technical, and less difficult to construe.[37] Seneca may well have found in them an important model for his own project in philosophical letter writing.

More specifically, we can connect Seneca's use and occasional misuse of Epicurus to the Epicureans' own practice of memorizing and reflecting on brief summaries of doctrine.[38] Seneca recognizes in Epicurus a skillful handler of written texts as a vehicle for philosophical training and seeks to appropriate some of those techniques for his own program of written therapy. Epicurus's interest in providing short, easily memorized texts is explained in *Letter to Herodotus* 83 and evidenced in the *Key Doctrines*.[39] The *Letter to Menoeceus*, in addition to its summary of ethical teachings, offers explicit instruction on how one is to assimilate the material. One is to memorize, but also to "reason out" and "accustom oneself to believing" each point; then at the end, to "rehearse these and the related points day and night, with yourself and with a person like yourself" (*Menoeceus* 135). To Seneca, who spent much of his life as a teacher of oratory, the instruction to "rehearse" (μελετᾶν) would suggest the process of rehearsing before delivering a speech – not memorization as we think of it, but mulling over one point at a time so as to be ready to deliver them when the time comes.[40] Seneca's frequent quotations from Epicurus may be meant to recall this characteristically Epicurean way of reforming a person's character through meditation on brief ethical *sententiae*. Their significance is procedural, not doctrinal.

Seneca clarifies his intentions concerning the use of maxims in philosophical instruction in letter 33, after giving over his previous practice. Although in the preceding letters he had sometimes provided excerpts from authors who were not Epicureans, he now makes the philosophical

---

[37] Inwood (2007b: 142–45). In addition to the collection of personal letters, of which he knows at least eight in some detail (*Letters* 9.1, 9.18, 18.9, 21.3, 22.5–6, 52.3–4, 79.15–16, 81.11–12, 98.9, 99.25–26), Seneca must also have access to a *gnomologion* (referred to in *Letters* 13.17), some or all of the *Key Doctrines* (*Apoc.* 8, *Happiness* 7.1, *Letters* 30.14) and apparently also the *Letter to Menoeceus* (*Letters* 14.17, 66.45). The evidence is systematically reviewed in Setaioli (1988: 171–256).

[38] This line of interpretation is adumbrated already in Griffin (1976: 352); see also Schmid (1984: 130).

[39] The *Key Doctrines* are a prime instance of this Epicurean initiative whether they were compiled by Epicurus himself or not, since they were circulated as his from an early date. It is worth noting that Philodemus, writing over a century before Seneca, treats the *Key Doctrines* as a work of Epicurus's own (*De ira*, col. 43.20–1). See Clay (1983: 78–81).

[40] As Phaedrus does with the speech of Lysias in Plato, *Phaedrus* 228b (ἵνα μελετῴη); and see Chrysippus apud Galen, *PHP* 3.7.34 (*SVF* 2.250).

maxim the basis of a contrast between Epicurean and Stoic authors. While not voicing any objections to Epicurean texts in terms of content, he remarks that they are more easily excerptable just because their mode of expression is less tightly structured than Stoic texts.[41] He then aligns this difference of style with a difference in attitude toward philosophical study. The Epicurean assumption, he says, is that the learner will be subservient to the authority of Epicurus, while Stoic texts require more intellectual independence. The latter are thus more suitable for advanced students, the former only for beginners. However, Seneca does not definitively reject the model of therapeutic reading he has built up in relation to Epicurean texts. He does promise to send "by the fistful" the extracts Lucilius requests (33.6), and he wants these to be read with the kind of thoughtful intensity these early letters have demonstrated. But he seeks now to dissociate that procedure from Epicureanism, and at the same to add to it a new dimension of critical assessment and reasoning. The entire sequence, from letter 2 through letter 33, thus becomes an exercise in creative adaptation at the level of literary form. Seneca appreciates the psychological efficacy of the reading method promoted by Epicurus and by the form of Epicurean texts, but he also means to alter that method to suit his rather different therapeutic objectives.

Human Nature and the Tactics of the Therapist

We have seen that Seneca's usual hostility to the main principles of Epicurean thought does not prevent him from showing appreciation for the brief, memorable maxims he finds in Epicurean texts and for the practice of meditative reading Epicurus recommends. I now consider a series of passages in which Seneca expresses respect for Epicurus's psychological insight and for the practical efficacy to some of his arguments in managing desire, fear, anxiety, and grief. In some instances, he even goes so far as to endorse an Epicurean claim, taking it on board for his own project in advancing Lucilius and other readers toward Stoic wisdom. He can do this without conflict, since the points in question are not core philosophical commitments so much as empirically developed observations of how minds operate. In essence, he treats these Epicurean assertions as describing real psychological phenomena that any philosophical system would need to account for.

---

[41] *Letters* 33.3–5; see further page 285 and following.

A particularly clear-cut example is his treatment of the fear of penalties in letter 97. Commenting that it is elegantly phrased, Seneca gives his endorsement to Epicurus's view that wrongdoers inevitably experience anxiety about possible punishment, even if they have escaped thus far. However, he does not agree with the role that wrongdoer anxiety plays in Epicurean ethics as the principal penalty for unjust conduct. For him, an intelligent agent does not refrain from harming others merely because he wants to avoid subsequent anxiety, but rather because the act is inherently wrong: *sceleris in scelere supplicium est* (*Letters* 97.14). Still, the criminal's anxiety can be a secondary penalty, and the Stoic need not liberate him from that. Indeed, the persistence of this anxiety tells in favor of the Stoic view that justice exists in nature.[42]

> We should disagree with Epicurus when he says that there is nothing that is just by nature, and that the reason one should refrain from misdeeds is that one cannot avoid the anxiety resulting from them; we should agree with him, though, that the wrongdoer is tormented by conscience and that his worst penalty is to bear the hounding and the lash of constant worry, because he cannot trust those who guarantee him security. This is proof in itself, Epicurus, that we have a natural horror of misdeeds: every criminal is afraid, even in a place of safety. Fortune exempts many from punishment, but none from anxiety. Why, if not because we have an innate aversion to what nature has condemned? (*Letters* 97.16)

Confident that the point is adaptable to a Stoic ethical framework, Seneca proceeds in letter 105 to repeat the Epicurean claim as an assertion by his own authorial voice.

> Anyone expecting punishment undergoes punishment, and anyone who deserves it expects it. Safety is compatible with a bad conscience, but security is not.... The wrongdoer sometimes has the chance of concealment, but never the confidence of it. (*Letters* 105.7–8)

Given the similarity in wording, Seneca can hardly be unaware of Epicurus's influence in this second passage.[43] Clearly, though, he is not committing himself to Epicurean consequentialism. His borrowing is of the psychological observation only.

---

[42] It should perhaps be pointed out that the Latin word *conscientia* refers only to one's awareness of what has been done; it is not equivalent to "moral sense." For the argument, compare *Ben.* 4.17.1–18.4.

[43] Compare the last words of letter 105, *nocens habuit aliquando latendi fortunam, numquam fiduciam*, with the words quoted from Epicurus in 97.13: *potest nocenti contingere ut lateat, latendi fides non potest*.

A similar progression can be observed in some of his remarks on the fear of death and pain. While he cares nothing for the "Epicurean song" that is supposed to address fears of eternal torment in Tartarus (*Letters* 24.18), he does want to address the more elemental fear of death, and for this he finds some efficacy in the usual Epicurean arguments. In letter 30, he recounts a conversation with an elderly Epicurean named Aufidius Bassus, who he says is facing the approach of death with enviable tranquility. Giving his own version of Bassus's words, he reports a series of arguments that run parallel to those in the *Letter to Menoeceus* and in book 3 of Lucretius: that it is foolish to fear what you will not be present to experience, that nature reshuffles and reuses our components, though without any continued consciousness on our part, that the sated diner is content to leave the banquet.[44] Bassus refers also to Epicurus's principal defense against the fear of pain in *Key Doctrine* 4:

> In fact he used to say, in conformity with Epicurus's teachings, "First of all, I hope there will be no pain in that last breath; but if there is, it will be short, and that itself is some comfort. For severe pain is never of long duration. But if there is torment in the moment when mind separates from body, I will console myself thus: after that pain, I can no longer experience pain." (*Letters* 30.14)

These are not the arguments given by Stoics against the fear of death and pain; those are rather that neither makes any difference to the human good, which has to be conceived of solely in terms of human excellence. But Seneca can reasonably claim that the Epicurean arguments can be adopted by a Stoic without creating any complications for his own doctrinal position. He does not himself hold any strong views on what happens to any given person's soul at the time of death. He is not committed to the Epicurean position on the extinction of consciousness, but he is open to it as one alternative. "Death either consumes us or sets us free. If we are released, then better things await us once our burden is removed; if we are consumed, then nothing is waiting for us at all: both goods and evils are gone."[45] Consequently, he is quite willing to state the Epicurean arguments elsewhere as his own opinion. Shortly after the

---

[44] *Letters* 30.5–6, 9–12; cf. *KD* 2; *Menoeceus* 124–26; Lucretius 3.830–42. Compare also the version of the satiety argument given by Diodorus, "an Epicurean philosopher" preparing for suicide, in *On Happiness* 19.1. Seneca notes that there are those who question whether Diodorus's suicide is consistent with Epicurean doctrine. Of course the questioners are correct: see *Menoeceus* 126–27 and the fragments quoted by Seneca in *Letters* 24.22–23, together with Warren (2004: 205–12).

[45] *Letters* 24.18. In some contexts (e.g., at *Letters* 79.12 and 92.30–34), Seneca takes the Stoic view that the souls of the wise ascend to a dwelling place in the upper air. But none of us can be certain

Bassus letter, we find him giving in his own voice the argument from *Letter to Menoeceus* 125: "Death holds no disadvantage, for a disadvantage must be that of some existing person."[46] Not long afterward, in letter 54, he supplies a fairly exact version of Lucretius's symmetry argument, applying it to his own situation.[47] Similarly, he makes frequent use of *Key Doctrine* 4 on the endurance of pain, quoting it as if it were part of Stoicism in letters 24, 78, and 94.[48]

Concerning pain, he is also familiar with a second Epicurean claim: that in times of bodily pain, one can maintain one's state of blessedness by directing one's attention away from one's present sufferings toward good things one has experienced in the past. This approach to pain is attested for Epicurus by Cicero in *Tusculan Disputations* 3.32–33.[49] Two specific components are mentioned: first, "distracting the mind from the thought of suffering," and second, "redirecting it to the contemplation of pleasures." These should be compared with what Seneca writes in letter 78.18, immediately following another paraphrase of *Key Doctrine* 4. Like Epicurus, Seneca recommends a twofold manipulation of attention: one should both "turn the mind toward other thoughts" and "depart from the pain." However, where Epicurus had suggested directing one's thoughts specifically toward remembered pleasures, perhaps especially the pleasures of discussing philosophy with one's friends,[50] Seneca has in mind a very different kind of mental satisfaction:

> It will also be beneficial to turn the mind toward other thoughts and depart from the pain. Think of honorable deeds, brave deeds you have performed; reflect on what is good in your character. Let your memory range over everything you have most admired. Then bring to mind some great example of courage and victory over pain. (*Letters* 78.18)

Moreover, Epicurus specifically denies that one should try to anticipate future pain or distress, and this is the position we should expect him to take, since doing so would increase our psychological distress over time.[51]

---

whether this inspiring prospect is what is in store for *us*. For those who fail to achieve wisdom in life, death means "returning to the universe"; that is, dissolution (*Letters* 71.16, 76.25).

[46] *Letters* 36.9; compare *Letters* 4.3. It is worth pointing out that from an Epicurean perspective, Seneca's uncertainty about postmortem survival removes nearly all force from the argument.

[47] *Letters* 54.4–5.   [48] *Letters* 24.14, 78.17, and 94.7.

[49] For the Epicurean material in Cicero, see Tsouna (2009: 261); and in more detail, Graver (2002b).

[50] This is stated in Cicero's account and is also present by implication in the deathbed letter to Idomeneus. The emphasis on pleasures derived from past experience is found also in *Ben.* 3.4.1–2, where Epicurus is named. See also *Letters* 81.11–12 on the gratitude of the wise in Metrodorus.

[51] Cicero, *Tusc.* 3.32.

Seneca, however, frequently recommends such "pre-rehearsal of future ills" as a way of preparing oneself to face trials with fortitude:

> Fix your mind on whatever it is that you are afraid might happen as a thing that definitely will happen. Whatever bad event that might be, take the measure of it mentally and so assess your fear.[52]

Once again, he is willing to take on an Epicurean technique that he believes can be efficacious but is unconcerned with closely related elements in Epicurus's system of thought.

Other examples can be given. Seneca agrees with Epicurus that it is beneficial to remind the one making progress in philosophy that there is a natural limit to the pleasure that can be derived from eating and drinking. The point appears already among the maxims provided for Lucilius in the early letters and resurfaces frequently thereafter, even as late as letter 119, where a direct quotation confirms that Seneca still has in mind the Epicurean origins of the thought.[53] He also recommends several of Epicurus's practical expedients for improving one's moral character, such as restricting one's diet on specified days or visualizing some good person as a constant spectator for one's actions.[54] He cites with approval Epicurus's classification of students into those who make good progress in philosophy without aid, those like Metrodorus who easily follow where another leads, and those like Hermarchus who need to be driven and compelled to do the right thing (*Letters* 52.3–4). In all these cases, he follows Epicurus out of respect for his sensitivity to the ins and outs of human nature, believing that his observations are grounded in real phenomena of human experience that a Stoic therapist ought likewise to consider.

Correspondingly, Seneca will sometimes reject an Epicurean claim on grounds that it lacks a sound observational basis. Like Cicero in *Tusculan Disputations* 2.17, he understands Epicurus to have said that a wise person under severe torture is able not only to maintain a state of blessedness but actually to derive pleasure from the experience: when roasted in the bull of Phalaris, he will say, "It is pleasant; it does not matter to me at all."[55] This claim he rejects indignantly; he finds it psychologically implausible and

---

[52] *Letters* 24.2. For the technique, see further Armisen-Marchetti (2008).
[53] See *Letters* 4.10, 16.7–8, 119.5–7, and compare *Menoeceus* 127–8, *KD* 21. One can hardly suppose with Lana (1991: 285) that Seneca's interest in Epicureanism waned after *Letters* 92. Clear references in fact continue practically to the end of the extant collection, with *Letters* 123.10.
[54] *Letters* 18.9; 11.8–9; 25.4–5.
[55] *Letters* 66.18. The utterance credited to Epicurus here and in *Letters* 67.15 is recognizably the same as the one reported a number of times in Cicero, but the wording in Latin is significantly different, as if independently translated from the same Greek source. Usener (1887: 338–39), section 601,

philosophically problematic, since it suggests that wisdom not only perfects but actually alters human nature. Similarly, in a discussion of grief and consolation, he takes exception to a claim he finds in a letter of Metrodorus, "that there is a pleasure which is akin to sorrow and that in situations like this one should try to catch that pleasure."[56] As Seneca understands it, the consolation Metrodorus offers is not the usual Epicurean recommendation for neutralizing mental pain by diverting one's attention or by finding compensatory sources of pleasure. Rather it is a novel form of pleasure derived from the experience of grief itself: it comes "in the very midst of grief – indeed, through grief" (*in ipso luctu voluptatem, immo per luctum*) and to pursue it is "to try to snare a pleasure right in the midst of grief" (*voluptatem in ipso dolore aucupari*).[57] Again, the Stoic author rejects the claim, not only because he finds it morally reprehensible but also because he denies its empirical basis: it is "hard to believe."[58] In both instances, reflection on the Epicurean inheritance proves valuable to Seneca primarily in helping him clarify his formulation of the Stoic position on the impassivity of the wise person under conditions of physical pain or personal bereavement.[59] The aim is not strictly polemical; rather it is to make clear that Stoic *apatheia* does not alter or eliminate any essential capacity of the human being.

***

Epicureanism is a complex body of doctrines, techniques, and practices, and Seneca's response to it over more than a decade of study and writing necessarily takes many forms. Yet when we consider his reactions across the board, a definite pattern does emerge. Seneca has thoroughly internalized the principles of Stoicism, and wherever he deals with the main elements of Epicurus's philosophy, he finds himself in disagreement with them for reasons he can explain. At times, he takes a strongly polemical tone, seeking to dissuade his contemporaries from the libertinism and nihilism for

---

groups the Latin passages together with Diog. Laert. 10.118, which, however, reports a different Epicurean claim, that the wise person is *eudaimōn* while being twisted on the rack but will cry and groan.

[56] *Letters* 99.25. I treat the passage in more detail in Graver (2015) and its context in Chapter 7, pages 172–73.

[57] Pressing the validity of his attribution, Seneca quotes the passage in Greek as well as in his own Latin translation. Clay (1998: 66) connects the pleasure identified by Metrodorus with the "peculiar form of pleasure" (ἰδιοτρόπῳ ἡδονῇ) mentioned in Plutarch, *Non Posse* 16.1097e.

[58] *Letters* 99.26.

[59] Concerning the wise person's experience of corporeal pain, see *Letters* 71.27 together with Courtil (2015: 382–94).

which members of the Roman elite sometimes used Epicureanism as a pretext. In so doing, he speaks out of conviction, not out of partisanship, for just as he will sometimes reject views offered by Stoic authors that he deems inconsistent with Stoic foundations, so also he adopts certain elements of Epicurean thought as his own when he thinks there is no inconsistency. That these adopted elements are invariably matters of psychological insight and therapeutic practice will serve to indicate the level at which he was impressed and inspired by Epicurus's achievement.

CHAPTER 5

Refuting the Peripatetics
Seneca and the School of Aristotle

The depth of Seneca's engagement with Peripatetic thought is a point better known to specialists on Aristotelianism at Rome than it is to Seneca scholars themselves, who have more often concerned themselves with his professed Stoicism and his numerous references to Epicurus.[1] But mention of the Peripatetics and of distinctively Peripatetic ideas is in fact quite frequent in his writings, and with good reason. For while Peripatetic ethics is substantially different from Stoic ethics, it lies much closer to Stoicism than Epicureanism does. The virtues are essential to happiness, but not exclusively so; the emotions are to be subordinate to reason, but not eliminated by it; even philosophical hedonism may be tolerated on some accounts, though only in certain manifestations. It is often important to Seneca, then, to differentiate Stoic doctrines from their Peripatetic counterparts and to refute the latter. This relatively sophisticated task gives rise to some of his most energetic philosophical discussions.

Of particular interest is the 92nd of the *Letters on Ethics*, a long and meandering defense of Stoic ethics against a series of pointed objections. Here the identity of Seneca's opponents has not usually been recognized, but is crucial for a correct understanding of Seneca's position.[2] The omission is understandable, for on such a point, modern readers generally like to have clearer indications than any Seneca provides. That the positions criticized are indeed Peripatetic from start to finish becomes plain, however, when we compare Seneca's letter with the Peripatetic ethical doxography

---

[1] For the historical development of Aristotelianism during the Roman period, see Moraux (1973), Gottschalk (1987), Barnes (1997b), Hahm (2007), Gill (2012), Inwood (2014). It is significant that the sourcebook of Peripatetic philosophy compiled by R. W. Sharples (2010) includes no fewer than eighteen passages from Seneca's philosophical writings.
[2] The role of the Peripatetics is discussed in Inwood (2007a) and Kidd (1988: vol. 2, 665–69). Trapp (2007: 32–35) juxtaposes letter 92, which he calls "a straightforward sermon on the sufficiency of virtue," with the Peripatetic ethics found in Stobaeus, but his remark is of a general nature and does not supply any details.

found in Stobaeus 2.7, 116–30 Wachsmuth, known to modern scholarship as Doxography "C" and usually attributed to Arius Didymus.[3] In view of the range of topics treated and the manner in which they are presented, that comparison will show that Seneca in letter 92 responds point by point to a summary account of Peripatetic ethics that is similar in nature to Doxography "C." The doxography Seneca consulted seems to have differed in certain ways from Doxography "C" itself – a point that should be of interest for Peripatetic studies – but its main contentions were those of the Peripatos, not the Garden. Recognizing this fact yields significant benefits for Seneca studies in the form of a better understanding of Seneca's polemical strategies and a more fine-grained account of his positions on some core issues in ethics: the relation between upper and lower divisions of the psyche, the status of the so-called bodily and external goods, and the sufficiency of virtue for happiness.

A well-educated man and one who seems to have enjoyed frequent philosophical discussions with similarly well-educated friends, Seneca was undoubtedly capable of explaining doctrines of more than one philosophical school from memory alone. But a man of his wealth and interests must also have owned an extensive library, and mentions of reading and of the contents of specific treatises are frequent enough in his work to suggest that consultation of sources, many of them in Greek, was a regular part of his process of composition. Sometimes, though, he writes in a way that seems to a modern interpreter to suggest dependence on some kind of written source, but fails to indicate how the material comes to him. Such reticence is easily explained by his literary sensibilities and by the nature of his philosophical project. He mentions a source only when he feels that the name will contribute in some way to the elegance of his artistic product or to the edification of his reader. It is up to us, then, to make such determinations as we can about the works Seneca has consulted, attending first and foremost to such explicit citations as he provides, but also to the presence of characteristically Peripatetic ideas and terminology and to the way such ideas and terms are arranged within a particular context.

One point that strikes the eye immediately when surveying Seneca's works is that his explicit citations of Peripatetic material (where he gives them) do not all follow the same pattern. In the relatively early treatise *On*

---

[3] A complete translation can be found in Sharples (2010: 111–33), as well as in Tsouni (2017). In what follows, I give my own translations, following Tsouni for the Greek text and for section numbers within the text but supplying the page numbers of Wachsmuth (1884–1912) in parentheses.

Anger, his references are always to "Aristotle" or "Theophrastus," never to the Peripatetics, even though the doctrines referred to are recognizably the same as are attributed by Cicero to the Peripatetics.[4] Later on, in the *Letters on Ethics*, doctrines concerning ethics and psychology are consistently attributed to the *Peripatetici*, even on points similar to those mentioned in *On Anger*; letters 58 and 65, however, on substance and causation respectively, speak again of *Aristoteles*.[5] Meanwhile, the *Natural Questions*, written at about the same time as the *Letters on Ethics*, refers frequently to Aristotle and Theophrastus and once to Strato, but never to the *Peripatetici*.[6]

Such variety in citation practice is just what one would expect to see if, in composing works on different subjects, Seneca consulted works written by different Peripatetic authors or using different systems of reference for Peripatetic material. He may also have taken over some information at secondhand from earlier Stoic authors polemicizing against the school. A direct dependence on Cicero's reports in the *De Finibus* and *Tusculan Disputations* is less likely. For Seneca diverges from Cicero in his handling of the material, and on at least one point he has knowledge of the Peripatetic tradition that he could not have gained from Cicero.[7]

Explicit Citations

Although my central concern will be with letter 92, an important preliminary is to establish some benchmarks concerning Seneca's knowledge of Peripatetic ethics. To that end, we need to review all the passages in Seneca that link an explicit mention of the *Peripatetici* with topics treated in Doxography "C." The most important of these are concerned directly with the Peripatetic system of value.

Both in the *Letters on Ethics* and in the treatise *On Benefits*, we find passing remarks indicating some familiarity with the Peripatetics' threefold

---

[4] Aristotle is named in *Anger* 1.3.3, 1.9.2, 1.17.1, and 3.3.1; Theophrastus in 1.12.3, 1.14.1. Setaioli (1988: 141–52) brings out the important differences between these citations and the actual views of Aristotle and Theophrastus. See also Inwood (2014: 90–103).
[5] *Letters* 58.9, 65.4–6.
[6] Aristotle in *NQ* 1.1.2, 1.1.7, 1.3.7, 1.8.6, 2.12.4, 6.13.1, 6.14.1, 7.5.4, 7.28.1, 7.30.1; Theophrastus in *NQ* 3.11.4, 3.16.5, 3.25.4, 3.25.7, 3.26.1, 4a.2.16, 6.13.1; Strato in *NQ* 6.13.2.
[7] See page 9. An especially significant point is the complete absence of Antiochus of Ascalon from Seneca's treatment of the "Old Academy"; see pages 118–19. Conversely, *Letters* 85.2–3 show knowledge of the same syllogism as is quoted by Cicero in *Tusc.* 3.18, but Seneca, unlike Cicero, also knows a Peripatetic refutation.

classification of goods. *Letters* 88.5 encapsulates the characteristic doctrines of several philosophical schools: as the Epicurean typically "praises civic repose while living amid songs and parties" and the Academic "says there is no certainty about anything," so the Peripatetic "posits three types of goods." *On Benefits* 5.13.1 is somewhat less transparent, since Seneca there speaks at first of "goods of the mind, of the body, and of fortune" as an element of *Stoic* doctrine. Immediately afterward, however, he correctly assigns that threefold classification to the Peripatetics, adding tendentiously that *Peripatetici* "greatly expand the boundaries of human happiness." The misleading implication that Stoics, too, might recognize goods of the body and of fortune is cleared up later in the paragraph.

Three passages in the *Letters on Ethics* show familiarity with arguments used by Peripatetics to support their views. These occur in polemical contexts in letters 85 and 87. In letter 87, Seneca promises to share some Stoic reasoning to support the claim that virtue is sufficient for happiness. The Stoic has claimed that the only things that should be regarded as good are those that make *people* good – that is to say, the virtues. To support his view, he offers a craft analogy in syllogistic form:

> That which is good makes people good, just as in musical skill that which is good makes one a musician.
> Things depending on fortune do not make a person good.
> Therefore, such things are not goods. (*Letters* 87.12)

He then introduces the *Peripatetici*, whose task it is to rebut the Stoic argument. Their tactic is to insist that the craft analogy is misused, that in fact some elements of music are good apart from those that make the performer good – good musical instruments, for instance.

> Against this the Peripatetics argue that our first premise is false. "People do not automatically become good from what is good. In music, there are things that are good, for instance a flute, a lyre, or an organ well-suited for playing, but none of these makes a person a musician." (*Letters* 87.12)

The comparison of non-psychic goods to musical instruments is reminiscent of a type of argument that has its ultimate origin in Aristotle, *Nicomachean Ethics* 1.10, 1100b27. According to this argument, at least some non-psychic goods are required as instruments for the activation of the virtues in the same sense as flutes are required for flute-playing or medical instruments for the practice of medicine. This is to say that they are necessary conditions: one cannot perform generous actions if one does not possess at least some of the goods of fortune, and so on. Versions of it can be found in several of the later Peripatetic sources including Doxography "C."[8]

A closely related line of thought underlies the Peripatetic position reported by Seneca in *Letters* 85.30–31. Here, too, there is a debate between two speakers, one upholding the Stoic view that only the vices are bad, the other favoring the Peripatetic position that bodily and external circumstances may also be considered bad things. Now the Stoic reasons this way:

> Whatever is bad does some harm.
> Whatever harms a person makes him worse.
> Pain and poverty do not make a person worse.
> Therefore, they are not bad. (*Letters* 85.30)

A nameless interlocutor now intervenes with an objection to the second premise, remarking that wind and storm harm the helmsman without making him worse. Seneca then provides both a Stoic defense against the objection and a Peripatetic counter:

> Some of the Stoics respond to this objection as follows. Wind and storm do make the helmsman worse, since he cannot achieve what he set out to do; that is, to hold his course. He is not made worse as concerns his skill, but he is made worse as concerns his activity (*in opere*).
> To this the Peripatetic replies, "By that reasoning, even the wise person is made worse by poverty, pain, and everything else of that sort, for such things will impede his activities (*opera eius inpediet*), even though they do not take away his virtue" (*Letters* 85.31)

Aided by incautious Stoic dialecticians, the Peripatetic here makes effective use of the helmsman analogy to support his own view. Just as the storm does not make the helmsman worse but does impede the exercise of his craft, so pain and poverty do not keep the sage from being virtuous, but do in a sense make him worse, since they will impede his achievements (*opera eius inpediet*). Again the craft analogy draws ultimately on Aristotle's in *Nicomachean Ethics* 1.10, that great misfortunes "oppress and spoil blessedness" not only because they involve pain but also because they impede (ἐμποδίζει) the activation of the virtues.[9]

---

[8] It is stated with great clarity in Aspasius, *On Aristotle's Ethics* 24.3–9 (for which see Sharples 2010: 162, 167–68) and appears also in Doxography A, Stobaeus 2.7, 46.13–17 Wachsmuth. In Doxography C, section 12 (129.19–130.12 Wachsmuth), the external goods are compared to "the use of tools" (τὴν τῶν ὀργάνων χρῆσιν) and are called "necessary conditions" (τὰ ὧν οὐκ ἄνευ).

[9] Aristotle, *Nic. Eth.* 1.10, 1100b29–30, trans. Irwin (1985).

A more cryptic reference to Peripatetic argumentation is found in *Letters* 87.38. This time the Peripatetics speak first, stating an argument *against* their view. Naturally this is an argument which they claim to be able to refute.

> That which is good is not made up of things that are bad.
> But many instances of poverty make up one instance of wealth.
> Therefore wealth is not a good.
>
> This syllogism is not recognized by our school; it is both devised and solved by the Peripatetics. Posidonius says, however, that this sophism, which has been bandied about among dialecticians from every school, is refuted by Antipater as follows...

Seneca does not explain how the Peripatetics set about refuting the argument; he is more interested in an alternative refutation by Antipater. From our perspective the passage is of interest because of its dialectical format, which is very like that of the two passages just quoted. In all three we see the Peripatetics right in the thick of the fray, challenging premises, turning arguments on their head, and even propounding a bad argument on behalf of their opponents.[10] This is to say that here, at least, Seneca's presentation brings to mind the kind of debates we can imagine taking place in the second century BCE. His immediate source in both letters may be Posidonius, who is named also in *Letters* 87.35, but in that case Posidonius himself must be drawing on an older treatise, since it is he who quotes Antipater.[11]

In addition to these passages that deal directly with the system of value, there are two passages in the *Letters on Ethics* that connect the *Peripatetici* with a particular doctrine on the emotions. One is *Letters* 85.3, where "certain Peripatetics" (*Peripatetici quidam*) respond to a Stoic syllogism favoring impassivity by stating their own position on that issue: that the wise person does experience emotions, but only "occasionally and in moderation" (*raro perturbatur et modice*). Similarly, *Letters* 116.1 says that the *Peripatetici* "restrain" (*temperant*) the emotions, and mentions the term "moderate amount" (*mediocritas*).[12] We have already noted the

---

[10] On the argument, see Sharples (2010: 166); further on the role of Posidonius in letter 87, Kidd (1986, 1988: 626–37).

[11] Posidonius is named in *Letters* 87.35 and 87.38. His name does not occur in letter 85, but the manner of presentation, quite different from Seneca's expository style in other letters, carries some weight. See Leeman (1954). Inwood (2007a: 257–58) suggests that refutation by Antipater points to Critolaus as the originator of the argument. On Critolaus's position and methods, see Hahm (2007).

[12] The term is attested in Cicero, *Acad.* 2.135, *Tusc.* 4.46. On limitation and "moderate amounts," see Annas (1993: 59–66).

resemblance of these doctrines to those attributed in *On Anger* to Aristotle and Theophrastus.

Moreover, *Letters* 89.10 shows awareness that Peripatetic authors acknowledged as areas of philosophical study not only ethics, physics, and logic but also politics, household management (*partem quam οἰκονομικὴν vocant*), and "kinds of life" (*de generibus vitae locum*). Finally, *Letters* 117.11 attributes to the *Peripatetici* a rather subtle claim that a substance, such as wisdom, cannot be differentiated from the associated predicate, such as "being wise." Nothing much need be said about these passages here; they do, however, have some significance in that they provide further evidence that Seneca possessed an extensive, if rather disparate, knowledge of Peripatetic thought.

Implicit References

The overview just given includes all of Seneca's explicit references to the Peripatetic school; it does not, however, take in all the passages in which our author knows himself to be repeating Peripatetic doctrines. I turn now to some instances in which Peripatetic influence is evidenced even without explicit citation, either by the content of a paragraph or by the structure of Seneca's argumentation.

That the Peripatetic material in the *Letters on Ethics* is in fact more extensive can be inferred from the flow of the argument in two letters that have already been quoted. The more straightforward case concerns letter 87. That letter as a whole has to do with the value to be assigned to wealth. After some anecdotal material, the issue is stated formally as being about the sufficiency of virtue for happiness. Having promised some reasonings of the Stoics (*interrogationes nostrorum*, 87.11), Seneca proceeds in the remainder of the letter to deliver no fewer than six arguments, each followed by an attempted refutation and then a counter-refutation. The first argument is the one quoted earlier from 87.12; there, as we have seen, the refutation is attributed to the *Peripatetici* with their point about musical instruments. The second through fifth arguments are similarly in support of the Stoic view, but are not labeled as such, and the refutations likewise carry no label but are introduced in each case merely with "they say" (*inquiunt*) or "he says" (*inquit*). In *Letters* 87.15, the interlocutors insist that goods may be possessed by such lowly persons as grammarians; in 87.22, that a good thing, namely financial gain, may come from a bad act such as robbery; in 87.28–29, in a more involved argument, that it is improper to say that wealth is bad merely because the desire for it leads to many bad actions. The fifth Stoic argument is attributed to Posidonius; responding to it, the nameless interlocutor points out that if, as Posidonius claims, riches and the like always produce bad qualities of mind, they should not be counted even as preferred indifferents (*commoda*, 87.36). The sixth argument is the one given earlier from 87.38, where, as we have seen, Seneca notes that both the argument and the refutation originate with the Peripatetics. But Inwood is surely correct in identifying the preceding refutations as likewise reporting Peripatetic views,[13] both because the position represented is consistent throughout and, more specifically, because Seneca's management of the speaking voices here serves in lieu of explicit citations.

The structure of letter 85 is similar in the main to that of its companion piece, but with some meandering that requires close attention to follow. Here too the thesis is stated abstractly at the outset, that virtue is sufficient to fill out happiness, and here too the discussion proceeds as a series of arguments interspersed with efforts at refutation. The first of the refutations has already been mentioned, since it is labeled for the Peripatetics; it is the one concerned with the emotions in 85.3. Following a lengthy counter-refutation, Seneca returns to the abstract issue and reports two other philosophical views on the sufficiency of virtue for happiness. Xenocrates and Speusippus, he says, hold that a person can be made happy by virtue alone, but still deny that the honorable is the *only* good; while Epicurus believes that one who has virtue is also happy, but that virtue itself is not sufficient for happiness, since "it is the pleasure that arises from virtue that makes one happy, not virtue itself" (*Letters* 85.18). Epicurus is answered briefly, then the view of Xenocrates and Speusippus is restated ("that a person will indeed be happy through virtue alone and yet not completely happy"). Seneca then argues at greater length against the Xenocratean/Speusippan view, noting that for Stoics, "there is no respect in which the happy life can be raised to a higher degree" (*Letters* 85.19).

At this point, Seneca proceeds to a second formal argument for the Stoic position, again followed by an attempt at refutation. This time, however, the originators of the refutation are unnamed:

> Anyone who is courageous is without fear.
> Anyone who is without fear is without sadness.
> Anyone who is without sadness is happy.

---

[13] Inwood (2007a: xiv and 218).

This line of reasoning belongs to our school. Trying to refute it, they respond that the premise we take for granted, that anyone who is courageous is without fear, is actually false and controversial. "How's that? The brave person won't fear impending evils? You're talking about someone who is crazy and out of touch, not someone who is courageous. To be sure, the courageous person experiences a very moderate degree of fear, but he is not completely beyond fear." (*Letters* 85.24)

The most recently named philosophers are Xenocrates and Speusippus, mentioned earlier, but we have no reason to believe that it is they who are intended here. On grounds of content, we should think of the Peripatetics, for the position on fear given by the refuters in 85.24 is exactly the one stated for the emotions generally in 85.3: "a very moderate degree of fear" (*moderatissime timet*) corresponds to "troubled only very occasionally and in moderation" (*raro perturbatur et modice*).[14] It seems, then, that with the new departure in the argument, Seneca has returned to the main discursive frame of the letter. Apparently he considers the letter as a whole to be presenting a debate between Stoics and Peripatetics, despite the intrusion of other philosophical views in 85.18–23.

In both letter 87 and letter 85, then, we see that Seneca sometimes states a Peripatetic position without identifying it as such. The absence of citation does not indicate that he has no specific philosophical school in mind. Where these two letters are concerned, he may imagine that the way he has structured the argument makes it clear where the objection comes from, even if in fact it does not. Or he may not care who owns the objection, since his main interest is in the argument itself. Either way, the omission of citation in these instances should alert us to the possibility that other passages in the *Letters on Ethics* may also refer *sine nomine* to views Seneca knows to be Peripatetic.

One such instance is to be found at *Letters* 71.17. The context is a long explanation of the Stoic position on goods. For Stoics, all goods are equal to one another: as long as one's own behavior exhibits the relevant virtue, winning an election or a battle is not a greater good than losing it, and an honorable life is not a greater good than an honorable death. Realizing that not everyone will accept this view, Seneca explores the consequences of disagreement. If one does not concede that Regulus, tortured by enemies for preserving his honor, is experiencing just as choiceworthy a good as if he had been free of pain, one will be saying in effect that pain is a bad thing, since

---

[14] Compare the usual Peripatetic position on "moderate amounts" (*mediocritates*) of emotion as stated in *Letters* 116.1–3. Sharples (2010: 147) is overly cautious on this point.

anything that can diminish a good has to be bad in its own right. Regulus will still have his good, but he will also have an evil, and in fact a great one, since the pain is great. Yet no philosopher has ever been so bold as to say that a virtuous person can be made miserable by adverse circumstances.

> For if you accept that there is inequality, even such that you would consider the courageous endurance of torture to be one of the lesser goods, then you will also be regarding it as a bad thing. You will be saying that Socrates was unfortunate in his prison, that Cato was unfortunate when he reopened his wounds even more bravely than he made them, that Regulus was more terribly afflicted than any of them, in that he kept a promise even to his enemies and paid the penalty for doing so. Yet no one, not even the most fainthearted, has dared to say that: they say that Regulus was not happy yet insist that he was not miserable either. (*Letters* 71.17)

Who are these "fainthearted" philosophers (*mollissimi*), who say that Regulus was not happy and yet not miserable either? Clearly the position is one held by some historical persons, and these persons cannot be Epicureans, even though *mollissimi* is the kind of polemical epithet Seneca sometimes applies to Epicureans. For Epicurus, too, holds that the tortured sage remains happy.[15] That the *mollissimi* are in fact Peripatetics becomes clear when we compare their betwixt-and-between view with Doxography "C," section 14 (Wachsmuth 133.6–11):

> The person from whom happiness is taken away is not miserable, like the one who does not have happiness at all; sometimes he is in the middle. For both the wise and the non-wise person sometimes live what is called the middle life, the one that is neither happy nor miserable.

The origin of the view is in Aristotle's statement in *Nicomachean Ethics* 1.10, 1101a8, that the happy person could never become miserable but is not blessed either. Admittedly "the so-called middle life" may not be quite what Aristotle had in mind. But it is easy to see how someone might have gleaned that idea from the passage, and a dictum of Solon that is also cited in this portion of "C" is from the same context.

In *Letters* 71.18, immediately following the passage just quoted, Seneca brings in some philosophers he calls "Old Academics":

> The Old Academics admit that Regulus was happy even amid such torments, but not to the full and perfect extent of happiness. This is completely unacceptable. If one is not happy, one cannot have attained the highest good.

---

[15] Diog. Laert. 10.118; compare Seneca, *Letters* 66.47–48, 92.25.

> The highest good does not admit of any further degree of goodness, as long as there is virtue in it; as long as adversity does not diminish that virtue; as long as virtue remains intact even when the body is maimed. (*Letters* 71.18)

This is the same position as is given in *Letters* 85.18–19 to Xenocrates and Speusippus, and as in that letter, Seneca's argument against it targets the notion of a lesser degree of happiness. Here, it stands in contrast to the view of the "fainthearted" Peripatetics, since the Old Academics, like the Stoics, hold that someone like Regulus is happy amid torment. They are criticized only for denying that Regulus is happy "to the full and perfect extent of happiness"; that is, for claiming that there is a "further degree of goodness" that is attainable over and above happiness itself.

Interestingly, this "Old Academic" view also has a plausible origin in *Nicomachean Ethics* 1.10, following a different interpretation of Aristotle's intent. Where Aristotle writes,

> If this is so, then the happy person (εὐδαίμων) could never become miserable. Still, he will not be blessed (μακάριός), if he falls into misfortunes as bad as Priam's,[16]

this alternative interpretation draws a distinction between εὐδαίμων ("happy") and μακάριος ("blessed") and takes the latter to denote a higher degree of happiness. Aristotle would then have said that virtue is indeed sufficient for happiness, but not for the highest degree of happiness. Julia Annas presents this reading as an innovation by Antiochus of Ascalon in the first century BCE.[17] But Seneca never mentions Antiochus in any of his writings. Antiochus might just as well have drawn it from an earlier tradition of interpretation that has found its way to Seneca by some other channel.

The pairing of Peripatetic and Old Academic views is perhaps natural; after all, Seneca is looking for views on the sufficiency question that can be compared with his own Stoic view. It is remarkable, though, that both here and in *Letters* 85.18 we find recognizable but unattributed Peripatetic material supplying the context and introduction for an Old Academic position that is identified as such. The latter, it seems, is something of a curiosity and requires the specific label; after all, Seneca remarks in *Natural Questions* 7.32 that the Old Academic position in ethics had no adherents in his day. By contrast, the Peripatetics are the usual and expected opponents for the core Stoic position in ethics. They will sometimes

---

[16] *Nic. Eth.* 1.10, 1101a8 (trans. Irwin 1985).   [17] Annas (1993: 420–23).

appear by default, as it were, stating a view Seneca knows is theirs but does not take the trouble to name.[18]

Letter 92 and Stobaean Doxography "C"

Comparison with Doxography "C" is again valuable when we turn to letter 92. That letter, too, is concerned with the sufficiency of virtue for happiness, and here again the opponents to Seneca's Stoic position are not named. When we review the philosophical doctrines that are assigned to these opponents, however, we find that they are, one after another, the characteristic doctrines of the Peripatetics, listed in a manner very similar to that of Doxography "C." We can infer that the letter as a whole contends against Peripatetic thought, although the source Seneca worked from cannot have been Doxography "C" itself.

The letter begins with a claim of agreement between Seneca and an unspecified "you" on certain points about human nature: that externals are pursued for the sake of the body, that one cares for the body to honor the mind, and that the mind includes a directive faculty (*principale*) and subordinate parts responsible for movement and nutrition. Further, the directive faculty itself is divided into non-rational and rational elements, with the non-rational serving the rational (92.1). If there is agreement on all this, Seneca continues, then there should also be agreement on the thesis he means to defend: that happiness consists solely in perfected rationality, without any further necessary conditions (92.4). But clearly there is no such agreement, for some people (*quidam*) take the view that "the supreme good is such as to be increased, because it does not attain its greatest fullness when circumstances are unfavorable" (92.5). Seneca does not say who these people are. He does mention the Stoic Antipater, saying that he grants something to externals. But Antipater is not the sole or even the principal exponent, since the phrase is "*even* Antipater" (*Antipater quoque*, 92.5).

For the remainder of the letter, Seneca proceeds to single out specific elements of the view or views he is arguing against and to respond point by

---

[18] For other instances in which Seneca states a Peripatetic position as an unlabeled objection to his own view, see *Letters* 74.22, where the interlocutor insists that since Stoics recognize "devoted children, good customs in one's homeland, and good parents" as genuine goods, they should also allow for emotional disturbance at the loss of these; and 118.13, where the objection is that since Stoics make accordance with nature the distinctive property of goodness, they should count everything that accords with nature as a good. Compare *Anger* 1.12.3 (citing Theophrastus); Cicero, *Tusc.* 4.38; Doxography C, section 2 [Wachsmuth 118.15–17].

point. In sections 5 and 6, he unpacks the notion of increase, first via an analogy to the improvement a candle flame makes in the light of day, then by specifying two things that the opponent is bound to want as additions to virtue: either "repose" (*quies*) – that is, absence of distress, "which the Greeks call ἀοχλησία" – or pleasure (92.6). Arguments against the inclusion of pleasure continue to the end of section 10, with some pungent polemic: pleasure is "the good of a grazing animal" and "a mere tingling in the body"; to add it to virtue is to create a monstrous amalgam like Vergil's Scylla. The earlier addition, *quies*, though it did not supply the mind with anything, at least removed impediments; pleasure, though, actually weakens the mind.

The opponent now responds: If good health, repose, and freedom from pain are not impediments to virtue, will not the Stoic pursue them as well? This point Seneca cheerfully concedes, but without allowing that such objects are therefore to be considered goods. For him, goodness is involved only in that such objects are *well* selected. If given an opportunity for selection, the Stoic will prefer health, strength, and so on, but what is good in that selection will reside in the mind, in the propriety of its intention and judgment (92.13).[19]

To this, an opponent replies with a fuller version of the claim that virtuous knowledge might make one happy and yet not perfectly happy. Without some "natural goods" or "tools" (*instrumenta*), among which are included health and soundness of the limbs, one cannot be supremely happy, even though a person who has virtue cannot be miserable (92.14). Seneca objects: in his view, it makes no sense to speak of being happy and yet not supremely happy, since, if there are circumstances that can prevent the virtuous person's happiness from being perfect, severe adversity could abolish it altogether. He compares the happiness of the good person to the light of the sun, which receives not the slightest augmentation from that of a tiny flame or spark. "But," says the opponent, "even the sun has its light blocked by certain things" (92.17). The cloud, Seneca replies, does not actually prevent the sun from shining, but only prevents us from seeing its radiance; and similarly, disasters, losses, and unfair treatment might make the exercise of virtue less apparent, but they could not make it less virtuous.

In sections 19–23 Seneca revisits the claim we saw in letter 71, that a wise person who is afflicted in body will be "neither miserable nor happy"

---

[19] In Stoic terminology, "selection" (ἐκλογή) is impulse directed toward a preferred or dispreferred indifferent as such (see Chapter 1, note 9). Note that Seneca's phrase *si electio detur* implies that one will sometimes not be able to rationally choose preferred indifferents.

(92.19). Following this, the opponent raises the possibility that living longer, while free of pain, might make a person happier (92.24). Seneca denies this, which raises the possibility that the Stoic account of happiness might be "incredible and beyond human nature" (92.25). He counters this objection by appealing to the testimony of Epicurus in his deathbed letter. If even a hedonist philosopher can consider himself happy in extreme pain, then philosophers who say that the wise person in extreme adversity is neither miserable nor happy come out as "base-minded degenerates" (*degeneres et humillimae mentis*, 92.26).

Finally, the opponent states the view that human happiness differs in character from divine happiness. All humans can achieve is a "shadow and semblance" (*umbra quaedam . . . et similitudo*) of divine virtue and happiness: "we approach, but we don't actually reach them" (92.27). As might be expected, Seneca defends the Stoic conception of the divine element in human nature, and the letter ends with an elaborate peroration on disdain for the body.

Side-by-side comparison of this Senecan letter with Doxography "C" makes it plain that virtually all the specific claims against which Seneca is arguing emanate from the Peripatetic school. The principal target of the letter is a pluralistic account of the human good that sees happiness as a combination of virtue with other kinds of goods. Doxography "C" takes just such a combination view of the end, stating it directly in section 8 (Wachsmuth 126.12–24). There, the Peripatetic author Arius Didymus defines the *telos* as "living in accordance with virtue amidst the bodily and external goods, either all of them or most of them and the most important" and states also that goods belonging to the body are productive of happiness "by contributing something through their presence" (τῷ συμβάλλεσθαι τι παρόντα).[20] In addition, Didymus's listing of what are meant to be standard Peripatetic doctrines includes all the following points:

- The mind (or soul, ψυχή) has both a rational and an irrational part; each of these is then subdivided into two further parts: section 1 (Wachsmuth 117.4–118.4])
- Goods that are choiceworthy for their own sake include pleasure and absence of distress (ἀοχλησία): section 15 (Wachsmuth 137.4–5)

---

[20] I take the view that the denial in this section that bodily and external goods "constitute" (συμπληροῦν) happiness means only that they do not by themselves make up happiness, that is, not in the absence of virtue.

- The goods that are "in accordance with nature" are also called "instruments and equipment," as of a craft: sections 12 and 14 (Wachsmuth 129.19–130.12 and 132.19–21)
- A good person in adverse circumstances will fail to obtain happiness, but even so "is not wretched like the one who does not possess it at all, but is sometimes found between the two": section 14 (Wachsmuth 133.6–11)
- Happiness is dependent on living to an advanced age, since "a short period of time will not make happiness": section 13 (Wachsmuth 131.19–132.8)
- Happiness is not the same for a god as for human beings: section 14 (Wachsmuth 132.21–133.2)

As all of these doctrines appear in letter 92, it is an easy conclusion that Seneca is giving a series of rejoinders to a miscellany of Peripatetic claims, even though he does not name the Peripatetics anywhere in the letter.

The reference to absence of distress (ἀοχλησία) and the pungent language about "tickling of the flesh" and "gratification from the trough" have sometimes been taken as indications that the critique in *Letters* 92.6–10 is directed against Epicurean hedonism.[21] That interpretation should be rejected out of hand. The word ἀοχλησία is indeed used by Epicurus for freedom of pain in the body (*Menoeceus* 127), but it is by no means restricted to Epicurean contexts. It is in fact lingua franca, widely attested among philosophers of various persuasions from Speusippus to Sextus Empiricus; among Peripatetics, it was favored especially by Hieronymus.[22] As for the polemical phrases, there is no question that they are an attack against hedonism, but not every hedonist is an Epicurean. In this instance, the criticism is leveled specifically against those who bring pleasure in as an addition to virtue with other kinds of goods, producing what Seneca considers to be a hybrid account of the end. The point of the polemical language is that anyone who includes pleasure in the end *at all*, even in the smallest degree, is subject to the kinds of criticism usually leveled against Epicureans. Parallels can be supplied for this kind of argument.[23] Only in *Letters* 92.25 do we see a clear reference to

---

[21] As is assumed by Costa (1988) and Préchac (1945–64); see also Inwood (2005: 40).
[22] Speusippus (fragment 77 = Clement, *Stromata* 2.22.133), the Megarians (Alexander, *De Anima* 2.150), Hieronymus (Stobaeus 1.49, 383.8–10 Wachsmuth), and Sextus Empiricus (*Outlines of Pyrrhonism* 1.10). Its role as philosophical lingua franca is well illustrated in Posidonius, fragment 187 Edelstein and Kidd. The term is discussed in White (2004: 397–98).
[23] The tactic was used by Chrysippus in attacking rival accounts of the *telos* (Cicero, *Acad.* 2.138; see White (2004: 401) and also in a polemic against Academic and/or Peripatetic positions on the life of contemplation. See page 22.

Epicureanism. There, however, the example of Epicurus is invoked a fortiori against the Peripatetics: since even Epicureans are found in support of the sufficiency of virtue, the Peripatetics can hardly reject the Stoics' case as implausible.[24]

Once these points are established, there should be no hesitation in recognizing letter 92 as the third of three large-scale, unified attacks on Peripatetic ethics within the *Letters on Ethics*. With that said, we should also take into account the substantial ways in which the presentation of issues in letter 92 differs from that of letters 85 and 87. Each of those earlier letters takes up a single thesis and treats it in a dialectical manner, with formal arguments for the thesis pulled apart and assessed for the strength of their premises. The subject matter of letter 92 is much more diverse, and the close dialectical argumentation is lacking; in its place, we have a series of loosely related claims offered by the opponent with little or no argumentative support. In a word, the account Seneca criticizes throughout this letter proceeds in a doxographical manner very much like that of Doxography "C." However, I do not claim that Seneca has read "C" itself, but only that he was familiar with a doxographical account of a generally similar kind. There are points of difference to be considered as well, and these are not merely in the ordering and level of specificity within the presentation. They concern more substantive philosophical issues.

Seneca's Version of the Tripartite Mind

A point of particular interest is the division of mind or soul that is posited in letter 92.1 and Doxography "C," section 1. Here there are some obvious similarities between our two texts, since both speak of "parts" within a person that are responsible for our various functions, and both prominently mention both "rational" and "irrational" parts. But there are also important differences in the relationship that is established among the parts, reflecting quite different philosophical motivations.

Doxography "C" posits quite an elaborate partitioning of the psyche. After the initial division into rational and irrational parts, each of those parts is subdivided: the rational into "scientific" (ἐπιστημονικόν) and "deliberative" (βουλευτικόν) parts and the irrational into "appetitive" (ἐπιθυμητικόν) and "spirited" (θυμικόν) parts. The determination of impulse belongs to the irrational part, which is thus also called the "impulsive" (ὁρμητικόν) part, but it is the rational part that deliberates about the objects of desire. Hence it

---

[24] Similar arguments are used by Seneca at *Constancy* 16.1 and *Letters* 66.45–48.

is especially important to note how these parts relate to one another. That the relationship is not entirely harmonious is adumbrated early on, when we are told that what is meant by saying that the spirited or emotional soul-part is irrational is that it is "able to obey reason" (οἷόν τε πείθεσθαι λόγῳ) and "capable of receiving virtue" (τῆς ἀρετῆς δεκτικόν). It is irrational, then, in that it does not *always* obey reason: it is capable of doing so, but actually does so only when virtue is present in it. The potential for conflict between this part and the rational part is explained lower down in section 10 (Wachsmuth 128.17–25), which states that emotion and reason are sometimes "discordant and at strife with one another" (στασιαστικῶς διαφωνεῖν) and that the non-reasoning part exhibits "lack of self-control" (ἀκρασία).

The opening of Seneca's letter partitions the *animus* in a way that at first looks quite similar to the Peripatetic doxography. Seneca writes:

> You and I will agree, I think, that one pursues outward things for the body's sake, that one cares for the body in order to show respect for the mind, and that the mind includes subservient parts, responsible for our motor and nutritional functions, which are given to us on behalf of the directive faculty itself. This directive faculty includes both a non-rational and a rational component. The former is at the service of the latter, which is the one thing that does not look to anything else but rather refers everything else to itself. As you know, divine rationality is similarly at the head of all things, subordinate to none of them; and this rationality of ours, which derives from that divine rationality, is just the same. (*Letters* 92.1)

Again we find the soul divided into heterogenous parts, with one part responsible for reasoning and other, non-rational parts responsible for movement and nutrition. However, Seneca does not commit himself to a model of psychic conflict in which the impulse-generating part of soul is sometimes at odds with the reasoning part, making us behave in ways that reason does not agree to. Rather, he states that the lower elements *serve* the higher, and this not as a fact about the virtuous person only, but as a description of how all human minds are arranged. In his account, then, the lower parts serve the higher not merely when they are so inclined or when they are forced to do so, but always, in their very nature as subordinate parts. It is the rational part alone that determines what the creature should pursue and does pursue. The emphasis falls on the supremacy of reason as the sole element that refers everything to itself.[25]

---

[25] Just below, in *Letters* 92.8, Seneca moves closer to conceding the possibility of mental conflict when he sets up a contrast between two parts within the mind's non-rational part, one "spirited, ambitious, and wayward, consisting in emotions ... unruly" (*animosam, ambitiosam, inpotentem, positam in adfectionibus...effrenatam*), the other "base, idle, devoted to pleasures" (*humilem,*

The partitioning of the *animus* at the beginning of letter 92 has long been an issue in Seneca studies.[26] Why would an author who is elsewhere strongly committed to a single directive faculty allow himself to speak of parts at all? Having now seen that the remainder of letter 92 is targeted consistently against the Peripatetic position in ethics, we are at last in a position to make some progress on this question. Given the rhetorical aims of his letter, Seneca has good reason to begin with premises he believes his opponents would accept. In effect, he allows his straw Peripatetics to choose the terms of the debate, feeling that he has argumentative resources to defeat them on their own territory. Yet his statement need not be seen as a dialectical step that he agrees to merely for teaching purposes, as Inwood has suggested.[27] On the contrary, it is an account that a Stoic thinker can willingly endorse. For in Seneca's version of the psychic division, the mind's functions are arranged in such a way that the very possibility of disharmony and conflict among the parts is conspicuously absent. Moreover, this account of the mind's structure does not undermine Seneca's Stoic position on the sufficiency of virtue; rather it supports it. For since it is only the reasoning part that determines what objects are to be pursued, there is no reason why anything external to virtue has to be considered good in its own right. The reasoning part can order the pursuit of food and the like for merely instrumental reasons, nurturing and protecting the body and subordinate mind-parts for the support of its own virtuous ends.

Seneca's expressed openness to psychic tripartition thus appears as a deliberate accommodation to Peripatetic thought. Whatever source he used must have included a tripartition along the lines we see in Doxography "C," with a division of mind into (at least) three heterogenous parts. Because of his commitment to Stoicism, however, he does not accept that type of mental conflict into his own account: he does not grant that human nature is set up for strife between one mental function and another. We cannot now tell what exactly his source might have said on that score, but if it resembled Doxography "C" closely, then Seneca has

---

languidam, voluptatibus deditam). Seneca's point there, however, is that the pluralistic account he is rejecting gets things wrong in terms of its *own* psychology, by preferring the objective of the mind's lowest part to that of the emotional part.

[26] See Setaioli (1988: 304–5), which argues for Posidonian influence, with further remarks in Setaioli (2014b: 246 n49); in earlier literature especially Grimal (1978: 400–1); I. Hadot (1969: 76, 91). Seneca generally resists efforts to explain the intransigence of emotion in terms of conflicting soul-parts; see page 52 and 139.

[27] Inwood (2005: 38–41).

found a specious agreement with it by doing some strategic reshaping of the Peripatetic view.

Distinctive Features of Seneca's Peripatetics

That the doxography Seneca used was not entirely congruent with C becomes clearer when we compare the latter with certain other features of the position Seneca gives to his opponents in letter 92. In particular, there are two themes in Seneca's letter that appear to have been taken over from the tradition on Peripatetic ethics but which could not have originated in Doxography "C" itself. The presence of these themes is suggestive as to the nature of Seneca's source, even if we cannot put a name to its author.

Consider first the following objection stated by Seneca as coming from his opponent:

> The wise person is happy, to be sure; yet he does not attain the supreme good unless he has some natural tools at his disposal. Thus while someone who has virtue cannot be miserable, one who lacks such natural goods as health and an unimpaired physical condition is still not supremely happy. (*Letters* 92.14)

The objector concedes that virtuous wisdom is sufficient to make one happy (*beatus*), while still insisting that even the most virtuous person cannot be supremely happy (*beatissimus*) without the bodily and external goods. He is thus at odds with Seneca, who proceeds to argue against the distinction between "happy" and "perfectly happy." But he is also at odds with the Peripatetic position that the wise person whose body is afflicted is neither happy nor unhappy (*Letters* 92.19). On the face of it, his view appears to be identical with the view Seneca assigns in *Letters* 71.18 to the *veteres Academici* and in *Letters* 85.18 to Xenocrates and Speusippus.

If this is an Old Academic account, however, then the mention of "natural tools" (*naturalia instrumenta*) comes as a surprise. We have already seen how Peripatetic texts, including Doxography "C," sometimes give the term "instruments" (ὄργανα) to bodily and external goods as part of an argument against the sufficiency of happiness. The thought is that just as the crafts require certain instruments to achieve their ends, so virtue cannot be activated without resources external to itself: virtue needs to use those other goods in the same way as a flute player needs to use a flute or a doctor needs to use medicines. This convenient argument is usable by the philosopher who denies the sufficiency of virtue whether or not he also holds that the bodily and external goods are actually constitutive of happiness. The same cannot be said, however, for the philosopher who takes the "Old Academic" line in favor of sufficiency.[28] If bodily and external goods are necessary conditions for the activation of virtue, one can hardly say that virtue is sufficient for happiness even in their absence. If they are *necessary*, then their absence should mean that virtue cannot be activated, with the result that the one who lacks them cannot be happy *at all*.

What then are natural tools doing in the middle of an objection that makes virtue sufficient by itself? It is possible that Seneca has just been careless – that he means to give a Peripatetic flavor to the discussion and imports a phrase characteristic of the school into a paragraph where it does not properly belong. But we should also consider the possibility that the "Old Academic" view might have been framed within a larger Peripatetic position in Seneca's source. For a Peripatetic author, it would represent a kind of fallback position, a place to which a member of his school might retreat under dialectical pressure without giving up anything really important. Sufficiency would have been conceded, but in such a way as to maintain some status for the bodily and external goods. Strictly speaking, that would not be the status of instruments but rather of constituents; the Peripatetic author, however, might regard those terms as more or less interchangeable, since he is in the habit of using both to refer to externals.

This is not a theme Seneca could have extracted from Doxography "C." In fact Didymus explicitly refuses to take this gambit. For him, the possession of bodily and external goods is "entirely necessary" (πάντως ἀναγκαῖον) for happiness:

> The activity of virtue is primary in that it is entirely necessary for it to take place amid the goods that are in accordance with nature. For a morally serious person would use virtue even among evils, but would not then be blessed, and would give evidence of nobility even under torture, but would not then be happy. (Doxography "C," sections 13–14 (Wachsmuth 132.8–12))

Being "blessed" (μακάριος) is equivalent to being happy (εὐδαιμονήσει); a person deprived of the bodily and external goods will be neither blessed nor happy. Moreover, happiness is not a matter of degree: "it cannot be increased, as a skill can, by an abundance of instruments and equipment" (section 14 (Wachsmuth 132.21)). Thus, Didymus's understanding of

---

[28] As implied by the analysis in Sharples (2007: 627–28).

Peripatetic ethics is different from the "Old Academic" interpretation; indeed, it reads like a rather emphatic rejection of it. We catch a hint of a controversy that must have gone on at some point in the later Hellenistic period, in which Didymus (or his source) took one position and some Peripatetic or Academic opponent took the other. Antiochus of Ascalon would no doubt have participated enthusiastically in such a debate; we need not think, though, that the conversation began with him.[29]

A second feature that distinguishes Seneca's Peripatetics from those of Doxography "C" can be seen in the passage concerning absence of distress, where Seneca helpfully supplies the Greek term ἀοχλησία:

> If you are not satisfied with honorable conduct on its own, you are bound to want the addition of either repose (which Greeks call ἀοχλησία) or pleasure. The former of these is admissible in any case, for the trouble-free mind is at leisure for studying the universe; nothing distracts it from contemplating nature. (*Letters* 92.6)

As we saw earlier in connection with "natural tools," the underlying argument is that virtue cannot be activated unless conjoined with some goods external to itself. In this case, the virtuous activity is contemplation of nature. Disturbance (*molestia*) has the potential to interfere with contemplation: the mind that is free of it is at leisure (*vacat*) and is not distracted (*nihil avocat*) from carrying out that virtuous intention.

Letter 92 also gives considerable attention to the Aristotelian idea that serious misfortunes might be impediments to virtuous activities. In addition to the passage just cited, we find it in three other places in the letter, with the impetus coming in each case from the Peripatetic side. In 92.10, it appears again in conjunction with repose (*quies*) as a less problematic addition to virtue than pleasure would be. "Their other objective, repose, though incapable of providing the spirit with any positive benefit, would at least remove any impediments" (*inpedimenta*).[30] Since repose was already mentioned in 92.6 as equivalent to ἀοχλησία, this statement clarifies that ἀοχλησία is strictly a privative notion consisting in the removal of impediments. The theme is renewed in 92.11, where the interlocutor suggests that good health (*bona valetudo*), repose (*quies*), and absence of pain (*dolorum vacatio*) might be things to pursue "as long as they are not impediments to virtue" (*si virtutem nihil inpeditura sit*). Here it may be

---

[29] Context for the suggestion made here is supplied in White (2002); Inwood (2002); Sharples (2007); Hahm (2007); Inwood (2014).

[30] *Letters* 92.10 *Illa utcumque altera quies nihil quidem ipsa praestabat animo, sed inpedimenta removebat.* The imperfect indicatives recall the prior mention of the concept in *Letters* 92.6.

significant that two of the three suggested objects of pursuit are privatives – three, if one thinks of health as an absence of illness. Finally, in 92.17, the interlocutor appears to have a notion of impediments in mind when he objects to Seneca's sunlight analogy.

> As I was saying a bit ago, a spark makes no contribution to the light of the sun; for the sun's brightness obscures anything that might shine in its absence. "But even the sun has its light blocked by certain things." Yet the sun is unimpaired, even when it is obstructed; and even if there is something in between that stops us from seeing it, it is still at work and still proceeding on its round. Every time it shines out between the clouds, it is no smaller or slower than when the sky is quite clear. There is a lot of difference between an impediment and a mere obstruction. (*Letters* 92.16–17)

The Senecan response makes it clear how the objection is supposed to work. The opponent allows Seneca's point that nothing external to virtue can make any positive contribution to happiness (the spark does not contribute to the light of the sun) but retains the weaker claim, that some externals can prevent virtue from achieving its ends.

Now, for Aristotle, the capacity of severe misfortunes to impede virtuous activity is a kind of inverse notion to the instrumentality of external goods, one that works "conversely" (ἀνάπαλιν) to the way strokes of good fortune are available for fine and excellent use. It takes only a moment's reflection, however, to realize that the philosophical notion of an impediment is in fact distinct from that of an instrument. An instrument, as involved in many of the craft analogies, has properties specific to the purpose for which its use is required: a flute, with its specific properties, is required for flute-playing but not for paddling a boat. An impediment merely prevents: the broken arm that impedes flute-playing also impedes boat-paddling, house-building, and much else. A version of Peripatetic ethics that made happiness consist only in virtuous activity plus a lack of impediments would be quite austere, though still distinct from Stoicism. It would allow that virtue can work with any circumstances that come to hand – a poor person can be generous, a weak person courageous – but it would insist that distress of body or mind can prevent even the best people from activating their virtues. A Stoic might object at this point that the business of avoiding anything that would genuinely impede the activities of virtue is just part of virtuous activity itself. But the austere Peripatetic does not have to allow this. For he might restrict his notion of impediments to Aristotle's "misfortunes like those of Priam"; that is, to events that would plausibly be debilitating to the mind itself.

The privative notion of ἀοχλησία as an absence of debilitating distress had an advocate in the Peripatetic tradition in Diodorus of Tyre, who "supplemented virtue with absence of distress" in his account of the end, making happiness consist in "living trouble-free and honorably."[31] Hieronymus, a contemporary of Arcesilas and Chrysippus, must also have emphasized ἀοχλησία to the exclusion of the positive external goods, since his account spoke of ἀοχλησία alone.[32] In Doxography "C" itself, however, the idea of impediments is barely mentioned at all. The notion surfaces only once, in a string of definitions for εὐδαιμονία that looks to have been culled from earlier works.[33] While the notion of unimpededness was not unknown to Arius Didymus, there is much else in his doxography that favors the less-austere account, and we can hardly think that such a glancing mention could have provided the impetus for what we find in Seneca.

Thus, we have noted two features of the Peripatetic position attacked in Seneca's letter that are significantly different from that laid out in Doxography "C": a readiness to make use of the (putatively) Old Academic gambit on degrees of happiness, and a subtle but unmistakable emphasis on impediments to activation. When we place these features alongside what we have already observed about the views Seneca seeks to refute in letter 92, we can discern at least the broad outlines of the source he must have used. This source must have laid out a comprehensive array of Peripatetic claims, including claims about the structure of the psyche, claims about the non-sufficiency of virtue for happiness, and at least one claim about the nature of happiness itself, namely that it is different for a god than for a human being. It must have mentioned the possibility that one could be neither happy nor wretched, and it must have argued at some point that external goods are needed as tools for activation, and again that some degree of longevity is required for a complete life. This range of inclusions suggests a doxographical account resembling Doxography "C" in many ways. Unlike "C," however, the account known to Seneca made positive use of the "Old Academic" reading of *Nicomachean Ethics* 1.10; also, it emphasized the austere Hieronyman or Diodoran version of

---

[31] Cicero, *Fin.* 5.14 *adiungit ad honestatem vacuitatem doloris;* Clement, *Stromata* (ed. Früchtel, Stählin, and Treu (1960)) 2.21.127 ἀοχλήτως καὶ καλῶς ζῆν.

[32] See White (2002, 2004). It is of interest that Hieronymus denied that pleasure is intrinsically choiceworthy (Cicero, *Fin.* 2.9). It may be that he was falsely portrayed by his opponents as more of a hedonist than he really was.

[33] Doxography C, section 13 (Wachsmuth 130.20–21): εὐδαιμονία is "the unimpeded use of virtue among things in accordance with nature" (χρῆσιν ἀρετῆς ἐν τοῖς κατὰ φύσιν ἀνεμπόδιστον).

pluralism, allowing only absence of impediments as the adjunct to virtuous activity. In brief, what we meet in Seneca's letter is a second Peripatetic doxography with its own distinctive emphases.[34]

***

This summary of Peripatetic themes in Seneca has shown him to be deeply engaged with that rival school of thought. He consulted multiple textual sources to gain knowledge of Peripatetic positions, and he studied those sources carefully for terminology and for specifics of argumentation. Most importantly, he takes Peripatetic ethics seriously as a worthy opponent to Stoic ethics. Whereas his attitude to Epicurean material is uneven, frequently hostile but at times smilingly indulgent or even playful, his handling of the Peripatetics is quite different. He shows little interest in names and personalities (if he indeed has that information), but pays close attention to the ideas themselves, working through the arguments at length with quiet concentration. The sufficiency of virtue for happiness is not a point on which he can compromise. He respects the opponents of that doctrine, but his resistance to them is firm.

---

[34] In the longer version of this chapter published as Graver (2018), I consider in an appendix the possibility that the unusual classification of goods in letter 66 also reflects Peripatetic influence. That particular threefold classification, though argued to be consistent with Stoic thought, is unparalleled in Stoic sources; while the first class of goods, which Seneca calls "primary goods" (*prima bona*), bears a striking resemblance to the "primary actions" (πράξεις προηγουμέναι) and "primary activity" (προηγουμένη ἐνέργεια) that appear in three passages in Doxography C. Further to letter 66, see page 186 and following.

PART III
Models of Emotional Experience

CHAPTER 6

Seneca's Therapy for Anger

"A brief insanity." With this phrase, already a familiar dictum of philosophers writing on anger, Seneca expresses the main idea of his own *On Anger* and also its most pervasive tension.[1] On the one hand, anger is brief: it is episodic, coming on strong at one moment and off again in the next. It is that temporal structure that gives an opportunity for the philosopher to address it. For anger can listen to reason: in contrast to the continuous irrationality of the dispositionally insane, it is a judgment formed at a particular time, and as such it affords opportunities for discursive intervention. But on the other hand, anger is a kind of insanity. The judgment that it makes is so powerful as to be inherently ungovernable for as long as the episode lasts. Like every emotion, but to a much greater degree and in a much more dangerous way, anger takes us beyond our rational control, to a realm of action where philosophy can no longer intervene.

The earliest of Seneca's major works, written either just before or just after his period of exile, *On Anger* already sets its author up as a philosophical writer with a firm commitment to Stoicism.[2] The Stoic definition of anger is "our definition"; the authors of Stoic books are "some of our people."[3] And in the explicitly theoretical discussions that fill roughly the first half of his work, Seneca in fact adheres quite closely to the Stoic analysis of emotion. Emotions for him are certainly embodied responses, in that they can be felt within the chest and read

---

[1] *Anger* 1.1.2, indicating that the expression is inherited from "certain philosophers" (*quidam e sapientibus viris*). Seneca does not specify which philosophers he has in mind. Numerous works had been written on anger management; Harris (2001: 88–128) offers an overview of the tradition. For Seneca's sources in *On Anger*, see notes 16 and 34 in this chapter.
[2] The three *Consolations* are also from this period. For the date see Griffin (1976: 398), setting the *terminus ante quem* in 52. Grimal (1978: 270–76) favors a date in 41, because of the attitude toward Caligula; others, including Harris (2001: 112–13) n132, think it must have been written after Seneca returned from exile, that is, in 49–50.
[3] *Anger* 1.3.3; 2.19.3. Note also 1.6.5, in adding an argument of Plato: *quid enim nocet alienis uti ea parte qua nostra sunt?* ("What's the harm in using others' views on points where we hold the same opinion?").

in one's facial expression, gestures, and gait; but their essence is mental. If they lead us to act contrary to our better judgment, it is not because they come from some region of the self that is essentially different from our decision-making part, but because they are flawed decisions of an especially vehement kind. The centrality of this view of anger to the theoretical portion of *On Anger* is, I think, indisputable, and the case is strong that Seneca means to present himself throughout the work as an advocate for the canonical Stoic position.[4]

But philosophical thought is not expressed only in explicit statements about the nature and causation of anger. Seneca's ways of understanding that emotion are evident also in his recommendations for how to cure oneself and others. In the latter part of this chapter, I take a close look at the working assumptions that undergird the therapies presented in the second half of book 2 and throughout book 3. To what extent do those assumptions accord with the Stoic understanding of emotion that Seneca explains in the earlier, more theoretical portions of the treatise? Does his approach to the management of anger still adhere to the psychological model that makes anger "a brief insanity"?

What one would expect on the basis of Seneca's Stoic-inspired psychological theory is that any therapeutic strategies he offers should respect the temporal structure of anger. If he believes that anger cannot be hindered in its moment of greatest force, he should not offer any techniques to combat it in that moment; rather, he should limit himself to strategies for prevention and delay. It is therefore something of a disappointment when book 3 suggests a strategy for arresting an angry impulse midway.[5] That suggestion in itself indicates that the rhetorical objectives of the work have not been fully integrated with the philosophical analysis. But Seneca also shows signs of discomfort with this aspect of his work, and these can be read as promising for his further philosophical development.

Anger Theory in Book 1

From its preface onward, the first book of the treatise is concerned not with the *how* of anger management but with the *why*. Novatus has

---

[4] On the philosophical content of the work, see now especially the papers in Laurand, Malaspina, and Prost (2021). Earlier treatments include Huber (1973), Cupaiuolo (1975), Fillion–Lahille (1984), Malchow (1986), Nussbaum (1994), Ramondetti (1996). Specific issues are treated in Inwood (2005), Vogt (2006), Graver (2007), Kaufman (2014), Braicovich (2015), Gartner (2015).

[5] For the concern, see Cupaiuolo (1975: 82), who finds the theoretical and practical sections of the work largely unconnected. Others, including Nussbaum (1994: 402–38), and Ramondetti (1996), find a more integral relation.

requested a work on "how anger can be soothed" (1.1.1), and Seneca approves this aim with a powerful indictment of that emotion. Putting on display the lavish rhetoric that had already won him a reputation at Rome, he elaborates on the lack of self-control, the inability to hide one's feelings, the damage to public and private interests, and all the other features that make anger the ugliest and most dangerous of all the emotions. Following the preface, however, he proceeds in quieter style to make the philosophical case for eliminating anger from one's life. Here, despite a gap in the received text, it is evident that the book began by inquiring into the nature of anger and that it quoted typical Stoic definitions of anger as "a desire to take revenge" or "a desire to punish one by whom you think yourself unjustly harmed."[6] Defending these definitions, Seneca next distinguishes true anger from other forms of aggressive behavior. Neither a crowd of people nor a young child can properly be considered a rational agent, and for this reason, the roar of an excited mob and the temper tantrums of young children are not real instances of anger. Similarly, the fierce attacks of certain wild animals are not anger, because the animal does not intend its attack as retribution for an offense. Animals can do many things, but for Seneca they are not capable of conceiving a desire for revenge, any more than they are capable of forgiveness or of human vices. What they have are not emotions but emotion-like reactions.[7] Seneca thus maintains that "although anger is inimical to reason, it occurs only in those in whom reason has a place" (1.3.4).

In taking this position, Seneca has already aligned himself with the Stoic tradition. But his most characteristically Stoic claims are yet to come. Beginning with section 1.5, he argues against the conciliatory stance that speaks of "moderate emotion," a stance that he attributes here to Aristotle and Theophrastus, although elsewhere he labels the same position as "Peripatetic."[8] According to this view, all emotions are in accordance with nature, which implies that they serve some useful purpose. Consequently they should not be eliminated but only moderated; that is, experienced in some proper degree. Against this view Seneca asserts first of all that anger,

---

[6] Both definitions are quoted by Lactantius in *De ira dei* 17.13 as being from this work; the second, Lactantius says, was quoted by Seneca from Posidonius. See Reynolds (1977: 42). Seneca refers back to the missing material in *Anger* 1.4.1 and 1.5.3.

[7] *Anger* 1.3.8: *his quaedam similia*. Compare Chrysippus *apud* Galen, *PHP* 5.6.37 (LS 65I, SVF 1.570), Cicero, *Tusc.* 4.31. The position is consistent with the respect for animals' cognitive abilities Seneca displays in *Letters* 121.5–13, 17–24.

[8] See *Anger* 1.9.2, 1.12.3, 3.3.1; and for the same view attributed to the Peripatetics, *Letters* 85.6–16 and 116; Cic. *Tusc.* 4.38–47. See Laurenti (1979). More broadly on μετριοπάθεια, see now Wildberger (2021) as well as Graver (2002a: 163–65); Dillon (1983).

as a desire for revenge, is actually incompatible with human nature. Humans are by nature gentle, sociable, and inclined toward mutual aid; anger prompts us to behave contrary to that nature. Although we may have to correct one another, there is no need for us to do so in anger, for just as medical treatment is sometimes painful, so even severe punishments can be imposed out of kindness.

He then turns to the claim that anger and other emotions are useful in our lives. His argument to the contrary turns upon our ability to subject the emotions to conscious control. The Stoic Chrysippus had put forward that the emotions, properly so called, are all voluntary impulses and yet cannot easily be controlled while in progress. Chrysippus had drawn a comparison to the action of running downhill: the movement is difficult to stop even though the initial impulse to run was a decision for which one can be held accountable.[9] Seneca makes exactly the same point, but strengthens the image. In his version, the decision that initiates an emotional impulse is compared to the action of stepping off a cliff:

> With some things, the beginnings are in our power, but after that they carry us on by their own force, not allowing a return. Bodies allowed to fall from a height have no control of themselves: they cannot resist or delay their downward course, for the irrevocable fall has cut off all deliberation, all repentance; they cannot help but arrive where they are going, though they could have avoided going there at all. Even so the mind, once it propels itself into anger, love, and other emotions, is not permitted to check its impulse. Its own weight – that is, the naturally downward tendency of its faults – must carry it to the bottom.[10]

Just as running or jumping off a cliff is the kind of action that necessarily carries the body forward, so anger, love, and the other passions are the kind of movement that inevitably carries the mind forward until that force is spent. Whether or not one has the emotion is still a matter of decision: one does not have to step off the cliff. On this point Seneca is emphatic: the beginnings are "in our power" (*in nostra potestate*); we "could have avoided going there" (*quo non ire licuisset*); and in the following paragraph, we give entry to anger "of our own will" (*voluntate nostra*, 1.8.1). But once the emotion gets going, we cannot simply tell it to stop. And if we cannot limit the degree or duration of the emotional response to what reason deems appropriate, then clearly we cannot make it serve a useful purpose.

---

[9] See page 45.
[10] *Anger* 1.7.4. My translation treats the phrase *et vitiorum natura proclivis* as epexegetic, an effort to explain the significance of weight in the analogy.

But Seneca has not yet explained why he thinks that reason cannot regulate the emotions while they are going on. To clarify, he continues with a further point, also Chrysippan, about the underlying psychology. He now explicitly rejects the model that represents the emotions as belonging to a separate part of the mind from the part that reasons and makes judgments:

> The mind is not off by itself, observing the emotions from outside, so as not to allow them to proceed further than they should; rather it is itself changed into the emotion. For that reason it cannot regather its useful and salutary force after it has been betrayed and weakened. As I said, it does not have its own separate and disjoined location; no, emotion and reason are alterations of the mind for the better and for the worse. (*Anger* 1.8.2–3)

If it were the case that emotion and reasoning emanate from different regions within the person, then reason would be extraneous to the emotions and in a position to combat them. But in fact, says Seneca, that is not how emotions work. Instead, the reasoning capacity is directly implicated in the production of the emotional impulse: if that impulse is out of line, then reason itself is out of line. Having made the poor decision to become agitated and aggressive in response to a perceived offense, the mind has no further resources with which to control its own behavior.

The psychological basis has now been established for the arguments of book 1. Seneca fills out the book with further arguments against the supposed usefulness of anger. A good person, he says, will have other ways of dealing with injustice. Just as hunters and soldiers can wield their weapons most effectively when guided by cool reason alone, so one can rely on courage, not anger, to respond appropriately to others' acts of aggression, including even such terrible acts as the murder or rape of a member of one's family (1.12.1). Will that response then be completely calm? Seneca concedes that the wise person will feel "suspicions and shadows of the emotions," but he insists that these feelings are not really emotions.[11] In its context, this last point is intended only to forestall the objection that a complete absence of anger would make a person inhumanly callous.[12] It is only in book 2 that Seneca will explore the implications of these "suspicions and shadows" for how anger itself is to be understood.

---

[11] *Anger* 1.16.7. In connection with this claim, Seneca reports an observation of Zeno of Citium, that "in the mind of the wise person also there remains a scar even after the wound has healed."

[12] This emphasis is similar to that of *Cons. Marc.* 7.1 and of numerous passages in the *Letters*. See page 54.

Book 2: The Causal History of Anger

The second book of the treatises opens with the promise of a more technical treatment. The subject matter of book 1 was relatively easy, Seneca says, but the present book must take up the more difficult question of how anger is generated. In particular, it must consider whether it arises spontaneously or with the consent of the reasoning mind.[13] The latter is the Stoic position, and Seneca has already indicated that it is his as well. Now he must explain what the Stoic claim is meant to refer to within the causal history of anger and other emotions.

As in book 1, Seneca is most interested in defining what mental events count as anger, or "what anger is" (2.2.1). Once again, he proceeds by contrasting reactions that satisfy the criterion for genuine anger from others that do not. This time, however, he is much clearer about what that criterion is. Drawing on the Stoic theory of action, he specifies that anger requires not only an impression that one has been harmed, but also assent to that impression.

> That anger is stimulated by an impression of injury is not in doubt; what we are asking is whether it follows immediately upon the impression itself, rushing forth without the mind's agreement, or whether it is generated when the mind assents. We hold that anger dares nothing on its own; rather, it comes about with the mind giving its approval. For to gain an impression of injury received, and to conceive a desire for revenge, and to link together the two ideas that one ought not to have been harmed and that one ought to take revenge – none of this is characteristic of that impulse that is stirred involuntarily. The one is simple, the other composite, made up of many things: it understands something, thinks it wrong, condemns it, and punishes it. (*Anger* 2.1.3–4)

Here, as in earlier Stoic theory, the word "impression" (*species*) designates a mental event in which one registers some way of seeing the world.[14] The impression already involves some processing of what is registered by the senses, for it is an impression "of injury received"; that is, of the proposition *that I have received an injury*. Still, it is a relatively simple event, one

---

[13] The intent of the passage is clear despite a difficulty with the received text in 2.1.1, *utrum sua sponte moveatur an quemadmodum pleraque quae intra nos insciis nobis oriuntur*. Interpreting *sua sponte* to mean "of their own volition," Reynolds (1977) accepts the insertion of <*non*> ("not") before *insciis*, to establish a contrast between the two classes of phenomena. This is unsatisfactory, however, because *pleraque* ("many things") is surely meant to index the multiplicity of involuntary reactions that will be listed in sections 2.2–3. Kaster and Nussbaum (2010) rejects <*non*> and offers parallels to show that *sua sponte* can mean "of one's own volition."

[14] See page 42.

that Seneca is willing to describe as involuntary.¹⁵ Anger requires more than this: for anger, the mind must link together two or more propositions in the further event known as assent. Actually to become angry is to endorse the conclusion that one should indeed take revenge, and should do so because of the injury one has received. Seneca is thus exactly in accord with Stoic psychology, that makes impression and assent the two basic functions of the rational mind. For him as for earlier Stoics, the impulse that determines how one should act at a given moment is a subspecies of assent, in which one says to oneself either more or less consciously *this is what I should do now*.¹⁶

A long list of examples in sections 2.2 and 2.3 aids the reader in mapping Seneca's theoretical distinction onto the manifold gradations of experience. There are many reactions that are at least quasi-emotional in nature, from autonomic responses like vertigo to high-level cognitive events like blushing at obscene language or bristling at potentially bad news. For Seneca, though, none of these qualifies as an emotion unless it accompanies the formation of the relevant belief. One may experience a momentary dampening of spirits at the passing of a funeral procession, but real grief is more than that. In the same way, there may be a flash of irritation even in that moment when the thought that one may have been wronged first crosses the mind, but this is not yet anger.

> Hence that first agitation of mind, the one instilled by the impression of injury, is not anger, just as the impression of injury itself is not. The impulse that follows, which does not merely receive the impression but also endorses it – that is anger: the agitation of a mind that moves toward revenge through volition and judgment. (*Anger* 2.3.5)

---

¹⁵ The "impulse that is stirred involuntarily" (*impetus qui sine voluntate nostra concitatur*) in *Anger* 2.1.4 is not equivalent to the ὁρμή of Stoic moral psychology. *Impetus* is used in an attenuated sense, for want of any better term for such low-level mental events. By contrast, *Anger* 2.3.4 states firmly that an *impetus* (properly so called) can never occur without the mind's assent.

¹⁶ While there is broad agreement among scholars that Seneca's anger theory in book 1 is essentially Chrysippan, there is much less agreement about book 2. Concerning the early chapters of book 2, some scholars have questioned whether the position there expressed is compatible with early Stoic doctrine, notably Holler (1934), Fillion-Lahille (1984), and Setaioli (2021). However, the arguments for Senecan heterodoxy, and in particular for Seneca's having adopted a heterox position previously taken by Posidonius, become much weaker when it is recognized that Posidonius is not likely to have been the originator of the pre-emotion concept put forward in *Anger* 2.2–3; on this point, see Graver (1999a). My argument here follows up on that of Graver (2007: 85–93), that Seneca's position in these chapters, if read correctly, is consistent with that of Chrysippus; a view I share with Inwood (2005: 41–64) and Tieleman (2021). This does not preclude Seneca's having made use of Posidonius elsewhere in the treatise; on this point, see note 34 in this chapter.

Anger begins just at the moment when one decides that yes, the situation is such as calls for revenge-taking in some form. At this point, it is appropriate to speak of "volition and judgment" (*voluntate et iudicio*).[17]

Seneca has now gone on for some time on the distinction between a first and a second mental event: first, the involuntary feeling that accompanies a certain kind of impression, and then, with assent to that impression, anger itself. It is thus a bit of a surprise when we are told in 2.4.1 that anger takes us through a series of *three* events.

> Let me tell you how the emotions begin, or grow, or get carried away. The first movement is non-volitional, a kind of preparation for emotion, a warning, as it were. The second has volition, but a non-contumacious volition, like this: *It is appropriate for me to take revenge, since I have been injured;* or *It is appropriate for this person to be punished, since he has committed a crime.* The third movement is now beyond control. It wants to take revenge not if it is appropriate, but no matter what; it has overthrown reason. (*Anger* 2.4.1)

The first of these events is designated as "non-volitional" (*non voluntarius*) and as a sort of premonition (*quaedam comminatio*); this, obviously, is the involuntary feeling that accompanies the impression. But what are the second and third? Prima facie one would expect that the second movement, since it is volitional and a desire for revenge, must be anger itself. This is consistent with its being "removed by judgment" (*iudicio tollitur*, 2.4.2), since it is essential for Seneca that anger will yield to philosophical argumentation.[18] The new addition would then be a further mental event that goes on beyond anger. In favor of this interpretation, one can point out that the third movement is different in character from what Seneca has been saying about the rational nature of anger impulses. For while anger has consistently been linked to the idea that revenge is warranted by another person's actions, this third movement wants revenge "no matter what" (*utique*); and while anger has been tied to the possession of reason, this movement "has overthrown reason" (*rationem evicit*). But we have not yet seen what an impulse that goes beyond anger could consist in.

Some interpreters have argued that the second movement cannot be anger because it is said to have a "non-contumacious volition" (*voluntate non contumaci*).[19] After all, we were told in 1.9.2 that contumacy

---

[17] Compare *Anger* 1.8.1 *voluntate nostra*; 2.4.1 *non voluntarius ... cum voluntate*; similarly Cicero, *Tusc.* 3.64, 3.66, and 3.83. For Seneca's use of volition language, see page 50.

[18] Compare *Anger* 2.2.1 *rationi succumbet* and 2.2.2 *praeceptis fugatur*. The reading offered here is defended in more detail in Graver (2007: 120–32) and (2002c: 225–34).

[19] Sorabji (2000: 61–63); Vogt (2006); Kaufman (2014: 119–26); Gartner (2015: 219–25), Malchow (1986: 48–51).

(*contumacia*) is the very hallmark of anger, its *proprium*.[20] They note also that in the third movement the emotions "get carried away" (*efferantur*), an expression that closely resembles the Greek ἐκφέρεσθαι, used by Chrysippus of the recalcitrance of emotions generally.[21] These interpreters therefore take Seneca to be saying that there is a type of impulse that comes between the involuntary feeling and full-blown anger. There would then be a point in the causal history of anger at which one judges in favor of revenge but is not yet carried away, a *controlled* desire for revenge. This, however, would be a major alteration in Stoic psychology and would present a glaring inconsistency with the position Seneca has defended up to this point. For it has been his contention that one cannot assent to the impression that revenge is called for without proceeding to vengeful conduct – that angry behavior is, precisely, the behavior that comes of such an assent.[22]

The puzzle is solved when we continue on to section 2.5. For Seneca goes on to say that there is indeed a form of behavior that goes on beyond anger.[23] This is what takes place when people have actually gone insane and are no longer reacting to an impression of injury. These are not cases of anger; instead they are *feritas*, brutishness, a non-rational condition like that of a wild animal.[24]

---

[20] For the term *contumacia*, see examples of Seneca's usage in *Constancy* 12.3, *Anger* 2.26.5 (horses), 3.34 (mules), *Clemency* 16.4 (horse); *NQ* 3.30.6 (flood waters); *Letters* 119.2–3 (hunger). For the application of the word to emotion, note especially *Cons. Marc.* 8.1, *Cons. Helv.* 17.1.

[21] As noted in Graver (2007: 131), there is a striking resemblance between this *efferantur*, from *efferri* "to be carried away," and *efferentur*, the corresponding form of *efferari* "to become brutish," a rarer word but one that Seneca uses elsewhere. (Compare especially *Letters* 83.26 *ebrietates continuae efferant animos*.) We should consider the possibility that Seneca actually wrote *efferentur* here, in which case most of the difficulties with the passage disappear. Assuming, though, that *efferantur* is retained, the resemblance creates a chilling play on words, as if the unruliness of anger changes before our very eyes into the incurable wildness of insanity.

[22] Donini (1995: 206–9) is particularly vehement on this point. Gartner (2015) attempts to rescue Seneca's orthodoxy by making the second movement something less than assent. Both Vogt (2006: 57–74) and Kaufman (2014: 119–26) concentrate on the element of rightness or appropriateness in the beliefs of movement two, forgetting that a belief as to the appropriateness of one's action is definitive of anger (cf. *Anger* 2.1.3-4) just as it is of every impulse in Stoicism. To be sure, Seneca also has a category of non-emotive action, which may take the form of dispassionate punishment (*Anger* 1.9.4), but that can hardly be the thought here, where he means to tell "how the emotions grow" (*quomodo adfectus . . . crescant*). Inwood (2005: 61–64) recognizes the second movement as assent to the hormetic proposition, then makes the third movement "the uncontrolled form of this," leaving it unclear in what sense there are *three* successive events.

[23] Most of the confusion in the secondary literature is explained by the habit of treating section 2.5 as a completely new departure, rather than as following naturally from the preceding section. This interpretive move can be traced back to Justus Lipsius (1632) 20. Lipsius recognized that section 2.4 prepares us for an explanation of the *tertius motus* but did not realize that section 2.5 supplies that explanation; consequently, he posited a lacuna; see Malchow (1986: 57–59).

[24] For this concept of *feritas*, compare especially *Ben.* 7.19.7–9.

> And we must still inquire about those people who rage about at random and delight in human blood, whether they are angry when they kill people from whom they have not received any injury and do not believe that they have – people like Apollodorus or Phalaris. This is not anger, but brutishness. For it does not do harm because it has received an injury; rather, it is willing even to receive an injury so long as it may do harm. It does not go after whippings and lacerations for punishment, but for pleasure. (*Anger* 2.5.1–2)

Examples include the tyrants Apollodorus and Phalaris when they killed people for no reason at all, or, just below, the moment when Hannibal saw a ditch full of blood and said "What a beautiful sight!" Such behavior is highly erratic: it lacks even the flawed logic of the angry person.[25] Still, the condition is causally related to anger.

> What then? The origin of this evil is from anger. Once anger has been exercised and satiated so often that it has forgotten about mercy and has cast out every human contract from the mind, it passes in the end into cruelty (*in crudelitatem transit*). (*Anger* 2.5.3)

Seneca, like Epicurus and some other Greek and Roman authors, believes that extreme anger will cause a person to become insane, destroying the rational nature in the same way as alcohol or drugs or mental illness might destroy it.[26] A single episode of anger may thus be a step along the path to the disintegration of our rational condition. Such loss of rationality is an even worse evil than anger, and is incurable.[27]

We can now see why Seneca says here that anger is not contumacious. It is a question of what one contrasts it with. When it is put alongside the ordinary, non-emotional impulses of rational agents, it is indeed contumacious: while it lasts, it does not listen to any other decision. But when contrasted with the erratic violence of an insane person, anger is relatively tractable. The angry person is not in fact behaving like an animal. Actions taken in anger are still driven by a judgment: they arise from the belief

---

[25] Their behavior is attributable to "empty" impressions, as in *Tranq.* 12.5. Seneca's treatment of the subject has some points in common with discussions of brutishness (θηριοτής) in Aristotle (*Nic. Eth.* 7.1, 7.5) and Theophrastus (*apud* Simplicius, *On Aristotle's Categories* 8.235).

[26] Epicurus's statement is reported by Seneca in *Letters* 18.14: *inmodica ira gignit insaniam*. Compare Ennius in Cicero, *Tusc.* 4.52, and compare *Anger* 2.36.5 (on Ajax). See further Gill (1996). For the effect of alcohol, drugs, and mental illness in Stoic theory, see Diog. Laert. 7.127; Simplicius, *On Aristotle's Categories* 102a (*CAG* 402.22–26, *SVF* 3.238).

[27] *Anger* 2.5.5: *non fuit haec ira sed maius malum et insanabile*. While Cicero in *Tusc.* 3.11 speaks of custodial care for those who cannot manage their own affairs, Seneca in *Anger* 1.16.3 suggests that such individuals, if they have committed acts of violence, should be killed, not as punishment but out of pity.

that some particular person, the object of one's anger, has committed an offense and deserves reprisal. Such a judgment is always highly problematic, Seneca thinks. It cannot accord with Stoic values; it is especially resistant to rational correction, and in the end it may even be corrosive to the reasoning faculty itself. But because it is still a judgment, and not the snarl of an animal or the raving of a lunatic, there will be ways for the philosopher to address it.

The Predicted Therapy

We have seen how carefully book 1 and the first part of book 2 work through the Stoic account of what anger is, explaining its essential nature and distinguishing it from other mental events that resemble it in various ways. Before proceeding to the therapeutic treatments recommended in the later parts of *On Anger*, we should now pause to reflect on what therapeutic approach a philosopher of Seneca's commitments would be expected to take. For the view of anger laid out in books 1 and 2 does have some clear therapeutic implications.

The fact that anger is a distinctively rational phenomenon, beyond the reach either of animals or of the insane, implies that anger will yield in one way or another to a well-designed program of argumentation. At the same time, the headstrong and exceptionally violent force of anger means that in most cases it will not be possible to work with a patient who has already become angry. The angry person is not yet irrevocably insane, for he still knows why he acts as he does, and when his feeling abates, he will again be able to listen to reason. But just in this moment, he is not able to reverse the decision he has made. It follows that the prospects of a philosophically grounded therapy for anger are very much dependent on timing. A philosophical teacher who wants his arguments to be effective will need to think about what can be expected from the human mind at each moment in the generation of an angry reaction.

Reviewing Seneca's Stoic account of the causal history of anger, we can identify two periods of time that should be targeted by therapeutic arguments. First, and with perhaps the best prospect of success, one might concentrate on the period before any impression of injury has occurred. Taking this approach, one would try to head off even the opportunity for anger, offering safeguards against it rather than philosophical arguments per se. For instance, one might teach a person to avoid the kinds of situations in which conflicts arise, or to break off connections with the kinds of people who are prone to give offense. Alternatively, one might address the period in which a triggering impression has occurred but the potentially angry person has not yet given assent to it. This second approach would intervene in the process of practical reasoning that converts the impression of injury into an impulse to take revenge. In effect, the therapist would grant that an impression of injury will sometimes occur, but would offer reasons not to assent to it; that is, not to conclude that revenge-taking is called for. These reasons might have been taught to the pupil ahead of time, or they might be offered in the moment of deliberation itself.

In fact it is possible to be even more specific about the elements of practical reasoning that this second approach would need to address. Seneca's remarks about assent in book 2 suggest that he is familiar with a typical Stoic analysis of the reasoning that underlies all instances of emotion. In order to generate anger, he says, one needs not only to have the impression that an offense has occurred, but also "to link together the two ideas that one ought not to have been harmed and that one ought to take revenge" (2.1.4). This is quite similar to the general version of the pathetic syllogism that can be reconstructed for the Hellenistic Stoics.[28] In the general Stoic account, an impression of one's present circumstances links up with two beliefs already resident in the mind: first, an evaluative belief that objects of a certain type are either good or bad for oneself; and second, a belief that it is appropriate to respond to such objects in an emotional way. All three components are needed in order to yield the conclusion that one ought to respond emotionally in the present circumstances. Consequently, it should be possible to eliminate the emotional response by refuting any one of them. Thus, Chrysippus, in seeking effective remedies for grief, suggests that the philosopher should leave alone the evaluative belief that the death of a family member is bad, which would be difficult to address in a time of bereavement, and instead argue against the belief that grief is the appropriate response.[29]

Although Seneca's anger-specific treatment of assent is less neat than the Chrysippan analysis, it proceeds along the same lines. Again, the key step in generating the emotion is the linking of a new impression to at least two prior beliefs. The first belief, that *I ought not to be harmed*, corresponds to Chrysippus's evaluative belief, and arguably is a belief of the same kind, in that it implies a certain way of thinking about harm and about one's own

---

[28] The general version of the pathetic syllogism is laid out in Graver (2007: 35–48), drawing on Cicero, *Tusc.* 3.24–25, 3.61, 4.14–15, Diog. Laert. 7.111–14, and Stobaeus 2.7.10b, 90 Wachsmuth (*SVF* 3.394).

[29] Cicero, *Tusc.* 4.60; cf. 3.76, 79. Compare the fragment quoted by Origen, *Cels.* 8.51 (*SVF* 3.474) concerning the emotions generally, and see Tieleman (2003: 166–70); Graver (2007: 198–99).

worth. The second belief, that *I ought to seek revenge* because of the slight, concerns the appropriate response. As in the Chrysippan account, an effective strategy for preventing the emotion would be to reverse one or the other of these dispositional beliefs so that a new impression of injury will not result in an impulse to take revenge. If the impulse can be prevented, all is well: the person may have become agitated to some extent by the impression itself, but that agitation would have been only the involuntary or first movement.

The one thing that we would not expect to find in an approach based on Seneca's Stoic analysis is a therapy meant for the period after assent, when the impulse toward revenge has already been set in motion. From what Seneca has said, it seems clear that once assent has been given, the angry person is difficult or impossible to address. Although anger is intrinsically a rational phenomenon, its vehemence is such as to override arguments to the contrary, even more than is the case with other emotions like fear or grief. Even if the therapist were to persuade an angry person that revenge is not a good idea, he or she is not likely to be able to stop what has been set in motion. As soon as real anger begins, therefore, the intelligent therapist will not waste his efforts on a lost cause. Perhaps if the offense is minor and the feeling very mild, there might be some point in making the attempt, but those are relatively unimportant cases. With full-blown, vigorous anger, his only recourse is to wait until the full force of the impulse has expended itself and then begin afresh, hoping things will go better the next time around.

The Therapies of Book 2

The question then is whether Seneca adheres to this philosophically grounded program for anger management in his own therapeutic endeavors. It appears at first that he will not. At the midpoint of book 2, just where he turns from the theoretical to the practical treatment of his subject, he offers the following statement of purpose:

> Having now dealt with the inquiries into the nature of anger, let us proceed to the remedies for it. In my view there are two: that we not fall into anger, and that we do no wrong when in anger. Just as in caring for our bodies there are precepts for preserving health and different ones for restoring it, so we should use one method to prevent anger and another to curb it. In order for us to avoid it, there are some precepts that concern the whole of life; these are divided into the bringing up of children and the stages of life that follow. (*Anger* 2.18.1)

The promise given here is to instruct the reader not only on methods of avoiding anger, but also on methods for controlling anger after it has begun. The words "that we do no wrong when in anger" (*ne in ira peccemus*) clearly imply the mitigation of a full-fledged desire for revenge, as does the medical analogy and the word "curb" (*compescere*). This is the very objective that ought to be impossible according to Seneca's stated views on the nature of anger.[30] However, the paragraph also indicates that this second objective is to be deferred until later in the project. The immediate aim, according to the last sentence of the paragraph, is only to show how to avoid getting angry in the first place. Seneca has planned for his treatise to include some advice that is in conflict with his philosophical position, but he does not promise to deliver that advice right away.

And in fact the remainder of book 2 is devoted entirely to the aim of keeping any angry impulse from forming. Seneca first concerns himself with methods of child-rearing, aiming to forestall the development of any pronounced tendency toward angry reactions. He freely admits that some individuals are biologically disposed to hot-temperedness, through the particular balance of humors they are born with. He thinks, though, that such "beginnings and causes" (*initia causaeque* 2.20.2) can be counteracted by physical regimen, for instance by restricting the child's diet and by assigning hard work and games in alternation.[31] And all children, regardless of initial temperament, will be less inclined to anger if their upbringing fosters an appropriate sense of self. By ensuring that privileges are tied to good behavior, by not indulging every whim, and by scolding any shortcomings, parents can teach their children to properly evaluate their own worth and thus to refrain from taking offense for trivial causes.

He then turns to suggestions for how to prevent anger in adults. Here his reliance on a Stoic-influenced account of the pathetic syllogism is very much in evidence. As we have seen, that account sees the anger response as depending on a combination of the impression that one has been wronged with two dispositional beliefs, the belief that one ought not to have been injured and the belief that one ought to react in a certain way, that is, by seeking revenge. Taking these in order, Seneca first offers a series of considerations to weigh against the impression of injury itself. If one

---

[30] Setaioli (2021) notes the discrepancy and takes it as support for his thesis that book 2 in particular draws material from Posidonius. See note 34 in this chapter.

[31] Although the material on temperaments in *Anger* 2.19–20 is not specific to Stoicism, there is no need to believe, with Braicovich (2015), that it is a Senecan innovation. Earlier Stoics had allowed for antecedent causes of temperament: see Graver (2007: 170), referring especially to Chrysippus in Cicero, *De Fato* 7–9.

considers the matter carefully, one may realize that no injury has in fact occurred. The report of someone's behavior could have been false, or a chance remark could have been misconstrued, or the supposed offense might have been unwilling and unintended.[32] Next, we are given reasons to think that there may have been nothing unfair in our being slighted: we might have received the same treatment as others, or we might have done something to deserve the harsh treatment. From these points, Seneca turns in 2.31.6 to the third required premise, the belief that aggressive, vengeful behavior is the appropriate response to an injury. Appealing to widely shared beliefs about community and the kinship of all human beings, he argues that it is inherently wrong to harm another person. Further, he denies that revenge is either pleasurable or advantageous to oneself, citing anecdotes from history and literature as counterexamples. Toward the end of the book, he also stresses the sheer ugliness that anger imparts to one's outward appearance and by extension to the mind itself.

The book ends with a reminder that responding with anger may also endanger one's sanity. "Many people have continued from anger directly into madness," Seneca says, "and have never got back the mind they drove out" (2.36.5).[33] He cites the mythological example of Ajax, whose anger over the arms of Achilles unseated his reason, bringing on a hallucinatory killing spree followed by suicide. The passage reiterates what was said in 2.5.3 about the causal link between anger and insanity, remarking, "It was insanity that drove Ajax to suicide – and it was anger that drove him to insanity." But the difference between those two states is not stated as clearly as it was in the earlier passage. At this point, Seneca is no longer seeking to define what anger is; he is more interested in exposing its similarity to the insane condition.

There can be no doubt that the therapeutic recommendations of book 2 incorporate some material from earlier works on anger. Considering how many anger management treatises were available for Seneca to read, it is quite possible that his array of tactics for preventing anger draws not only on Stoic authors like Chrysippus and Posidonius but also on authors from outside the Stoic tradition.[34] A number of the tactics Seneca suggests have

---

[32] Intent (*consilium*) is a precondition for injury: *Anger* 2.26.4.
[33] *Anger* 2.36.5. *Multi continuaverunt irae furorem nec quam expulerant mentem umquam receperunt* (for the dative in *irae*, see *OLD* s.v. *continuo₂* 1b).
[34] Speculation about Seneca's sources was the primary occupation of an older generation of scholarship. Fillion-Lahille (1984) gives a résumé of the main arguments and contributes her own, not always convincing, account. A case in point is her list of similarities between remarks in the surviving portions of Philodemus's treatise *On Anger* and the first four chapters of Seneca's book

nothing specifically Stoic about them. The point of interest, though, is that he has made a serious effort to fit what he says in book 2 into a Stoic framework. His remarks are organized in accordance with the propositional analysis of 2.1.4, and they refrain from any attempt to curb anger while it is in progress. If there is to be such an attempt, it must be in book 3.

The Preface to Book 3

We will see before long that book 3 does indeed take up Seneca's unfulfilled promise to provide techniques for limiting or controlling active episodes of anger. At the opening of the book, however, we find no mention of any such purpose. On the contrary, everything from the beginning down through 3.5.1 seems intended to convince the reader that restraining anger in progress is simply not an option.

Some readers have taken the very first sentence of book 3 for a restatement of the objectives listed in the *divisio* at 2.18.1.[35] On close reading, however, the natural sense of Seneca's words is at odds with this assumption. Seneca writes,

> *Quod maxime desiderasti, Novate, nunc facere temptabimus, iram excidere animis aut certe refrenare et impetus eius inhibere.*
>
> We will now attempt to do what you wanted most of all, Novatus: to excise anger from our minds, or at any rate to bridle it and inhibit its attacks. (*Anger* 3.1.1)

3: these are certainly not fortuitous, but neither can they be claimed as evidence of direct dependence, since both authors were familiar with multiple earlier works in a tradition rife with commonplaces. The same is true for the treatise by Sotion of Alexandria that is attested by several brief quotations in Stobaeus (see Garbarino (2003: 146)) and favored as a source by Fillion-Lahille (1984: 261–72) and earlier by Rabbow (1914: 82–83); see also Huber (1973: 127). We have no compelling reason to believe that Sotion of Alexandria is the same person as the Sotion whom Seneca names in *Letters* 49.2 and 108.17–22 as his teacher and the inspiration for his youthful vegetarianism; in any case, note that Sotion of Alexandria's remark on feigning quoted in Stobaeus 3.20.54a is actually contradicted by the Senecan passage at *Anger* 2.17.1. Given Seneca's doctrinal commitments, we should assume that his principal influences were works on anger within the Stoic tradition, quite possibly including those by Antipater of Tarsus (*SVF* 3 p. 257) and/or Posidonius (fragment 36 Edelstein and Kidd), either of which might also have supplied information about Chrysippus's position. For Posidonius, note the citation of his definition in *Anger* 1.2.3, and see Setaioli (2021), with note 16 in this chapter. Other treatises Seneca may possibly have consulted include the work by Aristotle mentioned in Diog. Laert. 5.23, and others by Hieronymus of Rhodes and Bion of Borysthenes; for these see Kidd (1998: vol. 1, 178–79) and in more detail Setaioli (1988: 141–52).

[35] Interpreters who make this assumption include Fillion-Lahille (1984: 283–94), Cupaiuolo (1975: 70), Kaster and Nussbaum (2010: 9). An exception is Ramondetti (1996).

In that the sentence states two goals, it bears some resemblance to the rhetorical device of the *divisio*. But standard rhetorical practice does not place a *divisio* in the opening sentence of a book. Moreover, the sentence does not have the balanced structure that normally characterizes a *divisio*. Instead, it states a primary goal that is what Novatus wants most of all, and then a secondary goal to be aimed at if the first cannot be achieved. This is aspiration; it is not an outline of the book that follows. The goal of excising anger from our minds (*iram excidere animis*) is more ambitious than that of avoiding active episodes of anger: it suggests the complete elimination of that mental trait that inclines a person to experience anger.[36] But if this preferred goal cannot be achieved, then one still has the option "to bridle it and inhibit its attacks." The verb *refrenare*, "to bridle," is perhaps ambiguous; it is at least plausible, though, that it states a goal of preventing any outburst of anger.[37] Seneca is saying that if one cannot eliminate the underlying disposition toward anger, then what one should try to do is to hinder the disposition from being actively exercised. Thus the first objective from 2.18.1 (to prevent anger, *repellere*) becomes a subordinate goal for book 3, while the second (to curb it, *compescere*) is not mentioned at all. There is, as yet, no promise to tell Novatus how to arrest an angry outburst in mid-career.

And in fact it is this way of stating the objectives that accords with the continuation of the preface. There, Seneca is far from granting that there is some means of controlling an occurrent episode of anger. If the feeling is merely a mild irritation, one might be able to combat it openly; in the more serious cases, however, the therapist must work behind the scenes (*ex occulto*, 3.1.1) or simply retreat until the storm is past. For of all the emotions, anger is the most refractory, the least receptive to argument. Other emotions can at least pause for reflection, but anger, Seneca says, is at full force from the moment it begins: it does not merely trouble our minds, but carries them off. All this is just what he needs to say to contend against the Peripatetic position on the usefulness of anger, which he now restates from book 1. As before, he objects particularly to the claim that anger should be retained within limits because it is useful, a "spur to courage" whose removal would render one "weaponless and ill-suited for

---

[36] Seneca's later account of emotive traits of character in *Letters* 75.8–15 makes it clear that one could rid oneself of the vice of irascibility but still occasionally experience the emotion of anger. See page 52.

[37] The conjunction *et* ("and") functions epexegetically, as often in Latin: the phrase *et impetus eius inhibere* does not add a third goal, but rather explains the metaphor in *refrenare*.

any great endeavor."[38] Countering this view, he argues that anger is in its very nature illimitable. If one experiences it at all, one is susceptible to all its dangers. The best option will be to get rid of it.

In keeping with his argument, Seneca fills this preface with an extraordinary range of figurative language. Anger is like some powerful natural force, a fire or a thunderstorm or a flood. It burns us, sweeps us away, plunges us into the pit.[39] It is a fierce animal that cannot always be beaten back with the whip, a biting animal that sinks its teeth into itself, a crazed mount that has slipped the bridle, a monster, a brute.[40] Itself ungovernable, anger renders us unfree: an angry person is not powerful, as some suppose, but is a captive of the emotion.[41] This powerful language creates an interesting puzzle concerning the term "brutishness" in section 3.3.2, with its related remarks on insanity and self-destructive behavior.[42] The word brutishness (*feritas*) was used also in book 2; in the earlier passage, however, anger and brutishness were said to be distinct states. "This is not anger, but brutishness," Seneca says in 2.5.2, and remarks that the mind of a Hannibal or a Phalaris is no longer responding to a perceived slight. Here, by contrast, he speaks of brutishness as an attribute of anger, saying, "it is necessary to expose the foulness and brutishness of anger."[43] Despite the similarity of language, it is clear throughout the later passage that the behavior Seneca is now targeting still belongs to the passion of anger that Aristotle and his followers seek to defend. Frenzied as it may become, it is anger-madness, not madness itself.

The twinning of terms may be compared with the dual definition for cruelty (*crudelitas*) that Seneca gives in *On Clemency* 2.4. There he is primarily interested in the sort of cruelty that stands in opposition to the virtue of clemency, when someone who is in a position to punish tends to be excessively severe. This is a characteristic of rational agents and needs to be distinguished from the sort of cruelty that causes pain not as punishment for any offense but just for the pleasure of it, as was said to be the case with the tyrant Busiris and the highwayman Procrustes. That second form of cruelty is a subrational condition, which Seneca says may also be

---

[38] *Anger* 3.3.1. Compare *Anger* 1.7.1, 1.9.2, 1.17.1. For the limitation strategy, note also *Anger* 3.42.1: *quod enim malae rei temperamentum est?*
[39] *Anger* 3.1.1 *ardet . . . secum ferat*; 3.1.4 *praecipitat*; 3.1.5 *deiectus animorum est.*
[40] *Anger* 3.1.1 *reverberanda et agenda retro*; 3.1.5 *in se ipsa morsus suos vertit*; 3.3.6 *rabies effrenata*; 3.3.2 *quantum monstri . . . feritatem.* The comparison to animal behavior here has been insightfully treated in Berno (2021).
[41] *Anger* 3.4.4 *ne liber quidem dici possit irae suae captivus.*
[42] *Anger* 3.3.2 *furens . . . non sine pernicie sua perniciosus.*
[43] *Anger* 3.3.2: *necessarium est itaque foeditatem eius ac feritatem coarguere.*

termed "brutishness" (*feritas*) or "insanity" (*insania*).[44] Thus, while the two conditions resemble each other and can be referred to by the same name, they are fundamentally different and carry different moral implications. The same is true of the brutishness of anger in *On Anger* book 3.3.2: it resembles the bestial condition of the criminally insane and yet is not that condition. There is still a place for therapy – provided that therapy does not attempt to do the impossible.

The Therapeutic Program of Book 3

The question is what more Seneca believes his philosophical therapy can achieve. Although he promised in section 2.18 to deliver strategies for curbing an active episode of anger, he has thus far concentrated only on means of prevention. It is of interest, then to read the formal *divisio* that immediately follows the preface to book 3. Once again, he promises Novatus a means of arresting anger after it has begun:

> But since the first aim is not to become angry, the second to cease from anger, and the third to remedy another's anger as well, I will explain first how we may keep from falling into anger; second, how we may rid ourselves of anger, and finally how we may restrain and placate the angry person and bring him back to sound mind. (*Anger* 3.5.2)

There is now no ambiguity. The first objective, Seneca says, is to prevent anger from occurring in oneself; then, separately, there is the objective "to cease from anger" (*desinere*); and third, an objective to placate anger in others. The aims are then restated: Seneca wants to show not only "how we may keep from falling into anger," but also "how we may rid ourselves of anger" (*quemadmodum nos ab illa liberemus*), as well as how to soothe other people. It should be noted that success in the second of these objectives would invalidate much of what was said in book 1 and again in the preface to book 3 about the impossibility of curbing anger within oneself. But Seneca does not appear to be troubled by this flaw in his reasoning; at least not yet. It may be, though, that there is a discrepancy between the aims he lays out for his book and the actual content of his discussion. We should therefore consider what recommendations he has to offer in the remainder of book 3.

---

[44] *Clemency* 2.4.2. For cruelty as bloodlust, compare *Clemency* 1.25.1; also *Anger* 1.6.4, where taking pleasure in punishment is called *inhumana feritas*. It is interesting that in the continuation of *Clemency* 2.4.2, Phalaris is offered as an instance of the vicious but rational condition, whereas in *Anger* 2.5 he exemplifies the insane condition.

Since the first aim is once again to prevent anger from occurring, one would expect Seneca to proceed at first in the same vein as the latter portion of book 2. It is thus not surprising that the paragraphs following the *divisio* urge us to consider "all the faults of anger": how it costs us money, loses elections, ruins marriages, and in general comes up short of what is best in human existence. This gambit recalls that of book 2, sections 32–35, which seek to preclude assent to the anger-inducing impression by reversing the belief that anger is sometimes an appropriate response. Also reminiscent of book 2 is the gambit that begins at 3.6.3, where Seneca offers advice for keeping oneself clear of situations in which an offense might be given. He suggests, for instance, that one should reduce the number of activities in the day, so as to limit the possibility of some offense that might "prepare the mind for anger" (*in iras paret*). Similarly, he advises readers to choose tasks that are within their capabilities, to avoid people who might be annoying, to withdraw from any discussion that is becoming heated, and to avoid unneeded frustration, irritation, and fatigue (3.7.1–3.9.5). This entire group of recommendations is essentially prophylactic, in that it seeks to prevent even the impression that an injury has occurred. Again, the aim is to keep oneself from becoming angry, rather than to rid oneself of an active episode of anger.

It appears inevitable that at some point Seneca must finish with the first of his three objectives and take up the second. However, the text provides us with no indication of where that transition takes place. Most modern editions make some kind of division just before 3.10.1, where Seneca says, "The best thing, then, is to heal oneself at the first perception of evil, then to give a minimum of freedom to one's own words and check the impulse."[45] As a marker of transition, however, this is entirely arbitrary and unconvincing. If one reads carefully the sequence of thought from 3.9.5 to 3.10.1, it is clear that there is no new departure at that point. Seneca has been describing the beginnings of a quarrel, using a medical metaphor and speaking of the "littlest things" (*minimis*) that seem provoking when one is tired, hungry, or thirsty. This idea continues in 3.10.1, where the words *primum mali sensum* ("the first perception of harm") pick

---

[45] Bourgery (1922) indicates a division at this point, as do Cooper and Procope (1995), Wildberger (2007: 315) and somewhat reluctantly Kaster and Nussbaum (2010: 122 n282). Cupaiuolo (1975: 70) laments the lack of clarity as concerns the transition to the second theme. In general, it is important in reading Seneca's works not to assume that the section numbers inserted by the earliest printers accurately represent the structure of his thought. For the history of these divisions, see Cupaiuolo (1975: 78–79).

up on the idea in *minimis*, and *mederi sibi* ("cure oneself") and *morborum signa* ("symptoms") continue the medical metaphor. The sentences that follow have to do again with methods of keeping anger from beginning, not with methods of controlling it after it begins. Thus we find in 3.10.2–4 a brief reprise of the preliminary feelings discussion from book 2, drawing the therapeutic application,[46] while 3.10.4 and 3.11.1 continue the discussion of how to head off the initial impression that an offense has occurred. So if there is a transition, it must take place somewhere after 3.11.1.

Some scholars have accordingly identified a transition point either right after 3.11.1 or somewhere in 3.12 or 3.13.[47] At none of these points, however, do we find a clear intention of transitional intent like what we see at 3.5.3 and later at 3.39.1. And even if one were to identify a point where a structural marker has dropped out or been obscured, that would not be enough to establish the orderly arrangement of ideas that was implied by the *divisio*. There simply is not any major division of the book that is devoted to methods for restraining anger. The train of thought moves backward and forward, sometimes favoring narrower standards for what counts as an offense, sometimes urging us not to yield to the earliest stages of anger, sometimes attacking the dispositional beliefs that incline us to assent.[48] Meanwhile, the vivid narratives of sections 3.14–23, though given specious justification at 3.13.7 and 3.24.1, in fact provide almost nothing in the way of practical guidance.

It is instructive to read through sections 3.10–38 looking specifically for recommendations on how to stop one's anger after it has begun. There is, in fact, very little that addresses this point directly. Instead, we are told a great deal about how to reassess a situation so as not to see the other person's actions as an affront. This is helpful advice, but it is not advice for restraining anger; rather, it seeks to prevent anger from coming into being. By contrast, the anecdotes of Praxaespes, Harpages, and others do tell us

---

[46] One can emphasize the linguistic similarities between *Anger* 3.10.2, with its "symptoms" and "premonitions" (*morborum signa ... quaedam praenuntia*) and specific expressions in book 2: at 2.2.5 "beginnings that precede the emotions" (*principia proludentia affectibus*); at 2.4.1 a "preparation and a certain warning" (*praeparatio affectus et quaedam comminatio*).

[47] Ramondetti (1996) and Huber (1973: 104) favor 3.12.4; this is perhaps the best answer philosophically, but note the lack of transitional sentence as well as the repeated wording from 3.12.2 *nemo ... atqui*. Fillion-Lahille ((1984) 288–89) argues for 3.13.1, emending the text, but see the deeper analysis of the passage in Malaspina (2020, 2021).

[48] Tightening of standards for instance at *Anger* 3.11.1–12.3, urging not to yield to the earliest stages for instance at 27.4–5, attacking general dispositional beliefs for instance at 3.29.2.

how anger may be restrained – namely, by fear; but one can hardly read this as a recommendation.[49]

The one stretch of text where Seneca does offer suggestions on how to deal with a full-blown anger impulse is in sections 3.12–13. In 3.12.4, he begins speaking of the importance of delaying one's retaliation:

> The greatest remedy for anger is delay, so that its initial heat may subside and the fog that oppresses the mind may clear or become less dense. A day, or even an hour, will mitigate some of the things that were carrying you away; others will vanish altogether. (*Anger* 3.12.4)

At this point the anger impulse is already in full swing: it is in its "initial heat" (*primus fervor*); it is a "fog that oppresses the mind" (*caligo quae premit mentem*); the provocations "were carrying you away" (*te praecipitem ferebant*). The same situation is implied in the continuation of the paragraph, where Seneca retells an old story about Plato. Plato grows angry with his slave and orders him to prepare for a beating, then freezes with his hand in midair; and when a friend asks what he is doing, he replies, "I am punishing an angry person."[50] Finally he instructs his nephew Speusippus to punish the slave, saying, "I am angry (*irascor*), and I will beat him too much or too eagerly." Concluding, Seneca recommends, "Do nothing while you are angry (*dum irasceris*). Why? Because you want to do everything."[51]

In the same vein, the following section suggests that one should hide one's anger, "for if it is allowed to reveal itself outside us, it gets the better of us" (3.13.2). Again, the plain sense of the passage is that at this point the anger is fully in existence: after all, one cannot hide what does not exist.[52] An alternative is to authorize one's closest friends to intervene if one should become angry, just as those who misbehave when they are drunk might prearrange with friends to escort them home from a party. Naturally, the arrangement has to be made ahead of time, "while we are lucid and in control of ourselves" (3.13.4).

Now, suggesting that an irascible person seek assistance from friends is very much in conformity with Seneca's earlier statements that anger

---

[49] *Anger* 3.14.3–4, 3.15.3–4. For the possibility that one emotion might be displaced by another, see also *Anger* 1.10.1, *Letters* 13.12, and compare Cicero, *Tusc.* 3.66. See further Kaufman (2014: 111–18).

[50] *Anger* 3.12.5–7. For other uses of the anecdote, see Harris (2002: 317–36), and within *On Anger* compare the Socrates anecdote in 1.15.3.

[51] *Anger* 3.12.7. Delay is also emphasized in book 2, especially in 2.29.1. There, however, the delay is prior to assent, as in Epictetus, whereas 3.12.4 has in view a delay after assent but before retaliation.

[52] I owe this observation to Jula Wildberger (personal communication).

cannot be controlled by the one who is angry. But this is not the case with the counsels of delay and of concealment. In these two recommendations, Seneca appears to be thinking of anger in a way that is incompatible with the position he stated in books 1 and 2.[53] One can compare especially section 2.3.4:

> Someone thought he was injured and wanted to get revenge, but immediately settled down when some reason persuaded him otherwise: I do not call this anger, this movement of the mind in obedience to reason. Anger is that movement that overleaps reason and drags reason along with it. (*Anger* 2.3.4)

Here, the person who refrains from acting on a wish for revenge is simply not angry. If the reaction is obedient to reason, if it settles down when one sees an argument against it, then it is not anger but only a preliminary agitation. In 3.12.4–13.6, by contrast, a person can be fully angry in thought alone. It is now possible for the angry person to prevent his emotion from moving even into the face, let alone into the realm of action. Like Plato, he can keep a full-blown anger impulse to himself while he decides whether his anger will have any deleterious effect. In a word, he has a stopping-place – the very thing that Stoic theory had denied him.

One might try to rescue Seneca's theoretical position by claiming that in these sections, Seneca is referring all along to the involuntary feeling that precedes assent. In support, one would point out that the verb *irascor* can have inchoative force: "begin to be angry" rather than "be angry." What Plato feels would thus be only the beginnings of anger, not anger itself, and the same would be true of the person who successfully hides his anger. But *irascor* is the preferred verb throughout the treatise, used in many contexts where the argument requires it to refer to genuine anger. To insist on an inchoative sense here would be to charge Seneca with a very confusing equivocation. On the whole I think it is better to admit that in this passage Seneca is just inconsistent with his earlier stance. He tries to fulfill the promise he made in 3.5.2, but cannot do so without contradicting his own view.

In his favor, one can say that this stretch of text is quite brief and finds no corroboration later in the treatise. Immediately afterward, the discussion veers off into the historical anecdotes of 3.13.7–23.8, and when those are over, it returns not to the counsels of delay and concealment, but to further advice of the kind we saw in the second half of book 2: find reasons to

---

[53] The conflict with early Stoic psychology is noted in Huber (1973: 104–5, 124–27), and in Setaioli (2021).

overlook the offense, don't assume it was intentional, remember how dangerous anger is, think of more appropriate responses, work on one's underlying disposition. Once more Seneca advises his readers not to accept the view that vengeful conduct is appropriate, and hence not to become angry at all. We hear nothing more about stopping anger after it has begun.

The inconclusive treatment of the second objective stands in contrast to the concise and firm handling of the third objective in 3.39–40. There, we find a clear transitional sentence, and Seneca's treatment of the theme makes explicit reference to the points that have already been made about the inability of angry persons to listen to reason. Because anger is "deaf and unthinking," the therapist "will not dare to caress it with speeches"; instead, he will "give it room" (3.39.2). Just as one allows an inflammation of the eyes or any similar condition to subside before attempting treatment, so one should allow the angry person to calm down a bit before offering advice. If it is possible to affect his behavior at all, it will be by deception, or, if one is in a position of power, by exercise of authority. For instance, one might pretend to be angry oneself but advise a tactical delay in implementing revenge; or, if one is a ruler like Augustus, one might use force to frighten the angry person into submission. What one cannot do is ally oneself with any resources *within* the person who is experiencing the full force of anger. It seems now that there are no such resources.

***

In this chapter I have sought to determine whether the Seneca of *On Anger* is a consistent thinker, in two ways: first, whether his theoretical position is in accordance with the Stoicism he professes; and then, whether the therapeutic program he outlines is in conformity with the theoretical view he has laid out. For in this work we see not only his first extensive efforts to explain a challenging philosophical position to his reading public, but also some of his earliest attempts at translating that position into specific applications. In order to call his project an unqualified success, one would like to see that there is, at least, no conflict between the advice he gives and the theoretical view to which he claims allegiance. Even where he draws material from older works, he should exercise authorial control in the selection and arrangement of that material so as to bring it into conformity with his Stoic view of anger.

What we have seen is that even on a charitable reading, there are some elements of *On Anger* that are at odds with their alleged theoretical foundation. However, these elements play only a very limited role. Both in book 2 and in book 3 Seneca states as one of the aims of his therapy the control of angry impulses in progress, an objective that his Stoic theory of anger regards as impossible. But this goal is not actually implemented in book 2, and although there is an attempt at implementation in book 3, it is handled in a much less focused and confident way than the book's other therapeutic objectives. Seneca never tells us when he means to begin addressing the topic, and when he finally does so, he speaks hastily and unconvincingly, then does everything he can to divert attention from what he has said.

We can read this weakness in the argumentative structure of book 3 as an indication of unease, an awareness of having arrived at an impasse. Seneca has tried to deliver on what he considers to be the standard objectives of an anger treatise, but he realizes, perhaps too late, that these are at odds with the theoretical position he has endorsed. No doubt following the example of earlier works on the subject, he has promised to provide techniques for mastering one's own anger; but at his intellectual core, he is reluctant to deliver on that promise and gives it short shrift. The result is not entirely satisfactory from a philosophical standpoint. We do not see here the disciplined philosopher of the *Letters on Ethics*, in full control of his creative medium, ready to engage his Peripatetic opponents in elaborate debates on emotion theory, as he does in letters 85 and 116, or to devise a new Stoic approach to the management of emotion, as he does in letter 99. Yet already in *On Anger* we see him beginning to develop the habits of mind that will enable him to do those things in the work of his maturity.

CHAPTER 7

The Weeping Wise
Stoic and Epicurean Consolations in Seneca's 99th Letter

The consolatory letters and treatises of antiquity are not, on the whole, philosophically ambitious. They may appeal to What Philosophy Says, but their content usually tends toward platitudes of general application, such as will find ready acceptance with the bereaved and perhaps provide some comfort. Yet consolation does sometimes cross-fertilize with serious intellectual endeavor. We can identify instances in which philosophers of the Hellenistic period refer to the success or failure of particular consolatory techniques to establish a premise in moral psychology. For example, Epicurus rejected on theoretical grounds the tactic of prerehearsal favored by the Cyrenaic hedonists; Carneades challenged Chrysippus on the therapeutic efficacy of quoting a particular passage of Euripides; and Posidonius appealed to the consolatory chestnut about grief diminishing over time to support his own thesis about the causal history of emotion.[1] We might expect, then, that a philosopher with strong interests in moral psychology would at some point explore the possibility of composing a consolatory epistle on a more doctrinal basis, assuaging his addressee's distress while simultaneously defending the position of his school.

This is essentially what we find in Seneca's letter to Marullus, the last and least conventional of his five consolations. Shorter and more focused than the three freestanding consolations of his early period, the work is presented as a long enclosure in the 99th of the *Letters on Ethics*.[2] In keeping with others of Seneca's letters that explore theoretical questions in

---

[1] For Epicurus and the Cyrenaics, see Cicero, *Tusc.* 3.28, 32–35; Diog. Laert 2.89–90; for Carneades and Chrysippus, *Tusc.* 3.59–60; for Posidonius, Galen, *PHP* 4.7.4 (*SVF* 3.481) and 5.6.29–31 (fragments 165(A) and 166 Edelstein and Kidd). See further Graver (2002a: 198, 217–18). For background on the consolatory tradition, see Kassel (1958), Johann (1968), Manning (1981: 12–14), and Scourfield (1993: 15–23).

[2] The three consolatory treatises are dated by Griffin (1976: 395–98) to between 39–49. For a detailed overview of Seneca's consolations, see Manning (1974). Regarding Seneca's approach to the task of consolation within the *Letters on Ethics*, see Wilcox (2012: 157–74).

Stoicism, the letter to Marullus takes a disciplined philosophical line, closely integrated with Seneca's Stoic positions on the emotions and on friendship. Its closest kinship is with letter 63, a consolation addressed to Lucilius himself upon the death of his friend Flaccus. The 99th is, however, considerably more careful than the earlier letter in drawing distinctions between phenomenologically similar forms of affect. Toward its end, the letter also engages in a limited polemic against a recommendation made by Metrodorus, the colleague of Epicurus. Metrodorus, it seems, had written his own consolatory letter along Epicurean lines, mentioning a form of pleasure that exists in the midst of grief. In combatting this claim, Seneca is able to clarify his own position on the affective responses of the wise.

Mourning without Grief

From the outset, Seneca's approach is remarkably bold. In his introductory note to Lucilius, he observes that the enclosed consolation does not conform to the usual model in that it declines to treat its addressee with gentleness. Marullus has lost a young son (a *filius parvulus*, though in view of 99.23 not actually an infant) and is bearing the loss "softly" (*molliter*); that is, with less firmness of self-command than befits a man of estimable character.[3] For this reason Seneca deems that he merits reproach rather than consolation. At least that is what he tells Lucilius, and the opening sentences of the consolation itself are certainly very aggressive:

> Do you expect solace? Here is chastisement. Are you so soft in bearing the death of your son? What would you be doing if you had lost a friend? (*Letters* 99.2)

We should not suppose, however, that this unusual rhetorical gambit is in token of some intention other than that of consoling the addressee.[4] The letter that follows does seek to assuage Marullus's grief; it merely does so in an unusually rigorous way.

---

[3] The word connotes failure to uphold the standard of masculinity and so is rendered by some translators "like a woman"; see page 242. Compare *Letters* 63.13, where Seneca interprets old Roman law to have said that while women may be permitted a year's mourning, there is no period of mourning appropriate to a man.

[4] I have not been convinced by the arguments of Wilson (1997) to this effect. Nor do I see any reason to doubt that Marullus is fully as real as other individuals named in Seneca's letters. It is possible that he was the Junius Marullus who as suffect consul in 63 AD came into conflict with Thrasea Paetus (Tacitus, *Ann.* 14.48.2; the suggestion is made in Griffin (1976: 92, 495)); or he may have been a relative.

The most committed Stoic might have enough tact to make some concessions when dealing with the bereaved; and indeed Seneca's earlier works of consolation regularly give some leeway to grief experienced in moderation.[5] Even letter 63 settles for urging Lucilius not to grieve "excessively" (*plus aequo*): "Not grieve at all? That I will not venture to ask of you, though I know it would be better" (63.1). But the present letter deliberately breaks with that convention (*non sum solitum morem secutus*, 99.1). It takes a stern line, arguing in essence that grief, properly so called, is not the appropriate response to bereavement. Insofar as it is *grief* that Marullus feels, he needs to be corrected. Seneca has no objection to the brief, low-level sensation that he calls a "biting," but a more robust grief has a voluntary aspect to it (*sibi lugere sumpserunt*, 99.1), and Marullus's emotion is at that level.[6] "What you feel is not grief but only a biting: it is you who are making it into grief" (99.14).

Consistent with Stoic values, Seneca denies both implicitly and explicitly that any real evil has befallen Marullus such as would justify his grieving. To modern sensibilities, and to many ancient sensibilities as well, this is a radical view: as Stefan Schorn suggests, it is a position specifically for those with some commitment to philosophy.[7] Thus it is in keeping with the general tenor of the letter when Seneca refers in 99.14 to Marullus's training in philosophy – and does so in a sarcastic manner: "A great lot of good philosophy has done you, if your strength of mind consists in missing a boy who was better known to his wet nurse than to his father!" Strong medicine indeed; but we can see why this form of admonition is thought to be an effective consolatory technique. In effect, Seneca appeals to Marullus's own self-concept, by describing his recent behavior as a temporary departure from his real nature as a morally excellent person. The rhetoric is of a piece with the compliment to Marullus's virtue (or manliness, *virtus*) in the preceding sentence, and with the explanation at the end: "I am sure you have already said all these things to yourself. My purpose was, rather, to chide you for having forgotten yourself for a short time" (99.32).

To develop his case, Seneca appeals repeatedly to the contrasting case of the virtuous person who has lost a lifelong friend. Such a friendship

---

[5] The "moderate emotion" position was especially connected with the Academic and Peripatetic philosophers; nonetheless, Seneca makes the same concession in his consolatory essays: see *Cons. Marc.* 7, *Cons. Polyb.* 18, *Cons. Helv.* 16. See further page 137.
[6] Contra Gloyn (2017: 194), it is not *only* the indulgent and performative element in Marullus's grief that Seneca disapproves of; it is indeed "grief *per se*."
[7] Schorn (2009: 358–61).

instantiates what Seneca considers to be real goods, that is, goods of character; hence this death is a "the greatest loss of all," whereas that of a child whose character is still unformed is merely one of "those illusory troubles at which people groan for the sake of custom" (99.3).[8] Yet even if a friend had died, the bereavement would still not be an occasion for grief; rather, one should rejoice that one has had the privilege of friendship. A fortiori, grief cannot be an appropriate response to the death of the child. There is no occasion for rejoicing, given the absence of positive goods in the relationship, but neither is there any justification for believing oneself harmed. One should bear the loss with equanimity.

Having taken such a strong position, Seneca must now respond to the expected objection that the attitude he recommends is harsh and unfeeling:

> What's this? Am I now advocating harshness? Do I want your countenance to be frozen even at the funeral ceremony – do I forbid you even to experience a contraction of mind? Not at all. That is inhumanity, not virtue: looking upon the bodies of your loved ones with the same expression as beheld them in life, failing to be moved at the first moment when your family is wrenched apart. But suppose I did forbid it: some things are independent of our command. Tears fall even when we try to suppress them, and shedding them is a relief to the mind. (*Letters* 99.15)

The complaint about "harshness" and "inhumanity" is an old one. Cicero credits it to the fourth-century Academic Crantor of Soli, also writing on grief and consolation:

> I cannot by any means agree with those who extol some kind of impassivity (*indolentiam*). Such a thing is neither possible nor beneficial. I do not wish to be ill, but if I am, and if some part of my body is to be cut open or even amputated, let me feel it. This absence of pain comes at a high price: it means being numb in body, and in mind scarcely human.[9]

Crantor's "impassivity" is in Greek ἀπάθεια, a term used both by the Cynic philosophers and, as Cicero knows well, by the Stoics.[10] Seneca does

---

[8] For the value of friendship in Stoicism, see Stobaeus 2.7.11i, 101–2 Wachsmuth (*SVF* 3.626); 2.7.11m, 108 Wachsmuth (*SVF* 3.630); Diog. Laert. 7.124; Cicero, *Fin.* 3.70. Seneca demonstrates his knowledge of the doctrine in letters 9 and 109. On the friend's death, see esp. *Letters* 9.4–5.

[9] Cicero, *Tusc.* 3.12. As the passage is also quoted in Greek in [Plutarch], *Cons. Ap.* 102d, it is likely that Crantor's work was available in Rome in the original language. See Graver (2002a: 187–94).

[10] See the references to *apatheia* in Cynic contexts in Diog. Laert. 4.51, 6.2, 6.15 and in *Cynic Epistle* 12, and compare *Brevity* 14.2 *hominis naturam cum Stoicis vincere, cum Cynicis excedere* ("to conquer human nature with the Stoics, or with the Cynics to go beyond it"). The Cynic version of *apatheia* is treated in detail in Graver (forthcoming).

not concede, however, that the attitude recommended by Stoics amounts to being numb or, worse, inhuman. In letter 9, he had drawn a distinction between Cynic and Stoic meanings of impassivity: the Stoic wise person, he says, "conquers all adversities, but still feels them," whereas the Cynic wise person "does not even feel them" (9.2). His point is that one can be free of grief in the Stoic sense and yet give evidence of humanity through tears, changes of facial expression, and other responses at that level. Such reactions are involuntary, and not to have them would indeed be unnatural, as Crantor says: it would mean that one is insensate, like a stone as in *On the Constancy of the Wise* 10.4. By the same token, one may also experience a "contraction of mind" – the twinge of mental pain – as long as one does not commit to the response, letting it become a voluntary action. The latter is what people do when they conform to cultural expectations of grieving behavior. Loud sobbing, beating oneself on the head, rolling off the couch, and praying aloud for death are all additions to the natural response, conditioned by a morally compromised society. A sign of this is that people cease to behave in such ways when no observers are present. "Without a spectator, grief comes to an end" (99.16).

"A Necessity of Nature"

Confirming his acceptance of involuntary tears, Seneca adds in section 18 that such weeping is also characteristic of the wise person or *sapiens*, that ideal human being who serves as a convenient thought construct for all the ancient schools of ethics after Aristotle. Tears, at least in some form, belong to the condition of virtuous wisdom, even though grief and many of its attendant behaviors do not. The ideal human must be assumed to exhibit every characteristic that is natural in us; ergo, if tears are a natural phenomenon, the wise person will shed them, either willingly or unwillingly:

> The wise man too sheds tears, I believe, sometimes when he allows them to flow and sometimes when they well up of their own accord. I will explain the difference. When we are first assailed by the news of an untimely death, when we are holding the body that is soon to pass directly from our embrace into the flames, tears are squeezed out of us by a necessity of nature: just as the breath, when struck by grief's blow, shakes the entire body, so does it press upon and expel the moisture in the vicinity of the eyes. These tears are shed due to internal pressure, against our will. (*Letters* 99.18–19)

The involuntary tears are the ones that "well up of their own accord." They are expelled from the eyes by a physiological process that begins with the breath, here functioning both as the center of consciousness and as the primary vehicle of all bodily change.[11] Not only does the breath take in "grief's blow" (*ictu doloris*) – that is, the impression of loss, though without assent in this case – but it also operates on the remainder of the body, producing sobs (*totum corpus*) and also the tears. All this is blameless, fully compatible with wisdom and virtue. It is merely a "necessity of nature."

This claim about involuntary tears and "bitings" has deep roots in Stoic thought as attested in other sources. A fragment of Chrysippus quoted by Galen indicates that the Stoic founder had an interest in the causes of involuntary weeping and also of unintended cessation of weeping, which he attributes, obscurely, to certain "impressions" and to the presence or absence of "impediments."[12] More helpful for our purposes, though, is a group of passages that mention tears, mental pain, and "biting" in conjunction with the inner experience of the wise and virtuous person. Plutarch in *On Moral Virtue* 449a provides evidence that Zeno and Chrysippus drew a distinction between actual grief and fear – paradigm cases of emotions – and another, non-culpable level of response for which they employed a special terminology. For Plutarch, this usage is hypocritical, a facile name-switching device meant to gloss over the indisputable fact that Stoics have the same emotions as other people. He writes:

> But when, refuted by their tears and tremblings and changes of colour, they [Zeno and Chrysippus] say, instead of grief and fear, "bitings" and "troublings," and use "eagernesses" as a euphemism for desires, they seem to contrive sophistic switches and shifts away from reality, by their terminology.[13]

Reading through Plutarch's polemic, we can discern that the early Stoics must have offered "biting" as a suitable term for a mental reaction that gives rise to tears, but which is not properly characterized as grief. A similar assertion is to be found in Cicero's third *Tusculan Disputation*, in a passage representing Stoic views. Throughout this portion of his work, Cicero has been explaining why he believes, following the Stoics, that the wise person is not susceptible to grief. Near the end he recapitulates the main points in

---

[11] Compare *Letters* 50.6, quoted on pages 48–49.
[12] Galen, *PHP* 4.7.16–17 (LS 65O, *SVF* 3.466), quoting apparently from Chrysippus's treatise *On Emotions*. See the edition by De Lacy (1978). The fragment is translated in Graver (2007: 90), with some attempt at interpretation.
[13] Plutarch, *On Moral Virtue* 449a. The word "troublings" is my rendering of συνθροήσεις, correcting the MS συνέορσις; for the emendation, see Sorabji (2000: 40).

support of this thesis, saying that grief is "empty," serves no good purpose, and is not in accordance with nature, being caused by false beliefs. At the same time, however, he allows that a lesser response, which he calls "a bite and a small contraction," is natural even in the wise:

> Once this entirely voluntary belief [viz., that grief is appropriate] is removed, distress will be eliminated – the real, unhappy distress, that is, but the mind will still feel a bite and a small contraction from time to time. This last they may indeed call natural, provided they do not use the name "distress." (*Tusc.* 3.83)

It should be noted that "bite" (δῆξις) and "contraction" (συστολή) are also securely attested terms in the usage of both Zeno and Chrysippus for the sensations experienced in the actual emotion of grief.[14] Here, though, as in the Stoic writings criticized by Plutarch, the terms refer to a feeling that lacks the definitive characteristic of grief, namely its belief structure. This feeling is what we might call a *mere* biting or contraction, in a way resembling grief and yet devoid of ethical significance.

Remarkably, both the concept of a non-culpable grief-like response and the specific terminology of "biting" and "contraction" are known also to Philo of Alexandria, the first-century Jewish scholar. Philo finds the Stoic distinctions convenient in his own work of Scriptural exegesis. For instance, it enables him to explain how it is that Abraham, who for Philo is the exemplar of human excellence and ought therefore to be untouched by grief, nonetheless "came there to mourn" for his wife, Sarah (Genesis 25:2).[15] In another passage (on Genesis 9:3), he solves the puzzle of how God can have instructed Noah to consume reptiles – in his system representative of the "poisonous passions" – by arguing that God was not recommending the emotions themselves, but only certain emotion-analogues that he regards as harmless. Instead of grief, which is a poisonous passion, God recommended only "biting" and "contraction."[16]

Admittedly, neither Philo nor Cicero speaks explicitly in these contexts of tears or changes of facial expression; their words concern inner sensations, which are not the same thing. But the expectation that inner sensations of this sort will sometimes be manifested in tears, trembling, paleness and so on, whether or not an actual emotion occurs, is probably implicit in their statements. It is this expectation that underlies the repeated device of the philosopher observing someone's tears or change

---

[14] Plutarch, *On Moral Virtue* 450a; Galen, *PHP* 4.3.2 (LS 65K, *SVF* 1.209); 5.1.4 (*SVF* 3.461).
[15] Philo, *Questions on Genesis* 4.73. See further Graver (2007: 102–7) and (1999).
[16] Philo, *Questions on Genesis* 2.57. See further Graver (1999a: 316–18).

of countenance and refusing to conclude that an emotion has occurred.[17] That device, clearly known to Plutarch, is used also by Origen, who has independent knowledge of Stoic writings, to explain the weeping of Jesus at Gethsemane in Matthew 26:38–39. Because Jesus is fully divine, Origen wants him to be untroubled by any emotion. It is therefore an advantage for him to be able to say that despite his evident agitation, Jesus did not grieve "with the grief of emotion itself."[18] It is in Origen, too, that we find this involuntary reaction labeled *propatheia* ("pre-emotion"), the term that has become standard in modern discussions of this Stoic doctrine.

Seneca has already demonstrated his familiarity with the concept of involuntary affective response on several occasions. As noted in Chapter 6, he explains it in considerable detail in *On Anger* 2.2–3, where tears, changes of expression, trembling, and paleness figure as examples alongside more obviously mental events such as a momentary wish for revenge. Both in *On Anger* and in the *Letters on Ethics*, he lays particular emphasis on the claim that such phenomena are natural and not to be eliminated from human beings.[19] Thus, in *On Anger* 2.2, tears and other quasi-emotional reactions prior to assent are called "things which come about through some requirement of the human condition and which, for that reason, befall even the wisest persons." Similar observations are made in the *Letters on Ethics* in connection with blushing (11.1), changes of color (57.2), trembling, and other corporeal manifestations (71.29). In *Letters* 99.18, as we have seen, the phrase "a necessity of nature" (*naturalis necessitas*) marks the continuation of this theme.

Eupathic Tears?

More surprising is the other form of weeping mentioned in sections 18 and 19. In the passage quoted on page 164, Seneca states that the wise person can shed tears either willingly ("when he allows them to flow") or unwillingly ("when they well up of their own accord"). Continuing in the same paragraph, he writes:

> These tears are shed due to internal pressure, against our will. There are others, though, to which we give egress when we revisit the memory of those we have lost and find an element of sweetness in our sorrow – when

---

[17] As also in the western tradition in Aulus Gellius, *Attic Nights* 19.1, citing Epictetus fragment 9.
[18] Origen, *On Matthew* 902b (*Patrologia Graeca* 12.1741) *non est tristatus tristitia passionis ipsius, sed factus est secundum humanam naturam tantum in ipso principio tristitiae et pavoris.*
[19] See page 141.

> we think of their pleasant conversation, their cheerful company, their devoted service. At that time, the eyes release their tears, just as in joy. These we indulge; the others conquer us. (*Letters* 99.18–19)

While the wise person can and sometimes does weep involuntarily, it is also consistent with wisdom to shed tears in a more deliberate way, "giving them egress" (*exitum damus*), or "indulging" them (*indulgemur*).[20] These willing tears express positive rather than negative feelings: they are a response to the "element of sweetness" that inheres in the memory of the pleasant conversations, the cheerful company, and the devoted services of the departed. They are like tears of joy. As such, they manifest the very attitude Seneca has already identified as the correct response to the death of a friend: rejoicing in the goods one has experienced through the friendship.

For the possible Stoic background to these remarks, we can look to the doctrine of the *eupatheiai* ("good emotions" or "proper feelings"), full-scale affective responses belonging to the Stoic sage.[21] Eupathic responses, like the emotions of the nonwise person, are impulses that come about when an agent assents to impressions concerning objects conceived as either good or evil. For instance, the *eupatheia* of joy is defined as a "well-reasoned elevation" of mind in response to present goods, just as the emotion of delight is defined as an "irrational elevation" in response to present goods. Being impulses, these eupathic responses count as voluntary actions, ones in which the movement consists especially in alterations of the size or shape of one's psyche, that is, of the sensitive breath in the heart region.

This supposition is confirmed by the mention of joy in section 19: "[T]he eyes release their tears, just as in joy" (*tunc oculi velut in gaudio relaxantur*). For joy figures prominently in Seneca's philosophy as that feature of the wise person's inner experience that corresponds to pleasure or delight in the nonwise person. He refers to it often, and he sometimes makes a point of explaining its relation to goods of character.[22] His conception of joy may not be entirely consistent, but it is fair to say that in many contexts, his word *gaudium* is a term of art signaling his familiarity with older Stoic accounts of wise affect.

---

[20] Compare *Letters* 104.3 *Indulgendum est enim honestis adfectibus*.
[21] Cicero, *Tusc.* 4.12–15; Diog. Laert. 7.115; Plutarch, *On Moral Virtue* 449a; see also Plutarch, *Stoic Self-Contradictions* 1037f–1038a. The suggestion that the voluntary tears are eupathic has been made in Reydams-Schils (2005: 140–41).
[22] *Happiness* 4.2–5; *Letters* 23.1–6, 27.2–3, 59.2. See page 180 and following.

As a matter of procedure, I must emphasize that here, as often in Seneca's writing, our best indication that he means to refer to an existing doctrine is less in his exact choice of words than in the inclusion of a key word within the relevant conceptual frame. If he had used the word *gaudium* without clear indications of a philosophical intention, one would not be justified in seeing a reference to eupathic joy. Even in this same letter, Seneca is capable of writing "excessive griefs, like excessive joys, belong to the foolish," where the reference is unquestionably to the pathological delight (ἡδονή) of the nonwise (99.21). Here, though, the philosophical intention is clearly marked, since the response is said to belong to the *sapiens* (99.18) and since it is occasioned by the deceased person's remembered excellence of character. So for Seneca to say that the eyes let themselves go "just as in joy" (*velut in gaudio*) is not an assertion that these tears manifest anything other than joy itself. What is at issue is the full-scale eupathic response, which the nonwise ("we" as well as Marullus) should approximate as best we can.

If this analysis is correct, it tells us something interesting and important about how at least one Stoic author conceives of eupathic response. Our most comprehensive report on the *eupatheiai* is that of Cicero in *Tusc.* 4.12–14, which names and defines three genera of eupathic response: joy, in which the wise psyche elevates itself in response to present goods; caution, when the psyche retracts itself from prospective evils; and wishing, when the psyche extends itself toward prospective goods.[23] Cicero also makes it clear that these are the natural affective responses of the normative human being, of which the emotions we ordinarily experience are merely the perverted versions. But his report is not very informative about the phenomenological characteristics of these normative affective responses. He says only that the three genera involve the same psychophysical movements as the emotions – that is, elevation, extension, and retraction of the psyche – and that in joy, the mind is moved "quietly and consistently" in contrast to the "hollow" sort of elevation that is delight. Because the movements are the same in each case, it has seemed to me most logical to suppose that the *eupatheiai* were conceived as being phenomenologically quite similar to the ordinary emotions. They should lack the sense of struggle that comes of conflict among one's beliefs, but this need not mean either that they are lacking in intensity or that they are exempt from corporeal manifestations. Given the theory, it looks as though the wise

---

[23] The genera are listed in Diog. Laert. 7.115 and Cicero, *Tusc.* 4.12–15. There is no *eupatheia* corresponding to distress.

person could sometimes weep with joy in a genuine present good, tremble with anticipation of some genuine prospective good, shudder or blanch in cautious aversion from some genuine prospective evil.[24] But Cicero does not say this much, and our Greek sources, which are schematic in nature, leave the question open.[25] It is interesting therefore to find that Seneca describes the joy of the wise person as the sort of powerful feeling that might bring tears to the eyes.

Should we regard this tearful aspect of eupathic joy as an innovation by Seneca, taking his Stoic inheritance in what is perhaps a new direction, or should we rather believe that this is one of those points where Seneca takes over an older position and makes it his own? Development on Seneca's part is certainly a possibility. But the absence of any explicit reference to tears of joy in the fragments of the old Stoa does not count as evidence that the early Stoics conceived of the good emotions as devoid of corporeal effects.[26] It may be that they simply failed to comment on what might have seemed an obvious point, or it may be that they did comment and their comments failed to make it into the historical record. Or perhaps there is evidence we have heretofore failed to consider. David Konstan draws attention to the following passage from Philo's *On the Migration of Abraham*:

> But the devotees of virtue too have the tendency to groan and weep, either because they bewail the misfortunes of the foolish, thanks to natural community and sympathy, or because of exceeding joy. This latter occurs when a multitude of good things that were previously unanticipated suddenly rain down and flood one. It is due to this, I believe, that the poetic phrase "laughing tearfully" was pronounced. For since "joy, the best of the good emotions" lighted unexpectedly upon her soul, it rendered it larger than it was before, so that because of its bulk the corporeal part could no longer contain it. Crushed and pressed, it dripped forth streams, which it is the custom to call tears (...).[27]

---

[24] See further Becker (1998: 131–32) and (2004); Graver (2007: 52, 81–83).
[25] Hence Cooper (2005: 179) describes phenomenology of the good feelings as "calm, steady, equable, smooth, and so on."
[26] Brennan (2003: 275–78) argues that the Stoics were not particularly interested in how emotions feel but only in their characteristic belief structure; presumably he would make the same point about the *eupatheiai*. On the whole I agree with this: the phenomenology is largely taken for granted. Nonetheless, in those instances where it does become an issue, there is no reason it must be lacking in intensity.
[27] Philo, *On the Migration of Abraham* 156–57 (2.299 Wendl; SVF 3.436). See Konstan (2009: 314), which also supplies the translation given here.

The paragraph is one of many bits of Philo included by von Arnim in his massive compilation of Stoic fragments. Here the phrase "joy, the best of the good emotions" (εὐπαθειῶν ἀρίστη χαρά) is unquestionably Stoic in origin and is marked as such by von Arnim. But there are additional elements here that are equally suggestive of influence from the Hellenistic Stoa. A minor point, but worth mentioning, is the use of the Homeric tag "laughing tearfully" (δακρυόεν γελάσασα), referring to Andromache in *Iliad* 6.484. Citations of Homer are extremely infrequent in Philo but very much in the manner of Greek philosophers. A characteristically Stoic element is the mention of a "natural community and sympathy" (τὸ φύσει κοινωνικὸν καὶ φιλάνθρωπον). Chrysippus in particular is said to have asserted in virtually every one of his treatises that human beings have a natural sense of community and affinity to one another.[28] Still more striking is the notion that a sudden access of joy would cause a physical expansion of the psyche (μείζονα αὐτὴν ἢ πρότερον ἦν ἐποίησεν), which would then produce weeping by a physical process, the psychic material being "crushed and pressed" (θλιβόμενον δὲ καὶ πιεζόμενον) through the tear ducts. These words bear a distinct resemblance to a remark securely attested for Chrysippus, that in anger we have a sensation of "something evaporating from the heart and blowing outwards toward the hands and face."[29] And we have indications in Galen that Chrysippus gave similar physical explanations, now lost to us, for other affective sensations including those of fear, distress, confidence, and joy.[30] So it is reasonable to suppose that Philo's explanation for tears of joy is one he remembered from reading in Chrysippus or in some compilation or doxography that gave evidence of his views.[31] The resemblance to Seneca's letter can hardly be denied. Not only do both make eupathic joy the kind of response that can produce tears, but both list two possibilities for virtuous weeping, and both offer a physicalist explanation for the production of tears – though in Seneca's case "internal pressure" (*per elisionem*) explains the involuntary tears rather than the joyful ones. So if Philo's language reflects old Stoic material, Seneca's presumably does as well.

---

[28] Plutarch, *Stoic Self-Contradictions* 1038b; and see Stobaeus 2.7.11m, 109 Wachsmuth (*SVF* 3.630); Cicero, *Fin.* 3.68; Diog. Laert. 7.123.
[29] Galen, *PHP* 3.1.25 (*SVF* 2.886).
[30] Galen, *PHP* 4.2.4–6 (LS 65D, *SVF* 3.463), 4.3.2 (LS 65K, *SVF* 3.462), 5.1.4 (*SVF* 3.461). See Graver (2007: 28–34).
[31] Philo's immediate sources for Stoic thought are not known (but better than ours!); for informed opinions, see Dillon (1996: 140–41) and Runia (2008). Winston (2008) emphasizes the detailed extent of his knowledge of Stoic views on emotion. I treat some additional Philonian passages on eupathic joy in Graver (1999a: 312–18).

An Epicurean Expedient

Toward the end of letter 99, Seneca turns to criticize a rival strategy for consolation advanced by Metrodorus, the colleague of Epicurus. As Marcus Wilson observes, Seneca appears to have been reading some volume that contained Epicurean material, for in *Letters* 98.9 he quotes with approval the line "every good thing for mortal beings is likewise mortal," which he says is from a letter that Metrodorus addressed to his sister on the loss of her son.[32] Now he reports an additional line, almost certainly from the same letter but containing a thought he finds less acceptable:

> I do not by any means approve of what Metrodorus says, that there is a pleasure that is akin to sorrow and that in situations like this one should try to catch hold of that pleasure. Metrodorus's exact words are as follows: "From Metrodorus's letters to his sister. 'For there is a pleasure akin to grief which one ought to go hunting for in this situation.'"[33] I am not in any doubt as to what view you will take of these words. For what could be more shameful than to try to catch pleasure in the very midst of grief – indeed, through grief – and to go looking for something delightful even amid one's tears? And these are the people who reproach us for excessive rigor and complain that our teachings are harsh, just because we say one should either not admit grief into the mind or else cast it out quickly. Which, pray tell, is harder to believe, and which is less human: not to feel grief when one loses a friend, or to try to snare a pleasure right in the midst of grief? (*Letters* 99.25–26)

What is it in Metrodorus's recommendation that Seneca finds "shameful," "hard to believe," "inhuman"? We must assume that he understands "pleasure" here to refer to some form of *bodily* pleasure, some "agreeable movement that delights the senses," as in Cicero, *De Finibus* 2.8. The pleasure that is akin to or born with sorrow (*cognatam tristitiae*), would then be a corporeal sensation, perhaps some physical release in yielding to sobs. Metrodorus seems to be advising his sister that she should recognize and appreciate this pleasure as a kind of compensation for the mental pain of bereavement.

---

[32] Wilson (1997: 57). The *Letters on Ethics* quote frequently from a collection of Epicurean letters; see page 90. The inclusion of the identifier Μητροδώρου ἐπιστολῶν πρὸς τὴν ἀδελφήν at *Letters* 99.25 perhaps indicates the source is a florilegium, rather than a continuous text. See Ferguson (1990: 2280–81) and Setaioli (1988: 171–82).

[33] Seneca quotes in Greek: Μητροδώρου ἐπιστολῶν πρὸς τὴν ἀδελφήν. Ἔστιν γάρ τις ἡδονὴ <λύπῃ συγγενής, ἣν χρὴ θηρεύ>ειν κατὰ τοῦτον τὸν καιρόν. The fragment is not otherwise attested; the bracketed words are an editorial supplement to match Seneca's Latin rendering.

The notion of a compensatory pleasure is at home in a hedonist system. For Epicureans, the aim of philosophical thought is to make intelligent use of the available sources of pleasure so as to achieve a life which is pleasurable on balance; that is, a life in which one's total pleasure exceeds ones total pain.[34] But the particular recommendation made here – assuming Seneca understands it correctly – is different from Epicurus's own recommendation for the management of unavoidable mental pain. Epicurus seems to have conceded that the pain occasioned by the death of a close friend or family member is a veridical pain that cannot be eliminated simply by correcting one's false assumptions about value.[35] But his own recommendation for counteracting this pain was that one should "direct the mind away" from the evil and "redirect" it toward goods, by remembering the pleasure experienced through the friendship.[36] In other words, one is to compensate for mental pain by drawing upon a mental pleasure in much the same way as, in the famous letter to Idomeneus, he claims to be able to compensate for the pain of his fatal illness by drawing upon the memory of philosophical conversations.[37] Metrodorus's consolation strategy is different in that he suggests compensating for a mental pain with a corporeal pleasure. It may be that he, like the Cyrenaic hedonists of the same time, rejected Epicurus's thesis that mental pleasures and pains are always of greater magnitude than corporeal ones.[38]

For Seneca himself, an important advantage of raising the Metrodoran claim is to clarify his own assertion about tears of joy. Metrodorus's remark on the pleasure that is akin to pain bears some resemblance to Seneca's own observation about "an element of sweetness in our sorrow" (*inest quiddam dulce tristitiae*, 99.19). In letter 63, also, he had spoken of the pleasure that comes from remembering loved ones:

> Let us try to make the memory of those who are gone a pleasant one. If the thought brings torment, one does not willingly return to it, and so here: we are bound to feel a biting when the names of loved ones come to mind. But even this biting has its own pleasure (*hic quoque morsus habet suam voluptatem*). (*Letters* 63.4)

---

[34] The doctrine is best known from Epicurus, *Menoeceus* 129–30.
[35] This is reported in Cicero, *Tusc.* 3.28 and 3.32. See also Plutarch, *Non posse* 1101a–b (fragment 120 Usener).
[36] Cicero, *Tusc.* 3.32–35; Plutarch, *Non posse* 1091b (fragment 423 Usener) and 1105e (fragment 213 Usener). A parallel text in Philodemus (*De dis* 3 col. 2.25–27 Diels) uses the Epicurean term ἐπιβολή; see Asmis (1984: 124). On Epicurean methods of consolation, see further Kassel (1958: 29–32), Manning (1974: 79–81), Sorabji (2000: 233–37), and Graver (2002b).
[37] Diog. Laert. 10.22.   [38] Diog. Laert. 10.136–137.

Continuing the thought, he had cited a remark by his own Stoic teacher Attalus, that the memory of friends who have died gives a pleasurable (*iucunda*) sensation "like that of apples that are both tart and sweet, or like the pleasing acidity of an old wine" (63.5). He himself, however, had rejected this comparison, insisting that the pleasure of memory is only "sweet and comforting" (*dulcis ac blanda*, 63.7). So he, too, seems initially to favor the idea of seeking out some kind of positive feeling in times of bereavement.

In fact, the substance of the position is quite different. Seneca does not endorse the idea that pleasure can somehow come *through* grief, or that joy and grief can be mingled in any way. The idea of mingling is that the two things one is experiencing simultaneously are in some sense comparable with one another, so that the more intense of the two will predominate in the mix. This is the essence of Epicurean consolation: one is to find a greater pleasure, whether a mental pleasure, as for Epicurus, or a physical pleasure as is apparently the strategy of Metrodorus. For Seneca, there can be no such comparison, and no counteracting. The joy experienced by the wise person in the memory of his friend is unalloyed. The tears he shed may be involuntary tears, in which case they are completely inconsequential in comparison to the glad feeling that arises from the memory of the goods of friendship; or they may be voluntary tears that are actually part of that glad feeling. Either way, these are tears in which there is no bitterness.

***

The task of consolation is culturally specific, and it is highly specific also to the circumstances of the bereavement and to the character of the bereaved. We cannot tell now how the real Marullus might have reacted to Seneca's consolatory gambit: whether he would have found comfort in its austerity, whether he might have wished to explain the extremity of his feelings, as Cicero once did in a letter to Servius Sulpicius Rufus, or whether perhaps he appreciated being named as a philosopher – even with admonition – in a letter of such depth and sophistication. What we can see is that Seneca himself is intellectually engaged in his topic. In his consolation to Marullus, more than in any of his previous consolatory ventures, he probes deep into the implications of a Stoic understanding of emotion and of personal relationships. Though fully aware that his "chastisement" (*convicia*, 99.2) will be a shock to certain cultural expectations, he does not concede that a Stoic *consolatio* must be hard-faced and inhumane. On the contrary, he insists that tears born of affection may be fully consistent with virtuous wisdom. What matters is the nature and meaning of the tears. When weeping represents the common but incorrect assumption that proximity to death is inherently bad, he is unwilling to sanction it even in moderate amounts. Still less can he make any concession to weeping whose real purpose is display, or to a kind of self-indulgent weeping that finds a paradoxical pleasure in the release of tears. But tears that are involuntary and uncontrollable cannot be criticized at all, while those that arise from remembrance of the good qualities of the one who has died are in fact virtuous. They are the corporeal manifestation of a properly conceived affective response to the goods of friendship.

CHAPTER 8

Anatomies of Joy
Seneca and the *Gaudium* Tradition

> Cast aside those things that glitter on the outside, those things that are promised you by another or from another, and trample them underfoot. Look to your real good, and rejoice in what is yours. What is it that is yours? Yourself; the best part of you.
>
> (*Letters* 23.6)

One of the most difficult problems in studying Seneca concerns his working methods as a philosopher. We know by his own admission that much of his philosophical material came to him from Stoic sources – mostly written sources, though live discussions with contemporaries must also have been a factor – and we can see the depth of his commitment to Stoic ethics.[1] It is much harder, though, to grasp the internal process by which he assembles and re-presents the content of his tradition. To what extent does he retain the exact contours of ideas he has encountered? Is his a receptive intellect, tolerant of inconcinnities, or does he tend rather to reshape the inherited body of thought to the model of his own understanding or that of some admired teacher? This is the kind of thing we need to know if we are to assess his personal philosophical achievement, and also if we are to assess his value as a source.[2] To make progress on such questions, one promising strategy is to trace the exact parameters of a single inherited concept as it appears in multiple contexts in his work. This is what I propose to do here, taking as the object of study a notion that plays a major role in Seneca's corpus: the notion of wise, normative, joy.

Our own scholarly canons regarding "classical" or "orthodox" Stoicism are only partly useful here. The real issue is the extent to which our reconstructions of early Stoic philosophy – or more specifically the

---

[1] A basic resource is Inwood (2005: 7–22). Much valuable detail may also be found in Griffin (1976).
[2] Worth noting in this regard are Seneca's own accounts of how he proceeds; for instance, in letters 6 (voluminous reading), 33 (revision and innovation), 84 (amalgamation and assimilation). But it is not safe to assume that his descriptions tell the whole truth.

philosophy of Chrysippus – can aid us in any detailed study of Stoic thought across a broader historical spectrum. Faced with a large but scattered array of partially overlapping fragments and doxographical summaries, the modern historian of philosophy will usually proceed by collecting reports relevant to a particular point and determining what coheres with other known elements of the system, guided by her own philosophical acumen: in brief, she will *assemble and harmonize*. The result is a neat, undoubtedly too neat, account of Stoic orthodoxy, useful in itself but with much that is less neat left at the periphery. Yet we have known all along, in part through Seneca's own descriptions of Stoic practice, that Stoic-identified authors often felt free to restyle and develop the school's positions to suit their own philosophical tastes.[3] A departure from core principles would have been a different matter; but there were many topics that could be analyzed in more than one way while retaining the essential insights of the founders. Such divergences must have given rise to some interesting discussions, of which the main outlines may still be recoverable. To see this, we must *atomize and anatomize*.

In this chapter, I first review what the reconstructive method has been able to tell us about the best represented Stoic position on joy and other positive emotions, then compare that account with the numerous assertions about normative joy that we find in Seneca's work. Seneca's handling of *gaudium*, I find, is not like what might be observed in a rigorous thinker who takes hold of a specialized term and uses it consistently thereafter. In many passages, he does make use of a conception of wise joy that is at least very similar to the one that has come to be regarded as standard within Hellenistic Stoicism. But other passages give evidence of additional philosophical possibilities for the concept that are distinct from that standard conception and yet consistent with the core principles of Stoic ethics. Moreover, one extended passage deploys an understanding of wise joy that is not compatible at all with the usual Stoic account but coheres in an entirely different way with the ethical principles of the school. I argue that these divergences within Seneca's usage reflect intellectual habits that favor the reproduction of earlier lines of thought, even quite distinctive ones, over the imposition of an admirable but less interesting consistency.

The Convergent Stoic Account

It is often observed that while some of the more prominent modern approaches to ethics deal primarily with kinds of action, asking what is

[3] See Reydams-Schils (2011); Sedley (1989: 97–99).

the right thing to do in certain situations, classical moral philosophy is more centrally concerned with agents, thinking of moral action as just whatever an ideally virtuous person would do.[4] The general concern about agency motivates inquiries into human psychology on two broad fronts: descriptive inquiries, that try to understand how minds typically work so that ethics can be grounded in reality; and normative inquiries, that try to understand what a perfectly functioning human mind would be like so that ethics can direct us toward what is best for us. So also when asking specifically about the emotions, the philosophers of antiquity ask both about the emotions ordinary people typically experience – what they are, what causes them, how they are to be managed – and about ideal emotions, what our emotional lives would be like if we were functioning as optimal agents.

Joy has a natural place in the latter sort of discussion. Unlike the hedonists, who by definition valorize all positive affect, philosophers in the Platonic-Stoic tradition draw a distinction between ordinary forms of pleasure and the positive affect experienced by the ideal agent. The former, termed pleasure (ἡδονή, *voluptas*), belongs to the morally questionable realm of actual experience; the latter, joy (χαρά, *gaudium*), to the normative realm. As such it invests the experience of the ideal agent with an intuitive appeal, and this in itself makes it structurally important for descriptions of optimal human functioning, even if one does not hold that the good feeling is the very reason why optimal functioning is desirable.

It was within this philosophical context that one or more Stoics of the Hellenistic period developed what became the dominant account of joy within that school, which is to say, the account found in Cicero, *Tusculan Disputations* 4.12–14 and Diogenes Laertius, *Lives of Eminent Philosophers* 7.116. In all likelihood this account belongs to the theory of emotional response worked out in detail by Chrysippus of Soli in his widely influential treatise *On the Emotions*.[5] In this convergent account, joy is an affective response occurring in the wise person in response to present goods and consisting in an "elevation" or "effusion" of the material psyche, or, as we might put it, a lifting of spirits.[6] As such it is an occurrent phenomenon, not merely a state or characteristic of the agent, although

---

[4] A good general discussion is Annas (1993: 27–46).
[5] For the reconstruction of Chrysippus's treatise, see especially Tieleman (2003).
[6] The terms "elevation" (ἔπαρσις) and "effusion" (διάχυσις) are both also used with regard to ordinary delight: Diog. Laert. 7.114; Galen, *PHP* 4.2.4–6 (LS 65D, *SVF* 3.463); 4.3.2 (LS 65K, *SVF* 3.462); 5.1.4 (*SVF* 3.461). The Latin equivalent to ἔπαρσις is *elatio*, as in Cicero, *Tusc.* 4.66–67. See further Graver (2007: 29–34, 201–6). For διάχυσις, see also note 22 in this chapter.

the stable characteristics of the wise agent do play a role in generating the response on any given occasion.

Thus defined, joy occupies a particular place within the classification of affective responses that looms large in our major sources. It is not one of the ordinary emotions (πάθη), which depend on erroneous judgments concerning the value of externals and which accordingly are repudiated by Stoic ethics. Rather, it belongs among the eupathic responses (εὐπάθειαι), normative versions of emotion that occur in the optimal agent on the basis of correct judgments of value. It thus ranks alongside caution (εὐλάβεια) and wish (βούλησις) at the level of genus, and has subordinate to it several more specific eupathic responses to present goods, including "enjoyment" (τέρψις), "cheerfulness" (εὐφροσύνη), and "good spirits" (εὐθυμία).

Neither Cicero nor Diogenes Laertius says explicitly whether joy is a reaction to external objects (what the Stoics call "preferred indifferents") or to what may be termed *integral objects*, features of the virtuous agent's own character or conduct. However, a simple inference gives strong support to the latter interpretation. Since only integral objects count as genuine goods or evils within the Stoic system of value, it must be these that an optimally wise agent recognizes as present goods. For no external object could be regarded in that way by a wise person. Further support can be derived from the logic of a classification that lists joy as the wise response for present goods, wish for prospective goods, and caution for prospective evils, but pointedly declines to name any response for present evils. The person of perfect wisdom and virtue does not need the fourth type of response, since he or she cannot logically be in the presence of anything bad – provided we are speaking of integral objects. But if the missing genus is missing for this reason, then the other three responses must be conceived along the same lines.[7] On this Stoic view, then, joy must be a response to virtuous qualities or activities exhibited by oneself.

Seneca and the Convergent Account

Evidence that Seneca was familiar with the main outlines of the foregoing account is found in the 59th of the *Letters on Ethics*. At the beginning of that letter, Seneca draws a contrast between the pleasure experienced by the ordinary person, which he says is a fault (*vitium*), and the response that

---

[7] See further Graver (2007: 51–55) but the same interpretation was already given in Long and Sedley (1987: vol. 2, 407).

is properly termed *gaudium*; the latter, he says, is experienced only by the wise. From there he goes on to offer a definition of joy in language unmistakably of Stoic origin:

> I know, say I, that if we make words adhere to our statutes, then pleasure is discreditable, while joy pertains only to the wise person, for it is the elevation of a mind confident of goods that are real and its own. (*Letters* 59.2)

Both the restriction to the wise and the phrase "elevation of mind" (*elatio animi*) recall the convergent, probably Chrysippan, account. So also does that element in the definition which specifies that the mind's elevation is directed toward "goods that are real and its own" (*suis bonis verisque*). The goods that are real and are the mind's own can only be integral objects, traits or activities of the agent, as opposed to the external objects that give pleasure to ordinary persons. In this, Seneca makes explicit what is implied in the accounts of Cicero and Diogenes Laertius, that joy relates only to circumstances that belong inalienably to the agent.

The restriction of joy to integral objects is indeed a point Seneca makes over and over in the *Letters on Ethics*. The theme is stated emphatically quite early in the collection, near the beginning of letter 23:

> Reaching the heights means knowing what to rejoice in – finding prosperity in that which no one else can control. Anyone who is enticed by hope is anxious and unsure of himself, even if hope is for something close at hand or not difficult to get, even if the things one hoped for never prove disappointing. Do this above all, dear Lucilius: learn how to experience joy. Do you now suppose that because I am removing from you the things of fortune, and think you should steer clear of hopes, those sweetest of beguilements, I am therefore taking away many pleasures? Not at all: what I want is that gladness should never be absent from you. I want it to be born in your own home – and that is what will happen if it comes to be inside of you. (*Letters* 23.2–3)

And a little lower down:

> Any joy lacks foundation when it has been imported from elsewhere. The joy of which I am speaking, to which I seek to direct you, is solid through and through, and has its widest scope within. There is only one course of action that can make you happy. I beg you, dearest Lucilius, to do it: cast aside those things that glitter on the outside, those things that are promised you by another or from another, and trample them underfoot. Look to your real good and rejoice in what is yours. What is it that is yours? Yourself; the best part of you. (*Letters* 23.5–6)

Anatomies of Joy

Similarly, letter 27 speaks of a good that the mind "discovers for itself from out of itself"; letter 72 of joy as a happiness that "lives at home"; letter 98 of a joy "that arises from oneself"; and letter 124, in the last paragraph of the extant collection, instructs Lucilius, "Do not judge yourself to be happy until all your joys arise from yourself."[8]

In all of this, Seneca is very much in harmony with the complex of ideas that is now usually designated the principal Stoic account of joy. At the same time, it may be doubted whether Seneca has read the very same Stoic work that lies behind the convergent accounts of Cicero and Diogenes Laertius. For anyone who knows those accounts, it is a startling realization that Seneca, who knows so much, never makes any effort to situate joy within the Stoics' elaborate classification of affective responses. Among the numerous remarks on *gaudium* in his prose writings, there is not one that lists it as one of three eupathic responses; indeed, so far as I have been able to determine, there is no word equivalent to *eupatheia*, no general term for normative affective response, in Seneca's philosophical lexicon. His *gaudium* does not function as a subtype of any more general conception of normative affective response, and neither does it have any further species of positive affect subordinate to it.

Kinetic versus Static Joy

Seneca's relation to the convergent tradition comes into question again when one studies his accounts of joy in connection with a distinction that is commonly made in the modern literature on emotion between occurrent emotions, like being sad when a beloved companion dies, and persistent emotional states: being depressed, being a timid person, being prone to anger or anxiety over a long period of time. This same distinction is found in ancient psychology, where the usual language is of mental events (κινήσεις, *motus*) as opposed to conditions or states (ἕξεις, *habitus*).[9] As we have seen, the definition of joy as an "elevation" or "effusion" of the material psyche suggests a mental event and thus an occurrent emotion. On one way of thinking, then, the joy of the Stoic wise should be the feeling they have in particular moments of their experience when they recognize the presence of some good. For instance, they might rejoice in each new opportunity to exercise one of the virtues. A just person would be gladdened when achieving an equitable

---

[8] *Letters* 27.3; 72.4; 98.1; 124.24.
[9] For *habitus* in this sense in Seneca, see *Anger* 3.26.5; *Letters* 16.6; 85.14–15.

resolution to some conflict (exercising justice) or when standing up for a victim of abuse (exercising courage).[10]

In Seneca we sometimes find clear statements that treat joy as kinetic in just this way. In letter 23.3–4, one experiences "real joy" when engaging in specific virtuous actions: despising death, opening one's home to poverty, reining in pleasure, and rehearsing the endurance of pain. This is "not a smooth or seductive feeling," and yet it is a glad feeling, one that does not merely "smooth the brow" but rather "fills the heart." Still more explicit is a passage in letter 76, where the good person experiences a necessarily brief joy in dying for his country:

> Sometimes from an extremely beautiful object one experiences great joy even in a tiny space of time; and although no profit from the act performed accrues to the one who is deceased and removed from human life, still there is satisfaction in the very contemplation of the deed ahead. A just and courageous man, when he envisions the benefits of his death – the freedom of his homeland, the safety of all those for whom he lays down his life – is at the height of pleasure, and is gladdened by his own danger. But if one is deprived even of this joy that the doing of this greatest, last deed provides, even then one will still plunge down into death, finding satisfaction in acting correctly and with due devotion. (*Letters* 76.28–29)

Joy is not the motive for the courageous action: a good person would act courageously even without it. But when joy does occur, it is occasioned by the wise person's own action, "the doing of the deed" (*tractatio operis*).

But this kinetic understanding of joy takes turns in Seneca's writings with an alternative understanding that makes joy rather a condition or state, something that persists for the entire time one is wise. It is a thought he likes to invoke when he wants to draw a contrast with the transient delights of the foolish. While the main objection to the foolish person's delight is that it is experienced for the wrong reasons, it is also suboptimal in that it is at best intermittent. By contrast, those who derive joy from objects within their own control have a source of gladness constantly available to them. Thus in *On Tranquility of Mind* 2.4, joy "remains in a tranquil state"; in *Letters* 27.3, it is a good "that will remain"; in *Letters* 59.16, it is marked by "steadiness"; in *Letters* 98.1, it "stays with us to the end," while other forms of gladness "are goods only for a day."[11] Cloud

---

[10] Virtuous activities are themselves goods: Stobaeus 2.7.5e, 70 Wachsmuth (*SVF* 3.97).

[11] Especially in *On Tranquility of Mind*, Seneca's interest in the continuity of joy seems to resemble Epicurus's notion of katastematic pleasure. But compare also Democritus's εὐθυμία and Zeno of Citium's εὔροια ("good flow of life"). For the combination of Stoic and non-Stoic elements in the treatise see Gill (1994).

and sky metaphors strengthen the point: as the high heavens are always bright even when clouds obscure our view, so the joy of the wise is always present to them even when other thoughts momentarily get in the way.

> We are inquiring how the mind may proceed always on a level and favorable course; how it may be kind to itself, look with gladness on what is its own, and have no intermission in this joy but remain in a tranquil state, neither elevating nor lowering itself. (*Tranq.* 2.4)

> Look about, rather, for some good that will remain. There is none but that which the mind discovers for itself from out of itself. Virtue alone yields lasting and untroubled joy. Even if something does get in the way of that joy, it is interrupted only as daylight is by clouds, which pass beneath but do not ever overcome it. (*Letters* 27.3)

> So ponder this: the result of wisdom is steadiness of joy. The wise mind is like the superlunary heaven: eternally serene. Thus you have reason to desire wisdom, if wisdom is always accompanied by joy. But this joy has only one source: a consciousness of the virtues. A person is not capable of joy unless he is brave, unless he is just, unless he is temperate. (*Letters* 59.16)

This same conception of joy as a steady state is to be found in *On the Constancy of the Wise* 9.3, "uplifted by continual joy" (*continuo gaudio elatus*).

In connection with this static form of joy, Seneca also expresses a further thought about the relation between joy and virtue. It is a point he uses to combat the Epicureans, for whom positive affect, both corporeal and mental, is the very thing that constitutes the blessedness of the wise. Speaking in *On Happiness*, Seneca concedes that virtue brings pleasure, but he insists that the virtuous person does not choose to be virtuous for that reason. As in the passages quoted previously, glad feelings are continuous and arise from deep within, "since one is rejoicing in what belongs to oneself" (*ut qui suis gaudeat*, *Happiness* 4.4). But the point here is that this positive mental affect is only superadded to what is essential: it "necessarily follows" (*velit nolit sequatur*, 4.4). In more technical language, it "supervenes" (*supervenit*) or is an adjunct (*accessio*) to virtue, not a reward or motivation for it (9.1). It is like the wildflowers that spring up unbidden at the edge of a cultivated field.[12] By taking this position, Seneca preserves the intuition that a truly rational being would choose virtuous action for its

---

[12] The use of the word *voluptas* in *Happiness* 9.1, rather than *gaudium* as in preceding sections, is triggered by the Epicurean context. A similar but less developed account is found in *Happiness* 14.1; and note also *Happiness* 4.4 *velit nolit*. The point appears again later in *Letters* 85.18, again in an anti-Epicurean context, and again using only the word *voluptas*.

own sake and not for any further results it produces.[13] Returning to the same thought further on in the treatise, he adds that although *gaudium* arises out of virtue and is a good in its own right, it is not constitutive of the highest good.

> Not even the joy that arises out of virtue – though it is itself a good – is part of the absolute good, any more than gladness and tranquility are, though they are born from very beautiful causes. For those things are goods, but concomitants *(consequentia)* of the highest good, not constituents of it *(consummantia)*. (*Happiness* 15.2)

To give yet another analogy, we might compare virtue to a tree and joy to the tree's shadow, which belongs to it without adding in any way to its bulk. Joy is merely a further characteristic of the virtuous life, something that turns out always to be true of the virtuous person within Stoic theory. It is a good in its own right, as are impassivity (ἀπάθεια), inner strength (ῥώμη), and many other qualities of the normative agent; but the goodness that is in this positive affect does not contribute to the human good in the sense of making it better than it already was.

Mutual Joys

In view of the pronounced emphasis on oneself and one's own actions that we have seen in the *Letters on Ethics* and *On Happiness*, it comes as a bit of a surprise to read in *On Benefits* that joy may also be a response to the actions of other people. Prominent within that work is a definition of the *beneficium*, the act of disinterested kindness, as understood within the Stoic tradition. According to this definition, a benefit is "a well-intended action that is such as to confer joy and to take joy in conferring it."[14] Like other Stoic definitions, this one is meant to capture the best-case scenario, what the object of definition is conceptually, as seen in the ideal agent. The actions of ordinary people may approximate it but cannot fully instantiate it. It seems, then, that the joy mentioned in the definition must be the positive affect of the wise person who either gives or receives some gift or disinterested service.

---

[13] Compare Diog. Laert. 7.94, where joy and cheerfulness are similarly said to be "supervenients" (ἐπιγεννήματα); also 7.86, where a similar statement is made about pleasure; and Stobaeus 2.7.6d 77 Wachsmuth (*SVF* 3.113), where joy, cheerfulness, and the habitudes are "not necessary for happiness."

[14] *Ben.* 1.6.1 *benevola actio tribuens gaudium capiensque tribuendo.*

In his discussion, Seneca distinguishes clearly between the benefit itself, consisting in a well-intended action, and what he calls "the material of the benefit"; that is, the item that is given or the service that is performed. Logically, the recipient's response is to the benevolent action itself, for the same material gift or useful service would evoke a very different response if provided by some other kind of action; for example, in some churlish way, or with strings attached. Joy for the recipient relates to the goodwill (*voluntas*) of the giver, just as the giver's own joy relates to her own act of giving and to the gratitude of the recipient. The two of them thus share a very similar satisfaction in the same moment of giving: it is "a transaction between minds" that brings "mutual joy."[15]

A similar claim appears in the 109th of the *Letters on Ethics,* a letter devoted to the problem of mutuality and relationship among the wise. Because Stoic ethics holds that the wise person is fully self-sufficient, it may seem that there is no role for friendship in the wise life. Like other Stoics, however, Seneca holds not only that friendship exists among the wise, but that theirs is the truest form of friendship, which the relationships of nonwise people can only hope to emulate. To give meat to this idea, he identifies a number of ways wise friends can be helpful to one another without detriment to the self-sufficiency of each. The primary answer, which is also found in *Letters* 9.8, is that each provides the other with "occasions for honorable action" – not that opportunities to behave well are ever lacking in life, but friendship can be the context for specific kinds of virtuous action that are good to include. Beyond this, though, there is also an affective dimension in wise relationships, just as there is in the negative interactions of the nonwise.

> A bad man harms a bad man and makes him worse by arousing his anger, approving his gloom, and praising his pleasures. Conversely, one good man will help another. "But how?" you say. He will bring him joy and strengthen his confidence, and each one's delight will grow from the sight of their mutual tranquility. (*Letters* 109.4–5)

Joy, confidence, and delight are all affective responses, here occasioned simply by the appreciation of the other person's character. Again, we see the wise reacting to goods outside of their individual selves.

These joys belonging to wise friendship are rather different from the self-directed joy that Seneca so often stresses. But while the wise friends are indeed responding to the goods in another person, these are not, for them,

---

[15] *Ben.* 2.34.1 *res inter animos geritur;* 2.31.2 *mutuo gaudio adfecit.*

external goods like those that are the objects of pleasure for ordinary flawed agents. In keeping with Stoicism, Seneca's position seems to be that virtuous friendship involves such a close linking of interests and perspectives that the two friends can be said to share a collective agency.[16] It is not only that such friends counsel one another by means of their particular knowledge, but that they are actually linked in volition, "having the same wishes and the same aversions" in what letter 6 calls "a companionship of honorable intentions."[17] In a real sense, the wise friend is responding to goods that are indeed his or her own, even though those goods also belong to someone else.

Joys as "Primary Goods"

By now it should be clear what it is that distinguishes joy as a philosophical concept from joy in the common or pre-theoretical sense of that word. While non-philosophers might speak of joy (χαρά or *gaudium*) as a response that anyone might have to perceived good fortune, Stoic philosophers restricted the term to the inner experience of the optimal agent. That philosophical restriction is observed also in letter 66, where joy figures prominently in a rather technical discussion of Stoic moral theory. However, the treatment of joy in that extraordinary letter is in other respects quite different from what we have seen.

In letter 66 Seneca adapts what may have originally been a Peripatetic classification of goods to fit within the framework of his Stoic commitment. Within the classification, joy is the preeminent example of what are called "primary goods."[18] Initially there is some lack of clarity as to how joy relates to the other items in its class, for Seneca at first lists the primary goods as "joy, peace, the safety of one's homeland" (*gaudium, pax, salus patriae*) but later replaces that phrase with "rejoicing in the devotion of one's children, in the safety of one's homeland" (*gaudere liberorum pietate, patriae incolumitate*).[19] The difference is significant. In the earlier formula, it looks as if joy is just one of those circumstances that might prevail in an agreeable life, whereas in the second, rejoicing is clearly the agent's own response to such circumstances. It must in fact be this second formulation that Seneca has in mind throughout, for that is what corresponds structurally to the other two classes of goods. Just as the first class consists in the joy that responds to favorable situations, so the second class consists in patient

---

[16] See page 69.   [17] *Letters* 109.16 *idem velle atque idem nolle*; 6.3 *societatem honesta cupiendi*.
[18] See note 34 in Chapter 5.   [19] *Letters* 66.5, 66.37.

endurance of adverse situations like illness or torture, and the third class in virtuous mental activities where the circumstances are neither preferred nor dispreferred. Moreover, Seneca's solution to the problem studied in the letter actually requires this interpretation. He argues throughout that the classification does not delegitimize the Stoics' usual assumption that all goods are equal in magnitude. The goodness of an activity resides in the character of the agent, not in the circumstances of the action; those circumstances are only the material in which the corresponding good is expressed.[20] Since rejoicing in favorable situations, patiently enduring unfavorable ones, and generally virtuous behavior the rest of the time are all activities of the good person, they are all equally good.

We can see, then, what Seneca means by *gaudium* within letter 66. It is a response of the virtuous mind to circumstances that accord with nature – to seeing one's children behaving well or seeing one's country saved from danger.[21] In a word, it is the wise person's affective response to the sorts of objects Stoics call preferred indifferents. This joy is an occurrent phenomenon, not a steady state: it comes about when external circumstances are favorable and at other times is replaced by patient endurance or by some neutral activity. I note, too, that it is described as an *affective* response in language familiar from Stoic theory; that is, as one that involves a sensed alteration in the psyche itself. The joy of this letter is "effusive and expansive" (*remissa et laxa*, 66.12); it involves a "natural effusion and expansion of the mind" (*naturalis animi remissio et laxitas*, 66.14); it "pours out" the mind, whereas danger "bites" it (*diffundit . . . mordet*, 66.32).[22]

---

[20] The presentation of preferred and dispreferred indifferents as "material of the good" is Chrysippan; see Plutarch, *On Common Conceptions* 1069e (*SVF* 3.491).
[21] A question might be raised as to whether *gaudium* as used in this letter is perhaps a *corporeal* pleasure corresponding to corporeal pain. Support for such an interpretation might be alleged from several passages in which *gaudium* is paired not with the endurance of pain but with pain itself (*in hoc gaudio . . . in illis cruciatibus*, 66.15; *gaudium et dolorem*, 66.19; *moderate gaudere et moderate dolere*, 66.29), or even with the instrument of torture (*in gaudio an in eculeo*, 66.18). In the more precise parts of the letter, however, Seneca uses longer expressions linking joy not with pain itself but with the courageous endurance of pain (*fortis atque obstinata tormentorum perpessio*, 66.12; *dolorum inflexibilem patientiam*, 66.14; *obnixus animus ad perpetiendos cruciatus vulnerum aut ignium*, 66.40). It is not uncommon for Seneca to abbreviate his expressions where he thinks his intent is clear. In any case, *gaudium* and *gaudere* in the key passages at 66.5 and 66.37 cannot possibly concern bodily pleasure. Having good children, peace, or a safe homeland does not titillate the body.
[22] Compare the early Stoic usage of διάχυσις ("effusion") for the psychic change involved in positive affect (either delight or joy) as opposed to the "biting" of distress. See note 6 in this chapter; and compare *effuse* and *ecfusio* in Cicero, *Tusc.* 4.13, 4.66. *Diffusio* is used of *gaudium* also in *On Happiness* 4.5 (quoted on page 190), where Costa (1994), noting its rarity in Latin, likewise suspects a connection to διάχυσις.

This conception of joy is markedly different both from what we have seen elsewhere in Seneca and from the mainline Stoic conception. In all other Senecan and Stoic accounts, joy is a response to goods of character in some form. It does not track the preferability of situations and can be experienced even under torture. Here, joy responds specifically to preferred indifferents.[23] Yet it is not just another name for the emotion of delight such as ordinary people experience in the presence of preferred indifferents. It may involve the same kinds of inner sensations as the nonwise feel when danger is averted or when children turn out well, but unlike the nonwise response, it is not predicated on the assumption that these things are good. The wise person knows that a safe homeland is only a preferred indifferent and responds to it as such, yet with real feeling, not merely with calm decision making. We are indeed seeing a divergent account of how normative affect works.

Seven Senecan Joys

What this study reveals, then, is that the concept associated with *gaudium* as a term of art is strikingly inconsistent within Seneca's corpus. But this is not the sort of inconsistency that comes of having too loose a notion of what words mean. Instead, Seneca offers multiple properly philosophical conceptions, each of which is well worked out and consistent within its own context. Setting aside the misnamed "joy" of ordinary persons, we have so far seen five distinct conceptions of joy: (1) a glad feeling that comes of the realization that one is performing some significant good deed, which may sometimes mean taking on poverty, pain, or death; (2) a steady, serene beatitude that accompanies the possession of virtue, contrasting with the fleeting pleasures of the foolish; (3) a supervenient adjunct to virtue, a good in its own right but not, as in Epicureanism, constitutive of the highest good; (4) a feature of the interpersonal dynamics of wise friends who appreciate and mutually participate in one another's character and actions; and (5) an activity of virtue consisting in a "natural effusion of the mind" in response to preferred indifferents. To these five broad-based conceptions of joy, we can add two further notions that may be called special cases of Senecan joy. These, too, are theorized notions, and again they are restricted to the experience of the wise. (See Figure 8.1.)

---

[23] Wildberger (2014: 453–54) notes this difference in Seneca's treatment of *gaudium* but attributes it to "conceptual fuzziness."

Type	Senecan work	Modality	Objects
1. Active joy	Letters 23 and 76	Episodic	Integral goods in the self
2. Stable joy	*On Tranquility of Mind, On Happiness*, letters 27 and 59	Constant	Integral goods in the self
3. Supervenient joy	*On Happiness*, letter 85	Constant (by supervenience)	Integral goods in the self
4. Mutual joy	*On Benefits*, letter 109	Episodic	Integral goods in another
5. Primary joy	Letter 66	Episodic	Preferred indifferents
6. Joy in bereavement	Letters 63 and 99	Episodic (through memory)	Integral goods in another
7. Joy in contemplation	*On Happiness*	Constant (through reflection)	Integral goods in the self

Figure 8.1   The joys of the wise

Related to the mutual joys of friendship is a highly unusual joy that wise people experience when they remember friends who have died. Explaining this thought in the consolatory letter 99, Seneca at first says that joy, rather than grief, is the correct response to a friend's death, because one ought to rejoice in having had such a friend (99.3). He later observes that while the wise sometimes weep involuntarily, in the morally inconsequential reaction he sometimes calls a "biting," they can also weep voluntarily, "just as in joy," remembering the goods of past friendship, which is to say the cheerful and loving behavior of the deceased (99.19).[24] As in *On Benefits* and in letter 109, the goods to which this cheerful joy responds are another person's goods of character, experienced vicariously in the context of wise friendship. Here, though, there is an added feature, since in this case, the object of joy is present only in memory. Relatedly, *Letters* 63.5–7 quotes the Stoic Attalus on the "bittersweet" (*suaviter aspera*) pleasure that comes with the memory of a departed friend, but then rejects the component of bitterness from the analogy, claiming that in Seneca's own view the experience is entirely a sweet one. At that point, Seneca speaks of himself as if he were the Stoic sage.[25]

Finally, there is the "great and immovable joy" of *On Happiness* 4. The passage there begins by sounding a familiar theme of Stoic ethics, that only honorable conduct is good, and that other objects of pursuit make no real difference in one's ultimate happiness. As we saw earlier, the message is that deep satisfaction has to come from within. Self-examination and an investment in moral excellence necessarily yield "a continual gladness, a cheerfulness that is deep and that comes from deep within, since one is

---

[24] See pages 167–68.
[25] See page 173. The wise posture of *Letters* 63.7 is suited to the consolatory function of the letter. It is soon negated, however, when Seneca admits at the end of the same letter that he wept immoderately for a kinsman, as "an example of one conquered by grief" (63.14).

rejoicing in what belongs to himself and wants nothing more than what is at home" (*nec maiora domesticis cupiat*, *Happiness* 4.4). As he continues, however, Seneca brings in an idea that is a favorite of some other ancient philosophers: that pure intellectual activity yields an especially delightful form of pleasure.[26]

> Therefore one must escape to freedom. Then and only then will arise that inestimable good which is the quiet of a mind lodged in a place of safety, and which is also sublimity (*sublimitas*) and, now that errors have been eliminated, the great and immovable joy that comes from the recognition of what is real (*ex cognitione veri*), and cheeriness and relaxation (*diffusio*) of mind, in which it delights not as goods but as things arising from its own good (*non ut bonis sed ut ex bono suo ortis*). (*Happiness* 4.5)

The main idea is still that joy responds to goods of character; specifically, of one's own character after wisdom is achieved. But elements of the phrasing are strongly reminiscent of other passages in Seneca that speak more specifically of philosophical study as a form of relaxation after hard labor, as liberation for the mind from the imprisoning body, as raising the spirit to the level of the sublime, and as conferring pleasure.[27] This is very much the joy of contemplation (*theōria*) as described by Aristotle in *Nicomachean Ethics* 10.7. We catch the resonance of the thought in the language of escape and refuge, in the mention of "sublimity," and in the phrase "recognition of what is real." The associations lend a sense of grandeur and excitement to the familiar moral message. By linking his usual language of rejoicing "in one's own" to the ancient theme of pleasure in contemplation, Seneca suggests that reflecting on a truth about oneself can be as uplifting as natural science and other theoretical pursuits.

***

In closing, let me sketch briefly what new conclusions emerge from the texts we have studied. First, concerning Seneca himself. We've seen that although Seneca does not speak of the eupathic responses in the way that we see in Cicero and other sources, he is deeply engaged with the idea of joy as the affective response or state that especially characterizes the normative agent. He regards joy as a special form of affect, set apart from the ordinary person's gladness or delight. This feeling is not fully accessible

---

[26] See page 22, and compare the eupathic response called *euthumia* (εὐθυμία), a species of joy, defined in Ps.-Andronicus, *On Emotions* 6 (*SVF* 3.432) as "joy in the management or self-sufficiency of the universe."

[27] See *Leisure*. 2.1, 5.5–6.1; *Letters* 58.27, 65.15–20, 92.6, 95.10.

to us in our present condition: it is what we *should* feel, and in our best moments may begin to approximate, but it properly belongs only to the virtuous wise. The thought of it may serve as an enticement toward moral progress; however, Seneca is careful not to make the advent of joy the very point and purpose of moral progress. Virtuous wisdom itself continues to be the aim of existence.

As long as these principles can be maintained, Seneca has room for significant variation in his treatment of what joy is and how it works. He is content to speak of it sometimes as a response and sometimes as an unbroken state, and to associate it firmly with externals in one context even though insisting elsewhere on its relation to goods of character. The fact that he is untroubled by such inconsistencies, even on a topic he cares about, seems to me to be indicative of his manner of working and perhaps too of the way he understands his task as a philosopher. An avid reader, and if we may believe his own account an eager conversationalist as well, he is more concerned to capture the depth and excitement of others' views than he is to impose a system of his own thought upon the world. These priorities make him less of a philosopher by our standards, but a better recorder of philosophical ideas. His own not inconsiderable contribution is most often in the dramatic frame, the engaging manner of expression, and the justification of the enterprise as a whole.

We gain something also for the earlier period of Stoicism. To read Seneca in the way I suggest is also to read *through* him and his Roman interlocutors, casting our minds toward earlier analyses that he might have read. We catch a glimpse, maybe more than a glimpse, of a whole range of approaches to eupathic response within Hellenistic Stoicism. If what I have said here is correct, then we can posit several different Stoic accounts of joy: a static and supervenient version, adopted by Seneca in *On Happiness*; a kinetic version that responds to integral goods only, as defined in letter 59; a version concerned especially with the goods of friendship, adopted by him in letter 109 and in the treatise *On Benefits*, a consolatory version that he adopts in letters 63 and 99, and a highly intellectual version that crops up in discussions of the contemplative life. In addition to these, there was one version with which he was unfamiliar, but which was known to Cicero and Diogenes Laertius, classifying joy as one of four generic *eupatheiai*.[28]

Curiosity is naturally drawn to the atypical Stoic treatment of joy given in letter 66. I argued in Chapter 5 that the likeliest explanation for the

---

[28] A similar conclusion can be drawn (from very different evidence) about confidence (θάρρος, *fiducia*); see Graver (2007: 213–20).

unusual features of this letter is that its Stoic argument is directed against a Peripatetic opponent who sets the terms of the debate with his terminology of preferred or "primary" goods. It may not have been Seneca himself who made the adaptation, however. A likelier explanation is that he derives the main argument of the letter from one of the less-well-attested Hellenistic authors, perhaps from Hecaton, a pupil of Panaetius, who is known to have written a treatise on goods in at least nine books;[29] or from Antipater or Diogenes of Babylon, whose accounts of the *summum bonum* made explicit reference to preferred and dispreferred indifferents.[30] It would then be one of those authors who made rejoicing the proper response to preferred indifferents.

The richness and variety of these Stoic traditions on joy suggests in the first place that the psychology of the wise person, including his or her affective responses and states, was regarded within the school as a matter of real importance. Diversity of view suggests energy and discussion: where we find evidence of multiple treatments of a topic, we can be sure that more extensive work was being done. Motivation for taking up the topic of joy in a range of treatises may have come from the long-continued effort to combat hedonist approaches, that spoke of mental and physical pleasure as the sole motivation for moral action. Virtually anyone who wrote against Epicurus or the other hedonists must have found it advisable to provide an alternative account of what positive affect is for.

Such an account would need to be rendered on Stoic principles; it seems clear, however, that it did not need to conform in every detail to the treatment given by Chrysippus. When one reads the elaborate definition and classification systems in some surviving witnesses, it is easy to imagine that these represent a set of official dogmata espoused by everyone in the school. We may be nearer the mark, though, if we regard such classificatory ventures as opportunities for individual philosophers to display their ingenuity while maintaining a broadly Stoic allegiance. Dogma, at least in this school, consisted in a set of core intuitions that one could scarcely give up without ceasing to philosophize in the Stoic manner. Beyond that, the field was open.

---

[29] See Diog. Laert. 7.103; Veillard (2022); Setaioli (1988: 308–15). The suggestion that Hecaton might be the source for the classification of goods in letter 66 was made previously by von Arnim (1921–24: vol. 3, 27).

[30] See von Arnim (1921–24: vol. 3) Diogenes Babylonius pp. 44–48; Antipater Tarsensis pp. 52, 56–59. For Seneca's knowledge of Antipater, see *Letters* 87.38–41, 92.5.

PART IV

The Self within the Text

CHAPTER 9

The Challenge of the Phaedrus
Therapeutic Writing and the *Letters on Ethics*

> That book changed my heart; it changed even my prayers to you, o Lord, and made my wishes and desires other than they were.

So writes Augustine of Hippo in *Confessions* 3.4, about an event in his life as a reader. The words are a prayer, for the *Confessions* is a Christian text; but the book Augustine is remembering is not the Christian scriptures, but a text of Roman philosophy, the *Hortensius* of Cicero.[1] That book, Augustine says, caught hold of him in his youth, and it was Cicero's protreptic to philosophy that first set his feet on the path toward the priesthood. Of course, we cannot now assess the validity of this claim about an event that took place sometime around 371 CE, inside the mind of someone studying a now-vanished text. We can see, though, that in his self-representation as a reader, Augustine puts himself for a moment in the position of his own readers, that invisible public that, as it were, overhears his prayer throughout the work. His story of his youthful reaction to the *Hortensius* provides them with a model of openness and humility in the approach to a text, encouraging them to engage with the *Confessions* in the same way. For Augustine believes that written texts can exercise real influence over the mind and character of their readers, changing their values and their behavior, transforming lives far removed in time and space from the author's own.

This notion that written texts can sometimes be transformative for their readers appears very early in Greco-Roman antiquity. It is in evidence as early as the fifth century BCE, when Gorgias of Leontini credits early writers of meteorology with the ability to "take one belief away and create another in its place, making things that are incredible and obscure appear

---

[1] For aims of the *Hortensius*, see Cicero, *Tusc.* 3.6; *Fin.* 1.2. The fragments are collected in Grilli (1962); and see also MacKendrick (1989: 109–13).

before the eyes of belief."² Borrowing the language of medicine and of the philosopher-poet Empedocles, Gorgias speaks of both oral and written discourse as a powerful drug, a φάρμακον, that works on the mind rather than the body. Such a drug may be used to deceive, bewildering the other with "bad persuasion," but the effects may also be salvific: putting an end to disease, giving delight, rousing the audience toward courage.³ Much later, in the last century of the Roman Republic, we catch another echo of Empedocles in the promise of Lucretius to use the power of writing to reshape the mental universe of his reader. His poem will be a medicinal cup administered as to a reluctant child, with sweetness to elicit cooperation and reasoned argumentation to deliver the needed healing.⁴ Lucretius's nocturnal labor will thus be amply repaid in therapeutic benefits to Memmius, his addressee and internal reader.

Already in fourth-century Athens, though, there were voices ready to challenge any claim of therapeutic efficacy for doctrines presented in written form. In the last pages of Plato's dialogue *Phaedrus*, Socrates offers a well-argued indictment of the view that written texts, even philosophical texts, can ever change the character of a reader. For compelling reasons, Socrates believes that real ethical development does not ever come about through reading but only through the give-and-take of live conversation. In saying this, he gives more than just one person's view, for Plato's contemporary Isocrates, who makes some of the same points, indicates that they are widely shared.⁵ But the arguments given in the *Phaedrus* are especially important ones that require our attention in the first part of this chapter. For whether or not Plato himself means to endorse those arguments, he gives voice in them to a historically significant notion of what teaching, and in particular philosophical teaching, should consist in.

In the philosophical schools, oral delivery and live discussion remained the pedagogical norm even where books were in regular use. The enthusiasm with which philosophers of the fourth century, including Plato, took up the nascent genre of the prose dialogue as their vehicle of choice

---

² *Encomium of Helen* 13. That Gorgias is thinking of texts as well as oral delivery is confirmed by γραφείς ("written") in the same paragraph. While interpretation of the *Encomium of Helen* remains controversial, helpful resources can be found in Pratt (2015); Wardy (1996: 25–51); Poulakos (1983); Kerferd (1981: 78–82); Segal (1962).
³ *Encomium of Helen* 14. For the quasi-magical term φάρμακον in Empedocles fragment B111 Diels-Kranz, see Faraone (2019); Lloyd (1979: 33–35); for more generally on Greek incantatory or magical discourses, see Laín Entralgo (1970).
⁴ See especially Lucretius 1.935–50, 4.10–25. For Empedocles as the model for Lucretius's poetic project, see Sedley (1998).
⁵ Isocrates, *Letter 1* (*To Dionysius*) 2–3; *Oration 5* (*To Philip*) 25–26. See Sullivan (2007: 9), 18n12.

suggests an ideological commitment: paradoxically, orality is championed by its written mimesis.⁶ In the Hellenistic period there were some philosophers who wrote nothing; others wrote copiously but regarded written works as repositories of knowledge rather than as the instruments by which teaching is effected. While it is admitted that certain kinds of reading can be motivational for the study of philosophy – Plato's *Alcibiades*, for instance, or Aristotle's *Protrepticus*, or in one notable instance Xenophon's *Memorabilia of Socrates* – that effect is not sufficient for imparting the skills, attitudes, and intellectual commitments that make one a philosopher.⁷ The preference is always for direct tutelage by oral methods, through lectures, class sessions, or for the wealthy in one-on-one tutoring sessions. In the words of Pierre Hadot, "In matters of philosophical teaching, writing is only an aid to memory, a last resort (*pis-aller*) that will never replace the living word."⁸

In the *Discourses* of Epictetus, which supply our best evidence of instructional methods in philosophy during the Roman Empire, the act of reading is constantly called into question. Epictetus does not reject books altogether – he himself reads daily – but he restricts what can be expected from that kind of study.⁹ The main task, he thinks, is to bring the pupil's desires and aversions, impulses, and habits of assent into accord with nature; and books cannot do any of those things. For the writings of Chrysippus, he has a respect bordering on reverence, for he regards him as the one who "has discovered and brought to light the truth not for living, but for living well, and has conveyed it to all people" through his treatises.¹⁰ Yet making the acquaintance of Chrysippus's books will not in itself yield any benefit for the pupil. Reading is of use only insofar as the reader is guided by a live instructor who can judge his needs and abilities. Otherwise, it brings psychological sickness rather than health, causing the incautious reader to "vomit, or have bad digestion, then cramps, diarrhea, fevers."¹¹

---

⁶ For the rapid proliferation of prose dialogues or *Socratikoi logoi* during the fourth century, see Ford (2009).
⁷ According to Diog. Laert. 7.2, it was reading the second book of Xenophon's *Memorabilia* that inspired the young Zeno of Citium to begin studying (Cynic) philosophy with Crates of Thebes.
⁸ P. Hadot (1990: 497), trans. by Davidson and Wissing from P. Hadot (1981: 30).
⁹ Epictetus, *Discourses* 1.10.8; 1.4.6–17. Dobbin (1998: 95) compares Seneca, *Letters* 33.7–9 and Marcus Aurelius 2.3: "Away with your books! Do not be drawn to them any longer, it is not allowed" (trans. Dobbin). Further on Epictetus's methods of instruction, see Hijmans (1959: 41–46); Dobbin (1998: 130); Long (2002: 97–127).
¹⁰ Epictetus, *Discourses* 1.4.31.   ¹¹ Epictetus, *Discourses* 1.26.16.

Epictetus's own resistance to writing as the vehicle for philosophical teaching stands in contrast to the ambition of Arrian of Nicomedia, the historian and biographer who circulated the written version of Epictetus's teachings to the public. In the preface to his publication, Arrian explains that in producing the written version, he hopes to do the one thing that Epictetus himself sought to achieve in speaking, namely "to move the minds of his hearers toward what is best."[12] He is diffident, however, about the ability of his text, or indeed *any* written text, to draw readers toward ethical living.

> If in fact these *Discourses* were to achieve that aim, then they would have the ability that philosophical discourses ought to have. But if not, then may it be known to those who encounter them that when Epictetus himself spoke them, the hearers could not help but feel exactly what he wanted them to feel. If these *Discourses* do not produce that effect on their own, perhaps I myself am at fault, or perhaps there is even a necessity that it should be so.[13]

With his appeal to "necessity," Arrian acknowledges that his stated objective is in tension with the position that Epictetus himself seems to hold on the potentialities of written texts. No doubt aware of the irony, Arrian leaves the matter unresolved.

With Seneca, however, we have the opportunity to observe how a talented philosophical author not only registers the concern about the efficacy of his chosen medium but also seeks to resolve that concern. Well trained in rhetoric, familiar with the potential of formal speech to stir emotion and sway decision, Seneca is also an ambitious writer with a strong interest in literary achievement. Like Lucretius, he seizes on the notion that philosophical reading can be a transformative experience and frames his own projects accordingly, as efforts to heal and to inspire. Pressing the medical analogy, he often uses words like *prodesse* ("to benefit" or "to be of use") and *efficax* ("effective") to emphasize the curative potential of the written word. Unlike Lucretius, however, Seneca is also sensitive to the kinds of theoretical considerations that are expressed in Plato's *Phaedrus*. He speaks with some frequency about those challenges, sometimes even echoing (though perhaps unwittingly) the very words of Socrates. When he insists nonetheless on the therapeutic value of his writing, it is as one who has discovered ways to overcome the difficulties

---

[12] Arrian of Nicomedia *Preface to the Discourses* 5. One should not discount the possibility that Epictetus may have produced the written version of the *Discourses* himself or overseen its production: see Dobbin (1998: xx–xxiii).
[13] Arrian of Nicomedia *Preface to the Discourses* 6–8.

of the project. As early as the dialogue *On Tranquility of Mind*, but especially in the *Letters on Ethics*, he sets out consciously to adapt the style and format of his philosophical writing to better serve the needs of readers who do not have the benefit of in-person instruction. In the central part of this chapter, I trace out some of the strategies he uses to achieve that end.

An important and perhaps surprising aspect of Seneca's treatment of this issue is his interest in the emotions of readers. Since Seneca is an exponent of Stoic ethics and is committed to the Stoics' negative view of the emotions, one might expect him to eliminate emotional response from his account of therapeutic reading. Indeed, in the early treatise *On Anger*, he speaks of reader emotions as transient and inconsequential sensations that have no moral significance whatsoever. In the *Letters*, however, he makes a point of modeling an emotionally engaged kind of reading that responds particularly to the ethical content of the text being read. In the last part of this chapter, I consider how Seneca's treatment of reader emotions should be understood in relation to the Stoic theory he inherited. I argue that the representation is consistent with Stoic ethics, but not theorized by earlier philosophers, and further, that these reactions are modeled for Seneca's readers as part of his larger project in adapting therapeutic philosophy to the medium of writing.

Deficiencies of the Written Word

Near the end of his dialogue *Phaedrus*, following a long discussion of the proper use of rhetoric in the sense of public speaking, Plato has Socrates tell a story about the invention of writing. Theuth, the Egyptian god who first devised a system of writing, believes that he has invented an elixir, a φάρμακον, of memory and of wisdom (274e). But the god-king Thamos does not agree. Writing, Thamos says, can give people a semblance of wisdom, but it cannot give them real wisdom: those who learn by reading, without direct instruction, "will appear to be knowledgeable in many areas, but in fact they will be, for the most part, ignorant" (275b). Continuing in this vein, Socrates says that anyone who thinks writing can pass on a skill must be "brimming with naivety" (275c). Written works can remind people of what they already know, but they cannot teach, because teaching requires live interaction. In order to understand what is being said, the learner may need to ask questions, so as to have the thought explained in some different way or to hear the response to various objections. A book cannot meet this need, any more than a painted portrait can carry on a conversation.

> Writing has a strange characteristic, Phaedrus, that is very like painting. The offspring of painting stand there as if they were alive, but if anyone asks a question, they maintain a dignified silence. It's the same with [*sc. written*] discourses: you would think they were speaking from some intelligence, but if you ask them anything, wanting to learn their meaning, they keep on signifying one and the same thing forever. Once it is written down, the discourse is carted around everywhere, to those who understand and to those who are unsuited to it. It doesn't know who it should speak to and who it shouldn't. When it is mishandled or unfairly criticized, it needs the help of the parent, for on its own it isn't capable of defending itself or helping itself. (*Phaedrus* 275d–e)

Written philosophy is thus a mere imitation of real teaching, "the living and breathing discourse of one who has knowledge." The latter is "written in the mind of the learner, along with knowledge, being capable of defending itself, and knowing to whom it should speak to whom it should say nothing" (276a). Then, switching the metaphor, Socrates compares written philosophy to the sort of pseudo-agriculture that is practiced by women at the festival of Adonis. As the tiny container gardens planted in the heat of summer grow up rapidly but yield no fruit, so words written with pen and ink "cannot defend themselves with reasoning and cannot adequately teach the truth" (276c). It is only the oral method of instruction, "using the skill of dialogue" (276e), that can produce any real result. Just as serious agriculture "sows its seeds in appropriate soil and is pleased when they come to maturity in the eighth month" (276b), so real philosophical discourse chooses an appropriate hearer, one who will not only take in the arguments but also go on to reproduce them for others:

> Taking a mind that is suited to it, he plants and sows discourses along with knowledge, ones that are able to help both themselves and the one who planted them. These are not without fruit; they produce seeds, and from those, yet more discourses are able to grow in yet more characters. (*Phaedrus* 276e–277a)

The result is that where writing may be a "very fine amusement" for the philosopher with stories to tell about justice and the like (276e), it is only live conversation that can produce happiness (εὐδαιμονία) for those who possess it (277a).

From this densely imagistic passage, we can extract three observations about features that Socrates regards as essential in oral teaching but that are lacking in the written counterpart. The first is a matter of *proximity*. Much of the behavioral impact of the philosopher's discourse is dependent on the physical presence of the philosopher as a living person, whose conversation is likewise "living and breathing" (ζῶντα καὶ ἔμψυχον, 276a). In part, the effectiveness of in-person teaching may be attributed to direct behavioral modeling: when we know a person well, we can imitate and even anticipate their behavior without need for explanation. But in describing the discourse *itself* as living and breathing, Socrates appeals more specifically to the fact that much of face-to-face communication is not encoded in the words themselves, but in tone of voice, facial expressions, body language, and other nonverbal signals. When he calls the written word a mere image – an εἴδωλον (276a), better translated "wraith" – he emphasizes that in a written message, this rich stream of information is greatly attenuated.[14]

A second important feature of oral communication is its *adaptability* to characteristics of the hearer. In Socrates's conception of teaching, it is essential that the philosopher identify which individuals are ready to hear the discourse and speak to them alone. Oral teaching knows "to whom it should speak to whom it should say nothing" (276a). More broadly, an in-person teacher has the opportunity to alter the style and manner of the discourse to suit the needs of individual hearers, in the same way as the skilled agriculturalist chooses different seeds for different soils (276b): a more complex philosophical discourse for one sort of mind, a more straightforward account for another. While written philosophy might seem to have the advantage in that it can be duplicated and distributed to a wide audience, Socrates feels that availability to all and sundry can be an impediment to teaching. The very fact of dissemination means that the text is bound to come in contact with some who are not ready to receive it, with the result that it is "mishandled or unfairly criticized" (275e). Without some reasonable discrimination as to the recipients, the work loses effectiveness even with those who might stand to gain by it.

Third, Socrates is strongly interested in that aspect of oral teaching that we now call *interactivity*. A speaker can pause for questions and can even think on the spot to answer objections or resolve confusions. For those in attendance, that give-and-take may be especially important as an opportunity to participate in the thought process and to develop their own critical thinking skills. But written works cannot pause their flow of language to hear the questions of the recipient, and they cannot change whatever it is they are saying in order to respond to individual concerns.

---

[14] In contrast to an εἰκών ("likeness," from ἔοικα, "resemble"), an εἴδωλον (from *εἴδω, "see") is an "image" in the sense of a ghost or phantom; that is, that which gives the visual appearance of something without the substance of it (LSJ⁹ s.v. εἴδωλον IA).

When it is time to stop and listen, they "keep on signifying one and the same thing forever," and when it is time to reply to the reader's questions, they "they maintain a dignified silence" (275d). Consequently the written word seems to Socrates to be an ineffectual replica of real philosophical instruction, beautiful and entertaining perhaps, but incapable of engendering productive change in those who receive it.

Socrates's case in favor of orality is a powerful one. It expresses with clarity and force a set of concerns that many philosophers have had about the teaching of reasoning skills, and more generally about any teaching that is to have a major behavioral impact. These concerns are ones that it is incumbent on Seneca to address, if he means to pursue the therapeutic program he has laid out for the *Letters on Ethics*, regardless whether he first became aware of them through direct reading of Plato's dialogue, or from elsewhere in the philosophical tradition, or even by his own reflections.[15] For Seneca's claim is very bold, bolder even than the promise Lucretius had made for his poem. Where Lucretius had offered enlightenment to one contemporary, the praetor Gaius Memmius, Seneca declares his intention to alter the lives of a wide readership, including some readers long in the future. He writes "for the greater number" and "for posterity," meaning to supply "healthful admonitions" to subsequent generations (8.1).[16] In this way he hopes to preserve his name and, with it, the names of those to whom his books are dedicated (21.5). The advantages of oral discourse in terms of proximity, adaptability, and interactivity thus present him with a major challenge.

In what follows, I mean to show that Seneca's offer to benefit readers through the written word is made with full awareness of the reasoning that denies literature that capability. Indeed he expresses his own reservations about the therapeutic potential of books, sometimes echoing the concerns of Plato's Socrates. These reservations tell in favor of teaching and learning in person, and indeed face-to-face communication is constantly mentioned in the *Letters* as the best way to promote moral progress. But while he allows that oral teaching would be preferable, Seneca also maintains that a therapy conducted entirely through the medium of writing is a real possibility. He does this not because he is unreflective about the potentialities of the written word, but because he has hit upon ways of crafting the

---

[15] While Seneca appears to have had direct knowledge of some Platonic dialogues (see Setaioli (1988): 117–40), there is no compelling evidence that the *Phaedrus* was one of them. Tieleman (2007): 141–42) notes a quotation from *Phaedrus* 245a in *Tranquility* 17.10, but suggests, plausibly, that Seneca might have found the line "in a thematically arranged anthology."

[16] The passage is quoted at more length on page 28.

reading experience to make it more immediate, more flexible, and more interactive than reading a dialogue can ever be. His confidence on this point is not a matter of "naivety," as Socrates charged; instead, it relates directly to a series of choices he has made regarding the style, the rhetorical address, and the literary form of his work.

Speaking across Time and Space

In the 94th letter, as part of a theoretical discussion of pedagogical method in philosophy, Seneca remarks on physical proximity as an avenue of communication. The mere presence of the wise is beneficial, he says, even if the philosopher never utters a word. He then cites Phaedo of Elis – the pupil of Socrates, who was himself a composer of dialogues – for a curious comparison:

> Just how this happens would be hard for me to tell you, but I am sure that it has happened. As Phaedo says, "There are some tiny creatures whose attacks are so miniscule and insidious that we don't even feel them when they bite us. Their bite is marked by a swelling, but even the swelling itself shows no wound." The same will happen to you in associating with men who are wise. You will not realize how or when it helps you, but you will realize that it has. (*Letters* 94.41)

Midge-like, the wise affect others by avenues that cannot be traced: their influence is not reducible to some specific utterance or argument that might be spelled out in so many words. Seneca has in mind, perhaps, the kind of communication that comes through nonverbal signals: gestures, facial expressions, and the like. Alternatively, he may be referring to the example of the philosopher's personal life and to the ability one has, when one knows a person well, to envision how they would react in a given situation. Both ideas are present in letter 6, where the reference is to Seneca's own influence on his addressee Lucilius. In that letter, he represents himself responding to a request from Lucilius for copies of "the things you have found so efficacious"; that is, for the books he has been reading (6.4). These he is very willing to send, with helpful annotations. He comments, though, that face-to-face contact with himself as teacher would be far more effective:

> But formal discourse (*oratio*) will not do as much for you as direct contact, speaking in person and sharing a meal. You must come and see me face to face – first of all, because humans believe their eyes much more than their ears, and second, because learning by precepts is the long way around. The

> quick and effective way is to learn by example. If Cleanthes had merely listened to Zeno, he would not have been molded by him; instead, he made himself a part of Zeno's life, looking into his inmost thoughts and seeing whether he lived in accordance with his own rule. Plato and Aristotle and the whole crowd of philosophers who would later go their separate ways all derived more from Socrates's conduct than from his words. (*Letters* 6.5–6)

Even books that have already proven their worth, and that come with some guidance as to their use, seem not to be comparable to in-person instruction; or, as Socrates had it, "the living and breathing discourse of one who has knowledge" (*Phaedrus* 276a).

A priori the effect Seneca is describing would seem to be impossible to reproduce in a written text. The divide between writer and reader is a necessary consequence of the use of writing to reach a wide audience. In the language of the *Letters on Ethics*, what represents that gap is the Strait of Messina that separates Italy from the province of Sicily where Lucilius serves as civil governor. In letter 45, Seneca again expresses his desire to meet with his pupil in person: "I'd send myself over to you if I could," he writes (45.2). Like Ovid's Leander, he imagines himself swimming the distance, heedless of danger – though in his case, old age makes the wish absurd rather than heroic:

> If it weren't for my hope that you will soon obtain leave to conclude your duties there, I would resolve on travel, elderly as I am. Even Scylla and Charybdis, the fabled straits, would not frighten me away. I would not only cross them; I'd swim them, if it meant that I could embrace you again, and see for myself how much your mind has grown.[17]

As in letter 6, the books of philosophy that he promises to send instead are distinctly a second choice. Even if they are Seneca's own books, as Lucilius requests, they cannot possibly replace the loving companionship of the author himself or do his work as a teacher.

And yet Seneca repeatedly claims that the divide can be bridged by means of the written word. While entire books – *libri*, that is, whole scrolls of continuous writing – cannot make the connection, the individual letters that make up the *Letters on Ethics* can do so. Indeed, that should be part of the reader's expectation, for Greco-Roman conventions assigned this task to the letter writer: to render the absent present, to conjure up the sensations of

---

[17] *Letters* 45.2. Compare Ovid, *Heroides* 18, and see Altman (1982: 13); Lindheim (2003: 18–23). Compare also Isocrates, *Letter 1* (*To Dionysius*), 1 "If I were younger, I would not be sending a letter, but would have sailed to you myself and would be conversing with you there" (i.e., in Syracuse).

The Challenge of the Phaedrus 205

in-person communication within a distance medium.[18] Creating a vivid impression of character – "a likeness almost of one's own mind," according to the stylistic theory of Demetrius – was the aim of epistolography and was something that a writer could consciously promote, just as public speakers practiced the technique of character depiction (*ethopoieia*).[19] Seneca sometimes finds occasion to advertise this potentiality of his chosen medium. "I am letting you into my private room," he writes (27.1), and "I wish my letters to be like what my conversation would be if you and I were sitting or walking together" (75.1). In the same way, he makes a point of exclaiming over the successful self-depiction he finds in the letters of Lucilius to himself. In letter 67, his ongoing conversation "with books" is seamlessly integrated with his epistolary conversation with his friend: "Every time a letter arrives from you, it seems to me that I am with you. I feel as though I were actually answering you and not just writing back" (67.2).

In letter 40, Lucilius's letters provide "a moment of recognition" (*agnoscere*) that is more powerful than any visual image:

> I am grateful to you for writing so often, for you are showing me yourself, in the only way that you can. It never fails: I receive your letter, and right away we are together. If portraits of absent friends are a delight, refreshing our memory and easing the pain of separation with a kind of comfort, though false and empty, how much more delightful are letters, which bring us real traces, real news of an absent friend! For what is sweetest about seeing someone face to face is also to be found in a letter that bears the imprint of a friend's hand – a moment of recognition. (*Letters* 40.1)

In what sense is the epistolary presence of the other "real" while that created by a painted portrait is "false and empty"? A single visual image supplies a vast amount of information, much more than can be coded into a verbal message of any reasonable length. But verbal missives are not limited to the messages they convey in so many words. By means of description or by metaphors and other figurative language, they can conjure up mental images that are rich in quasi-sensory content. Just a few words, working as signals or "traces" (*vestigia*), may be enough to engage the reader's memory and

---

[18] Thraede (1970: 65–74) documents Seneca's awareness of earlier epistolary conventions, noting in particular the ἀπών-παρών trope of *Letters* 55.9–11 and 40.1. See also Edwards (2018: 327–28); Edwards (2015); Cambron-Goulet (2014); Wilcox (2012: 4–22 and 139–42); Inwood (2007b).

[19] Demetrius, *On Style* 227 "The letter, like the dialogue, should have in abundance the element of character (τὸ ἠθικόν). For one writes a letter as a likeness almost of one's own mind (σχεδὸν γὰρ εἰκόνα τῆς ἑαυτοῦ ψυχῆς), and while it is possible to see the character of the writer from every other form of discourse, one does not see it from any other so much as from the letter." On Demetrius and the rhetorical theory relating to epistolography, see Malherbe (1988: 2–14); Poster (2007).

imagination. In fact, the letter may permit an even closer connection in absence than normally occurs with geographical proximity, for what matters is a mind "that accommodates all things to itself" (55.8). The pleasure of spending time with Seneca in Campania is available to Lucilius as long as he holds on to his friend mentally. Even friends who live together will be in different spaces much of the time; the mind, though, "can converse with friends in their absence" and itself "is never absent" (*conversari cum amicis absentibus licet ... numquam abest*, 55.9–11).

The endeavor to create such a powerful impression in his own readers is one of the most obvious features of Seneca's own writing in the *Letters on Ethics*. Virtually every letter includes some description of small events of his day-to-day experience, often rich in evocative detail, together with an account of his thoughts and feelings in relation to them. Where his technique differs from that of other epistolographers is chiefly in the application of that lively self-characterization to the purposes of ethical teaching, when he extrapolates from anecdotes of his own represented experience to broader principle of ethics. Seneca's watching the mail boats come in gives way to a reflection on life's journey (letter 77); his being disturbed by the roar of a nearby stadium to the contest with fortune (letter 80); an attack of his asthma to courage in the face of death (letter 54); and so on. Literary self-fashioning is put at the service of philosophical instruction.[20]

It may indeed be that the presence of the author within the text goes beyond conscious self-depiction to a more intimate form of availability. In a passage to be treated in more detail later in this book, Seneca commits himself to a theory of discursive style whereby the mental characteristics of an author are necessarily and fully observable in the written composition.[21] Language, whether spoken or written, is a direct manifestation of the linguistic facility that inhabits the author's mind, the talent (*ingenium*). But the *ingenium* cannot differ in character from the mind itself, the *animus*: the one is "completely mixed" with the other, "and receives from it its shape, direction, and principle" (114.3). The debased prose style of Maecenas in letter 114 serves as a negative example, but there are also cases in which the style of writing gives evidence of an admirable character: a dry and sober style of writing is sure evidence of a mind that is serious and self-controlled; a lively style, just like an energetic walk, indicates a vigorous mind. Hence an attentive reader has direct access to the mind of

---

[20] A similar point is developed in Wildberger (2014); see also Schafer (2011) and (2009: 67–83).
[21] See pages 243–246.

the author: not only the self that the author chooses to reveal, but the self that *is* revealed in the very texture of the writing. What Seneca sees in the writing of Lucilius is not just a product made by Lucilius; it is Lucilius himself: "*You* are tall, upright" (46.2). By the same token, Seneca's own writings make him present to his readers in a real and meaningful way.

Finding the Right Audience

Let us now turn our attention to Socrates's point about the adaptability of spoken discourse and the corresponding lack of flexibility in written works. While a speaker can observe those who are listening and so knows when to speak and when to be silent, a writer produces the same text for all readers, including some who lack the ability to understand the discourse they have encountered and who may reject or even vilify it. As Martha Nussbaum has observed, the metaphor of philosophy as a healing art connotes responsiveness to the needs of the individual, in which regard, "written texts will always be inferior to personal communication."[22] Of course, Seneca's works are formally addressed to individuals of his acquaintance, as was typical in Roman philosophical writing; in reality, though, they are intended for a wide audience of readers whose mental characteristics he does not know and whose needs he cannot predict. The implications for his therapeutic claim would seem to be very serious.

Even if Seneca were writing for the named addressee alone, the value of his work would be limited by his lack of knowledge concerning that person's situation at the time of reading. "Over and over you consult me about specific matters," he writes to Lucilius, "forgetting that you and I are separated by a wide and empty sea" (71.1). In order for his advice to be specific enough to be of use, it must be formulated "on the spot" (*sub manu*, 71.1) or "in the ring" (*in harena*, 22.1), the way the gladiator observes every move of his opponent. Writing, though, can only consider the general case:

> What is customarily done, what duty requires, can be dictated in the general case (*in universum*), and also written down: such advice is given not only to those who are away but even to posterity. But on the further question, when or in what way it should be done, no one can give advice at a distance: one must make the determination according to circumstances. (*Letters* 22.2)

---

[22] Nussbaum (1994: 335–41).

Nor would his knowledge of Lucilius's character help him to advise even Lucilius himself in a sufficiently specific way. For he would need also to know Lucilius's current condition, what he is thinking and feeling in the very moment when advice is needed. "A doctor cannot appoint by letters the proper time for eating or bathing: he must feel the pulse" (22.1).

Clearly, Seneca is aware that the need for individualization presents a challenge for therapeutic writing. But he also offers some strategies that a philosophical author may use to achieve at least some of the aims of ethical therapy. Addressing the problem of specificity, he suggests that the role for the written text might be to provide a kind of general-purpose diagnosis and system of treatment, with the work of individualization being performed by the learners themselves. We have this in the treatise *On Tranquility of Mind*:

> How can this tranquility be attained? Let's investigate that question in the general case: you will then take as much as suits you from the public remedy. In the meantime, we need to expose this human failing in its entirety; from that, each person will recognize their own part. (*Tranq.* 2.4–5)

In the *Letters on Ethics*, the idea is developed further. Responding in letter 64 to a reading from Quintus Sextius the Elder, Seneca remarks that while the main principles of philosophy have all been discovered "by the ancients" (*a veteribus*), there is still much work to be done in terms of application to individual cases. At the level of metaphor, those principles are like the different substances that cure diseases of the eye: they are efficacious, but only if someone does the further work of compounding the salves and selecting the time and method of administration that is right for the individual (64.8). Similarly, in *Letters* 8.2, he says that the "healthful admonitions" that he is writing are provided to posterity "like the recipes for useful salves" (*velut medicamentorum utilium compositiones*).[23] In effect, his work is a philosophical recipe book, or more precisely a pharmacopoeia: a compilation of existing medical knowledge into specific instructions for the treatment of a range of possible ailments. His role as a philosophical author thus comes between the discoverers of philosophical principles and the ultimate users of those principles. Working with elements previously established by the founders of the Stoic system, he will spell out how their arguments address every kind of human failing; it is for

---

[23] *Compositio* and *componere* are technical terms for the preparation of medicaments, as also in *Ben.* 4.28.4; *Happiness* 17.4. Scarpat (161–62) notes precise parallels between the language of *Letters* 8.1–2 (*compositio, persanare, prodesse, efficax*) and the medical treatises of Scribonius Largus.

the readers of his book, though, to determine how those remedies are to be implemented to meet the particulars of their individual situations.

In order to fulfill their role in this three-stage philosophical cure, readers will need their own form of expertise. They need self-knowledge and knowledge of their current state, and they also need some method for bringing the words of the text to bear on their personal emotional and moral ills. Like the users of the pharmacopoeia, they must be able to choose from the book of medical knowledge what is applicable to their condition as well as to determine the time and manner of application. At a theoretical level, Seneca's whole project as a self-described therapist-through-literature depends on this. If there is to be therapeutic writing, there must also be therapeutic reading.

Now, a very noticeable feature of the *Letters on Ethics* is the obsessive frequency with which they comment on the act of reading.[24] Seneca and Lucilius are constantly reading books, talking about books, sending one another books, and Seneca very often delivers advice on the proper use of books for personal development. In the early letters, he recommends a meditative practice in which one restricts the number of authors read, selects just a few passages to concentrate on, and then continues to dwell on these through memorization and daily reflection.[25] He also models the practice by incorporating sample passages with brief comments of his own into his letters; for these, the author on whom he draws most often is Epicurus, though non-Epicurean authors also serve the purpose. The attitude he tries to promote is one of dedication to the task and receptiveness to new ideas, but it is not without critical distance, for his comments sometimes go in a different direction from the statements he quotes from books, and his handling of Epicurus in particular is tinged with irony.[26] So it is not really a reversal when, in letter 33, he shifts the emphasis toward reading texts – now especially Stoic texts – in their entirety, and toward independence of judgment. "Let there be some distance between you and the book," he writes (*aliquid inter te intersit et librum*, 33.9). In letter 84 his emphasis is again on developing one's own integrity of thought, which means both one's personal talent as a writer and one's moral character as an agent: in order to do this, one must start by absorbing deeply the words of the text, "digesting" them (*concoquamus illa* 84.7).[27] The reading of literary texts is included in Seneca's program along with the philosophical, notably in 108.24–35,

---

[24] As remarked also in Gunderson (2015: 14–36).
[25] On this practice, see also pages 98–100 and following.
[26] Wildberger (2014) traces some specific instances in which the use of Epicurean material in these letters departs from Epicurus's philosophical views.
[27] For the metaphor see page 274 with note 10 in Chapter 12.

where he gives examples of how passages of Vergil and Cicero may be read in ways that are either helpful or unhelpful for moral progress.[28]

Considered in the ensemble, these numerous remarks on methods of reading constitute a program of study in the reading of philosophy for therapeutic ends. Seneca is not content merely to deliver the concepts and arguments of Stoic ethics; he wants also to impart the strategies and habits of reading that will make the philosophical cure efficacious for a wide spectrum of readers. For engaged, thoughtful reading that looks toward one's personal and moral development is exactly the technique that will enable philosophical writing to get past the limits of its textual presentation.

One Half of a Conversation

There still remains the third advantage of speech as stated by Socrates. According to the *Phaedrus*, effective teaching requires the opportunity to interact with the learners and answer any questions they might have. Because written works cannot do this, they are not able to help anyone; indeed they themselves "need the help of the parent." Isocrates, who makes the same point in language similar to Plato's, adds that because the writer is absent, the written discourse is "orphaned" (ἔρημα) and is less likely to be believed.[29]

The opportunity for interaction is certainly an important aspect of orality. It would be overly simplistic, however, to treat it as an advantage of all oral discourse across the board. Everyone has heard speakers who never pause for questions, and indeed there are some kinds of speech that are not meant to include any sort of audience interaction. This point should be kept in mind as we consider Seneca's solution to the problem of interactivity in philosophical literature.

In letter 38, Seneca speaks directly to the therapeutic efficacy of the genre he has adopted. As often, he commences with a request made (he says) by Lucilius. As the format of his book does not include any letters authored by Lucilius, these rather stagey backward references supply us, the readers at large, with the clues we need to reconstruct the exchange. This time, the request concerns the exchange itself, and Seneca's short response – designedly the shortest letter in the book – constitutes a manifesto for the epistolary format.

---

[28] In addition to the passages cited here, see *Letters* 6.5, 45.1–2, 88.35–38, 108.1–2, with discussion in Graver (1996) and Schöpsdau (2005).

[29] Isocrates, *Letter 1* (*To Dionysius*) 3.

You are right to insist that we exchange these letters more frequently. The reason dialogue is highly beneficial is that it works its way into the mind bit by bit. Speeches prepared in advance and delivered before a crowd make for more noise, but less intimacy. Philosophy is good advice, and no one gives advice in ringing tones. There are times when one does need to deliver a campaign speech, if I may call it that, when someone is hesitating and needs a push. But when the aim is not to motivate learning but that the person should actually learn, then one has to revert to these less strident utterances. They get in more easily, and they stick; for one does not need a great number of words, but words that are efficacious.

They should be scattered like seeds. A seed is just a little thing, and yet when it lands in the right spot, it unfolds its resources and expands into a great and growing plant. Reasoning does the same: when you examine it, it is of small extent; but when you put it into effect, it grows. Only a few words are said, but if the mind receives them well, they become tall and strong. I say it again: words work like seeds. Though tiny, they achieve much. Only, as I said, the mind that receives them has to be suited to them, and has to absorb them. Then it will itself reproduce them, and many more than it received. (*Letters* 38.1–2)

One notices immediately the resemblance of the imagery in the second paragraph to Socrates's comparison of the words of the philosopher to seeds and the mind of the hearer to favorable soil. This may not be a conscious allusion, for the metaphor of words as seeds was commonplace enough.[30] Whether it is or not, the point of Seneca's seed image is rather different from that made in the *Phaedrus*. Where Socrates means to raise difficulties about the use of writing in philosophy, Seneca is more concerned with the brevity and simplicity of the type of writing that he currently favors. When philosophy is presented in letter format and is taken in by a suitable mind, the few words that make up the letter will take root and grow. Then, as in the *Phaedrus*, the discourse will go on to reproduce itself many times over.

The reasoning that supports this optimistic view of the letter is given in the first paragraph. Seneca's key move is to draw a contrast between two types of spoken utterance: prepared speeches (*disputationes*, also called *contiones*, "campaign speeches") and the dialogue or conversation (*sermo*). The prepared speech has some utility, but it is the quiet conversation that has real efficacy in ethical teaching, because it "works its way into the mind bit by bit" (*minutatim inrepit animo*). We are to understand that philosophical letters (*haec submissiora verba*, "these less strident utterances") are

---

[30] Cf. Schönegg (1999: 53–56). Armisen-Marchetti (1989: 148–50, 195–96) lists parallels in other authors and elsewhere in Seneca.

PLATO	
ORAL/INTERACTIVE	WRITTEN/CONTINUOUS

SENECA		
	oral	written
interactive	CONVERSATION	LETTER-EXCHANGE
continuous	DISPUTATION	TREATISE

☐ *effective*   ▨ *ineffective*

Figure 9.1 Modes of discourse in Plato, *Phaedrus* 274b–277c and in Seneca, letter 38

similar to the conversation, rather than to the prepared speech: they are intimate, quiet in tone, and of small extent, qualities that foster an exchange of ideas with the pupil. Although Seneca does not say so directly, he strongly implies that the pedagogical efficacy of the letter is in contrast to the continuous written work in a more elevated style; namely, the full-scale philosophical treatise. Such a work may serve an important function, just as oral disputations do, but it cannot "get in and stick."

Seneca's position on interactivity in philosophical teaching is thus different from that of Socrates and somewhat more complicated. In the *Phaedrus*, we saw a straightforward opposition between oral and written instruction, with the first being more interactive and consequently more pedagogically effective than the second. For Seneca, the important contrast is not between speaking and writing as such, but between interactive and continuous formats. In effect, he adds a dimension to the contrast between oral and written forms, and he also flips the axis that indicates which forms are considered effective (see Figure 9.1).

Where Socrates privileges orality as such, Seneca orients his discussion toward the characteristics that make some kinds of oral discourse efficacious with their hearers and others not. Provided the written work exhibits the right characteristics, there is no reason why it should not have the same efficacy. Letters are ideal for the purpose, because of the stylistic features conventionally recommended in letter writing, but above all because of the element of reciprocity that belongs to the very nature of a correspondence.

The word "exchange" (*commercium*), in the very first sentence of letter 38, highlights the interactive nature of epistolography, as does Seneca's backward reference to a preceding letter by Lucilius.[31] We are invited to imagine the two men in an epistolary conversation with one another, with Lucilius interposing his own questions, ideas, and experiences and even

---

[31] For the term, see *OLD* s.v. *commercium* 1, 4; for the financial metaphor see Armisen-Marchetti (1989: 74–75, 106); Wilcox (2012: 103–4).

influencing the structure of the correspondence by requesting a more rapid-fire exchange. However, this epistolary conversation, the one between Seneca and Lucilius, is not a sufficient answer to the question that is before us. For the *Letters on Ethics* are not simply the remnants of a historical correspondence between Lucius Annaeus Seneca and Gaius Lucilius Junior. The exchange of letters we see going on within the text belongs in reality to the more distant readers who are Seneca's actual audience.[32] And even if Seneca did send precisely these letters to the historical Lucilius and did receive his responses, the benefits of that interactivity would be only for one person. We would still need to consider how a reader who belongs to "the greater number" or to "posterity," as Seneca says in 8.1–2, may gain some of those benefits.

At this point, it is helpful to consider again the unprecedented literary form that Seneca adopted when he began circulating his books of letters to Lucilius. The idea of writing philosophy in letter form was not in itself new: both letters and pseudo-epistles had been used extensively in the Hellenistic period as a vehicle for philosophical thought.[33] But what Seneca produced was an extensive collection of letters all to one addressee and all from himself, with no examples of letters coming back from Lucilius. From his own remarks, he appears to have taken inspiration from the volumes that had perhaps only recently been published at Rome of Cicero's letters to his friend Atticus.[34] His project is to reproduce the effect of reading such a one-sided correspondence, but with philosophical content, and in a work addressed not to Lucilius alone but indirectly to the wider public.

That authorial decision brings to the fore the dynamics of the exchange itself. Consider: We have before us the letters of Seneca – one half of a dialogue, as Demetrius says.[35] Within those letters we see frequent references to questions posed by Lucilius and to his specific interests, but never the letters of Lucilius himself. As a result, distant readers like ourselves are induced to imagine those letters, reconstructing Lucilius's questions, his doubts, and his objections. We become, as it were, substitute authors for these invisible letters that we imagine him writing. In this way we come closer to the experience of Seneca's internal reader Lucilius than we could

---

[32] See page 9 and following.
[33] Sykutris (1931) provides a typology of Greek and Roman letters; see also Görgemanns (2006), and for pseudoepistolography P. Rosenmeyer (2001).
[34] Seneca refers to Cicero's letters in *Letters on Ethics* 21.4, 97.2–8, 118.1–2. See Wilcox (2012: 100–3); Inwood (2007c).
[35] Demetrius, *On Style* 223.

ever come to that of, for instance, Glaucon in Plato's *Republic*. Where a written dialogue gives us a mimesis of a philosophical conversation, with both parts written out for us, Seneca's unprecedented genre of philosophical writing enables us to construct one side of the conversation for ourselves. As we stand in for Lucilius, think his thoughts as it were, we enter into a more participatory relationship with Seneca the epistolographer than we can ever have with Plato.

Reader Emotions and Moral Progress

I would like now to attend more specifically to the emotional dimension of reading as we see it in the *Letters on Ethics*.[36] The intimacy and intensity of philosophical reading on Seneca's model gives ample scope for emotional involvement, and numerous passages, including some we have already seen, suggest that Seneca sees emotional response as an important part of reading. But there are questions to be asked about the way that he understands the affect-laden responses of readers. For Seneca is a Stoic author with a strong interest in emotion theory. If indeed he recognizes reader emotions as a category of experience, then it will be helpful for us to investigate how those feelings relate to his Stoic analysis. Further, we should consider whether it is reasonable for an author who often contends against emotion to encourage this kind of engagement with books, and what might be the implications for his therapeutic project.

Seneca had raised the subject of reader emotions already in the early treatise *On Anger*, in the context of a theoretical discussion of emotional response. There, his examples showcase the reading of historical narratives, and his point is that responses experienced while reading, like responses to the visual arts and to performances on stage, are not real emotions but belong rather to the class of involuntary feelings. Romans of his generation may feel themselves becoming angry when they read about Clodius driving Cicero into exile, about Sulla's proscriptions, and other similar events; they may feel something like fear when reading about Hannibal's siege of Rome (2.3–5). But such reactions are not real anger and fear; they are only "movements of minds that do not will to be moved" (*motus ... animorum moveri nolentium*), or "beginnings presaging the emotions" (*principia proludentia adfectibus*, 2.2.5). Crucially, the element of assent is lacking: these readers do not actually believe that they have been wronged by

---

[36] The topic of this section is treated in more depth in Graver (2017b), and see now as well Van Wassenhove (2021).

Clodius or that they are threatened by Hannibal's army, and consequently they are not motivated toward any retributive or aversive action. The feeling is essentially a trivial phenomenon that has no impact on behavior one way or the other.

By contrast, the experience of reading in the *Letters on Ethics* includes some strong feelings that have a clear connection to Lucilius's past and future behavior. Making use of the narrative and self-representational techniques of the epistolographer, Seneca repeatedly describes reactions that he himself claims to have had while reading letters sent to him by Lucilius. That these reactions are affective in nature is indicated both by the presence of emotion terms and by the heightened language, full of excited figures of speech and evocative comparisons:

> I am thrilled (*exulto*) every time I get one of your letters. For they fill me with great hope. No longer are they making promises on your behalf; now we have a solemn pledge. Do that, I beg – no, I beseech you (*oro atque obsecro*), for what better request can I make of my friend than what I would ask on my friend's behalf? (*Letters* 19.1)

> I swell – I exult – I shake off my years and feel again the heat of youth (*cresco et exulto et discussa senectute recalesco*), each time I learn from your letters and from your actions how far you have surpassed even yourself. For you broke from the pack some time ago. If a farmer takes delight when a tree bears fruit, if a herdsman is pleased when his animals bear young, if one who sees a protégé reach adulthood always feels as if it were his own coming of age, then how do you think a person feels when he has been in charge of someone's intellectual development and sees that immature mind grown up all at once? (*Letters* 34.1)[37]

In these examples, the reaction Seneca describes is in part to the sheer presence of the friend, since, as we have seen, creating an impression of one's own character is one of the aims of epistolography. But Seneca also responds to the content of Lucilius's letters, specifically in that they bring reports of promising developments in his friend's character. In Stoic terms, his feelings relate to a genuine good.

It can also be a book about ethics that stirs the reader's emotion. Seneca's affect-laden response to the book sent to him by Lucilius relates not only to the style of the work but also to its content. Comparing Lucilius's achievement in philosophy to those of Livy and Epicurus, he describes his response as

---

[37] Another instance is *Letters* 40.1, quoted on page 205.

one of joy occasioned by the author's talent and also by his "spirit" (*animus*), the latter term referring to expressions of courage in the face of misfortune.[38]

> The sunshine beckoned – hunger nagged – a storm threatened – and still I read it through to the end. It was not only delight that it gave me: it was joy (*non tantum delectatus sed gavisus sum*). What talent it showed – what spirit! (*Letters* 46.1–2)

He then refers to the content (*materia*) as essential for engaging the author's talent (46.2) and again commends Lucilius for stirring his reaction to that subject matter:

> I will write more about the book when I have been over it a second time; at present my judgment is hardly settled. It is as if I had heard these things rather than read them. (*Letters* 46.3)

Similarly, he reports feelings of excitement and confidence occasioned by a reading from the Roman moralist Quintus Sextius the Elder. Again, the exclamatory mode and the jerky rhythm are suggestive of a heightened emotional state:

> Then there was a reading. It was a book by Quintus Sextius the Elder – a great man, you may be sure, and a Stoic, even if he denies it. Good gods, what vigor there is in the man – what spirit! That's not something you'll find in every philosopher. Some of them are widely renowned and yet what they have written is dry and lifeless. They construct arguments, debate issues, and raise objections, yet they never rouse the spirit, because they are spiritless themselves. When you read Sextius, though, you will say, "He is alive – vigorous – free – he soars above humankind; he sends me away full of tremendous confidence" (*plenum ingentis fiduciae*). I will tell you what is my own state of mind when I read him: I yearn to challenge every stroke of fortune – to shout, "Why let up, fortune? Do your worst! See, I am ready!" (*Letters* 64.2–4)

Confidence (*fiducia*) signifies a firm motivation to face adversity without quailing, the opposite of fear in classical texts.[39] With a touch of humor, Seneca compares himself to the young Ascanius of *Aeneid* book 4, who gallops this way and that in his enthusiasm for the hunt, hoping to meet

---

[38] Both Livy and Epicurus are mentioned as voluminous (*levis* in 46.1 is "light," not "smooth"; see Alexander (1952)) but also as writers of moral philosophy; see *Letters* 100.9. For the expression "what spirit" (*quid animi*), compare *Letters* 64.3 *quantum animi*; 24.22 *quod dictum alicuius animosum*.

[39] See Graver (2007: 213–20).

some dangerous beast. "I yearn to have something to conquer – something I can endure as part of my training" (64.5).

These reactions of Seneca's are not just the inconsequential pre-emotions as in *On Anger* 2.3–5. For the element of assent that was lacking in *On Anger* is present here: Seneca believes what Lucilius says about himself, and he believes the principles of ethics. But neither are they instances of the ordinary emotions, since in the Stoic analysis the ordinary passions typically depend on mistaken assumptions about the value of indifferents (as, for instance, the threatened destruction of Rome by Hannibal's forces), while the objects Seneca is concerned with here are aspects of character and conduct, which Stoics treat very differently.[40] A better comparison is to the "good emotions" (*eupatheiai*) of Stoic theory. These arise from true beliefs about character goods: joy in the presence of the virtues or some present exercise of them; wishing (βούλησις) for future goods (for example, for some anticipated exercise of a virtue); caution at the prospect of real evils – that is, at some nonvirtuous action, which the wise person will proceed to avoid. For Seneca, the most important of the "good emotions" is *gaudium* (joy), which he often treats in ways that relate clearly to the concepts of Stoic philosophy. So it is probably significant when he says in 46.2 that the feeling he experienced was "not delight . . . but joy." That charged term is used in something approaching its technical sense as an idealized affective response.

One might object at this point that in this instance, and generally in the reactions he describes to Lucilius's letters, Seneca is not speaking of a reaction to some promising development in his own character, but to reported improvements in the character of his friend, and that, consequently, the objects in which he is rejoicing are still external to himself. Within the Stoic theory of friendship, however, there is a persistent emphasis on shared mental experience. Friends are good for one another, and there are legitimate affective responses to the presence of a friend and to the friend's virtuous activities. Seneca's response to Lucilius's letters might for instance be compared to the species of eupathic response called "good intent" (εὔνοια), "goodwill" (εὐμένεια), and "welcoming" (ἀγάπησις); or, in the genus "joy" (χαρά), one might call it "cheerfulness," (εὐφροσύνη), defined as "joy in the sensible person's deeds."[41]

---

[40] In the Stoic system of value, goods include the virtues and whatever else belongs to virtue, for example, courageous actions; evils include the vices (or flaws) and flawed actions. Moral progress is counted as an inherently preferred indifferent: Diog. Laert. 7.107, Stobaeus 2.7.7b, 80 Wachsmuth (*SVF* 3.136).

[41] For the goods within friendship, see Diog. Laert. 7.124; for the various species of eupathic response, see page 47.

There is another issue, however. Seneca has made it clear that the self he projects within the *Letters on Ethics* is not to be understood as the moral exemplar but is merely among those who aspire toward wisdom. We can hardly think, then, that the emotions he experiences as a reader are the *eupatheiai* of Stoic theory. For Stoic texts consistently state that the normative versions of emotional response occur only in the person of perfect wisdom. Seneca's thinking on this point is similarly restrictive. Concerning joy, he says several times that while ordinary agents may aspire to that exalted feeling, they cannot experience it in their present condition.[42] He is also well aware that his relationship with Lucilius cannot instantiate the ideal form of friendship that exists among the Stoic wise. The two of them may be called friends in the ordinary sense of the word, but true friendship is still beyond them (6.2–3, 35.1–2), and with it the joy and confidence that wise friends experience in one another (109.5–6).

Yet even though Seneca's readerly emotions cannot be eupathic, they share an important feature with the eupathic responses, in that they are directed at moral objects, not at misconstrued indifferents. This puts them in the category that in *Stoicism and Emotion* I labeled "progressor emotions": affect-laden responses of the nonwise toward the kinds of objects that Stoic ethics recognizes as genuine goods and evils.[43] An ordinary flawed individual perceives some aspect of his or her own character of conduct as being either valuable or reprehensible and responds with eagerness if it is something good, with shame or loathing if it is bad. Or, an ordinary person observes some encouraging or discouraging tendency in the behavior of a friend and reacts with gladness or disappointment. We can think of these feelings as bastard versions of the *eupatheiai*, promising in that they arise from correct opinions about value but deficient in that they occur in the nonwise, who may be gravely mistaken in their interpretations of their own and others' behavior.

Observe that the attitude of a nonwise person toward the real goods and evils of Stoic ethics will necessarily be different from that of the normative agent. In those who lack virtuous wisdom, a response to moral goods as present could only be on a contrafactual basis ("if I were wise") and a response to moral goods in prospect would be conditioned on personal transformation ("if I should become wise"). In contrast to the constant joy and confident eagerness of the wise, the most realistic forms of affect for these imperfect agents would be remorse for present wrongdoing and a vigorous distaste for

---

[42] *Letters* 23.1–6; 27.3–4; 59.1–4, 14–18.
[43] See Graver (2007: 191–211); Brennan (1998: 50–51) aptly calls them "veridical emotions."

the future errors that they are all too likely to commit. It is important to note, though, that feelings of this kind – remorse for wrongdoing, aversion from further error, yearning for personal goodness – are exactly the ones that are appropriate to the nonwise condition. Moreover, both the remorse and the yearning could be highly motivational for those who are being educated toward wisdom. The paradigm is the young Alcibiades, who weeps over his moral failings and begs Socrates to instill in him a better character.[44] Even if Alcibiades is hasty in his judgments and easily distracted from his resolutions, still these would seem to be the feelings that have the best chance of setting him on the road toward virtue. As such, they could potentially be quite important in a Stoic approach to moral education.

In the remnants that we have of Hellenistic Stoicism, however, there is only a little evidence that the progressor emotions were recognized even as a theoretical possibility. Authors earlier than Seneca sketch out the concept, but there is no attested terminology for affective responses of this type, and their potential utility does not seem to have been explored.[45] Seneca's interest in this category of feeling appears to come of his own initiative, prompted by his own rhetorical and philosophical instincts. While he fully agrees with his school's position on the dangers of anger, fear, grief, and pleasure, he senses that the emotional responses one might have to a philosophical letter or to a book on ethics are different in kind from those ordinary emotions. He never gives us an explanation of that difference – for he found none in his Stoic predecessors – but his awareness of it has shaped his self-representation in the *Letters*.

A curiously equivocal passage in letter 59 betrays the difficulty Seneca has in fitting his thoughts about reader response into the existing Stoic theory. As in other examples we have seen, the passage depicts Seneca having a strongly positive emotional response to a letter from Lucilius. This time, however, he considers how that reaction ought to be categorized within Stoic emotion theory:

> From your letter I derived great pleasure – for you must allow me to use common parlance; you mustn't recall my words to their Stoic meanings. It is

---

[44] Ancient sources for this anecdote regarding Alcibiades are listed in Graver (2007: 252n1). The motivational possibilities of nonwise moral shame are recognized by Epictetus; see *Discourses* 3.23, 3.27, with Kamtekar (1998) and Graver (2007: 254n27).

[45] According to Galen, Posidonius actually denied that feelings of this type ever occur (*PHP* 5.26–28 = fragment 164.12–25 Edelstein and Kidd). Cicero, who appears to have read the treatise on emotions by Chrysippus, speaks similarly to Posidonius in *Tusc.* 3.68–70, but elsewhere in the same work (3.77–78, 4.62) gives more scope to them, while still treating them as flawed responses that should be done away with. See further Graver (2002a: 114, 122–23, 203–6, 219).

> our doctrine that pleasure is a fault. Be that as it may, "pleasure" (*voluptas*) is the word we generally use to refer to a glad feeling of the mind. I know, say I, that if we make words adhere to our statutes, then pleasure is discreditable, while "joy" (*gaudium*) pertains only to the wise person, for it is the elevation of a mind confident of goods that are real and its own. (*Letters* 59.1–2)

Citing a Stoic definition of *gaudium*, he notes that if that word is used in its philosophical sense, then he himself is not eligible to feel it, since he is not wise. However, the alternative term *voluptas* will not do either, for in Stoic doctrine the emotion of pleasure is as much a fault as any other emotion, and he does not mean to say that his feeling is discreditable. Continuing, he notes that Vergil's phrase *mala mentis gaudia* ("evil joys of mind") represents a non-philosophical usage of *gaudium*: In Stoicism, delight in the wrong sorts of objects would instead be termed *voluptas*, signifying that people are glad of what is actually harmful to them (59.3). Ultimately he decides that his response to Lucilius's letter must also be termed pleasure rather than joy, arguing that even though the nonwise person may be rejoicing "for an honorable reason" (*ex honesta causa*), his emotion is still "set in motion by belief in a false good" (*opinione falsi boni motam*) and is uncontrolled, excessive, and quick to change to its opposite (59.4). This language expresses well the Stoic position on nonwise delight, but still hardly suits the purpose, for it leaves Seneca with the awkward implication that Lucilius's letter is a "false good" over which he, the reader, may soon come to grief. What he needs, rather, is a term that will allow him to preserve the usual tenor of his remarks on Lucilius's correspondence, expressing warm approbation of his friend's efforts at self-improvement. But the emotion theory he has inherited does not supply him with any such term.

Seneca's treatment of the emotions of readers is very much part of his endeavor to adapt the medium of epistolography to the purposes of philosophical therapy. Guided by his rhetorical training, his experience of the literary tradition, and the nature of his therapeutic project, he develops a habit of modeling in his own person the kind of response to a text that he wants his own readers to have: feelings of excitement at the thought of acquiring the virtues, eagerness to face adversity with courage, affection for the writer as a philosophical friend. The opening of letter 64 is particularly significant in this regard, for in describing his reaction to Sextius's book, Seneca is explicit about his expectation that Lucilius will go on to read Sextius himself and will experience just the same emotion (*cum legeris Sextium, dices* . . ., 64.4). Given Lucilius's position as Seneca's epistolary counterpart, we should assume in any case that the warm feelings Seneca expresses in response to Lucilius's letters are mirrored in

Lucilius's reaction to Seneca's. For readers who have learned already to place themselves in the role of Lucilius, trading letters with Seneca in a reciprocal relationship, there is strong inducement to allow the *Letters on Ethics* to engage their own affective capacities, in ways that, in theory at least, should support Seneca's therapeutic objectives.

***

Of all Seneca's works, the *Letters on Ethics* is the most frequently and obviously concerned with the potentialities of the written word. Earlier in this book, I argued that the *Letters* have a particular concern with this issue because, in the work's stated program, it is the therapeutic efficacy of written works that justifies the philosopher's expenditure of time in producing them.[46] In this chapter, I have tried to bring out some of the strategies that Seneca devises in the *Letters* for maintaining a plausible claim to therapeutic efficacy in the face of the well-reasoned preference for orality articulated in Plato's *Phaedrus* and in other places in the philosophical tradition. These Senecan strategies involve the use of rhetorical techniques to recreate a sense of authorial presence, together with attempts to train readers themselves in how to adapt the recommendations of the text to their individual situations, and with the manipulation of literary form to allow for quasi-dialogic engagement. Finally, they include a coordinated program, in keeping with Seneca's rhetorical training, to stir the emotions of the reader in ways that support Seneca's objectives while remaining consistent with his usual commitment to Stoic ethics.

---

[46] See page 28.

CHAPTER 10

The Mouse, the Moneybox, and the Six-Footed Scurrying Solecism
Satire and Riddles in Seneca's Philosophy

Flat-footed critics have too often failed to see the vein of humor that runs through Seneca's philosophical prose. Writing on the *Pumpkinification* farce, Martha Nussbaum once went so far as to call the philosophical Seneca a "sober killjoy," for which she was rightly scolded by a more perceptive reviewer.[1] And others have made the same mistake, seeing in Seneca the moralist, the rhetorician, and (sometimes) the intellectual, but missing entirely the wit. The resulting picture is defective, and not only in that it overlooks one stylistic register of the author. It also impoverishes our understanding of Seneca's objectives as a writer and sometimes of his actual philosophical views.

Previous studies have done something to reclaim Seneca's use of humor as a rhetorical device to engage his readers.[2] I hope here to contribute to that effort by bringing out Seneca's debt to Horatian satire and to the conventions of Roman invective humor. Still more important, however, are several specific passages in which sensitivity to Seneca's style of wit is required in order to properly assess his positions in philosophy. These include, among others, his management of Epicurean *sententiae* in letters 1–29; the attitude toward formal logic he displays in letters 45, 48, and 49; and an extraordinary riff on Stoic metaphysics in letter 113. In each of these cases, I will argue, Seneca directs his humor against a certain mode of philosophical discourse; and yet it would be a mistake to read his mockery as indicative of *philosophical* self-positioning. The aim is not to endorse or reject views of any particular school. Rather, the use of humor serves to mark and maintain boundaries within the project of the philosopher as a writer or speaker. In essence, humor functions as a disciplinary mechanism for the preservation of generic decorum.

---

[1] Nussbaum (2009: 112); the reviewer is Aldo Setaioli (2009: 12–13).
[2] See especially Armisen–Marchetti (2004a); also Grant (2000); Motto and Clark (1968).

Before making that case, however, I need to recover a more general picture of Seneca's characteristic style of humor and of his place within the tradition of Roman humor.

Seneca's Comic Style

In the *Letters on Ethics* especially, there are many passages where the humor is quite easy to recognize. Fond of verbal wit, Seneca occasionally brings in a cross-linguistic pun, naming with appreciation the originator of the witticism. In letter 29, for instance, he attributes to Mamercus Aemilius Scaurus a line about a *soi-disant* philosopher who rides everywhere in a litter: "Well, he's certainly not a *Peripatetic!*"[3] Probably traditional is the bon mot at the end of letter 51, where the pleasures of the flesh are compared to the Egyptian robbers called *phēlētai* or, homophonically, *philētai*, "sweethearts"; thus, "they embrace us just to throttle us" (51.13).[4] Another more difficult pun is attributed to Albinovanus Pedo, who was an associate of Ovid: the wastrel who is up half the night is called *lychnobius*, meaning either "one who lives by the lamp" (*lychnos*) or "one who lives greedily" (*lichnos*) (122.16).[5] An obvious species of humor, and one that draws more on Seneca's own imagination, is the incongruous juxtaposition. A troupe of stylishly mounted bon vivants meets Cato the Elder on his packhorse, hung about with various useful articles.[6] The provincial governor Pacuvius performs like Trimalchio his evening ritual of being carried off to bed on a funeral bier, as musicians play and the funeral chant is raised in handclapping rhythm – by his catamites.[7] Sattia, who died at age ninety-nine and boasted of her longevity on her tombstone, could easily have appeared in an epigram of Martial: "Who could have put up with her if she had lived to be a hundred?" (77.20).

Now and then we are treated to a more elaborate sketch of human folly in the harlequin style of verse satire. The bathhouse scene of 56.1–3 is especially memorable, with its many varieties of ridiculous behavior – the weightlifters grunting with pretended effort, the noisy masseurs, the swimmer who cannonballs into the *frigidarium*, the armpit-hair plucker

---

[3] *Letters* 29.6 *utique Peripateticus non est*. A "Peripatetic" is literally a *walking* philosopher.
[4] The pun is explained by Gummere (1917) ad loc., citing the occurrence of φηλητής in Callimachus's *Hecale*. But the word is much older, and the wordplay traveled with it; it is implied already in Aeschylus, *Choephoroi* 1001–4.
[5] The wordplay is explained by Summers (1910) ad loc.   [6] *Letters* 87.9–10.
[7] *Letters* 12.9; the humor is pointed out by Grant (2000) 321.

(*alipilum*) peddling his services in a screeching falsetto until he gets a client, who then screeches in his place.[8] Like the verse satirists, Seneca caps the scene with a snatch of dialogue. "You must be made of steel," says the interlocutor "or deaf, to retain your concentration" amidst all that noise: just think of Crispus, who died from an excess of guests! (56.3).[9] Even better is Calvisius Sabinus of *Letters* 27.5–8, a wealthy man, but ill-educated, who buys slaves to memorize poetry for him: "I never saw such a vulgarian with such a fortune," says Seneca. Here, too, the sequence culminates in a bit of witty repartee: Satellius Quadratus, the parasite, encourages Sabinus to take up wrestling next, and when Sabinus protests that he is a poor physical specimen, he replies, "Oh, please don't say that! Don't you see how many super-healthy slaves you have?" At more length, Seneca goes on about the "Antipodeans" of letter 122, strange-minded Romans who sleep during the daytime and are out and about in the wee hours of the morning. "They are as sinister as birds of the night" (*tam infausti ominis quam nocturnae aves sunt*, 122.3). Very much in the Horatian manner, Seneca first ridicules the behavior as a widespread fault, then singles out an individual as egregious in this regard: one Sextus Papinius, who does his accounts after nightfall, practices his vocal exercises at midnight, and finally gets to the dinner table as day is dawning. The entire passage is peppered with witticisms quoted from public figures of the preceding generation, perhaps drawn from a published collection or from the notebooks of Seneca's father, although an autoptic first person at 122.15 (*audieramus*) suggests the material is Seneca's own.[10]

In his more aggressive moments, Seneca's characteristic style of humor pillories its objects with a sharp-sighted and very personal cruelty that can make the modern reader squirm. That element of invective, frequently directed at a named individual, was quite common in Roman humor regardless of genre. A joke normally has a butt, who is exposed to ridicule: the reader or listener joins forces with the humorist against the targeted individual or group and enjoys the sensation of being included. In general terms, this form of humor is sometimes referred to as the *humor of*

---

[8] *Letters* 56.2.
[9] The manuscripts have *Crisipum*, sometimes taken to refer to Chrysippus, but this cannot be right. The correct reading must be *Crispum*, referring to Nero's stepfather Passienus Crispus. The *salutatio*, or morning visit, was a familiar though perhaps annoying experience for the Roman patron. The suggestion that it might actually be fatal seems likely to have originated in a witticism of Passienus Crispus himself, whose clever turn of phrase can be observed in Seneca's own anecdotes at *Ben.* 1.15.5 and *Natural Questions* 4a *praef.* 6.
[10] Corbeill (1996: 6–7) reviews the evidence for the circulation at Rome of collections of witticisms and maxims by well-known orators.

superiority.[11] Amy Richlin, in her 1992 monograph *The Garden of Priapus*, explores this typical mode of Roman humor through the paradigm figure of Priapus, the agricultural deity whose ithyphallic image symbolically threatens to rape the invader of garden or orchard. Richlin's thesis is that in Roman literary culture, the humorist assumes that same aggressive posture vis-à-vis some excluded and transgressive figure. The language used seeks characteristically to soil or degrade that outsider, and the response of laughter expresses solidarity with the satirist in his endeavor to protect the privileged domain.[12]

Again, it is instructive to compare this aspect of Seneca's writing with the techniques of verse satire. The invective element is particularly strong in satire: according to Horace, it was typical of Gaius Lucilius, the founder of the genre in the second century BCE.[13] The satirist thus has "hay on his horns" like an angry bull, or speaks "with black tooth" like a serpent.[14] Names may be used, and yet the satirist's aim is easily distinguished from that of the invective orator.[15] Where the orator seeks to diminish the social standing of an individual opponent, the satirist is concerned rather with some objectionable form of behavior that might be emblematized by the named individual. The broader interest creates the opportunity for thematized development, rich in pictorial detail, involving numerous persons, real or imagined, and enlivened with snatches of dialogue. The resemblance is very striking between Horace's standard satiric technique, as seen, for instance, in *Satires* 1.1 (social climbers), 1.2 (adulterers), or 2.8 (dinner parties), and such passages in Seneca as *Letters* 27.5–8, 95.22–33, and 122.2–16. Given that Seneca clearly knows Horace's work,[16] it is reasonable to suppose that his own invective technique has been directly influenced by his satiric predecessor.

Meanwhile, there is another side of the invective tradition that must be considered. Readers of Roman satire and of Horace's other invective collection, the *Epodes*, have been quick to point out that the tactic of aggressive verbal shaming is counterbalanced by a frequent impulse toward self-incrimination, in which the attack is humorously turned back on the

---

[11] Plaza (2006: 6–13) provides a useful summary of the psychological theories of humor that are most applicable to Roman verse satire.
[12] Richlin (1992: 58–59, 66–67).   [13] Horace, *Satires* 1.4.1–13; 1.10.1–4; 2.1.62–74.
[14] Horace, *Satires* 1.4.34, *Epodes* 7.15.
[15] Corbeill (1996) explores the dynamics of invective humor in the political oratory of the Roman Republic.
[16] He quotes from *Satires* 1.2 in *Letters* 86.13 and 119.13 and from *Satires* 1.3 in *Letters* 120.20.

speaker.[17] The paradigmatic figure of the humorist as threatening Priapus is then replaced by the transparently impotent vituperator of *Epodes* 8 and 12 or by the Saturnalian slaveholder of *Satires* 2.7, taken to task by his own servant. The strong first-person voice of verse satire makes this inversion a natural device for the humorist. The tables are turned; the social critic is implicated in his own criticism.

Remembering this element of self-caricature gives us a way to understand the moments of ignominious self-disclosure that are surprisingly frequent in Seneca's letters.[18] A particularly lively example is in letter 12, where an irate Seneca scolds his caretaker for the age of a grove that he himself had planted, and sneers at a toothless gaffer who turns out to be younger than himself:

> Turning to the door, "Who's that?" I asked. "He's decrepit! You were right to station him by the door – he's on his way out! Where did you get him? Is it some whim of yours to take a corpse off someone's hands?"
>
> But the man said, "Don't you recognize me? I'm Felicio! You used to bring your trinkets to show me. I'm the property manager Philostitus's son, your playfellow."
>
> "He's nuts!" said I. "Has he now turned into a little child, and also my playmate? Perhaps so! He's losing teeth enough!" (*Letters* 12.3)

Such exaggeratedly awkward self-portraits occur over and over: Seneca attending philosophy classes alongside the teenagers (*Letters* 76.1); Seneca beaten in a foot race by a six-year-old (83.4); Seneca lurching along the public highway in a mule cart (87.4); a dripping wet Seneca vomiting on the beach (53.1–5). But the undermining of Seneca's own authorial voice may also be more subtle, a matter of tone, a faint sense of the ridiculous. It may come out in the figurative language: Seneca venturing into a volume of Epicurus "as a spy" (*Letters* 2.5) or camping out like a "shipwrecked sailor" (87.1). Or it may take the form of an interruption by the internal reader, a constant but undifferentiated presence whom one is only rarely tempted to identify with the addressee Lucilius.[19] In letter 24, the reader's voice responds to a string of *exempla* for courageous death with a needling "I expect you'll now tell me about Cato." "Why shouldn't I?" says Seneca in his own voice, then proceeds undeterred, as if unaware that the interlocutor (who is of course his own creation) regards the narrative

---

[17] This aspect is brought out already in Richlin (1992: 59). For Horace's impotence as a defining theme in the *Epodes*, see Oliensis (1998: 68–77).
[18] This aspect is especially well brought out in Watson and Watson (2009).
[19] For discussion, see Roller (2015: 60–61).

that follows as overkill. These staged interruptions in the stream of discourse run the tonal gamut from entirely neutral to sharply confrontational. Even when they are mere requests for clarification, they serve to remind Seneca's readers that his authorial perspective is not the only one that matters. When the tone rises to a challenge, we see the moralist faring forward against a resisting wind.[20]

In what follows, I explore some instances of Senecan humor that are more specifically concerned with the writing of philosophy. When these are directed at others, they can be best understood in terms of the border-policing function of Roman invective humor. Like every author, Seneca has made certain choices about how his subject matter can best be addressed; from his point of view, these choices are norms of discursive conduct. On occasion he makes use of aggressive humor to punish other speakers and writers on philosophical topics for (as he sees it) violating the norms he, Seneca, wishes to uphold. In so doing, he notifies his audience of what those standards are, and gives them reason to appreciate his own observance of them. In other cases, the humor is self-directed, or directed simultaneously at other philosophers and Seneca himself. The policing function of invective humor then turns into self-policing. Instead of punishing the transgressive conduct of others, Seneca points out his own transgressions against norms he himself has established. In this way, he is able to maintain the boundaries he has set for the philosophical letter collection while *also* allowing himself the freedom to violate those expectations.

Tambourines and Riddle-Syllogisms

To illustrate the model, I begin with a relatively straightforward example of Seneca's aggressive style of humor against those whose approach to philosophical teaching differs from his own. The example comes from sections 12–13 of the dialogue *On Happiness*; those criticized are proponents of Epicureanism. In the preceding pages, Seneca has given an extensive critique of Epicurean hedonism, with particular attention to the fifth of the *Key Doctrines*, which states in part that it is impossible to live a pleasant life without also living prudently, honorably, and justly. Like Cicero in *De Finibus* book 2, Seneca is concerned about the use of this statement by his Epicurean contemporaries as a pretext for a sybaritic lifestyle. He grants that the real Epicurean pleasure was nothing of the kind; it was indeed

---

[20] For a few examples of the more challenging sort of interlocutor interruption, see *Letters* 45.2, 68.14, 71.21, 113.26, together with those listed in note 35 in this chapter.

sober and austere, *sobria ac sicca*. But he argues that the hedonist claim is corrupting nonetheless, just because it is misunderstood. The proponent of Epicureanism has misrepresented the doctrines of the founder in order to make them seem attractive, and in so doing has put himself in a dishonest position:

> For this reason, I do not say, as many of our authors do, that the sect of Epicurus promotes debauchery; but I do say this: it is ill spoken of; it is disreputable. "But it doesn't deserve it." Who knows that, if he has not yet got inside? The forefront of it gives credence to the story and stirs up nefarious expectations. You are like a strong man wearing a dress: your chastity is intact, your manhood unimpaired, your body is free of vile abuse – but in your hand is a tambourine! So let them choose an honorable placard, with a slogan that rouses the spirit, for the one that is there was devised by the vices. (*On Happiness* 13.2–3)

Seneca does not say that his Epicurean counterpart is effeminate; indeed, he *says* the reverse.[21] But when he dresses him in women's clothing, notes primly that he has never been raped, and then puts in his hand the instrument used in the worship of Cybele, there can be no doubt as to the implications. The effect is both ludicrous and acerbic, calculated to punish a transgression. Not, in fact, a sexual transgression; for while Seneca does object to what he calls debauchery (*flagitia*), he claims that those who seek opportunities for vice will not find them in the Epicurean community. The real transgression is in the discourse that falsely advertises Epicureanism as a source of such pleasures. The dishonest protreptic that seeks to gain adherents by such means is represented metaphorically as a form of prostitution.

A more challenging case of Seneca's satirical aggression spans a whole series of letters in book 5 of the *Letters on Ethics*. In these, Seneca explains and criticizes a particular mode of philosophical discourse that I refer to here as the *cavillatio*, or riddle-syllogism; as will be seen, the name is itself a point of interest. Examples include the "horn" syllogism mentioned in *Letters* 45.8 and spelled out in 49.8:

> What you have not lost, you have.
> But you have not lost horns.
> Therefore you have horns.

---

[21] For the ambiguous assertion, compare *Letters* 21.10, where a misleading placard attracts new adherents who are sadly disappointed by the austere reality (page 94). For the charge of effeminacy, see Gordon (2012: 160–62) and page 257.

Also, the "liar" syllogism of 45.10 (which must be some version of the Epimenides paradox) and the two "mouse" syllogisms of 48.6:

> Mouse (*mus*) is a syllable.
> But a mouse eats cheese.
> Therefore a syllable eats cheese.
> *Mouse* is a syllable.
> But a syllable doesn't eat cheese.
> Therefore a mouse doesn't eat cheese.

These conundrums were not of Stoic origin; they seem to have been propounded first by the Megarian dialecticians; but they were of interest to the Stoic founders as well.[22] And Seneca certainly associates them with Zeno and Chrysippus, for *illi quoque* in 45.4 must refer to the leaders of his own school. In presenting them, he complains again and again of the waste of time they represent, comparing them to a whole series of pointless, picayune, and mildly cruel pastimes: tying knots, knitting ambiguous meanings into words and then unraveling them again (45.5); "the conjurors' shells and pebbles" (45.8); "twisting words on the rack, pulling syllable from syllable" (48.5); "childish pranks" (48.7); "delving into minutiae" (49.6).[23] "For shame," he says, "that we who are mature men should play games with such serious matters!" (48.5).

> Sure, I'd have to watch out – someday I might find myself catching syllables in mousetraps! Better be careful – my cheese might be eaten by a book! ... Is this what makes us knit our brows? Is this why we let our beards grow long? Are we pale and earnest in our teaching of *this*? (*Letters* 48.6–7)

The recipient of this sort of philosophical discourse is put in a ludicrous position, feeling his own forehead to see if he has horns (45.8) – but no, that incongruous image is denied; it is the philosophers themselves who are made ridiculous, with their long beards and their pale, earnest complexions bending over the children's game.

There is some slippage in Seneca's choice of terms that may prove instructive here. In introducing the riddle-syllogism for the first time in *Letters* 45.5, he refers to it first as *cavillatio* and then in the plural as *captiosae disputationes*; just below, in 45.8, he claims that *captiones*

---

[22] Cicero in *Lucullus* 75 names the Megarian philosophers Stilpo, Diodorus, and Alexinus as the originators of "certain convoluted and needle-sharp *sophismata*." In the same context he offers *conclusiunculae* ("misleading little syllogisms") as a Latin rendering for *sophismata*. For the interest of the Stoic founders, see Plutarch, *Stoic Self-Contradictions* 1034f.
[23] On letter 49 in particular, see (Berno 2020), which argues that Aristo of Chios has influenced Seneca's handling of this theme.

("riddles") is the best translation for the Greek term *sophismata*. But later, at the beginning of letter 111, he returns to the point and cites Cicero as his model for preferring the term *cavillationes*.

> You asked me what is the Latin for *sophismata*? There have been lots of attempts to find a word for them, but no single term has stuck. We don't, of course, like actual sophisms or make use of them, and we don't like the word either. I think Cicero's word *cavillationes* is the most apt. (*Letters* 111.1)

This is a peculiar claim, because in fact, our texts of Cicero never use *cavillationes* or any related word in the sense indicated here. Cicero is familiar with the Greek *sophismata*, but has other terms for them; when he does use *cavillatio* or *cavillari*, it is in reference to verbal amusements in a much broader sense, essentially to any joke or quip that can raise a laugh from an audience.[24] So it must be Seneca himself who applies the term *cavillatio* to the riddle-syllogism.[25] Perhaps he simply misremembers which of his own preferred renderings was derived from Cicero. Still, his use of the word in this connection is significant, in that it establishes a link between verbal humor and this rather technical style of philosophical discourse. In calling the riddle-syllogisms *cavillationes*, Seneca alleges that they are humorous in intent, meant to discomfit some chosen interlocutor and raise a laugh from the crowd.[26] Seneca's own move is then to turn the tables on the proponent, shaming those who make use of such methods under the guise of philosophy.

Now, at one time it was common to allege that Seneca was simply hostile to logical argumentation as a way of doing philosophy; that he preferred a more rhetorical style and had no time for philosophy proper. That reading, however, was put to rest some time ago by Jonathan Barnes, in *Logic and the Imperial Stoa*.[27] Barnes argues convincingly that Seneca's objection in these passages is not to the study of logic in itself. Seneca's real attitude is comparable to that of Epictetus a generation after him: he complains about

---

[24] Cicero's renderings are *praestigia, captiones, fallaces et captiosae interrogationes, fallaces conclusiunculae* (*Lucullus* 45, 46, 75). For *cavillatio* and *cavillari*, see *De or.* 2.218.5, 3.122.7; *Nat. Deor.* 3.83.14; *Att.* 1.13.2; 2.1.5; *Q. fr.* 2.11.3. In five of the six occurrences, it is associated with *rideo, risus,* or *iocor*. Seneca knows this meaning of *cavillatio*: *Ben.* 2.17.1. See further Wildberger (2006: vol 2, 691–92).

[25] It may be relevant that in other passages, Seneca uses *cavillatio* and related words (*cavillari, cavillator*) either for arguments propounded in the form of syllogisms (e.g., *Ben.* 7.4.8, 82.8–10) or for sophisticated philosophical argumentation generally; for example, in *Letters* 64.3, 82.8, 102.20. At *Clemency* 2.4.3 the word means something like "sophisticated distinctions."

[26] For such aggressive use of dialectic, compare Plato, *Republic* 7.539b.

[27] Barnes (1997a: 12–23). Wagoner (2014) helpfully responds to the complaints lodged in Cooper (2004: 309–34) [= Cooper (2006)].

syllogistic reasoning used merely for the purposes of display, but he also has considerable appreciation for the systematic argumentation of the Greek Stoics. Indeed, he makes an effort to reproduce that sort of argumentation in his own work. Two of his longer letters, 85 and 87, proceed almost entirely in the format that propounds a syllogistic argument, explains the opponent's rebuttal, then proceeds with a counter-rebuttal. The same technique can be observed in the treatise *On Benefits*.[28]

Seneca's critique of Zeno of Citium in letter 82 appears disingenuous for this reason. Zeno is mocked for using an argument in syllogistic form to show that death is not an evil. Referring to such arguments as *cavillationes* (82.8), Seneca charges his Stoic predecessor with trying to rouse a laugh (*risum movere*, 82.9), and counters with his usual refrain: what matters is not the elegance of the philosopher's argumentation but the pupil's inner preparedness for death. But in fact his own interest is in the syllogism, for he goes on to quote in full an alternative version that takes the same form and appears to prove the opposite. Then he proceeds to analyze both arguments himself, showing the fallacy that slips in with the minor premise:

> You can see where this argument sneaks by a person. It is not death that is glorious but dying bravely. When you say, "Nothing indifferent is glorious," I concede the premise only with the stipulation that nothing is glorious which does not involve indifferents. (*Letters* 82.10)

And so forth: not an especially sophisticated discussion, but certainly one that uses some of the language and habits of mind that are associated with technical philosophy. The effect of the passage as a whole is ambiguous. On the one hand, it pits Seneca's own expansive style of rhetoric against the pinprick manner of the Stoic founders; but simultaneously, it demonstrates Seneca's ability to use their style himself. In mocking the Stoics for their "perversity" (*ineptias*), Seneca indeed marks a distinction between their precise and logical way of speaking philosophy and the way he deems appropriate for his own letters. Yet he himself is sometimes seen wielding the pin.

The Pilferer in the Garden

I return now to the early books of the *Letters on Ethics*, to pick up an especially elaborate instance of Seneca's self-directed mode of humor. The

[28] See *Letters* 85.1–35, 87.14–40, and, in *On Benefits*, especially book 3.

game begins with an act of discursive trespass. Following on a discussion of meditative reading in letter 2, Seneca recommends selecting a single maxim from some book to memorize and reflect upon throughout the day. To illustrate, he gives a sample maxim from his own reading – in the works of Epicurus, which he says has invaded, like an enemy's camp, "not as a deserter but as a spy" (2.5). The move is repeated at the end of letter 3 with an example from Pomponius, and then again at the close of letter 4, drawing once more from Epicurus. "This too," says Seneca, "is lifted from another's Garden" (*hoc quoque ex alienis hortulis sumptum est*; 4.10).

The pattern has now been established, and Seneca begins to play with it. In each of the subsequent letters down to letter 29, he closes with a similar maxim, usually from Epicurus or a writer of Epicurus's school. The implications of thievery in "lifted from another's Garden" rapidly devolve into a series of financial metaphors. Material from other people's books becomes first a commodity, "the daily dole" (*diurnam mercedulam*) or "little gift" (*munusculum*) (*Letters* 6.7, 10.5, 16.7); then an actual "bit of money" (*peculium*) or "money owed" (*aes alienum*) or "travel money" (*viaticum*) or "payment" (*pensionem*) (12.10, 23.9, 26.8, 29.10). The act of quotation becomes a figurative borrowing (*mutuum sumere*) and, toward Lucilius, the payment of a debt (*liberare*) (17.11, 26.8, 23.9). "You know whose money-box I use," Seneca says, referring to Epicurus's book (26.8). Lucilius is soon co-opted into the game. In 12.11 he recognizes the source and chides his friend for taking other people's material; in 16.7 he looks ahead to the end of the letter, peeking like a child for his "little gift"; in 18.14 he demands outright, "Pay what you owe!" By the twenty-ninth letter, he has become importunate, and Seneca makes only a token show of resistance:

> If you had any shame, you would excuse me the final payment. But since my debt is so nearly at an end, I won't be a cheapskate (no, not even I!), but will pay you what I owe.... "Who said that?" you say, as if you did not know where I get my funds. Epicurus said it. (*Letters* 29.10–11)

Lightly, but with an undercurrent of seriousness, Seneca makes his interlocutor challenge his right to retain and repeat Epicurus's well-phrased sentiments.[29] It is as if he as epistolographer has become both a trespasser and a thief, taking for his own use what does not belong to him.

---

[29] The confrontational tone is especially evident in *Letters* 12.10, 15.17, 18.14, 25.1, 29.11. The humor of these interactions is recognized by Richardson-Hay (2006: 95) and by Motto and Clark (1968: 40–41).

Failing to catch on, interpreters have sometimes marked Lucilius for an Epicurean because Seneca says to him, "I can give you a saying of your dear Epicurus (*Epicuri tui*) in payment of this day's bond" (*Letters* 23.9). This suggestion goes back to an earlier generation of scholars but has more recently been reiterated, notably by Miriam Griffin.[30] Griffin is aware, however, that Seneca's manner of addressing Lucilius in other contexts does not indicate that the real Gaius Lucilius Junior was an adherent of Epicurus; if anything, he is a Stoic or one strongly interested in learning about Stoic thought. Her suggestion, then, is that in the *Letters on Ethics*, Seneca deliberately misrepresents his friend as an Epicurean in order to provide a surrogate for the popularity of Epicurean views within the reading public. But it would surely be a strange gesture for a Stoic author to publicly assign Epicurean views to a friend who did not actually hold such views. The better answer is that Lucilius's proprietary interest in Epicurus has nothing to do with his philosophical adherence, real or imagined, but belongs rather to the humorous imagistic pattern that Seneca has established in this group of letters. Just as the Seneca whom we encounter within the letters has been found in possession of stolen goods, so Lucilius appears as the creditor who is to be paid off with those ill-gotten gains.

One cannot but wonder at Seneca's readiness to represent himself as a pilferer from the Garden of Epicurus. After all, within the conventions of Roman humor, the fruit thief is paradigmatic for the butt of the joke, the one whose trespass is subject to symbolic rape by the aggressive humorist. But we have seen already that Seneca's authorial presence in the letters is often tinged with self-mockery. Moreover, there is at least one end that is served by self-directed humor in this instance. While Seneca has good reason to instruct his readers in the method of meditative reading he associates with Epicurean authors, he also wants to raise questions about an overly submissive approach to philosophical reading. By representing his own use of Epicurean *sententiae* as transgressive, he can take advantage of the Epicurean achievement in therapeutic reading while also signaling his readers that there is something not quite right about that practice. The growing discomfort will eventually be explained and dispelled in letter 33, which puts in a plea for a very different practice of reading, a sustained and intellectually serious engagement with Stoic texts. At that point, Epicurus

---

[30] See Chapter 4, note 32. In addition to *Letters* 23.9, Griffin (1976) 351 cites *invideas licet* in 20.9, which belongs equally clearly to the discursive game.

and the Epicurean method of handling texts fall spectacularly out of favor, and the game begun in letter 2 is discontinued.

"Greek Shoes and Cloaks"

One further demonstration of Seneca's humor, and a particularly explicit one, can be found in the letter 113. One of the latest letters in the collection as we have it, the 113th is also one of only a dozen or so that venture outside the realm of ethics. The question addressed is a strange one: "whether justice, courage, prudence, and the other virtues are *animalia*," that is, whether they are animate creatures. It soon becomes clear that the issue is one of metaphysics. Within Stoicism, each of the virtues is simply the mind of some particular human disposed in a certain way: justice does not have independent existence but is simply a mind disposed toward just actions.[31] Since the *animus* (i.e., the ψυχή) is what animates the body, it must itself be an animate thing, and thus a Stoic can take the position the virtues are likewise animate – incidentally so, as Aristotle would say. It appears that at least some Stoics did hold that view, although the central postulates of Stoic metaphysics do not require it, and there is evidence of relevant disagreements among leading members of the school.[32] If there was disagreement, however, Seneca may not be aware of it, for he speaks of "our school's doctrine" (*quid nostris videatur*) as if there were only one Stoic view. His stated aim in the letter is to explain the doctrines of his preferred school, responding (he says) to Lucilius's request; he gives notice, however, that his own opinion is different:

> I will comply with your request and expound our school's doctrine, but I warn you that I am of a different opinion. My view is that some topics are only right for people who go in for Greek shoes and cloaks. (*Letters* 113.1)

He does not say at this point whether his difference from the Stoics consists in taking a different metaphysical stance, with him as one participant in the debate, or in repudiating the debate altogether. As the letter proceeds, we will see that he means to do both.

---

[31] For the background in Stoic metaphysics, see especially Stobaeus 1.177–79 Wachsmuth (LS 28D); Sextus Empiricus, *Outlines of Pyrrhonism* 2.81–82 (LS 33P); with Long and Sedley (1987: vol. 1, 166–79); Menn (1999).

[32] The assertion is reported as Stoic doctrine in Stobaeus 2.7.5b7, 65 Wachsmuth (*SVF* 3.306). Inwood (2007a: 272–88) argues that Seneca's position is essentially that of Aristo of Chios, in controversy with Chrysippus.

At first, he seems intent on straightforward exposition. Without taking a position himself, he first explains two lines of reasoning that undergird the Stoic claim and then resolves two objections: that if virtue is animate, it must itself possess virtue (113.3) and that if the virtues are animate, so are all other mental states, with the result that each individual mind will also be a multitude of different creatures (113.3–5). Concerning the second, he at first defends the Stoics at some length, appealing to their mereology and to their concept of the distinctive property of a thing, its *proprium*. Quite soon, however, he turns against the Stoic position and begins to argue for his own view. The virtues are *not* animate creatures, because that theory would imply that not only all mental states but even all mental events must also be animate creatures, including all emotions, all thoughts, and all actions, with many different animals occupying the same space. Because the implication produces such counterintuitive results, Seneca prefers to say that although the mind undergoes many configurations, it remains a single animate being persisting through change (113.7).

Bolstering his position, Seneca wends his way through a series of important philosophical issues: the stability of virtue, the causes of action, the unity of the virtues, and the uniqueness of individuating qualities. But the argument that carries the most weight takes the form of a *reductio ad absurdum*. Bringing out some ridiculous consequences of his opponent's view, he argues in effect that the Stoic position in metaphysics is untenable *because* it is laughable.

> The point will go so far that you cannot stop laughing. Prudently holding your tongue is a good, <and so too is dining well>; therefore holding your tongue and dining are animate creatures. Indeed I will not stop playing around and amusing myself with these pedantic absurdities. If justice and courage are animate creatures, they are certainly earthly. Every earthly animate creature gets sick, and hungry, and thirsty. Therefore justice gets sick, courage gets hungry, and mercy gets thirsty.
>
> What next? Won't I ask them what shape these animate creatures have? Is it a human being's or a horse's or a wild beast's? If they give them a round shape like that of a god, I will ask whether greed, luxury and madness are equally round. For they too are animate creatures. If they make them round too, I will even ask whether prudent walking is an animate creature. They have to grant that and go on to say that walking is an animate creature – and in fact a round one. (*Letters* 113.20–22)[33]

---

[33] Reading *exibit* and <*cenare bene*>.

In this part of the letter, the humor has a function *within* the argument. The notion of courage being hungry or walking being round is amusing because it is silly, and silly because it is illogical: walking should not be the sort of thing that can be round, and a philosopher who says that it is must be mistaken. One can hold a view that runs contrary to ordinary intuitions. The Stoic paradoxes are just such views, meant to arrest attention until they can be explicated. But some statements cannot be right.

Now, it is one thing to argue against a position on grounds of absurdity, quite another to say that an entire controversy is absurd – that it is the sort of discussion in which all who participate make themselves ridiculous. As we are nearing the end of letter 113, we watch Seneca shift from the first assertion to the second. In section 25, he is still pursuing the *reductio ad absurdum*, drawing out ever more amusing consequences of his opponents' view:

> I too grant for the moment that the mind is an animate creature, deferring my final judgment on the matter to a later date. However, I deny that the mind's actions are animate creatures. Otherwise all words will be animate creatures, and so will all lines of verse. For if prudent speech is a good, and every good is an animate creature, speech is an animate creature. A prudent line of verse is a good, and every good is an animate creature, therefore a line of verse is an animate creature. In that case "Arms and the man I sing" is an animate creature – but they cannot call it a round one since it has six feet! (*Letters* 113.25)

But then, at the beginning of section 26, he uses the voice of his interlocutor to turn the whole discussion on its head.

> "For heaven's sake!" you say, "what a web you are weaving at this point!" I burst out laughing when I envision that solecisms, barbarisms and syllogisms are animate creatures and, like a painter, I give them suitable faces. Is this what we are discussing with bent brow and knotted forehead? Can I not quote Caecilius and say, "What solemn idiocy!" It's simply ludicrous. So let's instead turn to something that is useful and salutary for us, and ask how we can arrive at the virtues and what route will bring us to them.

This exchange with the interlocutor replicates a discursive move that Seneca makes repeatedly in the more ambitious philosophical letters. Dubbed by Brad Inwood the "pragmatic break," the device consists in an interruption by the interlocutor scolding Seneca for excessive technicality in a foregoing discussion.[34] The exposition of Platonic ontology in letter 58, the analysis of

---

[34] Inwood (2007a: 131); and see page 30.

causation in letter 65, and the treatment of Stoic metaphysics in letter 106 all are cut short by this device, after which Seneca returns in each case to his more usual themes in personal ethics.[35] The move calls attention to a departure from the rule of genre Seneca has established for the *Letters on Ethics*, which decrees that each and every letter must concern itself with the values and modes of conduct conducive to happiness. Here, the metaphor of the tangled web ("For heaven's sake! what a web you are weaving at this point!") recalls the pattern of imagery we saw earlier in connection with the *cavillatio*: intricate and pointless intellectual activity. The humor in Seneca's reply adds vigor to his argument, distancing the author from his own venture into technical philosophy.

Should we then say that the 113th letter expresses a hostility toward metaphysics, a belief that such studies should never be undertaken? Not at all. Humor serves two functions within the letter: it is first a means of refuting a philosophical opponent and then a way for the epistolographer to back out of a topic that has gotten out of hand. But of course Seneca himself is responsible for the choice of topic, as well as for having pursued the discussion with gusto. Even his raillery has brought in additional elements of Stoic metaphysics that display his knowledge of the subject: the analysis that makes "prudent walking" a disposition of the wise psyche and hence a material thing; the peculiar doctrine that deities and also some human minds are spherical in form.[36] So we can hardly read the little drama of self-ridicule in section 26 as a genuine effort to exclude technical material from the *Letters on Ethics*. All it does is remind the reader that not everything Seneca chooses to include is in keeping with the stated purpose of his work.

***

If we think of Roman humor as a means of policing boundaries, of othering certain individuals and certain ways of behaving, then the passage in *On Happiness* that makes the Epicurean into a transvestite with a tambourine is one such police action, serving to maintain a boundary around Seneca's preferred manner of explaining concepts in ethics. In

---

[35] *Letters* 58.25 "What have I to gain," you say, "from these fine distinctions of yours?"; 65.15 "What is the attraction for you in frittering away your time on these matters which do not eliminate any of your passions nor drive out any desires?"; 106.11 "Now that I have done what you asked of me, it is time for me to anticipate the remark that I see you making: 'We are just playing checkers here.'"

[36] For spherical deities in Stoicism, see Cicero, *Nat. deor.* 1.18, 2.46–48; for spherical souls of the wise, the scholiast on *Iliad* 23.65 (*SVF* 2.815); Jerome, *Letter* 109.23 (*SVF* 2.816).

these three case studies from the *Letters on Ethics*, we see on the face of things a similar dynamic. Seneca uses humor to criticize representatives of the Stoic school whose ways of practicing and teaching philosophy are not properly edifying. In all these cases, however, the practices Seneca seeks to exclude are ones in which he too is implicated. The quasi-Epicurean practice of meditative reading, the habit of syllogistic reasoning, and the disquisitions on metaphysics did not wander into his book by accident; he himself chose to include that material. My claim has been that the exuberant use of humor in these cases serves as a means for Seneca to establish boundaries within his own project. Humor serves to define legitimate and non-legitimate zones within his philosophical practice, thus marking just one mode of discourse as proper to the work even where several different modes are on display. We can read it, then, as a device for maintaining the generic decorum of the *Letters on Ethics*.

CHAPTER 11

The Manhandling of Maecenas
Senecan Abstractions of Masculinity

Gaius Cilnius Maecenas was many things: a magnet for wealth, a shrewd political player, a patron of exceptionally sophisticated taste, and to some, at least, a cherished friend. It is disconcerting, then, to see what a one-sided image of him appears in the philosopher Seneca. Although reasonably complete evidence was available, Seneca's account hardly gets beyond Maecenas's mannerisms of dress and deportment, "how he walked, how prissy he was, how he sought the limelight, how he refused to conceal his faults" (*Letters* 114.4).[1] And even these traits are boiled down, in the last analysis, to a matter of language: "Is not his prose style (*oratio*) just as loose as his tunic was unbelted?" (114.4).

The motive for this reductive treatment is well worth investigating. If Seneca passes too quickly over some aspects of Maecenas's character, it may be that his real object is not Maecenas himself but an abstract principle that Maecenas serves to illustrate. My aim here is to show that Seneca's literary thought does indeed become abstract in this way, and that the principle involved – essentially a point of hermeneutics – holds considerable interest both in literary studies and in moral philosophy. Writing about Maecenas gives him an opportunity to bring out certain ideas about what constitutes an admirable style in literature, about the relation between formal discourse and the mind that produces it, and ultimately about the ideal condition for the human psyche. This ideal condition he calls by the name *virtus*, a word that retains its culturally determined associations with the male gender and norms of masculine behavior even while it invokes centuries of philosophical and especially

---

[1] Other ancient sources for these aspects of Maecenas's personal life include Tacitus, *Ann.* 1.54; Dio 54.17.5, 19.3, 30.4; Velleius 2.88.2; *Elegiae in Maecenatem* 1.21–26, 59; see Kappelmacher (1930). On Seneca's conservatism regarding gender roles, see now Gazzarri (2014).

Stoic thought on the ethical goal.[2] The same complex notion of *virtus* can be traced in his remarks on what he calls the "virile" style and in other related metaphors extending well beyond those passages that are immediately concerned with Maecenas. The sometimes peculiar results can be seen as a by-product of the interaction between cultural mores of first-century Rome and serious philosophical thought on questions of character, action, and evaluation.

The notion of a "virile" style does not originate with Seneca himself. Recent work by Maud Gleason and Amy Richlin emphasizes the frequency with which terms borrowed from the realm of gender and sexuality are employed in rhetorical works as early as the *Rhetorica ad Herennium* and prominently in the works of Seneca the Elder.[3] The younger Seneca differs from his predecessors, however, in that he consistently attaches gendered language not to the deportment of speakers but to the style of written works.[4] Terms that Cicero had applied primarily to the pitch and modulation of the voice or the grooming, stance, and gestures of the speaker, Seneca transfers confidently to discourse received exclusively by reading: passages from Maecenas's memoirs (*Letters* 114.4–8) and Arruntius's histories (114.17–19), a book by his own interlocutor Lucilius (46.1–3), philosophical works of Epicurus and others (33.1–2), his own letters and those of Lucilius (75.1, 115.1–2).

This habit of imputing virility (or its absence) to writers, as opposed to speakers, requires Seneca to offer some further explanation of his thinking. For it is not at all clear that features of written style can be reliably linked with personal characteristics of the author. In fact, there was at Rome a strong current of opinion that regarded this assumption as a particularly egregious fallacy.[5] A theorist who insists upon it nonetheless must be either

---

[2] For this double signification, compare Cicero, *Tusc.* 2.43: *vide ne, cum omnes rectae animi adfectiones virtutes appellentur, non sit hoc proprium nomen omnium, sed ab ea, quae una ceteris excellebat, omnes nominatae sint. Appellata est enim ex viro virtus; viri autem propria maxime est fortitudo.*

[3] Gleason (1995: 103–30); Richlin (1996). Also relevant is the work by L'Hoir (1992) on the difference in connotation between *homo* and *vir*.

[4] It is not always easy to distinguish between *oratio* as prose style and *oratio* as simply speech. As reading was normally oral, Romans could refer quite naturally to the way a writing style "sounds" or "strikes the ear" (e.g., *Letters* 114.13, *sonantibus*). The line between the composition of a speech and its delivery is somewhat easier to draw. Seneca does maintain an interest in vocal training and delivery (the passages are well discussed by Gleason (1995: 111–13), but his gender terms are primarily reserved for *compositio* itself. His usage perhaps has its origin in gendered language applied to the Asianist manner of oratory, where both delivery and style are at issue. See esp. Seneca the Elder, *Controversiae* 2 *praef.* 1 (on Arellius Fuscus); Tacitus, *Dial.* 18.5 and Quintilian, *Inst.* 12.10.12 (both on Cicero); Leeman (1965: vol. 2, 137–67); Richlin (1996).

[5] The point was made with some frequency in regard to sexually explicit material in poetry, and must have been known to Seneca at least through Ovid (*Tristia* 2.323–60) and Seneca the Elder

very misguided or very thoughtful. Seneca shows himself to be the thoughtful sort of theorist in two ways: first, in specific passages of the 114th letter that attempt to justify the derogation of Maecenas through an unusually careful description of the role of the *ingenium* or literary talent; second, in a broad parallel between his stated views on propriety of style and his Stoic-derived position on probity of conduct.[6] Given their manner of articulation, even his most derisive remarks on "effeminacy" commit Seneca to a positive notion of stylistic excellence that can be linked to a recognizably Chrysippan ideal of coherence in action-guiding belief.

In laying out the texts I proceed as follows. First, I describe the position on style that is articulated in the 114th letter, paying special attention to the theoretical justification that Seneca offers for treating style as an index of character. Second, I assemble those portions of the *Letters on Ethics* that make reference to a virile manner of writing, a *virilis contextus* or *compositio virilis*, and identify the particular characteristics of style to which they refer. Next, I relate this conception of stylistic masculinity to a specifically Stoic understanding of the psychology of virtue. Finally, I point out one instance in which the combination of ethical thought with cultural assumptions gives genuinely odd results. This is the treatment of Epicurus at the beginning of the 33rd letter – a strange text, but one that brings us close to the center of Seneca's thinking on philosophical style.

The Condition of the *Ingenium*

The passage from the letter 114 is familiar to Latinists both as an important source for Maecenas's prose and as a classic statement of the principle *talis oratio qualis vita*, "as we live, so do we speak."[7] Seneca pillories Maecenas for his flamboyant metaphors and tropes, his fondness for special rhythmic effects, and his eccentricities in *compositio* or word order. All these are supposed to parallel certain habits of dress and deportment for which Maecenas was also known: the unbelted *pallium*, the Oriental-style bodyguard, the excessive attention to his wife. The relationship between

---

Controversiae 6.8: *Quid tu putas poetas, quae sentiunt, scribere? Vixit modeste, castigate.* Merrill (1893) commenting on Catullus 16, supplies additional references.
[6] For a more comprehensive treatment of Seneca's views on prose style, see Setaioli (2000: 111–218). Berti (2018) supplies an extensive and highly informative commentary on letter 114.
[7] *Letters* 114.1 makes this common opinion and "proverbial among the Greeks" (*proverbium apud Graecos*); cf. Cicero, *Tusc.* 5.47 (ascribing it to Plato); and see Berti (2018: 59–61).

style and character is supposed to be quite direct, so much so that a close study of the great minister's prose would provide reliable indications as to his personal characteristics even if these were otherwise unknown.

> Is not his diction just as flamboyant as are his dress, his attendants, his home, his wife? (*Letters* 114.4)

> That's what you will see in his discourse: the style of a drunkard – convoluted, wandering, full of liberties. (*Letters* 114.4)

> When you read these examples, does it not occur to you at once that this is the man who always went about the city in a loose tunic? For when he took command in Caesar's absence, he was without a belt even as he was giving the watchword. (*Letters* 114.6)

> These words, so wantonly combined, so carelessly thrown about, so far from normal usage in their positioning, demonstrate that his character was equally outlandish, equally depraved, equally perverse. He gets great praise for his clemency, for he spared the sword, and refrained from bloody deeds, displaying his power only in his licentious behavior ... Yet he spoils this very praise with the affectations (*deliciis*) of his grotesque prose, which make it clear that he was not gentle (*mitis*), but soft (*mollis*). (*Letters* 114.7)

The character traits to which the writings are supposed to provide a clue might seem to us an odd assemblage. Maecenas is charged with keeping an unusual entourage, with drinking too much, with uxoriousness, and with failing to wear a belt. In what way are these facts so much related that one can deduce them all from a few lines of art prose? For the Roman reader, though, the connections are easier to draw. The summary charge, that of *mollitia* or "softness," is most often leveled at atypical sexual behaviors, but the thought behind it is more general in its application: in essence, it has to do with a weakness of will or failure to discipline oneself.[8] In relation to pleasures, "softness" manifests itself as excess. Hence *mollitia* may be charged even against heterosexual behavior by males, although it is more

---

[8] Richlin (1992: 258 n3), lists passages in which *mollis* is used of an effeminate and/or pathic man. The broader ethical sense of *mollis* can be found in many passages cited by *OLD*, for example, Cicero, *Fin.* 1.33, *officia deserunt mollitia animi* (failure to perform unpleasant duties); Caes. *Gal* 1.11.5, *animi est ista mollitia, non virtus, paulisper inopiam ferre non posse* (inability to bear hardship); Plautus, *Pseudolus* 173, *vos quae in munditiis, mollitiis deliciisque aetatulam agitis* (excessive indulgence in pleasure); Ovid *Tristia* 4.10.65, *molle Cupidineis nec inexpugnabile telis/cor mihi* (susceptibility to emotion). Compare the close relation between Gr. μαλακία and ἀκρασία, as described by Aristotle: the former is a failure to hold out against pleasures and pains, the latter a failure to overcome them (*Nic. Eth.* 7.7, 1150a31). Still valuable here are the remarks by Boswell (1979: 76), and (on μαλακός) 339–40.

The Manhandling of Maecenas 243

often imputed to women and to the passive partner in sex between males.⁹ *Mollitia* in relation to emotion similarly implies a heightened susceptibility: the *mollis* person feels certain emotions especially often or especially strongly. Yet in other areas *mollitia* may imply a lack – a failure to perform unpleasant duties, or an inability to put up with pain or inconvenience. Moreover, all these versions of *mollitia* are interchangeable, so that a person who is without self-discipline in one area may be expected to display similar weakness in other areas as well. This assumption serves as a powerful instrument of interpretation. For instance, Maecenas showed himself unwilling to perform acts of cruelty when in command: does this result from a praiseworthy *mansuetudo* ("humaneness," "clemency"), or from *mollitia*?¹⁰ The prose, Seneca asserts, provides an answer: by its abundance of affectations, it demonstrates that the mind from which it issues is *mollis*, and this observation justifies a radical reinterpretation even of actions unrelated to sexuality. Thus, Maecenas's shortcomings as a writer actually strip him of credit for his clemency as temporary commander!

The theoretical basis for this extreme position on style is indicated in section 3 of the letter. One's personal habits, we learn, proceed like all actions from the conditions of one's mind (*animus*) and must be evaluated in accordance with them. Preeminent among these personal habits is the nature of one's writings, here referred to by the potentially ambiguous term *ingenium*:

> The condition of the talent (*ingenium*) cannot be different from that of the mind (*animus*). If the mind is healthy, well put together, serious, self-controlled, the *ingenium* is likewise completely sober; if the mind is flawed, the talent is likewise inflamed. Do you not see that if the mind has lost its vigor, the limbs trail along, and the feet shuffle? If the mind is effeminate, the softness is seen even in the walk; if it is energetic and fierce, the stride is quick; if it raves or is angry (a condition similar to raving), the movement of the body is disturbed and goes hurtling along rather than walking. Must not

---

⁹ For examples, see Richlin (1992: 93–94, 139). There is an extensive bibliography on this topic. A good discussion can be found in Edwards (1993: 63–97), except that *mollis* is there insistently rendered "effeminate"; cf. Edwards's own observation that "the terms referring to *mollitia* and related notions have a much broader frame of reference than the specifically sexual" (Edwards 1993: 68)).
¹⁰ Velleius reports (2.88) that while serving as regent in 31 BCE, Maecenas stifled the conspiracy of Lepidus the Younger "with amazing swiftness and without creating an uproar," that is, by executing the young man immediately. Seneca may not have known about this event.

this be all the more true of the *ingenium*, which is completely mixed with the mind, and receives from it its shape, direction, and principle?[11]

In some passages in Seneca, as often elsewhere in Latin, the word *ingenium* signifies "intelligence" or "character," broadly understood, or else some specific aspect of the personality: a *saevum ingenium*, for instance, is a warlike temperament.[12] But Seneca also uses *ingenium* in a much more restricted sense, to refer to a person's rhetorical and literary abilities as demonstrated in actual pieces of writing. In letter 2, for example, he instructs Lucilius to apply himself to "specific talents" (*certis ingeniis*, 2.2), meaning that he is to concentrate on just a few books; in 33.5, when he warns Lucilius against hoping to get "a quick sampling from the *ingenia* of the greatest men" (*summatim degustare ingenia maximorum virorum*), his point is that Stoic books should be read in their entirety; in 75.3, the remark that "philosophy does not forswear the *ingenium*" (*neque enim philosophia ingenio renuntiat*) conveys that philosophers can sometimes speak and write elegantly.[13] This latter sense is what is intended here. Seneca is saying that the literary style we can see in someone's book gives us a direct indication of how their mind works. On the one hand, the *ingenium* is a distinctly psychological entity, a relatively stable capacity or characteristic of persons, and as such is "completely mixed" with the mind;[14] on the other, it is something perceptible to the outside observer in the same way as one's gait and other bodily

---

[11] Letters 114.3 *Non potest alius esse ingenio, alius animo color. Si ille sanus est, si compositus, gravis, temperans, ingenium quoque siccum ac sobrium est: illo vitiato hoc quoque adflatur. Non vides, si animus elanguit, trahi membra et pigre moveri pedes? si ille effeminatus est, in ipso incessu apparere mollitiam? si ille acer est et ferox, concitari gradum? si furit aut, quod furori simile est, irascitur, turbatum esse corporis motum nec ire sed ferri? Quanto hoc magis accidere ingenio putas, quod totum animo permixtum est, ab illo fingitur, illi paret, inde legem petit?*

[12] Both senses were well established in Latin; see *OLD* s.v. *ingenium*. Examples in Seneca referring to general intelligence or aptitude for philosophy include 29.4 *magna in illo ingeni vis est, sed iam tendentis in pravum*; 52.6 *quaedam ingenia facilia, expedita*; 94.30 *alium esse ingenii mobilis et erecti, alium tardi et hebetis*; similarly 7.6, 11.1, 24.3, 34.1, 51.11, 52.3, 66.1, 70.24, 71.31, 90.13, and 94.50. For aspects of temperament with more specific qualifiers, note *saeva ingenia* in Letters 51.6, 27.5 *libertini ingenium*; 39.2 *neminem excelsi ingenii virum*; 56.12 *leve ingenium*; 71.25: *ingenio vegetum*; 95.5 *obsequens ingenium*; 105.4 *ingeni lenitas*.

[13] Additional examples from the *Letters* include 7.9: *gloria publicandi ingenii*; 19.3: *in medium te protulit ingenii vigor*; 21.5: *pauca ingenia caput exerent*; 21.6: *ingeniorum crescit dignatio*; 24.9: *non in hoc exempla nunc congero ut ingenium exerceam*; 46.2: *materia [...] quae capiat ingenium*; 79.7: *ingenii tui vires*; 82.16: *multorum ingeniis certatum est*; 92.35: *habuit enim ingenium et grande et virile*; 108.23: *propositum adferunt ad praeceptores suos non animum excolendi sed ingenium*; 114.12: *nullum sine venia placuit ingenium*. In Seneca's other works, see *Marc.* 1.3 *ingenium patris tui in usum hominum reduxisti*; 26.1 *illo ingenio quo civilia bella [Cremutius Cordus] deflevit*; *Clemency* 2.2.3 *ingenia in inmani et invisa materia secundiore ore expresserunt sensus*; *Tranq.* 11.8 *tragicis comicisque ingeniis*; 3.3 *prodesse velit singulis universisque ingenio, voce, consilio*. Seneca the Elder can call a book-burning an *ingeniorum supplicia* (*Controversiae* 10 *praef.* 7).

[14] It is not clear in the passage whether the *ingenium* is numerically distinct from the *animus*. If pressed to explain his psychological model, Seneca would presumably retreat to the usual Stoic analysis and say

movements are perceptible. It thus provides a means of observing the character of the *animus*, a link between the external and the internal.

Like the ancient physiognomists, then, who claimed to be able to deduce character from face-to-face observation of build, facial structure, gait, complexion, and the pitch and volume of the voice, Seneca theorizes that certain inner psychological states are open to observation by those who know the external signs.[15] His hermeneutics are even bolder than those of the physiognomists, however, for he argues that an assessment of character can be made from the written word alone. In fact, judgments based upon literary style are even more reliable than those made in person. This comes about because the relation between *animus* and *ingenium* is particularly intimate: the two are directly allied in such a way that the one can be assumed to have furnished the principles by which the other is seen to operate.

It could be objected that the argument Seneca is pursuing rests on an equivocation. For most of the passage quoted, the word *ingenium* must refer to one's literary achievement – that is, to one's linguistic ability as demonstrated in actual speech or writing, rather as we speak of a person's "art." *Ingenium* already has this sense in the first sentence of the letter, and no other meaning will do here: the passage is supposed to explain something about the vagaries of literary style, which it will hardly do if *ingenium* means anything very different from "the way people write." But an *ingenium* could also be an internal, psychological entity roughly synonymous with the *animus*. So it is tempting to suppose that in speaking of the *ingenium* as "completely mixed" with the *animus*, Seneca has merely slipped from the one meaning to the other, exploiting the flexibility of Latin usage in order to make his point.

But there is another way to read the total mixing of *ingenium* and *animus*. Stoic thought places great emphasis on a correlation between rationality, or the possession of a certain sort of *animus*, and the capacity to produce meaningful utterances. For Stoics, it is no exaggeration to say that it is the power of *logos*, both of speech and of reason, that distinguishes the human being from other animals. Language as heard or read has its source in thought or "internal speech" and bears in itself the "imprint or

---

that the *ingenium* just is the *animus* (the directive faculty or *hēgemonikon*) considered for its capacity to produce speech or writing.

[15] The theory of physiognomy seems to have exercised some fascination for Stoic thinkers, as evidenced in Clement, *Paedagogus* 3.11.74; as well as by the following peculiar story from Diog. Laert. 7.173: "After Cleanthes claimed that according to Zeno character could be securely cognized from appearance, some ingenious young men brought to him a cinaedus hardened by field work and asked him to pronounce upon his character. Being at a loss, he told the person to leave. But he sneezed as he was leaving, whereupon Cleanthes said, 'I have him! He is soft (μαλακός)!'" See Evans (1969: 6–11, 22–24).

stamp" of the thought behind it.[16] The qualities of the utterance may therefore function as a sign of the quality of the thought: since words can only issue from the mind, strong words must necessarily have come from a strong mind, and disorderly words from mental disorder. This idea surfaces toward the end of letter 114, where it is linked also to assertions about masculinity in prose style.

> Let us therefore care for the mind, for from it proceed meaning (*sensus*) and words, demeanor, facial expression, and walk. If the mind is healthy and sound, the prose (*oratio*) is likewise sturdy, strong, and virile; if the mind stumbles, the rest collapses as well. (*Letters* 114.22)

The passage goes on to compare the effects of moral weakness on language production to the effects of alcohol. As slurred speech signals a loss of mental function from the effects of alcohol, so also a languid or fluid quality in either the actions (*actus*) or creations (*artes*) of a person indicates reliably that his mind "has yielded to pleasure" (114.23). Intoxication, effeminacy, moral weakness, and bad prose thus interentail in a strange chain of equivalences.

The Nature of the Masculine

This much is reasonably clear. Relying on a particular theory of language production, Seneca denies any radical disjunction between the character of a literary product and that of its producer. Written works may thus be treated as a kind of window on the soul of the writer and may even guide an observer in evaluating actions performed outside the literary sphere. We are still left with questions, however. By what standard is good writing to be assessed? And what qualities are being referred to when terms like "health," "sobriety," and especially "virility" are applied to a piece of writing?

Here letter 114 provides only a limited understanding. The question is explored only so far as to reject the opinion of "some people," that masculinity means sheer inattention to style or even deliberate ugliness. In a passage heavily laden with gendered language, Seneca complains of the way prose stylists tend to run to opposite, and equally objectionable,

---

[16] Evidence concerning Stoic thought on the vocal faculty is collected in Long and Sedley (1987) chapter 53. See especially Aëtius 4.21.1–4 =LS 53H (utterance is one of eight "parts" or faculties of the soul); Panaetius *apud* Nemesius 202, 6–9 = LS 53I (the vocal faculty is governed by impulse); Sextus Empiricus *Against the Professors* 8.275 = LS 53T (internal speech differentiates humans from non-rational animals); Diogenes of Babylon *apud* Galen, *PHP* 2.5.11–12 = LS 53U (language has its source in thoughts within the chest and is imprinted with the conceptions present in thought).

extremes (*Letters* 114.13–15). Some cultivate archaic or poetic diction, while others reject all but the most familiar and common words, thus lapsing into slovenliness.

> As far as I am concerned, both are equally at fault. One grooms himself more than he ought, the other less; one plucks the hair from his legs, the other neglects even his armpits. (*Letters* 114.14)

Similarly, while some writers are fond of a too-melodious arrangement of words, so that their prose "glides along softly and seductively," others are excessively fond of clipped and harsh phrasing, awkward hiatus, and imbalance of rhythms, believing such traits to be masculine and strong (*virilem putant et fortem*, 114.5). That is, they falsely equate masculinity with deliberate untidiness, a neglect of the armpits. By implication, Seneca holds that the truly masculine stylist will pay at least some attention to the aural qualities of his prose. For such standard devices as balanced phrasing, the use of *clausulae* and periodic sentences, and the avoidance of hiatus, stylistic masculinity seems to consist in unobtrusive adherence to convention.[17] If Seneca has a further idea as to some particular quality that belongs to a properly masculine piece of writing, he has not yet expressed it.

Nor does the opening of letter 115 resolve the matter. There Seneca urges Lucilius not to be "too anxious" (*nimis anxium*) about diction and word-arrangement, since the sage speaks "somewhat casually and without troubling himself very much" (*remissius loquitur et securius*, 115.1). He continues,

> When someone's rhetorical style exhibits great care and polish, you may be sure that his mind is likewise occupied with trivial matters. The great man speaks more casually than that: his words are heartfelt, not carefully arranged. You know those prettified youths with their hairstyles and beard styles, straight from the salon: you don't expect anything brave, anything solid from them! Speech is the dress and grooming of the mind: if our style is all trimmed about and made up and fussed over, it shows that the mind does not ring true either, that there is something queer (*fractus*) about it. Melodiousness is no masculine ornament. (*Letters* 115.2).[18]

If melodiousness (*concinnitas*) is not a "masculine ornament," then what is? Here, the answer seems to be "no ornament at all" – for while the

---

[17] For analysis of the technical features of the passage, see Leeman (1965: vol. 2, 275–76).
[18] For the connotations of *fractus*, compare *Happiness* 13.4: *qui voluptatem sequitur, videtur enervis, fractus, degenerans viro*; Cicero, *Tusc.* 4.64, *ne quid humile, summissum, molle, effeminatum, fractum abiectumque faciamus*. See also Gleason (1995: 67–68, 112), on the Greek equivalent (κατά)κεκλασμένος.

comparatives in section 1 would seem to imply that some level of care and polish is permissible, the strong implication is that the "good man" (*bonus vir*, 115.3) thinks only about content. Ornamentation per se is the province of the "prettified youths" (*comptulos iuvenes*) whom Seneca ridicules in a rare echo of his father.[19] Masculinity in the use of language is thus a matter of possessing an internal constraint against what Romans habitually called the "darlings" (*deliciae*) or "flowers" (*flores*) of language, that is, tropes and figures.[20] Such a constraint may be called by another term with sexual overtones, *verecundia* or "modesty." The debased stylists of letter 114 employ metaphor "in an immodest manner" (*inverecunde*), and their doing so is a prime example of stylistic "wantonness" (*lascivia*).[21] The comparison with sexual behavior is predictably in accord with the cultural norm: effeminate behavior is not so much behavior of one kind or orientation, as it is behavior that calls attention to itself. Masculinity of style thus appears in purely negative terms.

Another passage, however, leaves this conclusion in doubt. The 75th letter, although it does not use the term *virilis*, does conform to the pattern of setting standards for prose style in language borrowed from sexual behavior. And here it is clear that correct behavior for the stylist cannot be described solely as a matter of restraint. Even a kiss can be chaste (*sanctus*), Seneca points out in letter 75. One does not have to embrace a child in the way that a person embraces his girlfriend, and yet the kiss will still be a kiss:

> People kiss a lover in one way and their children in another; yet even in that chaste and restrained caress there is a sufficient show of affection. (*Letters* 75.3)

Explaining the metaphor, he states that the writer "should not expend much effort over the words" but still should not be "jejune and arid," adding, "there is a place for literary talent (*ingenium*) even in philosophy" (75.3). If stylistic masculinity is strictly a matter of restraint, this statement will be difficult to reconcile with the passages we have seen in letters 114 and 115.

The difficulty here is created by the fact that all three of these letters have reference to masculinity only insofar as it is necessary to fend off a superficial conception of what the ideal style should be. For a substantive

---

[19] Cf. Seneca the Elder *Controversiae* 1 *praef.*; Leeman (1963: vol. 2, 273).
[20] Cicero, *Orator* 39; *Brutus* 233, 298.
[21] *Letters* 114.1–2; and compare *Letters* 40.14, speaking of a certain style of speech, "You cannot achieve it without losing your sense of propriety" (*salva verecundia*).

The Manhandling of Maecenas 249

description of stylistic "masculinity," it is more useful to look at letter 46. This very short letter offers a glowing assessment of a work on moral philosophy sent to Seneca by Lucilius. Seneca reacts to Lucilius's composition in part because of its content, but more particularly because of the manner of writing.[22] In fact, it is possible to read the letter as a capsule essay on literary style, in which judgments of similar tendency to those expressed elsewhere are referred to a standard that is both discernible and surprisingly reasonable.[23]

As in other letters, stylistic propriety is repeatedly described in sexual language. Lucilius's style is both *virilis*, "manly," and *sancta*, "chaste," and yet it is by no means devoid of appeal. "Sweetness" (*dulcedo*) is part of the overall effect, and even the verb "to seduce" (*blandior*), elsewhere associated with effeminate writing, makes an appearance.[24] The book is so eloquent that it seems brief, despite its actual bulk, and so winsome that it captures and holds the reader's attention.

> It was not only delight that I felt; it was joy. What talent it showed – what spirit! I would have said, "What impact!" had there been in it any quiet stretches – had it roused itself only at intervals. But as it was, it was not impact, but a steady state. The style is masculine and chaste (*virilis et sancta*); nonetheless, there came in from time to time that note of sweetness, that just-right gentle moment. You are tall, upright – this I would have you keep; this is how you should walk. (*Letters* 46.2)

With "nonetheless" (*nihilominus*), Seneca signals that masculinity and the "note of sweetness" pull in opposite directions. Yet the relation between them is not one of mutual exclusivity; rather it is a whole/part relation. The sweet and the gentle may be treated as desirable features of style just insofar as they have an orderly place within a more comprehensive stylistic program. The point Seneca emphasizes throughout is that while Lucilius's book does have its minor graces, it presents itself as a coherent whole, with no one passage taking precedence over another. Its appeal is in fact so seamless that the reader has been unable to lay it aside, but has taken it whole at a single sitting and feels afterward as though he had experienced the fluent delivery of a thrilling lecturer. The book has thus been able to

---

[22] On this letter, see also pages 215–16.
[23] For earlier discussions of this letter, see Wilson (1987: 104–7) and Habinek (1992: 196–98). The latter is particularly helpful in bringing out the intimacy of the author–reader relation but overplays the sexual innuendo to some extent; *erectus*, for example, is not used in a sexual sense in classical Latin.
[24] Compare *blanditur* in *Letters* 114.15. *Dulcis* is the regular epithet of the intermediate style; for examples, see the index to Leeman (1965).

exert tremendous power over its reader: even Seneca, who means to portray himself as a strong reader, still needs to pause and collect himself before he will be ready to ask questions. And that power is derived not from an affected vehemence, such as might invite bursts of applause, but from a careful fitting together of parts that makes the reading experience a single, uninterruptible moment.

This letter's narrative of a productive reading process does as much as anything in the corpus to characterize the style Seneca is willing to call masculine. The quality he has in mind cannot be defined at the level of the phrase, by its use or avoidance of figures of speech or special effects of sound or rhythm. It is rather a matter of overall coherence, what we might call integrity of effect. Tropes, special effects, and *sententiae*, the "sweet" and "gentle" bits of the stylist's work, may be employed just to the extent that they can be integrated into the tenor of the whole, contributing to an impression of sustained power. Such a style would be particularly effective as a vehicle of communication, since it holds the reader's attention throughout and does not permit any single ornament to detract from the message of the whole.

Support for this general understanding of "masculinity" may also be found in the critique of Maecenas. For although Maecenas's effeminacy is largely characterized in terms of excess – the frequency of metaphor, for instance, and the borrowing of poetic constructions into prose – there is one central characteristic of his "effeminate" style that Seneca considers a defect, and which ought, therefore, to be the inverse of the masculinity we are seeking to define. Seneca's objection to Maecenas's prose (one that the modern student will wholeheartedly endorse) is that it is difficult to construe. More specifically, it is diffuse, lacking in cohesiveness; that is, it fails to make clear those syntactical relations among words that enable language to convey thought. Maecenas "would have been a great writer, if he had taken the straight road with his talent, and not tried to evade comprehension, not let even his prose flow free" (114.4). The ties, we might say, are missing: not only the negative constraints that inhibit certain linguistic behaviors, but more importantly the ties that link one thought to the next.[25]

This objection can be illustrated to some extent even in the passages from Maecenas's *De cultu suo* that are cited in letter 114, although here our

---

[25] It is worth noting here that Cicero uses *virilis* of Stoic writing specifically in approbation of its logical rigor (*Tusc.* 3.22), and that Gr. μαλακός is used by Aristotle of "slack" reasoning; see LSJ[9] s.v. μαλακός III.2.g.

understanding is hampered by difficulties of transmission.[26] For instance, in the fragment Seneca quotes first, a series of vague ablatives leaves it to the reader to imagine how the river, the forests, the bank, and the boats are to be connected with the action of the verb.

> *Amne silvisque ripa comantibus vide ut alveum lintribus arent.*
>
> Upon [?] the river and among [?] the forests leafy along [?] the bank, behold how they plow the deep with skiffs. (Letters 114.5)[27]

A phrase like *fanantur nemoris tyranni*, in the next sentence, defies comprehension from any standpoint. What can serve as subject for the plural verb *fanantur*, following a string of singulars? And how are we to construe the genitive *nemoris tyranni*?[28] Too-frequent metaphors and precious neologisms are part of the complaint as well: the person who *labris columbatur* "pigeons with his lips," and the *crepacem molam* "clatterish mill." But the point to which Seneca keeps returning is that of syntactical weakness, the way words are not bound to any precise relation among themselves but are "wantonly combined," "carelessly thrown about," "far from normal usage in their positioning." It is the same objection Quintilian was later to make (*Inst.* 9.4.28). This looseness of syntax is directly compared to a peculiarity of Maecenas's dress that serves here and elsewhere as an emblem of his depravity: his failure to wear a belt. In passages already quoted from letter 114, Maecenas's prose style is "just as loose as his tunic was unbelted" (114.4), and his habit of appearing in public without a belt can be discerned even in his writing. An earlier letter cites an isolated saying of Maecenas with approval – and then retracts the compliment:

> Maecenas said it eloquently: "I care not for a tomb; Nature buries the abandoned." This looks like the saying of a man closely girded (*alte cinctum*). For he had a great and virile talent – or would have had, if easy circumstances had not unbelted it (*discinxissent*). (*Letters* 92.35)

Especially in this last passage, unbeltedness comes near to being the exact opposite of masculinity. As a point of dress, the absence of cincture indicates

---

[26] For discussion of the prose fragments, see Bardon (1956: vol. 2, 13–19); André (1983: 1768), and (1967: 104–14).

[27] The punctuation is that of Hense (1914), since I cannot agree with Reynolds (1965) that *vide ut* should be assigned to Seneca. But throughout 114.5 the punctuation and indeed the text must be treated as arbitrary, as editors struggle to bring order to a mishmash of tags selected by Seneca for their disorderliness.

[28] Harder (cited in Reynolds (1965) ad loc.) emends to *memoris tyranni*, without producing any improvement in the sense.

defiance of convention and also unreadiness for action, in particular the inability to wear a weapon.[29] Applied to writing, the term suggests a lack of structure that renders language ineffective as a vehicle for thought.

The Psychology of *Virtus*

Thus far we have been following a metaphoric pattern that associates the term "masculine" with writing that is tightly structured, well integrated, and consistent. We have also seen how Seneca asserts that qualities of style, including "masculinity," are directly related to personal qualities of the writer, that is, to assumed qualities of that person's mind. It remains now to ask what quality a mind might have that would manifest itself as stylistic "masculinity" in the sense we have identified. In other words, what is it that characterizes the masculine *animus* in the same way as coherence or integrity of effect characterizes the masculine style? For those familiar with Stoic psychology, the answer is not difficult to supply.

The missing term in the analogy can only be "virtue." For souls can be tightly integrated just as any system can, and a coherent structure for the soul is one thing the Stoic means by ἀρετή or *virtus*. Pressed to give an account of that quality of soul that he calls, variously, "virtue," "knowledge," or "health," the Stoic resorts as a matter of course to the notion of pneumatic tension (τόνος).[30] Tension, in Stoic physics, is that quality whose presence in differing degrees serves to explain the hardness of stones, the complex functioning of higher animals, and the rationality of humans. Tension in the soul may be understood as physical cohesiveness, since the soul is a physical object; it may equally well be described as moral consistency – that is, a recognizable pattern of principled action – or as logical coherence, since bringing order and coherence to the belief set is the chief task of the directive faculty. It seems reasonable, then, that if one were to look for a quality of the *ingenium* to correspond with tension in the soul, it should be something that tends to knit the writing together, to make it orderly and consistent.

Conversely, the stylistic vice of Maecenas, his erratic and patternless deployment of words and tropes without concern for the relations among

---

[29] The absence of cincture again figures large in the *Elegiae in Maecenatem*, 1.21–26, very possibly in response to Seneca's criticism; see Schoonhoven (1980: 40–47). On the connotations of *discinctus*, see also Richlin (1992: 92); Edwards (1993: 90); and Corbeill (1996: 160 n82).

[30] Cleanthes in Plutarch, *Stoic Self-Contradictions* 1034e (LS 61C). For a concise account, see Long (1986: 153–57); also very helpful is the discussion in Annas (1992: 50–55). The underlying notion may well be that of musical harmony; see Long (1996: 202–23); Long and Sedley (1987: vol. 1, 288n1, vol. 2, 348, 354, 376); and compare *Letters* 84.9–11.

them, is one that resonates strongly with the Stoic account of moral depravity. Just as virtue represents the optimal level of psychic tension (εὐτονία), so moral imperfection is a natural consequence of slackness (ἀτονία) in the psychic material.[31] Even in the average person, the tension is less than ideal: instead of a full, logical coherence, most people's belief sets exhibit some inconsistencies, and actions dependent on those beliefs are accordingly at variance with each other and with the divine plan or "right reason." Given the connection between rationality and language production, we should expect that slackness will also be evident in the average person's speech and writing. Now, inconsistency is not, technically, a quality that admits of degrees: just as every line that is not straight must be considered bent, so all non-sages must be classed as inconsistent, depraved thinkers and agents. Still, some individuals are especially far from the ideal state, drowning at the bottom of the sea, as it were, rather than a few feet below the surface.[32] If we can assume that the person whose conduct is egregiously bad is one whose mind-material is especially lacking in tension, then it should follow that that person's utterances will be even less coherent than those of the average person.

The same complex of ideas is implicit in Seneca's use of the word *ebrius* ("drunk" or "drunkard"). Chrysippus held that the sage loses his virtue when inebriated, and the remainder of his statement (inebriation is listed along with sleepiness, dizziness, depression, and the effect of certain drugs) suggests that alcohol is seen as a destructive agent that physically breaks down the tension of the mind.[33] We might predict that a Stoic would take the slurred or disjointed speech of the drunkard as a direct manifestation of this loss of tension, and Seneca appears to confirm this intuition in *Letters* 83.21, which recapitulates the Chrysippan position.[34] It is by analogy with the breakdown of logic in intoxicated speech that Maecenas's prose is repeatedly called *ebrius*: his is "the drunkard's eloquence – convoluted, wandering, full of liberties" (114.4); a

---

[31] Galen, *PHP* 4.6.2–3 (LS 65T).
[32] For these matters, see Long and Sedley (1987: vol. 2, 383–86), with Diog. Laert. 7.127, Cicero, *Tusc.* 4.29, 34–35, Plutarch, *On Common Conceptions* 1063ab (LS 611, O, T).
[33] Diog. Laert. 7.127 (loss of virtue); *SVF* 3.238, 239 (effects of alcohol). Chrysippus's statements do not represent a departure from Cleanthes's position on the immutability of virtue so much as a supplement dealing with cases that Cleanthes failed to consider; so Inwood (1985: 289). n32). See Schofield (1983: 41–43); Rist (1969: 17–19).
[34] In *Letters* 83.21, the slurred speech and unsteady gait prove that the "upright character" (*rectus tenor*) of the wise mind is fully susceptible to the effects of wine. Seneca is arguing against one who pretends to defend Zeno's position from earlier in the letter, but who is really just a crass hedonist. Compare *Letters* 123.15.

particularly illogical phrase from his *Prometheus* is "drunk talk" (*ebrius sermo*, 19.9). Later in letter 114 the term is again "drunkenness" (*ebrietas*):

> Just as when one drinks wine the speech does not begin to falter until the mind, overwhelmed by its burden, has swayed or succumbed, so also that drunkenness of his prose (what else can I call it?) does not affect a person unless his mind is already slipping.[35]

If this is what it is for prose style to be "drunk," then the style that would display a "completely sober" mind (*siccus ac sobrius*, 114.3) would be just the opposite. It would have good tension (again εὐτονία) in that it would establish clear and orderly relations among words and paragraphs.

Some further investigation of the effects of psychic tension may assist us to a more insightful reading of Seneca's other stylistic pronouncements as well. It is important to observe, first, that in Stoic thought, the ideal state of soul is self-perpetuating. The systematic and comprehensive way in which this soul holds its beliefs and values exercises control over its further assents so that it is no longer prone to accept and act upon false impressions.[36] The result is that virtue is a "steady state" or character (διάθεσις).[37] The fortunate possessor of this level of soul-tension will no longer be subject to the psychic upsets which we call emotions, not even to the seemingly positive emotion of delight, where delight means pleasure in external goods. He may, however, enjoy a stable satisfaction in the presence of real goodness within himself, and this "good emotion" is properly termed "joy" (χαρά, *gaudium*). Finally, the human soul in its ideal condition is both beautiful and awe-inspiring. For Seneca, its thoughts are "splendid and upright" (*magnifica et erecta*), and it has the beauty and sublimity of deep forests, natural caverns, or great bodies of water (*Letters* 41.2–4).

All these points should be compared with what is said in *Letters* 46.2. Seneca exclaims over the *ingenium* that is on display in Lucilius's book, but he will not speak of its impact (*impetus*), for that would suggest that the effect comes only at intervals, whereas here, excellence is a steady state (*tenor*). From this he infers that Lucilius himself is *grandis, erectus*, "great and upright," assuming without hesitation that a quality of the work can

---

[35] *Letters* 114.22. The transition to this point from the discussion of deliberate affectation that precedes it is not well thought out. Seneca is anticipating the point that follows: the effects of alcohol on speech are not relevant to deliberate errors, but only to the dependence of speech on the character of the *animus*.

[36] Stobaeus 2.7.5l, 73–74 Wachsmuth (LS 41H); see Long and Sedley (1987: vol. 1, 256–59), and compare *Letters* 75.8–18.

[37] Diog. Laert. 7.89; Plutarch, *On Moral Virtue* 441b.

be transferred to the mind of its author.[38] Meanwhile, he, the reader of the book, responds with joy (*gaudium*), as distinct from ordinary delight (*delectatio*), momentarily taking on the normative emotion that the Stoic sage experiences in the presence of moral excellence.[39]

The same background conception of psychological health informs Seneca's assessment of the style of Papirius Fabianus in letter 100.[40] Lucilius has complained that everything in Fabianus's prose seems to him "flat and insufficiently elevated" (*humilia et parum erecta*, 100.8). This Seneca strongly denies:

> His style is not flat, but calm, formed after the steadiness (*tenorem*) and quiet of his mind; it is level, not low. It does lack rhetorical intensity, the provocations you are looking for, and the sudden impact of aphorisms (*sententiae*). But the body as a whole is admirable, no matter what its grooming (*sed totum corpus, videris quam sit comptum, honestum est*). (*Letters* 100.8)

As in letter 46, the written work bears a predictable relationship to (is "formed after") the mind of the writer, and evenness and integration are preferred to flashy special effects. The mention of grooming again invokes the norms of sexual self-definition in support of the work Seneca admires; compare *Letters* 115.2. However, the effeminacy theme is here muted, perhaps out of respect for Cicero, whose style, "soft but without scandal," figures prominently in the previous paragraph (*sine infamia mollis*, 100.7). Seneca's chief aim is to win acceptance for a norm of internal stability or perhaps "tensility" as a positive characteristic that can be both recognized and appreciated. Properly read, he insists, such writing may be extremely powerful: the individual parts go without praise, yet the writing as a whole is *magnificus* (100.2).

Peculiar Results

It would have to be a strange principle of style that could find much to praise in Papirius Fabianus – a family friend, to be sure, but a writer whom even Seneca seems to find rather stuffy, judging by the repeated concessions in letter 100. Why, then, would Seneca, whose own career was so much indebted to the liveliness of his prose, develop an ideal so peculiar

---

[38] A point also noted in Wilcox (2012: 154–55).
[39] On the distinction between joy and delight, see further *Letters* 23.1–8, 59.1–4 and pages 219–20.
[40] On Fabianus, see Seneca the Elder *Controversiae* 2 *praef.*; Griffin (1976: 39–40). Leeman (1965: 261–70) gives a sample of his prose style, which he discusses largely in terms of fluency or continuous movement.

and unproductive?⁴¹ In part, we see at work the mechanism so well described by recent work in cultural history: alterity (female/homosexual/ rival) is stridently rejected as a means of defining a selfhood that is perpetually difficult to articulate within a male-dominated culture.⁴² Like many another Roman male of his class, Seneca is ready to denigrate a Maecenas or a Lucius Arruntius in terms that subsume to himself their opposites, yet offers only a rather feeble and unconvincing explanation for what masculinity is in itself. This telling picture is made more difficult to read, however, by Seneca's genuine commitment to Stoic psychology as he understands it. Stoicism has given him some grounds for believing that language, spoken or written, provides a clear index of mental states, so that excellence of style is simply the observable aspect of soundness of character. When this idea intersects with the familiar language of gender invective, the results are sometimes counterintuitive.

One particularly odd case is the beginning of letter 33. Here the Stoic writers whom Cicero characterizes as "squalid" (*Fin.* 4.3.6–7) appear as paragons of style, while Epicurus, surely one of the most determinedly graceless stylists of antiquity, is criticized for something akin to Asianism!⁴³ The context is a question concerning the use in philosophical texts of aphorisms or *sententiae*: brief, piquantly phrased statements or memory bits. In letters leading up to this one, Seneca has permitted Lucilius to enjoy *sententiae* on ethical themes; in fact, letter 2 urges that one should maximize the benefit of a daily reading program by extracting such aphorisms from one's books and pondering them throughout the day. This recommendation, already strongly reminiscent of Epicurean ascesis, has been reinforced by the inclusion of sample *sententiae* in letters 2–29, most of them taken directly from the writings of Epicurus.⁴⁴ Now, early in the fourth book, there is a reversal: *sententiae* are no longer to be taken

---

⁴¹ The perception that Seneca's own stylistic practice is out of line with his recommendations – by now a commonplace of scholarship – gains much-needed perspective from the comments of Leeman (1965: 277–78) on the importance of evaluating stylistic judgments in relation to contemporary fashions. For pragmatic discussion of Seneca's theory and practice in general, see, besides Leeman, Cizek (1972: 298–322).

⁴² Gleason (1995: 61), speaking of the orator's posture and movement, remarks that manliness "appears to be an ideal best expressed in the negative: the real man ... is known by the absence of effeminate signs as much as by any positive distinguishing marks."

⁴³ Highly relevant here is the suggestion made by Aldo Setaioli, that given the resemblance between Seneca's treatment of Maecenas and Cleomedes's treatment of Epicurus himself – in other words, that his style was corrupt in the same way as his character – we should perhaps infer that Seneca was familiar with a similar remark made by Posidonius, who was Cleomedes's main source. See Setaioli (2000: 191–92) and 255–74, together with Gordon (2012: 187–88).

⁴⁴ For the role of memorization in Epicurean ascesis, see page 101.

from context, even though (we learn to our surprise) they may be found in far greater abundance in the writings of Zeno and Cleanthes. Naturally, the exponents of the masculine philosophy express themselves in masculine prose; this does not mean, however, that they eschew the ornaments for which Epicurus is noted.

> You request that I should close these letters, as I did the earlier ones, with quotations, and that I should take them from the leaders of our own school. *They* did not busy themselves with flowery bits of speech (*flosculi*): their entire fabric is masculine. Where what is noteworthy stands out from the rest, you can be sure the quality is uneven. A single tree excites no wonder when the entire forest rises to the same height. Poems are stuffed with sayings of that sort, and historical writings too. So I do not want you to think of them as belonging to Epicurus: they are public property, and especially *our* property. But in him they attract more attention, just because they occur infrequently, because they are unexpected, because it is surprising that anything courageous should be said by a man who professed effeminacy (*ab homine mollitiam professo*). (*Letters* 33.1–2)

Having thus insinuated that whatever is associated with Epicurus must be anything but masculine, Seneca hastens to correct himself. Epicurus is effeminate only in the judgment of the many; in Seneca's own view, he "can even be considered brave – despite his long sleeves."[45] It is admitted that like Maecenas, Epicurus was not one of those who are "closely girded" (*alte cinctos*); still, one does find warlike types even among the Persians! The net result of these openly backhanded compliments is a strangely ambiguous position on Epicurus's sexuality. He is neither masculine like the Stoic founders nor effeminate like his own doctrines, yet he shows some characteristics of both.

The passage is best read as a working out of Seneca's *talis oratio* principle. Elsewhere, he may follow Cicero in registering approbation for Epicurus's frugal habits and for his courage in his last illness.[46] Here, though, he is willing to play up the popular image of a sexually ambiguous Epicurus, not for the purpose of making the usual cheap gibe about subservience to pleasure, but in order to pursue a particular point about writing and reading.[47] The goal is to persuade Lucilius, or rather the

---

[45] For sleeves as a sign of effeminacy, see Corbeill (1996: 59–63); Richlin (1992: 92–93).
[46] Cicero's approbation for Epicurus's personal life can be followed in *Off.* 3.116, *Tusc.* 3.46, *Fin.* 2.96–99. Seneca echoes the point esp. at *Happiness* 13.
[47] According to Cicero in *Fam.* 7.26.1, the sexual slander against Epicurus was devised by the Stoics, who cited his bouts with dysentery and colic as evidence of gluttony and "another worse form of intemperance."

general reader who is the real object of admonition, to give up skimming for aphorisms in favor of a more disciplined reading program.[48] Stoic writings, unlike those of Epicurus, are represented as unexcerptable and yet rewarding, most valuable when taken as wholes. Employing the same tactic he will later use to defend Fabianus, Seneca appeals to the organic unity of these writings: they are like the body of a lovely woman, whose individual parts, though lovely, are less esteemed than her appearance overall. Logical interdependence of parts – the Stoic strong suit – makes these writings like a building from which no stone can be safely extracted.

> <*Continuando*> res geritur et per lineamenta sua ingenii opus nectitur ex quo nihil subduci sine ruina potest.
>
> The meaning is conveyed <continuously>, and by its own outlines is constructed a work of the *ingenium* from which nothing can be removed without a collapse. (*Letters* 33.5)

Sua, in the phrase *per lineamenta sua*, can only refer forward to *ingenium*. The sentence must say that the "work of the *ingenium*," that is, the writing as product, is related to the structure of the *ingenium* itself in the same way as a building is related to its blueprint. That is, the cohesiveness of the Stoic text, the quality that makes it difficult to excerpt, is a kind of direct manifestation, even a sign, of the structured and systematic way these minds handle information. And the latter is in turn equivalent to a tensing of the soul-material. Since this is where the letter is going, it is expedient that texts which are essentially collections of *sententiae* should be dismissed on moral grounds, as expressions of minds less tight, less systematic, less virtuous in a Chrysippan sense of the word. The association of *sententiae* with oratorical flourishes provides a convenient, if not entirely convincing, basis for representing Epicurus's prose as unmasculine to some degree. Effeminacy in the philosopher himself is a necessary concomitant, albeit a somewhat embarrassing one in view of the earlier letters' preoccupation with Epicurus.

***

It should be evident by now that the concept of "masculinity" as Seneca employs it has little utility either as a practical principle of style or as an evaluative principle of criticism. The absurdity of pairing Epicurus with

---

[48] For a similarly programmatic use of gender rhetoric, compare *Constancy* 1.1., where the point is to urge readers to accept the "manly," that is, demanding and sometimes repellent, medicine of a Stoic treatise. On the importance of intellectual independence in Stoic therapy, see Nussbaum (1994: 345–53).

Maecenas as personalities is matched only by the impossibility of finding any common ground between the writings of Maecenas that are known to us and any work Epicurus is known to have produced or can be imagined producing.[49] On the other hand, a counterintuitive principle of style may provide insight into its author's deeper reflections on language and character. So we have seen in these texts from the *Letters on Ethics*. In this work in particular, Seneca proceeds beyond the rather tedious gender polemic that pervades the philosophical as well as the rhetorical discourse of antiquity, and does so for a plausible if not entirely satisfactory reason.[50] Clearly, he has made an attempt to work out something of the practical applications of Stoic theorizing on the psychophysical dimension of language production. The existence of the Latin term *ingenium*, which is capable of mediating between the strictly psychic realm and the external products of talent, is of assistance to him in this project, but the extensions he makes are very much his own.

Epilogue: Seneca and the *Malagma Moecharum*

An amusing postscript to Seneca's critique of Maecenas has been provided for us by Macrobius. Fond of gossip and scandal, Macrobius also had enviable access to texts from the principate of Augustus. In one case we can see how his familiarity with the *Letters on Ethics* has assisted him to an ingenious reading of a testimonial.[51]

In the second book of his *Saturnalia*, Macrobius quotes from a personal letter of Augustus the following playful valedictory to Maecenas:

> *Vale mi ebenum Medulliae, ebur ex Etruria, lasar Arretinum, adamas Supernas, Tiberinum margaritum, Cilniorum smaragde, iaspi Iguvinorum, berulle Porsenae, carbunculum Hadriae*, ἵνα συντέμω πάντα, μάλαγμα *moecharum*.
>
> Farewell, my Medullian ebony, my ivory from Etruria, my Arretine lasarpicium, my diamond Supernan, my pearl from the Tiber, emerald of the

---

[49] Seneca was familiar both with the Epicurean *gnomologia*, probably including the *Kuriai Doxai* known to us, and with samples of Epicurus's connected prose; see Setaioli (1988: 173–83). The suggestion that Maecenas was himself an Epicurean, argued at length by André (1967: 15–71) and recently reiterated by Ferguson (1990: 2263–65) depends too much on inference from Seneca to be useful here.

[50] For instance, Cicero complains of Zeno of Sidon, the Epicurean scholarch, who "always referred to Chrysippus as Chrysippa" (*Nat. Deor.* 1.34.93). Cicero himself is free with such invective, not only against Epicureans but also against Peripatetics, for example, at *Tusc.* 4.64. Reversals of such stereotypes in Persius and Juvenal certify that such language was familiar enough to provide grounds for humor.

[51] Macrobius's fondness for Seneca is expressed mainly through plagiarism: in particular, Sat. *praef.* 5–9 and 1.11.7–15 present long stretches of material taken directly from letters 84 and 47.

Cilnii, jasper of the Iguvini, beryl of Porsena, carbuncle of the Adriatic, and to sum it all up, emollient of adulteresses.[52]

In itself, this is not very enlightening. Clearly the princeps alludes to his friend's fabled wealth and also twits him in some way for his sexual prowess; he may also be referring to Maecenas's poem addressed to Horace.[53] The point of the final phrase is ambiguous, however. Μάλαγμα, here translated "emollient," is the noun form of the verb μαλάκειν, "to soften."[54] Does this mean that Maecenas is himself "soft," or that he has a "softening" effect on the women he seduces? Macrobius offers a third interpretation. The joke, he says, derives its point from the prose style of the two men: the princeps is venturing on a parody of Maecenas's effeminate style. His introduction to Augustus's remark reads as follows:

> *Idem Augustus, quia Maecenatem suum noverat stilo esse remisso, molli, et dissoluto, talem se in epistulis quas ad eum scribebat saepius exhibebat, et, contra castigationem loquendi quam alias ille scribendo servabat, in epistula ad Maecenatem familiari plura in iocos effusa subtexuit.*

> Because he knew that his friend Maecenas was lax, soft, and loose in his style, Augustus frequently adopted the same manner in the letters he wrote to him. Thus, in a personal letter addressed to Maecenas, he works in many extravagant expressions, for a joke, contrary to the chaste manner of expression to which he elsewhere adheres.

Μάλαγμα, in this reading, refers both to the "softness" (*mollitia* or rather μαλακία) of flamboyant sexual conduct and to *mollitia* as a quality of Maecenas's prose. Augustus is making a sophisticated play on words.

To arrive at this reading, Macrobius has had to pursue a complicated hermeneutic program involving both the manipulation of gender language and the characterization of a prose style. He has first applied the label "extravagant" (or "diffuse, *effusa*) to Augustus's own style in the passage before him, relying on its use of metaphors, its rhythmic affectations, and especially its paratactic structure. He then links that adjective to the more pejorative terms "lax" (*remissus*), "soft" (*mollis*), and "loose" (*dissolutus*), making use of the regular association of that which is loose and/or liquid with flamboyant sexual conduct. *Mollis* may then be teasingly compared with μάλαγμα, but the humor of this is not yet comprehensible. One must

---

[52] Macrobius *Saturnalia* 2.4.12; text in Willis (1970).
[53] Fragment 3 Lunderstedt; Courtney (1993: 276–77).
[54] For the interpretation as "emollient," that is, an ointment of some kind, see LSJ[9] s.v. μάλαγμα, and compare the "myrrh-dripping ringlets" (μυροβρεχεῖς *concinnos*) of Suet. *Div. Aug.* 86.

also believe three other things: first, that what is evident in the prose may be expected to be evident in the person as well; second, that Maecenas's own prose (probably not available for autopsy by Macrobius) would naturally be characterized as "soft"; and third, that Augustus was not himself a "soft" character. It is then quite easy to insist that Augustus's other prose was generally "chaste" and to see the present fragment as anomalous, and hence deliberately parodic .

Whether this is the joke intended by the princeps is a moot point. What is of interest for us is the ease with which Macrobius has moved, in a kind of literary divination, from observations about prose style to complicated inferences about the behavior of absent persons and even to inferences at a further remove about the style of unavailable prose. In this, Seneca has been his tutor.

CHAPTER 12

Honeybee Reading and Self-Scripting

Classicists have been intrigued to see the strong reaction of Michel Foucault to the philosophy of the early Roman Empire. In the opening essay to a volume called *Seneca and the Self*, A. A. Long speaks movingly of how fresh and challenging Seneca appears, even to those who know him well, when situated by Foucault at the center of an emerging discourse about the cultivation of one's own selfhood as the essential requirement of ethics.[1] It is with similar excitement that I engage here with a particular letter of Seneca that was of interest to Foucault. In his letter, Seneca speaks in a suggestive way about the activities of reading and writing and about the shaping of oneself as a person through these activities. Foucault picks up on this and speaks of a process of "scripting the self," by which he means constituting oneself as a better and more consistent moral agent through the act of writing and through the prior acts of reading on which writing depends. In this, I argue, Foucault was on the right track, though he may not fully have understood what Seneca had in mind. With deeper philological study, we can bring out what is radical and of great significance in Seneca's thought even as we recognize the embeddedness of that thought in Roman literary culture.

Caution is required, certainly, as concerns the psychological model to be attributed to an author who considers himself an adherent of Stoic thought. Brad Inwood, writing for the same volume, reviews the expressions cited by Foucault for a particular concern with the self in Seneca and concludes that there is no evidence for innovation in terms of mental ontology.[2] Seneca is not in general very inclined to multiply psychological entities in the way that Plato does, and we should not expect him to be adding extra parts or organs to the unitary rational psyche. Inwood thus

---

[1] Long (2009); the volume is Bartsch and Wray (2009). The essay was first published in Long (2006: 360–76).
[2] Inwood (2009), first published in Inwood (2005: 322–52).

rejects the implication he finds in Foucault that Seneca conceives of the self in a way that departs from the analysis of mind and action he inherited from the Stoic tradition. Yet Inwood also acknowledges that Seneca does at least give the impression of emphasizing selfhood in a novel and distinctive way, because of his frequent claims of intellectual independence and because of certain literary devices in his writing: his strong first-person voice and his habit of using his own experience to exemplify various points he is making. In these ways Seneca does create a kind of self, such that "Seneca" appears as a fully realized character throughout the prose works and especially in the fictive correspondence that is the *Letters on Ethics*.

Like Inwood, I read Seneca's moral psychology as Chrysippan in all its essentials. Nonetheless, I believe that in the 84th letter, and implicitly elsewhere, Seneca does envision a novel ontology of the self. While he does not posit any new psychological entities, he does make an innovative philosophical adaptation of some familiar Roman ideas about what can be achieved through the medium of writing. The scripted self in his conception does not consist only in a first-person perspective; nor is it merely a self-portrait. It consists rather in the use of writing to externalize one's locus of identity, one's very thoughts, reasonings, and reactions, fixing them for the future and making them available to others. And there is more, for in his thought writing also becomes a way to rise above one's current self. Artistic achievement surpasses and ultimately replaces one's unstable and fleeting sentience within the body with an externalized self that is more consistent and more admirable as well as more stable. This is what Foucault realized, at least in part, about Seneca, but his grasp was tentative and lacked the awareness of literary context that made it a natural thought for Seneca to have. I try here to fill in some of what is missing in his account.

Reading Like a Honeybee

Seneca opens his letter by mentioning a journey, or rather a series of journeys (*itinera*), perhaps a succession of day trips. It appears that Lucilius, the "you" of the correspondence, has suggested these, for *ista* in the first line gestures toward the second-person point of view. As the preceding letter had spoken of sedentary habits (*Letters* 83.3), we are perhaps expected to imagine an intervening letter from Lucilius urging Seneca to get out more. Moving about, Seneca now admits, has benefited both his health and his studies – more obviously the former, since it has aroused him from his scholarly lassitude, but also the latter. If this seems odd, he will explain: it is because "I have withdrawn from readings."[3] To be sure, reading is a necessary activity, which both informs and refreshes the mind of the writer; still, neither reading nor writing should be practiced to the exclusion of the other. Writing alone will "exhaust" our powers (*exhauriet*); reading alone will "dilute" them (*diluet*). The proper approach is to take what is collected by reading and "assimilate it to the body" by writing (84.2).

This imagery of transfer of fluids, collection, and digestion sets up an easy transition to the extended metaphor of bees and the hive, the most highly developed image in the letter and one that has made a deep impression on many readers.[4] Seneca's description of the work of bees is beautifully detailed. His bees first move about and seize upon flowers suitable for honey-making, then arrange what they have collected and distribute it through the hive, and finally, in the words of Vergil, "pack away the liquid honey, and swell the comb with sweet nectar" (*Aeneid* 1.432–433). All this serves as an analogy for the kind of reading Seneca envisions as beneficial for himself and for Lucilius. Readers, he says, should first store away the things they have gathered from their diverse reading, keeping them distinct in their minds, then combine those varied elements into a uniform product different in character from what existed before. Even if it is apparent where a thing is taken from, it should still appear to be different from that from which it was taken (84.5). A series of further metaphors then adds emphasis to the theme of assimilation and transformation. The process is like that of digestion in the body, which changes the mix of foods in the stomach into one's own flesh and blood; or like a numerical calculation that combines many numbers into one sum; or like human reproduction – for the later work should resemble earlier compositions in the way that a child resembles a parent, not in the way a statue resembles its model. "A statue is a dead thing" (84.8). When the process is carried out successfully, the features of the prior text will not be distinguishable at all, just as in a symphonic performance the sounds of bass and treble voices, trumpet, flute, and organ are all mingled into unison. This, Seneca says, is what the mind of a reader should be like. It should harmonize many skills, many precepts, many examples from every age, into one.

---

[3] I follow the received text. Some editors insert *non* before *recessi*; I argue against that assertion later in this chapter.

[4] Summers (1910: 284) traces the influence of the passage through a series of authors from Macrobius (who plagiarizes shamelessly from it in the preface to his *Saturnalia*) through Petrarch (*Epistulae de rebus familiaribus* 1.7). See further De Rentiis (1998).

To achieve such integration requires constant concentration and attentiveness to rational standards of conduct. One must act, or refrain from acting, only as reason directs (84.11). No longer speaking solely about reading and writing, Seneca at the close of the letter reflects more generally on the values that should inform one's behavior. One must abandon wealth, pleasure, and ambition, and seek wisdom instead. In so doing, one will find tranquility as well as excellence, for while eminence in civic life is achieved only by struggle and difficulty, the *summum bonum* of the moral philosopher is reached via "level ground" (84.13); that is, by consistency in thought and action.

Techniques of Selfhood

Foucault's interest in this letter belonged to the last two years of his life; it was part of a topic he would no doubt have pursued further if he had lived to do so.[5] He had become intrigued by the work of the Parisian classical philosopher Pierre Hadot on certain "spiritual exercises" that, according to Hadot, were practiced throughout antiquity by the philosophically inclined of all schools.[6] He thus approached letter 84 as just one witness (though a key witness) to widely shared habits of reading and writing in the ancient world, and reading and writing themselves as belonging to a larger set of cultural practices aimed at the cultivation and care of one's individual identity.

Of course, Foucault was not primarily a classicist, and his fascination with Hadot's exercises, which he relabels "techniques of the self," has more to do with his own philosophical concerns than with a strictly historical understanding.[7] His response to this particular letter is nonetheless instructive. He is quite taken with what Seneca says about the need to alternate between reading and writing: that neither is beneficial without the other and that the two processes both limit one another and aid one another. The idea that a reading program needs to be restricted is one that

---

[5] Davidson (1997: 16).
[6] Foucault knew Pierre Hadot's articles even before the first edition of *Exercices spirituels et philosophie antique* was published in Paris in 1981. The second edition (P. Hadot (1993)) is available in English translation as P. Hadot (1995). Compare Foucault (1984: 53–85).
[7] Hence the historically oriented critique in Strozier (2002: 139–74) is not entirely apposite. More attuned to Foucault's objectives is Veyne (1993: 7): "Greek ethics is quite dead, and Foucault judged it as undesirable as it would be impossible to resuscitate this ethics; but he considered one of its elements, namely, the idea of a work of the self on the self, to be capable of acquiring a contemporary meaning, in the manner of one of those pagan temple columns that one occasionally sees reutilized in more recent structures."

he had found elsewhere in Seneca, notably in the second letter, where Seneca recommends concentrating on just a few works and excerpting small portions of these for further reflection. In a lecture given in Paris in 1982, and again in his 1983 essay "L'écriture de soi" ("Self-Scripting"), Foucault connects this notion of a restricted reading program with the writing of *hypomnēmata*, personal notebooks filled with extracts copied out from a variety of sources.[8] *Hypomnēmata* as Foucault imagines them are not written merely as an aid to memory or a tool for developing one's understanding of the source text; rather, they are an aid to ethical living. By copying, rereading, and reflecting upon selected aphorisms, one trains oneself to recognize "scattered truth" (*la vérité disparate*) in writings from the past and then, further, to keep that truth always at hand to influence one's actions on future occasions. This is one of two ways in which writing can be a spiritual exercise. The other is epistolography; that is, the writing of personal letters, in which one reveals oneself to another through personal narrative. Letters are written partly to educate the addressee, and reciprocally oneself, toward right action, but also partly to "objectify" oneself; that is, to give oneself over to the gaze of the addressee and to the much larger number of people who may eventually come to read the letter. By teaching and exhorting another, or many others, one is also training oneself to live in the eyes of others, "as though some other person could gaze into our inmost breast," as Seneca says in *Letters* 83.1.

With his emphasis on the subsequent transformation of material learned through reading, Foucault goes a long way to resolve what might seem to be a striking discrepancy between the tightly controlled reading program recommended in *Letters* 2.1–4 and the *diversa lectio* of 84.5. Seneca regularly urges Lucilius not to indulge in a wide range of readings, pleasurable as that might be, but to concentrate on just a few volumes.[9] Ill-advised browsing in many different authors and genres is compared in letter 2 to pointless travel (which Lucilius prudently avoids in 2.1), to frequent changes of medication for the sick, and to the consumption of a medley of foods. All these are indications of inward restlessness (something *vagum et instabile*, 2.1) and will only make one's condition worse: where readings are "varied and diverse," they will not nourish the mind but "pollute" it (2.4 *inquinant non alunt*). By contrast, letter 84 speaks favorably of travel and appears also

---

[8] For the lecture, see Foucault (2001: 338–53). The essay was first published in Foucault (1983) and reprinted in Foucault (1994: vol. 4, 415–30). In what follows I supply my own translations; a complete English translation by Ann Hobart may be found in Davidson (1997: 23–47).

[9] For the theme see page 209.

to recommend an eclectic program of reading, for the model of the honeybee surely suggests movement from place to place and nourishment drawn from a wide variety of sources. As Foucault realizes, however, the underlying implication is the same in both letters. What is important to Seneca is not so much the choice of readings as it is the process that goes on afterward within the reader, as multiple elements are combined into a single substance. This is the thought that is expressed by the motif of many things becoming one, which appears constantly in letter 84, and in particular by the metaphor of digestion, which is prominent in both letters.[10] It is assimilation by digestion that makes reading successful. If letter 2 dissuades Lucilius from the *varia et diversa*, it is only because they are difficult to digest, and if letter 84 then endorses *diversa lectio*, it is only insofar as digestion can transform diversity into uniformity.[11] It is a single idea, even though this metaphoric digestion takes different forms: in 2.4 an entirely inward activity of meditation, in 84.7 the more visible activity of writing. For Foucault, the two processes are essentially the same:

> Writing, as a personal exercise done by oneself and for oneself, is an art of scattered truth. Or, more precisely, it is a reflective means of combining the traditional authority of the prior text with the singularity of the truth affirmed in it and with the particularity of the circumstances determining its use.[12]

On this model the composition of *hypomnēmata* is in itself essentially reflective and integrative. One copies down a miscellany of excerpts, as Seneca describes in *Letters* 2.4, then ponders each to find in it a personal truth that will be applicable to the circumstances of one's own life.

A further development of this idea brings Foucault to the insight that is at one and the same time the most valuable of his essay and the most problematic. Studying the implications of the digestion metaphor, he points out that digestion is not merely a process of assimilating what one has ingested to one's own existing nature. It is also the process by which one's own nature is constituted and comes into being. The *corpus* to which one's reading is to be assimilated is thus in a real sense the very self that each of us is

---

[10] See *Letters* 84.4 *in unum diversa*; 84.5 *in unum saporem varia libamenta*; 84.7 *unum quiddam fiat ex multis*; 84.8 *in unitatem illa competant*; 84.9 *unus tamen ex omnibus*; 84.10 *multa in unum conspirata*; and compare *Letters* 2.4 *cum multa percurreris, unum excerpe*. Digestion is mentioned explicitly in 84.7 *concoquamus illa* and 2.4 *quod illo die concoquas* and is implied also in 2.3 *non prodest cibus nec corpori accedit qui statim sumptus emittitur* and 2.4 *fastidientis stomachi*.
[11] *Letters* 2.4 'Sed modo,' inquis, 'hunc librum evolvere volo, modo illum.' *Fastidientis stomachi est multa degustare; quae ubi varia sunt et diversa, inquinant non alunt.*
[12] Foucault (1983: 11).

constantly creating. It is not a body of doctrine, but rather "the actual body of the one who, by transcribing his readings, has appropriated them and made their truth his own."[13] This is to say that the writing that he calls "assimilative writing" (*l'écriture assimilatrice*) creates from the material of prior texts a new self, a new identity, which is in some sense the real identity of the writer. He traces the same idea in the sentence about resembling one's ancestors "as a son does, not as a statue does." Again, there is an idea of artistic creation, but the artifact is not separable from its creator. Artwork and artist are one:

> It is one's own soul that must be composed in one's writings. But as a man bears on his visage a natural resemblance to his ancestors, so likewise it is well that we should be able to recognize in his writings the ancestry of those thoughts which have been engraved on his soul. Through the interplay of selected readings and assimilative writing, one should be able to form for oneself an identity, upon which can be read an entire spiritual genealogy.[14]

Of course this notion of consciously creating an integrated self through deliberate spiritual practices of stylized reading and writing is one that combines easily with Foucault's own thoughts about self-actualization and an aesthetics of existence.[15]

As a generalization about Seneca's thought, this way of understanding letter 84 is problematic on several fronts. Even if it remains clear of the objections raised by Inwood to Foucault's other readings in the *Letters on Ethics* (and I am not sure that it does), it certainly encounters the objection raised in a response by Pierre Hadot, namely that Foucault is too quick to dismiss Seneca's commitment to Stoicism. Hadot objects strongly to Foucault's claim that therapeutic writing is eclectic by nature, so that it is "not a body of doctrine" but is actually opposed to the doctrinal unity of any avowed philosophical school.[16] In addition, Hadot and others have felt that Foucault's emphasis on reflexivity underemphasizes Seneca's larger concern with normativity. As Hadot reminds us, Seneca urges Lucilius not to turn toward himself as he is but to discover "the best part of himself" (*Letters* 23.6); that is, to learn what is required of him if he is to live as members of the human species were designed by the providential deity to live: rationally, virtuously, happily.[17]

---

[13] Foucault (1983: 12).   [14] Foucault (1983: 13).
[15] Helpful discussions include Davidson (1994); Bernauer and Mahon (1994: 152–56); Veyne (1993).
[16] P. Hadot (1989: 264–65), responding to Foucault (1983: 12).
[17] P. Hadot (1989: 262); but cf. Davidson (1994). Seneca's concern with normativity has been emphasized in (for example) Long (2009), who speaks of the "normative" versus the "occurrent" self, and Gill (2009), who speaks of the "natural" versus the "actual" self.

As an interpretation of letter 84 itself, however, Foucault's assertions have a good deal to recommend them. He is correct in believing that Seneca is promoting a kind of self-training toward moral action, for this model is clearly stated toward the end of the letter, where he urges the reader to examine the values that underlie his actions (84.11–13). The urgency of this recommendation should be kept in view even if, as will be seen, Seneca's point in some earlier paragraphs is rather different from what Foucault supposed. Even more important, Foucault is right to insist on the deeply personal and intimate nature of Seneca's metaphors of nourishment, bodily processes, and sonship. "It is *one's own soul* that must be composed in one's writings."[18] For in this letter more than any other, Seneca puts forward some definite ideas about how one creates a self out of the stuff of experience and how one may shape that self-in-progress for maximum impact upon the world.

The trouble with Foucault's account in my view is just that it does not go far enough to bring out the full implications of Seneca's thought on these issues. Although it is not wrong to speak of informal writing, such as journals and private letters, Foucault ought also to have considered the more ambitious and public literary forms favored by Seneca and Lucilius as members of Rome's educated elite. These are essential here, for at its core Seneca's notion of self-scripting is one of literary artistry, of harmonizing disparate stylistic inheritances within the written artifact. His criteria for success in this endeavor are aesthetic criteria, which appeal to the perceptions of those who read or hear what one has produced. Nonetheless, the product of this artistry is a real self, an "I" whose thoughts are one's own, but improved, stabilized, and externalized for the long term.

The Meaning of Study

The full understanding of Seneca's point necessarily begins with particulars of his language. I concentrate first on the word *studium*, a pivotal term in his discussion but one that lacks any precise functional equivalent in English – for the English word "study," though derived from *studium*, captures only part of its meaning. The difficulty both medieval and modern readers have had in understanding Seneca's usage of *studium* is indicated by a long-standing textual crux in the first paragraph of the letter. According to the received text, Seneca writes:

---

[18] Foucault (1983: 13).

> *Itinera ista quae segnitiam mihi excutiunt et valetudini meae prodesse iudico et studiis. Quare valetudinem adiuvent vides: cum pigrum me et neglegentem corporis litterarum amor faciat, aliena opera exerceor. Studio quare prosint indicabo: a lectionibus recessi. Sunt autem, ut existimo, necessariae, primum ne sim me uno contentus, deinde ut, cum ab aliis quaesita cognovero, tam et de inventis iudicem et cogitem de inveniendis.*

> Those trips are shaking the laziness out of me; they have been beneficial, I believe, both to my health and to my studies. Why they should improve my health is plain to you: since my love of letters makes me lazy and neglectful of my body, I get some exercise through the labor of others.[19] Why they should aid my study I will explain: I have withdrawn from readings. To be sure, reading is necessary, first that I may not be wrapped up in myself alone and second that after finding out about the inquiries of others, I may both judge concerning their discoveries and ponder what remains to be discovered. (*Letters* 84.1)

L. D. Reynolds, editing for the *Oxford Classical Text*, inserts *non* in angled brackets before *recessi*, making Seneca say, "I have *not* withdrawn from readings." François Préchac in the Budé edition and most other modern editors do approximately the same.[20] The preference for the negative is an old one, that goes back to the Renaissance edition by Justus Lipsius and that appears also in the manuscript tradition, though only in a few late copies.[21] Despite its long pedigree among textual critics, however, the insertion of *non* is certainly a mistake. Seneca has offered to explain a benefit to his studies, something he egregiously fails to do if we make him say no more than that he has "not withdrawn" from a previous activity. A person may say, if he wants, that he has improved his health by reducing his scholarly activity, but he can hardly claim to have made an improvement merely by continuing in his former habits. An improvement implies a change. The word *recessi* ("I have withdrawn") indicates that the change consists in at least a temporary cessation.[22]

---

[19] That is, his litter bearers. Seneca "exercises" via sedan chair.

[20] The exception is Beltrami (1937). Axelson (1939: 144–45) defends the negative, as does Berti (2018) 404–5. Gummere (1917) follows Hense (1914) in strengthening *non* to *nihil*. Summers (1910) omits the negative and interprets Seneca to mean "I have of late given them up, and now am encouraged to resume them." This saves the received text, but at the cost of making it say the opposite of what the words mean. Alexander (1941: 149) improves on Summers's interpretation by emphasizing the adversative force of *autem*, but still fails to draw an adequate distinction between *lectio* and *studium*.

[21] Lipsius (1632). Lipsius was influenced by *Letters* 15.6, as is shown by his comment ad loc: "Quare itinera prosint studiis? quia gestatio legere non impedit, vel certe legentem audire." For the MS tradition, I rely on the *apparatus criticus* in Reynolds (1965) and Préchac (1945–64).

[22] It is relevant that *recedere* in Latin frequently refers to a temporary withdrawal, like the waning of the moon or ebbing of the tides (*OLD* s.v. *recedo* 2ab, 4).

But can someone improve his studies – that is, his *studia* – by ceasing to read even temporarily? Not if *studia* and *lectiones* are synonymous, clearly, but when we look at the continuation of the paragraph, it seems quite clear that Seneca does not simply equate the two. In fact, he sets up an opposition between them:

> Reading nourishes one's *ingenium* and refreshes it when it is worn out with study, even though it does not do this in the absence of study. We ought neither to write exclusively nor read exclusively: the first – writing, that is – will deaden and exhaust our powers; the second will weaken and dilute them. One must do both by turns, tempering one with the other, so that whatever is collected through reading may be assimilated into the body by writing. (*Letters* 84.1–2)

"Study" now appears in a reciprocal relation to reading. Reading nourishes the *ingenium* when it is "worn out by study" (*studio fatigatum*), but reading "in the absence of study" (*sine studio*) would not have this effect. It turns out that there are two activities that must be done in alternation: one is reading, and the other is called at first "study" (*studium*) and then, in the second sentence quoted, simply "writing" (*scribere, stilus*).[23] One wonders, then, why Seneca chose the word *studium* here, and in what sense "study" can count as the opposite activity to reading books.

A brief survey of other passages in the *Letters on Ethics* will help to resolve the issue. As background, one needs to know that the word *studium* in Latin always signifies some form of dedication to a specific object: zeal for a cause, enthusiasm for a hobby, support for a candidate, or some other form of devotion.[24] The specific sense of energy and attention directed toward books and other intellectual pursuits may be expressed by *studium* without additional limiting words, but this meaning does not predominate over other uses. Seneca's own usage reflects his interests and priorities. Sometimes, he speaks of a *studium* for the kinds of pursuits that English speakers would call "study" or "studies." In *Letters* 8.1, for instance, it refers to Seneca's writing; in 21.2, to Lucilius's reading; in 15.6 and 26.6, it takes in a variety of intellectual pursuits: reading, giving dictation, delivering and listening to speeches, and conversing; and in 56.1, the point is about the quiet and seclusion needed to concentrate.[25] But he also often uses the word to refer to a zeal for virtue or a

---

[23] That *studium* is equated with writing is pointed out already in the note on this passage in Motto (1985); similarly Schöpsdau (2005: 98).
[24] *OLD* s.v. *studium* 1–6. For the broader sense of the term, compare *Anger* 2.12.5, where instances of *studium* include such activities as learning to walk a tightrope and learning to keep oneself awake.
[25] For *studium* as reading, compare also *Prov.* 2.11, on the *studia* of Cato's last night (referring to his reading of Plato's *Phaedo*).

commitment to moral progress. To take just one example, he says at the beginning of letter 16 that the study of wisdom (*sapientiae studium*) is the key to a happy life and that one's resolution should be strengthened by daily rehearsal and reflection (*cotidiana meditatione*). He adds, "One must persevere and add strength by constant study (*adsiduo studio*), until excellent intentions become excellence of mind."[26] In this passage there is no implication that the *studium* Seneca has in mind involves books and papers.

This latter sense of *studium* conveys the frequent Senecan theme of a reorientation of one's attitude and commitment to the fullness of human potential. In *Letters* 72.2–3, for instance, Seneca is speaking of the need to give over other occupations and to devote one's entire mind to philosophy, and of the excuses one might make for failing to do so. "As soon as I get through this troublesome task, I will give myself over to *studium*," he imagines the prospective philosopher saying, and he himself responds, "There is no time that is not well suited to this healing study (*studio salutari*); yet there are many who fail to study (*non student*) when caught up in the problems that give one reason to study (*inter illa propter quae studendum est*)." The usage is distinctive, a Senecan trademark, as it were. It is especially frequent at the beginnings of letters, where it has programmatic force.[27] *Studium* in this enriched sense refers to a kind of concentrated, time-consuming activity that may include book learning but is not defined by it. After all, Seneca as a Stoic does consider intellectual development to be essential to moral progress, and it seems inevitable that such development will entail mastering terms, concepts, principles, and the like either through reading or through oral instruction. But other forms of effort might equally well instantiate philosophical *studium* as long as they advance one toward what he regards as health and wholeness.

Not every activity one does with books will count as *studium* in the sense that matters most to Seneca. Literary or academic work that is pursued for the wrong reasons or directed toward the wrong topics is still "study" in the superficial sense, even though it is at odds with the form of "study" that is required for Stoic ethics. Thus, a scholarly endeavor pursued merely for ostentation would be a study, but not a "healing study" (*studium salutare*, 17.5, 72.3). Seneca likes to explore the ironies that result, especially when *studium* is paired with the similarly bivalent

---

[26] *Letters* 16.1. Here *sapientiae studium* is a calque for the Greek *philosophia* ("love of wisdom"); compare 89.5 *studium virtutis* ... *studium corrigendae mentis* ... *adpetitio rectae rationis*. For the emphasis on concentration, compare *Letters* 75.15 *adsidua intentione studii*, 124.12 *longo studio intentoque*.

[27] In addition to *Letters* 16.1 and 72.2–3 already cited, note 5.1 *pertinaciter studes*; 35.1 *te tam valde rogo ut studeas*; 56.1 *in studia seposito*; 62.1 *studia liberalia*; 78.2 *studia mihi nostra saluti fuerunt*.

adjective *liberale*, "befitting a freeborn person."²⁸ The phrase *liberalia studia* refers, as usual in Latin authors, to the various expensive forms of education favored by the elite, but Seneca also applies it to the one *studium* he continually recommends, commenting that it alone renders a person truly free:

> That sternness will turn out well with age, as long as he persists in working toward virtue and in imbibing the liberal studies. By which I do not mean those studies of which a smattering is enough; I mean *these* liberal studies. In these, the mind needs thorough steeping. (*Letters* 36.3)

> It's obvious why they are called "liberal" studies: because they are worthy of a free person. But there is only one study that is truly liberal, and that is the one that liberates a person, which is to say, the study of philosophy. (*Letters* 88.2)

Such doubling or twinning in the application of a term is a favorite device of Senecan rhetoric. A common word is invested with a special meaning in keeping with Seneca's ethical agenda, and this second meaning is then asserted as the dominant meaning on grounds of superior value. Thus, "real friendship" exists only where there is complete trust; "real well-being" is only what one gains by practicing philosophy; "real joy" is only the special satisfaction of the Stoic sage in possession of the "real good"; and so on.²⁹

We can now discern the progression of ideas that Seneca is developing in the first paragraph of letter 84. The recent day trips that occasion the letter benefit both Seneca's health, in the ordinary sense, and his "studies" in the special sense that a reader accustomed to Seneca's devices will easily recognize: they have helped his true intellectual endeavor, namely his progress in philosophy. With some irony, he proceeds to explain that this second benefit consists in a remission of his reading program, his "study" in the superficial sense of the word. His point is not that reading is detrimental to study, for in fact he holds that reading is an important part of philosophical activity. What he means is that *real* study consists in whatever contributes to his project of self-betterment. Sometimes that is reading, and sometimes it is putting aside his reading in order to write. Seneca did not have his books with him in the sedan chair; he had his notebooks.

---

[28] In claiming the term "liberal studies" for philosophy alone, Seneca aligns himself with Posidonius as reported in *Letters* 88.21–23. In addition to the passages quoted here, see *Letters* 59.15, 62.1, 88 *passim*, and 95.23.

[29] *Letters* 3.2 *vera amicitia*; 15.1 *valere hoc demum est*; 23.4 *verum gaudium*; 23.6 *verum bonum*.

Nourishing a Talent, Creating a Self

Also very important for understanding the letter is the correct interpretation of Seneca's word *ingenium*. The word appears a number of times, and always with some emphasis. Early on, when Seneca gives a positive role to reading, it is because "reading nourishes one's *ingenium*" (*alit lectio ingenium*, 84.1; cf. 84.6 *in his quibus aluntur ingenia*). As the letter proceeds to develop the metaphor of digestion, it is the *ingenium* that does the work of assimilation, as readers combine multiple elements into a single savor by "applying the care and ability of our own *ingenium*" (*adhibita ingenii nostri cura et facultate*, 85.5). Again, it is the *ingenium* that also receives the elements one has digested: in 84.7, "let us digest them; otherwise they will pass into the memory, not into the *ingenium*" (*concoquamus illa; alioqui in memoriam ibunt, non in ingenium*). Finally, the "man of great *ingenium*," in section 8, is one who is able to create an impression of unity from numerous elements collected from books.[30] Clearly this term is pivotal to the process of self-creation Seneca has in mind.

Translators sometimes assume that *ingenium* in these passages is just a synonym for *animus*, thus rendering it as "mind," "intellect," or the like. However, we have reason to reject that assumption. We saw in Chapter 11 how often in Seneca's writings *ingenium* refers specifically to the faculty of mind that generates spoken or written discourse – a mental characteristic to be sure, but one that is also observable to others in the speech or writing one actually produces.[31] In letter 114, Seneca goes so far as to assert that a debased style of writing like that of Maecenas provides incontrovertible evidence of the mental characteristics of the author, given that the *ingenium* "is completely mixed with the mind, and receives from it its shape, direction, and principle" (114.3). This remark in itself should tell us that *ingenium* is not merely synonymous with *animus*. Further, it gives some indication why Seneca, in keeping with his Stoic inheritance, gives particular significance to the linguistic faculty in the constitution of the self.

Taking these points into account, we can give a better interpretation of Seneca's statements about the *ingenium* in letter 84. When he says that reading nourishes the *ingenium*, he is not saying that reading makes a person more intelligent or better suited to put his philosophy into practice. He means that continued reflection on prior treatments of a theme will help a writer to develop his or her talent for writing, and thus the writing itself. Lower down, when he says that one should digest the things one has

---

[30] *Letters* 84.8. I follow Reynolds (1965) for the emendation. [31] See pages 243–45.

read lest they pass into the memory rather than the *ingenium*, he means that a writer needs not only to be able to quote passages from earlier works, but more importantly to create a richly allusive yet homogenous style in prose or verse. Similarly, his "man of great *ingenium*" is first and foremost a great writer, whose distinctive style is recognizable even when treating an often-used subject matter. For much of the letter, then, the idea Seneca is after is that a varied reading program, if properly handled, will enrich and enliven that aspect of oneself that will be open to the eyes of the public; that is, the *reading* public.

But this is not to say that the self that is so constituted is anything other than the real self of the writer. For the *ingenium* is not merely a represented self – an avatar, as when Seneca appears as a character in his own book. A clever writer can easily invent a character that bears his name and that speaks in the first person, as if on his behalf, while still being invested with a personality quite different from his own. What cannot be feigned is the way the book itself is written – the texture of the prose or verse, the design and progression of the whole, all the characteristics we respond to when we say that we "know" an author. A book can lie, in that it can offer fictions or misrepresentations of fact, but it cannot lie about its author's capacity to write: *that* capacity is just what the actual writing shows it to be. But this is just what Seneca means by the *ingenium*: that linguistic faculty that is essential to one's existence as a human being and as the very individual one is, a faculty conceptually but not numerically distinct from the *animus* itself. If we follow this line of thought, we arrive at a notion of selfhood revealed in written language: a scripted self.

The process that produces this literary and artistic self is elucidated primarily through Seneca's metaphor of digestion. In his sequence of images, the notions of change and stability, unity and diversity, internality and externality, the hidden and the observable mingle and interchange in a confusing yet richly productive matrix.[32]

> We also must imitate these bees, and taking the things we have gathered from our diverse reading, first separate them (for things are better preserved when they are kept distinct), then, applying the care and ability of our own *ingenium*, conjoin those various samples into one savor, so that even if it is apparent where a thing has been taken from, it may yet appear to be different from that from which it was taken. It is what we see nature do in our bodies through no effort of our own. For the nutriments we have

---

[32] A recent study by Tommaso Gazzarri gives in-depth treatment to Seneca's practice of accumulation and contiguity in the use of metaphor; see especially Gazzari (2021: 123–43).

> taken are burdensome for just so long as they retain their own character and swim as solids in the stomach, but when they have been changed from what they were, then at last they are added to our strength, passing into our bloodstream. Let us accomplish the same with these things that nourish the *ingenium*, not permitting the things we have consumed to remain whole, lest they be other than our own. Let us digest them; otherwise they will pass into the memory, not into the *ingenium*. Let us faithfully adjust our thinking to them and make them ours, so that from the many there may come to be some sort of unity. (*Letters* 84.5–7)

Like the human digestive system or like the mysterious inner organs of the bee, the reader is to take in a mélange of different elements; these, it seems, are both to be kept distinct in memory and to be altered from what they were before. Everything is to take place through inward reflection, and yet the changes should also be apparent ("it may yet appear to be different from that from which it was taken"). Items read should still be recognizable for what they were and yet *not* recognizable, for they are to become something else in the new substance that is being created. The *ingenium* is to be the producer of change ("applying the care and ability of our own *ingenium*") and yet also the product ("these things that nourish the *ingenium*"). In some sense it is we who are to change, for we must "assent to" or rather "adjust our thinking to" the things we have read, even as we "make them ours" (*adsentiamur illis fideliter et nostra faciamus*). One melds into the other.

If we go on to ask about the real-world procedure to which the metaphoric language is meant to refer, we find little to go on. At most, we can infer from the phrase "some sort of unity" (*unum quiddam*) that there should be some single principle operative throughout the written product. We could perhaps think in terms of a consistent set of preferences in diction or word order, or a certain rhythmic pattern that is regularly employed at the ends of sentences; or, more substantively, of a clear progression of thought from each word, sentence, or paragraph to the next. More certain is that a successful assimilative process will result in a work that makes a unified impression on its own readers. Selfhood has been achieved in its best form when the multiplicity of its origins is no longer discernible to the external observer:

> "What do you mean? Won't readers realize whose style, whose argumentation, whose well-turned remarks you are imitating?" It is possible they will not, I think, if a man of great *ingenium* stamps his own form upon all the elements that he draws from his chosen model so that they all fit together into a unity. (*Letters* 84.8)

Honeybee Reading and Self-Scripting

The appeal to the perspective of the observer is an interesting move and potentially a helpful one. For while it seems likely enough that the "man of great *ingenium*" will be aware of the principle of unity (whatever it is) and consciously apply it in the writing process, that might not be true in all cases. A less-accomplished writer, or one still in the process of development, might be able to make use of that observer perspective as a guide. For writers are also typically readers of their own work and can assess it from that perspective, revising as needed.

Postmortem Survival

There is now a further question to be asked about the nature of this writing that is to constitute and also to reveal one's inner nature. In his article, Foucault speaks of the composition of personal journals or commonplace books (*hypomnēmata*) and of day-to-day correspondence with an intimate friend, like Marcus Aurelius's correspondence with Fronto. But writings of this sort would not easily be described by Seneca's language of organic unity. For a classicist reading letter 84, it is hard to escape the impression that Seneca has in mind a more consciously literary activity, productive not of jottings and journals but of long poems or ambitious works of prose. In part, that impression comes from our awareness that this is the sort of writing Seneca himself produced, in his treatises and consolations, in the conspicuously literary *Natural Questions*, and in the *Letters on Ethics* themselves, which are certainly not the casual personal letters they pretend to be. But the more important signals that give rise to that impression come from letter 84 itself.

The image of the honeybee is itself suggestive of literary artistry. For bee similes are a standard *topos* of the more exalted forms of poetry, where they regularly evoke the figure of the author ranging freely among topics and sources and producing from them a new material of the highest quality. The image is as old as Pindar ("the finest of encomia darts from one theme to another like a bee") and figures prominently in Callimachus's famous *Hymn to Apollo*:[33]

> Not from every stream do the bee maidens carry water to Demeter,
> but from that which flows thin, pure, and undefiled from the sacred spring,
> the finest and best.

---

[33] Callimachus, *Hymn to Apollo* 110–12. The lines from Pindar are *Pythian* 10.53–54.

At Rome, the application to acts of reading is made had already been made both by the philosophical poet Lucretius and by Horace in his fourth book of *Odes*.[34] Seneca's manner of introducing the bee simile actually announces these antecedents, for he includes the phrase *ut aiunt* ("as they say"), marking the comparison as a *topos* borrowed from multiple sources. The passage is thus a cleverly self-referential gesture, enacting its own recommendation. It is Seneca in his most consciously literary mode.

Even apart from the honeybee, the middle portion of letter 84 is redolent of writerly ambition because of the repeated appeal to the *ingenium*. Like "talent" or "genius" in English, *ingenium* referring to the ability of writers is a strongly valorizing term, applicable to the most admired works of the past. When Seneca uses it in *Letters* 21.6 and 82.16, it is in reference to Vergil's *Aeneid*; in *Letters* 33.5, it refers to the treatises of his favorite Stoic authors. He also uses it a number of times to refer to Lucilius's growing reputation as an author and to praise his talents. At 79.7, for instance, he urges Lucilius not to curb his *ingenium* from writing his poem on Mt. Etna merely because the theme was already treated by Vergil, Ovid, and Cornelius Severus.[35] When he applies it to a more dubious literary achievement, the use is contrafactual. Of Gaius Maecenas, whose peculiar style he quotes with derision, he remarks more than once that he would have been a man of *ingenium* if he had not been corrupted by his luxurious manner of living.[36] The "man of great *ingenium*" of letter 84 will achieve what Maecenas failed to achieve. He will create a consistently impressive body of work – a *corpus*, as we and the Romans both say – in which there will be nothing that is not admirable.[37]

These belletristic implications of letter 84 are highly relevant to the notion of self-creation through the act of writing. For the concept of literary achievement was closely bound up with that of personal survival after the death of the body. The two ideas are linked already in Plato, in Diotima's speech in the *Symposium*, where Homer and Hesiod are called fortunate that their literary "offspring" perpetuate their names.[38] But the Romans gave the formula their own strongly first-personal cast, with the

---

[34] See Lucretius 3.11–12: "As bees in flowery meadows sample everything, so do I feed upon your [sc. Epicurus's] golden sayings." In Horace, note *Odes* 4.2.25–32.
[35] See also *Letters* 7.9, 19.3, and 46.2.
[36] *Letters* 19.9; 92.35; 114.4. Maecenas fails in that he does not control his diction nor establish clear syntactical relations among words: see pages 241 and following.
[37] *Corpus* in the sense of a single author's total literary production occurs in *Tranquility* 9.6 and *Letters* 46.1; *OLD* (s.v. *corpus* 16a) cites instances also in Ovid and Pliny the Younger.
[38] *Symposium* 209a, d.

circulated work taking on the identity of its author. Over and over in Latin poetry, the book speaks in the voice of its author and claims a life that continues beyond the author's death. The passages are known to every Latinist: Ennius's "Alive I roll through mouths of men"; Horace's "I shall not die entire; a great part of me will evade Libitina"; Ovid's "in the mouths of the people [...] I will live."[39] More obliquely, Vergil addresses two minor characters in his poem: "If my songs have any power, no future day will ever erase you from the memory of ages" – by which he means that his poems do have power and will last for many ages, carrying with them the names and reputations of anyone the poet chooses to include.[40] The ideology expressed in such claims is that a talented writer can create in his work a kind of external self that will speak with his voice and exercise his influence after his life in the body is over. The literary product will not be just an image or representation of himself; it will be a genuine self, something that he can call "me" and that readers will legitimately refer to by his name. As one's texts are replicated over and over by successive hand copying, this scripted self carries on its existence independent of any particular copy, for it "lives" not in ink marks on papyrus but in the voices and memories of generations of readers, the "mouths of men." It is not immortal: when the last copy is burnt and the memory of Roman culture is extinguished, it too will cease to exist. But a work that wins admiration may last for a very long time.

That Seneca recognizes and participates in this ideology is made clear in an extended passage from letter 21. "Your studies will make you famous," he tells Lucilius. Like Idomeneus, whom Epicurus addresses in several of his letters, or Atticus, who is addressed in so many letters of Cicero, Lucilius will win lasting fame not by anything he himself has done but because of the literary reputation of Seneca who writes to him.

> Deep is the abyss of time that will close over us. A few talented minds (*pauca ingenia*) will raise their heads above it, and although they too must eventually depart into silence, yet for long will they resist oblivion and lay claim to themselves. What Epicurus was able to promise his friend, I promise to you, Lucilius: I shall find favor with posterity, and I can bring others' names along with me, so that they will endure as well. (*Letters* 21.5)

---

[39] (Libitina is the funeral goddess.) Ennius's epitaph is quoted in Cicero, *Tusc.* 1.34, and imitated by Vergil in *Georgics* 3.9 as well as Horace, *Carmen* 3.30 and Ovid, *Metamorphoses* 15.871–879. Compare also Persius 1.37–43 and later Martial 1.107.

[40] *Aeneid* 9.446–449 (addressing Nisus and Euryalus); compare Propertius 3.9.32 (addressing Maecenas) *venies tu quoque in ora virum*.

He then quotes from Vergil the apostrophe mentioned earlier, and continues:

> Those whom fortune has thrust into the midst of things, who have been the members and partakers of others' power, have great prestige and many visitors – while they are on their feet. The moment they are gone, they cease to be remembered. But minds of talent are held in growing esteem (*ingeniorum crescit dignatio*), and this extends not only to the authors themselves but to anything that is associated with their memory. (*Letters* 21.6)

To one not familiar with Roman literary conventions, it might seem that this is not very complimentary to Lucilius, to be told that his own achievements are as nothing compared with what he gains by being named in someone else's book. But a remark that could have been derogatory in a private conversation comes out very differently when made as part of the literary work itself. The real Lucilius will understand that just as the dedication of a literary work is highly honorific to him, so the author's claim to lasting fame within the work redounds also to the credit of the addressee. And although Seneca here minimizes Lucilius's independent achievements, he does also take every opportunity to honor the products of Lucilius's own literary *ingenium*.[41]

The Rule of Reason

All these ideas are so familiar a part of the Roman literary tradition, and so well established already in Seneca's work, that it requires only a few phrases to bring them to mind in the context of letter 84. But Seneca is not merely evoking the cherished aestheticism of Rome's elite class. When he speaks of crafting one's own *ingenium* as a kind of self, and of high standards in doing so, he has more in mind than the usual idea of personal survival through literary achievement. As the letter proceeds, we realize that he has also been thinking all the time of the rational and linguistic mind in the Stoic sense, as the seat of consciousness and sole origin of ethically significant behavior. Right after the digestion metaphor of 84.5–7, we find a further comparison that is similarly focused on the production of unity:

> Do you not see how many voices combine to form a choir? Yet all of them sound as one. One is a high voice, another low, and another in the middle; women join the men, and flutes accompany them; yet one cannot make out

---

[41] Lucilius's writings are mentioned in *Letters* 8.10, 24.11, 46, and 79.5–7.

the voices of individuals but only the one voice of them all. [...] When the line of singers fills the aisles and the seating area is ringed with trumpeters and every kind of flute and water organ sounds together from the stage, then from the different sounds is produced a unison. This is what I want our mind to be like: in it are many skills, many precepts, examples from many ages, but all harmonized into one. (*Letters* 84.9–10)

As before, we have the notion of many components being combined into a homogenous artistic product; and as before, the success of the combination is to be judged by external observers. But here the point is about action-readiness as much as it is about literary talent, for the elements to be combined, the "many skills, many precepts, examples from many ages," are all such as might contribute to effective or principled agency. These are things that might indeed be gathered from books, but also things whose value can never be realized without some sort of action in the world.[42] The drawing into one is now the procedure of an orderly mind collecting and organizing various types of information, whether from books or from other sources, and integrating them into whatever it is in a person that produces moral acts – which is, once again, the *animus* itself.

The brief remainder of the letter confirms this observation. As Seneca goes on to consider how this last remarkable result can be achieved, he orients his account much with increasing clarity toward moral action. "Constant concentration" (*adsidua intentio*) and rational choice now play the role that literary artistry played earlier:

> "How is this to be done?" you ask. By constant concentration: if we do nothing except at the prompting of reason and avoid nothing except at the prompting of reason. (*Letters* 84.11)

In sections 11–13, he provides a little speech in the voice of reason, urging the moral agent to turn aside from the commonly accepted values of wealth, bodily pleasure, and high social status, and to turn instead toward wisdom, which promises great serenity and also great abundance. In particular, one should turn one's back on political ambition, which leads to nothing of real value and also involves a person in much difficulty and danger. The letter ends with a comparison between "what seems most eminent in human affairs" and the true eminence attained by the philosopher. The former is reached by steep and difficult paths, "even though in reality it is tiny and stands out only by comparison with what is the

---

[42] On the necessity of enacting that which is thought or spoken (*lekta*, "sayables"), see Wildberger (2006: 180–97).

lowest"; the philosopher's summit is far above all conventional goals, but the path to it lies "upon level ground."[43]

These last are familiar themes in Seneca's work: the appeal to rationally derived criteria, the inadequacy of conventional values, the inherent rewards of a life governed by moral philosophy. What is exceptional here is the way these themes are made continuous with the discussion of reading and writing that precedes. The transition from the honeybee and statue analogies of 84.3–8 (referring to literary style) to the orchestra analogy of 84.9 (referring to moral action) is virtually without seam; among modern editors, only Préchac indicates a paragraph division at that point. It is as if there is no clear distinction to be made between the first notion of self-formation, that of melding multiple literary influences to craft a unified and impressive voice in one's writings, and the second, that of applying a single rational standard to the business of living. And indeed Seneca may not wish to make such a distinction.

***

What happens in letter 84, then, is that Seneca superimposes one thing on another. He works at first with an idea about writing that would be familiar to his readers – for members of the educated elite, like the Lucilius of the letters, nursed their own writerly ambitions and were deeply interested in anything connected with literary achievement. He sketches for them a rich notion of the literary *ingenium* as a manifestation of intellectual capacity and force of character, and he elevates the familiar rhetorical task of homogenizing thoughts and expressions drawn from earlier works. When he speaks repeatedly of the carefully constituted *ingenium* as a kind of self, he perhaps reminds them as well of the potential of the written artifact to perpetuate not only one's name and influence but even one's very identity, the very nature of one's mind, through the long-enduring medium of textual transmission. But then, having done all this, he invests that same model with a further dimension of meaning that extends beyond the activity of writers to every activity of the human mind. The productive intellect that is responsible for a person's literary achievements is at the same time the faculty of rational choice that is responsible for all action and achievement. What has been said about the one applies also to the other. As reading alternates with writing, so discovery in general

---

[43] *Letters* 84.13 *per planum*. The last thought is made clearer by comparison with *On Anger* 2.13.1 *nec, ut quibusdam visum est, arduum in virtutes et asperum iter est: plano adeuntur.*

alternates with response, and as one's quality and ultimate survival as a writer depends on success in integrating multiple literary influences, so self-actualization as a human being depends on success in setting in order all the many impressions gained from experience.

The conception of self that is operative in this distinctively Senecan project is a strongly normative conception. Our present writings do not achieve the perfect integration that the man of great *ingenium* would exhibit: as the interlocutor points out, readers can generally discern whose style, whose argumentation, whose well-turned remarks we are imitating. But the proper task of the writer is to work toward that integration, because it is only in so doing that one stamps one's own form on all the elements drawn from one's chosen models. In the same way, our occurrent selves – the moral agents we are at present – fail for the time being to act consistently in accordance with normative reason: moral excellence, like literary achievement, is always a work in progress. Seneca insists nonetheless that the standards of reason are *our* standards, the only ones that enable us to become our best selves. In this, more than anything else, he betrays his Stoic allegiance.

Bibliography

Abel, K. (1981) "Das Problem der Faktizität der senecanischen Korrespondenz." *Hermes* 109.4: 472–99.
Accardi, A. (2015) *Teoria e prassi del beneficium da Cicerone a Seneca*. Palermo.
Alesse, F. (2008) *Philo of Alexandria and Post-Aristotelian Philosophy*. Leiden.
Alexander, W. H. (1941) "Seneca's Epistulae Morales: The text emended and explained (XCIII–CXXIV)." *University of California Publications in Classical Philology* 12.8: 135–64.
  (1952) "The interpretation of Seneca *EM* 46.1," in M. E. White (ed.) *Studies in Honor of Gilbert Norwood*. Toronto: 214–17.
Algra, K. (2003) "Stoic theology," in B. Inwood (ed.) *Cambridge Companion to the Stoics*. Cambridge: 153–78.
Algra, K., Barnes, J., Mansfield, J., and M. Schofield et al. (eds.) (1999) *Cambridge History of Hellenistic Philosophy*. Cambridge.
Altman, J. (1982) *Epistolarity: Approaches to a Form*. Columbus.
André, J. M. (1962a) *Recherches sur l'otium romain*. Paris.
  (1962b) "Otium et vie contemplative dans les Lettres à Lucilius." *Revue des Études Latines* 40: 125–28.
  (1966) *L'otium dans la vie morale et intellectuelle romaine: Des origines à l'époque augustéenne*. Paris.
  (1967) *Mécène: Essai de biographie spirituelle*. Paris.
  (1970) "Sénèque et l'Epicurisme: Ultime position," in *Actes du VIIIe Congrès de l'Association Guillaume Budé, 469–80*. Paris.
  (1983) "Mécène écrivain (avec, en appendice, les fragments de Mécène)." *Aufstieg und Niedergang der römischen Welt* 11.30.3: 1765–87.
Annas, J. (1992) *Hellenistic Philosophy of Mind*. Berkeley.
  (1993) *Morality of Happiness*. Oxford.
Armisen-Marchetti, M. (1989) *Sapientiae facies: Étude sur les images de Sénèque*. Paris.
  (2004a) "La signification de l'humour dans les Lettres à Lucilius de Sénèque," in L. Nadjo and E. Gavoille (eds.) *Epistulae Antiquae* III: 311–22.
  (2004b) "Mémoire et oubli dans la théorie des bienfaits selon Sénèque." *Paideia* 59: 7–23.
  (2008) "Imagination and Meditation in Seneca: The Example of Praemeditatio," in J. Fitch (ed.) *Seneca*. Oxford: 102–13. Previously

published as "Imagination et meditation chez Sénèque: L'exemple de la *praemeditatio*," *Revue des études latines* 64: 185–95 (1986).
Asmis, E. (1984) *Epicurus' Scientific Method*. Ithaca.
Atherton, C. (2009) "Epicurean philosophy of language," in J. Warren (ed.) *Cambridge Companion to Epicureanism*. Cambridge: 197–215.
Axelson, B. (1939) *Neue Senecastudien*. Lund.
Bardon, H. (1956) *La littérature latine inconnue*, 2 vols. Paris.
Barnes, J. (1997a) *Logic and the Imperial Stoa*. Leiden.
  (1997b) "Roman Aristotle," in J. Barnes and M. Griffin (eds.) *Philosophia Togata II: Plato and Aristotle at Rome*. Oxford: 1–69.
Bartsch, S., and A. Schiesaro (eds.) (2015) *The Cambridge Companion to Seneca*. Cambridge.
Bartsch, S., and D. Wray (eds.) (2009) *Seneca and the Self*. Cambridge.
Basore, J. (trans.) (1935) *Seneca: Moral Essays Volume III*. Cambridge, MA.
Becker, L. (1998) *A New Stoicism*. Princeton.
  (2004) "Stoic emotion," in S. K. Strange and J. Zupko (eds.) *Stoicism: Traditions and Transformations*. Cambridge: 250–75.
Beltrami, A. (ed.) (1937) *L. Annaei Senecae ad Lucilium epistulae morales*, 2 vols. Rome.
Bénatouïl, T. (2007) "Le débat entre platonisme et stoïcisme sur la vie scolastique: Chrysippe, la Nouvelle Académie et Antiochus," in Bonazzi and Helmig (eds.) (2007): 1–21.
  (2009) "Θεωρία et vie contemplative du stoïcisme au platonisme: Chrysippe, Panétius, Antiochus, et Alcinoos," in M. Bonazzi and J. Opsomer (eds.) *The Origins of the Platonic System: Platonisms of the Early Empire and Their Philosophical Contexts*. Leuven: 3–31.
Bénatouïl, T., and M. Bonazzi (eds.) (2012) *Theoria, Praxis, and the Contemplative Life after Plato and Aristotle*. Leiden.
Bernauer, J., and M. Mahon (1994) "The ethics of Michel Foucault," in G. Gutting (ed.) *The Cambridge Companion to Foucault*. Cambridge: 141–58.
Berno, F. (2020) "The importance of collecting shells: Intertextuality in Seneca's *Epistle* 49," in Garani, Michalopoulos, and Papaioannou (eds.) (2020): 142–60.
  (2021) "*Ferarum minus taetra facies est quam hominis ira flagrantis (ira 3, 4, 3)*," in Laurand, Malaspina, and Prost (eds.) (2021): 251–65.
Berti, E. (2018) *Lo stile e l'uomo. Quattro epistole letterarie di Seneca (epist. 114; 40; 100; 84)*. Pisa.
Bobzien, S. (1998) *Determinism and Freedom in Stoic Philosophy*. Oxford.
  (2021) *Determinism, Freedom, and Moral Responsibility: Essays in Ancient Philosophy*. Oxford.
Bonazzi, M., and C. Helmig (eds.) (2007) *Platonic Stoicism, Stoic Platonism: The Dialogue between Platonism and Stoicism in Antiquity*. Leuven.
Boswell, J. (1979) *Christianity, Social Tolerance, and Homosexuality*. Chicago.
Botros, S. (1985) "Freedom, causality, fatalism and early Stoic philosophy." *Phronesis* 30: 274–304.
Bourgery, A. (ed./trans.) (1922) *Sénèque: Dialogues I: De ira*. Paris.
Bradley, K. R. (2008) "Seneca and slavery," in J. Fitch (ed.) *Seneca*. Oxford: 335–47.

Braicovich, R. (2015) "Estrategias terapéuticas e intelectualismo en el *De ira* de Séneca." *Ideas y Valores* 64: 85–105.
Brennan, T. (1998) "The old Stoic theory of emotions," in Sihvola and Engberg-Pedersen (eds.) (1998): 21–70.
  (2003) "Stoic moral psychology," in B. Inwood (ed.) *Cambridge Companion to the Stoics*. Cambridge: 257–94.
  (2005) *The Stoic Life: Emotions, Duties, and Fate*. Oxford.
Brunt, P. A. (2013) *Studies in Stoicism*, ed. M. Griffin and A. Samuels. Oxford.
Cambron-Goulet, M. (2014) "Orality in philosophical epistles," in R. Scodel (ed.) *Between Orality and Literacy: Communication and Adaptation in Antiquity*. Leiden: 148–74.
Cancik, H. (1967) *Untersuchungen zu Senecas Epistulae Morales*. Hildesheim.
Chaumartin, F.-R. (1985) *Le De beneficiis de Sénèque: Sa signification philosophique, politique, et sociale*. Paris.
Cizek, E. (1972) *L'époque de Néron et ses controverses idéologiques*. Leiden.
Clay, D. (1983) *Lucretius and Epicurus*. Ithaca.
  (1998) *Paradosis and Survival: Three Chapters in the History of Epicurean Philosophy*. Ann Arbor.
Collette, B. (2022) *The Stoic Doctrine of Providence: A Study of Its Development and of Some of Its Major Issues*. Abingdon and New York.
Conradie, I. (2010) *Seneca in His Cultural and Literary Context: Selected Moral Letters on the Body*. Utrecht.
  (2004) *Knowledge, Nature, and the Good: Essays on Ancient Philosophy*. Princeton.
Cooper, J. (2005) "The emotional life of the wise." *Southern Journal of Philosophy* 43.Supplement: 176–218.
  (2006) "Seneca on moral theory and moral improvement," in Volk and Williams (eds.) (2006): 43–56.
Cooper, J., and J. Procope (ed./trans.) (1995) *Seneca: Moral and Political Essays*. Cambridge.
Corbeill, A. (1996) *Controlling Laughter: Political Humor in the Late Roman Republic*. Princeton.
Costa, C. D. N. (1988) *Seneca: 17 Letters*. Warminster.
  (1994) *Seneca: Four Dialogues*. Warminster.
Courtil, J.-C. (2015) *Sapientia contemptrix doloris: Le corps souffrant dans l'œuvre philosophique de Sénèque*. Brussels.
Courtney, E. (1993) *The Fragmentary Latin Poets*. Oxford.
Cupaiuolo, G. (1975) *Introduzione al* De ira *di Seneca*. Naples.
Damschen, G. and A. Heil (eds.) (2014) *Brill's Companion to Seneca: Philosopher and Dramatist*. Leiden.
Davidson, A. (1994) "Ethics as ascetics," in G. Gutting (ed.) *The Cambridge Companion to Foucault*. Cambridge: 115–40.
  (1997) "Structures and strategies of discourse: Remarks towards a history of Foucault's philosophy of language," in A. Davidson (ed.) *Foucault and His Interlocutors*. Chicago: 1–17.

Degand, M. (2015). *Sénèque au risque du don: Une éthique oblative à la croisée des disciplines*. Turnhout.
De Lacy, P. (ed.) (1978) *Galen: On the doctrines of Hippocrates and Plato* (= Corpus Medicorum Graecorum, vol. 5, no. 4.1.2). Berlin.
De Rentiis, D. (1998) "Der Beitrag der Bienen: Überlegungen zum Bienengleichnis bei Seneca und Macrobius." *Rheinisches Museum für Philologie* 141: 30–44.
Dietsche, U. (2014) *Strategie und Philosophie bei Seneca: Untersuchungen zur therapeutischen Technik in den* Epistulae morales. Berlin.
Dihle, A. (1982) *The Theory of Will in Classical Antiquity*. Berkeley.
Dillon, J. (1983) "Metriopatheia and apatheia. Some reflections on a controversy in later Greek ethics," in J. Anton and A. Preus (eds.) *Essays in Ancient Greek Philosophy*. Albany: vol. 2, 508–17. Reprinted in Dillon, J. (1990) *The Golden Chain: Studies in the Development of Platonism and Christianity*. Aldershot, UK.
  (1996) *The Middle Platonists*. Ithaca.
Dillon, J., and A. A. Long, (eds.) (1988) *The Question of 'Eclecticism': Studies in Later Greek Philosophy*. Berkeley.
Dionigi, P. (ed.) (1983) *L. Anneo Seneca: De Otio (dial. VIII)*. Brescia.
Dobbin, R. (1991) "Προαίρεσις in Epictetus." *Ancient Philosophy* 11: 111–35.
  (1998) *Epictetus: Discourses Book 1*. Oxford.
Donini, P. (1982) *Le scuole, l'anima, l'impero. La filosofia antica da Antioco a Plotino*. Turin.
  (1995) "Pathos nello Stoicismo Romano." *Elenchos* 16: 195–216.
  (2011) "The history of the concept of eclecticism," in M. Bonazzi (ed.) *Commentary and Tradition: Aristotelianism, Platonism, and Post-Hellenistic Philosophy*. Berlin: 197–210. Previously published in Dillon and Long (eds.) (1988) 15–33.
Dover, K. J. (1974) *Greek Popular Morality in the Time of Plato and Aristotle*. Oxford.
Dragona-Monachou, M. (1976) *The Stoic Arguments for the Existence and the Providence of the Gods*. Athens.
  (1994) "Divine providence in the philosophy of the Empire." *Aufstieg und Niedergang der römischen Welt* 2.36.7: 4417–90.
Dross, J. (2021) *Le philosophe dans la cité: Sénèque et l'otium philosophique*. Paris.
Edelstein, L., and I. G. Kidd (eds.) (1989) *Posidonius: The Fragments*. Cambridge.
Edwards, C. (1993) *The Politics of Immorality in Ancient Rome*. Cambridge.
  (2015) "Absent presence in Seneca's *Epistles*: Philosophy and friendship," in Bartsch and Schiesaro (eds) (2015) 41–53.
  (2018) "Conversing with the absent, corresponding with the dead: Friendship and philosophical community in Seneca's letters," in P. Ceccarelli, L. Doering, T. Fögen, and I. Gildenhard (eds.) *Letters and Communities: Studies in the Socio-Political Dimensions of Ancient Epistolography*. Oxford: 325–51.
Evans, E. C. (1969) *Physiognomics in the Ancient World [=Transactions of the American Philosophical Society 59, part 5]*. Philadelphia.

Faraone, C. (2019) "Empedocles the sorcerer and his hexametrical pharmaka." *Antichthon* 53: 14–32.
Ferguson, J. (1990) "Epicureanism under the Roman Empire." *Aufstieg und Niedergang der römischen Welt* 2.36.4: 2257–2327.
Fillion-Lahille, J. (1984) *Le De ira de Sénèque et la philosophie stoïcienne des passions.* Paris.
Fischer, S. E. (2014) "Systematic connections between Seneca's philosophical works and tragedies," in Damschen and Heil (eds.) (2014) 745–68.
Fögen, T. (ed.) (2009) *Tears in the Graeco-Roman World.* Berlin.
Ford, A. (2009) "The beginnings of dialogue: Socratic discourses and fourth-century prose," in S. Goldhill (ed.) *The End of Dialogue in Antiquity.* Cambridge: 29–44.
Foucault, M. (1983) "L'écriture de soi." *Corps écrit* 5: 3–23.
  (1984) *Histoire de la sexualité.* Vol. 3: Le souci de soi. Paris.
  (1994) *Dits et écrits, 1954–1988.* 4 vols. Paris.
  (2001) *L'herméneutique du sujet: Cours au Collège de France (1981–1982).* Paris.
Früchtel, L., Stählin, O., and Treu, U. (1960) *Clemens Alexandrinus.* Vol. 2 (*Stromata*). Berlin.
Gambet, D. (1970) "Cicero in the works of Seneca Philosophus." *Transactions and Proceedings of the American Philological Association* 101: 171–83.
Garani, M., Michalopoulos, A. N., and Papaioannou, S. (eds.) (2020) *Intertextuality in Seneca's Philosophical Writings.* Abingdon and New York.
Garbarino, G. (2003) *Philosophorum Romanorum fragmenta usque ad L. Annaei Senecae aetatem collegit I. Garbarino.* Bologna.
Gartner, C. (2015) "The possibility of psychic conflict in Seneca's *De Ira*." *British Journal for the History of Philosophy* 23.2: 213–33.
Gazzarri, T. (2014a) "Gender-based differential morbidity and moral teaching in Seneca's *Epistulae Morales*," in Wildberger and Colish (eds.) (2014) 209–28.
  (2014b) *The Stylus and the Scalpel: Theory and Practice of Metaphors in Seneca's Prose.* Berlin.
Gill, C. (1994) "Peace of mind and being yourself: Panaetius to Plutarch." *Aufstieg und Niedergang der römischen Welt* 2.36.7: 4599–4640.
  (1996) "Mind and madness in Greek tragedy." *Apeiron* 29.3: 249–67.
  (2005) "Competing readings of Stoic emotions," in Salles (ed.) (2005) 445–70.
  (2009) "Seneca and selfhood: Integration and disintegration," in Bartsch and Wray (eds.) (2009) 65–83.
  (2012) "The transformation of Aristotle's *Ethics* in Roman Philosophy," in J. Miller (ed.) *The Reception of Aristotle's Ethics.* Cambridge: 31–52.
Glare, P. G. W., and C. Stray (eds.) (2012) *Oxford Latin Dictionary.* Oxford.
Gleason, M. (1995) *Making Men: Sophists and Self-Presentation in Ancient Rome.* Princeton.
Gloyn, L. (2017) *The Ethics of the Family in Seneca.* Cambridge.
Gordon, P. (2012) *The Invention and Gendering of Epicurus.* Ann Arbor.
Görgemanns, H. (2006) "Epistolography," in H. Cancik and H. Schneider (eds.) *Brill's New Pauly.* Leiden: 1144–48.

Gottschalk, H. B. (1987) "Aristotelian philosophy in the Roman world." *Aufstieg und Niedergang der römischen Welt* 2.36.2: 1079–1174.
Goux, J. (2002) "Seneca against Derrida: Gift and alterity," in E. Wyschogrod, J. Goux, and E. Boynton (eds.) *The Enigma of Gift and Sacrifice*. New York: 148–60.
Grant, M. (2000) "Humor in Seneca's *Letters to Lucilius*." *Ancient Society* 30: 319–29.
Graver, M. (1996) Therapeutic Reading and Senecas Moral Epistles. Diss. Brown University.
  (1999a) "Philo of Alexandria and the origins of the Stoic προπάθεια." *Phronesis* 44: 300–25. Reprinted in Alesse (ed.) (2008) 197–222.
  (1999b) "Commentary on Inwood, 'God and human knowledge in Seneca's Natural Questions'." *Proceedings of the Boston Area Colloquium in Ancient Philosophy* 15: 44–54.
  (2002a) *Cicero on the Emotions. Tusculan Disputations 3–4*, Chicago.
  (2002b) "Managing mental pain: Epicurus vs. Aristippus on the pre-rehearsal of future ills." *Proceedings of the Boston Area Colloquium in Ancient Philosophy* 17: 155–77, 183–84.
  (2002c) "Review of Emotion and Peace of Mind by Richard Sorabji." *Ancient Philosophy* 22: 225–34.
  (2003) "Not even Zeus: A discussion of A. A. Long, Epictetus: A Stoic and Socratic Guide to Life." *Oxford Studies in Ancient Philosophy* 25: 345–61.
  (2007) *Stoicism and Emotion*. Chicago.
  (2015) "The emotional intelligence of Epicureans: Doctrinalism and adaptation in Seneca's *Epistles*," in Williams and Volk (eds.) (2015) 192–212.
  (2016) "Seneca the Younger's philosophical works," in D. Clayman (ed.) *Oxford Bibliographies in the Classics*. New York. URL = www.oxfordbibliographies.com/view/document/obo-9780195389661/obo-9780195389661-0224.xml
  (2017a) "Ethical psychology in the Hellenistic Stoa," in C. Bobonich (ed.) *Cambridge Companion to Ancient Ethics*. Cambridge: 200–17.
  (2017b) "Pre-emotions and reader emotions in Seneca," in D. Nelis and D. Cairns (eds.) *Seneca's Tragic Passions: Philosophical and Literary Perspectives* (= *Maia 69*). Brescia: 281–96.
  (2018) "Seneca's Peripatetics: *Epistulae Morales* 92 and Stobaean Doxography 'C'," in W. Fortenbaugh (ed.) *Arius Didymus on Peripatetic Ethics: Text, Translation and Discussion*. New York: 309–42.
  (2021) "Le *De Ira* de Sénèque et les *Tusculanes* de Cicéron," in Laurand, Malaspina, and Prost (eds.) (2021) 333–38.
  (forthcoming) "Cynic ἀπάθεια at Rome: Notes on the afterlife of Stilpo of Megara," in C. Guérin, M.-O. Goulet-Cazé, and J. Pià-Columella (eds.) *Le cynisme dans le monde romain*. Paris.
Graver, M., and A. A. Long (ed./trans.) (2015) *Seneca: Letters on Ethics*. Chicago.
Griffin, M. (1976) *Seneca: A Philosopher in Politics*. Expanded reprint 1992. Oxford.

(2007) "Seneca's pedagogic strategy: *Letters* and *De beneficiis*," in Sorabji and Sharples (eds.) (2007) 89–114.
(2013) *Seneca on Society: A Guide to* De Beneficiis. Oxford.
Griffin, M., and B. Inwood (ed./trans.) (2011) *Seneca: On Benefits.* Chicago.
Grilli, A. (1953) *Vita contemplativa: Il problema della vita contemplativa nel mondo greco-romano.* Expanded reprint (2002). Brescia.
(ed.) (1962) *M. Tulli Ciceronis Hortensius.* Milan.
Grimal, P. (1978) *Sénèque ou la conscience de l'Empire.* Paris.
Gummere, R. M. (ed./trans.) (1917) *Seneca: Ad Lucilium Epistulae Morales.* 3 vols. Cambridge, MA.
Gunderson, E. (2015) *The Sublime Seneca: Ethics, Literature, Metaphysics.* Cambridge.
Habinek, T. N. (1992) "Seneca on the beginnings of wisdom," in F. M. Dunn and T. Cole (eds.) *Beginnings in Classical Literature.* Cambridge: 187–203.
(2000) "Seneca's renown: *Gloria, claritudo,* and the replication of the Roman elite." *Classical Antiquity* 19.2: 264–303.
Hachmann, E. (1995) *Die Führung des Lesers in Senecas* Epistulae Morales. Münster.
Hadot, I. (1969) *Seneca und die griechisch-römische Tradition der Seelenleitung.* Berlin.
(2014) *Sénèque: Direction spirituelle et pratique de la philosophie,* Paris.
Hadot, P. (1981) *Exercices spirituels et philosophie antique.* Paris.
(1989) "Réflexions sur la notion de 'culture de soi'," in *Michel Foucault philosophe: Rencontre internationale, Paris 9, 10, 11 janvier 1988.* Paris: 261–70.
(1990) "Forms of life and forms of discourse in ancient philosophy", trans. A. I. Davidson and P. Wissing. *Critical Inquiry* 16.3: 483–505.
(1993) *Exercices spirituels et philosophie antique.* 2nd ed. Paris.
(1995) *Philosophy as a Way of Life: Spiritual Exercises from Socrates to Foucault.* Malden.
Hahm, D. (2007) "Critolaus and late Hellenistic Peripatetic philosophy," in A. M. Ioppolo and D. Sedoley (eds.) *Pyrrhonists, Patricians, Platonizers: Hellenistic Philosophy in the Period 155–86 BC.* Naples: 47–101.
Harris, W. V. (2001) *Restraining Rage: The Ideology of Anger Control in Classical Antiquity.* Cambridge, MA.
Henderson, J. (2004) *Morals and Villas in Seneca's Letters.* Cambridge.
Hense, O. (ed.) (1914) *L. Annaei Senecae Epistularum Moralium Qvae Supersunt.* Leipzig.
Heyd, D. (2019) "Supererogation," in E. N. Zalta (ed.) *Stanford Encyclopedia of Philosophy* (Winter 2019 edition), https://plato.stanford.edu/archives/win2019/entries/supererogation/.
Hijmans, B. L. (1959) *ΑΣΚΗΣΙΣ: Notes on Epictetus' educational system.* Assen.
Hine, H. M. (ed.) (1996) *L. Annaei Senecae Naturalium quaestionum libros.* Stuttgart.

Hine, H. M. (2010) "Philosophy and *philosophi* from Cicero to Apuleius," in Williams and Volk (eds.) (2015) 13–29. (ed./trans.) (2010) *Lucius Annaeus Seneca: Natural Questions.* Chicago.
Holler, E. (1934) Seneca und die Seelenteilungslehre und Affektpsychologie der Mittelstoa. Kallmünz.
Hosius, C. (ed.) (1914) *Seneca, Lucius Annaeus: Opera quae supersunt.* Leipzig.
Huber, R. (1973) *Senecas Schrift De Ira: Untersuchungen zum Aufbau und zu den Quellen.* Munich.
Huby, P. (1983) "Peripatetic definitions of happiness," in W. Fortenbaugh and S. White (eds.) *On Stoic and Peripatetic Ethics: The Work of Arius Didymus.* New Brunswick: 121–34.
Inwood, B. (1985) *Ethics and Human Action in Early Stoicism.* Oxford.
  (2002) "Comment on Stephen White, 'Happiness in the Hellenistic Lyceum'". *Apeiron Supplements* 35, 95–102.
  (2005) *Reading Seneca: Stoic Philosophy in Rome.* Oxford.
  (2007a) *Seneca: Selected Letters.* New York.
  (2007b) "The importance of form in Seneca's philosophical letters," in R. Morello and A.D. Morrison (eds.) *Ancient Letters: Classical and Late Antique Epistolography.* New York: 133–48.
  (2007c) "Seneca, Plato and Platonism: The case of letter 65," in Bonazzi and Helmig (eds.) (2007) 149–68.
  (2009) "Seneca and self-assertion," in Bartsch and Wray (eds.) (2009) 39–64.
  (2014) *Ethics After Aristotle.* Cambridge, MA.
  (2015) "The voice of Nature," in J. Annas and G. Betegh (eds.) *Cicero's De Finibus: Philosophical Approaches.* Cambridge: 147–66.
Inwood, B., and P. Donini (1999) "Stoic ethics," in Algra et. al. (eds.) (1999) 675–758.
Ioppolo, A.M. (1987) Il monismo psicologico degli Stoici antichi. *Elenchos* 8: 449–66.
Irwin, T. H. (1998) "Stoic inhumanity," in Sihvola and Engberg-Pedersen (eds.) (1998) 219–42.
  (trans.) (1985) *Aristotle: Nicomachean Ethics.* Indianapolis.
Johann, H. T. (1968) *Trauer und Trost. Eine quellen- und strukturanalytische Untersuchung der philosophischen Trostschriften.* Munich.
Kahn, C. (1988) "Discovering the will," in Dillon and Long, (eds.) (1988) 234–59.
Kamtekar, R. (1998) "Αἰδώς in Epictetus." *Classical Philology* 93.2: 136–60.
Kappelmacher, A. (1930) "C. Maecenas," in A. Pauly and G. Wissowa (eds.) *Paulys Realencyclopädie der classischen Altertumswissenschaft.* Stuttgart: XIV 214–15.
Kassel, R. (1958) *Untersuchungen zur griechischen und lateinischen Konsolationsliteratur.* Munich.
Kaster, R., and M. C. Nussbaum (ed./trans.) (2010) *Seneca: Anger, Mercy, Revenge.* Chicago.

Kaufman, D. H. (2014) "Seneca on the analysis and therapy of occurrent emotions," in Wildberger and Colish (eds.) (2014) 111–33.
Ker, J. (2006) "Seneca, man of many genres," in Volk and Williams (eds.) (2006) 19–41.
Kerferd, G. B. (1981) *The Sophistic Movement*. Cambridge.
Kidd, I. G. (1986) "Posidonian methodology and the self-sufficiency of virtue," in I.G. Kidd, Flashar, H., and O. Gigon (eds.) *Aspects de la philosophie hellénistique: Neuf, exposés suivis de discussions*. Vandœuvres-Geneva: 1–21.
  (1988) *Posidonius II: The Commentary*. 2 vols. Cambridge.
Kohn, T. (2003) "Who wrote Seneca's plays?" *Classical World* 96.3: 271–80.
Konstan, D. (2006) *The Emotions of the Ancient Greeks: Studies in Aristotle and Classical Literature*. Toronto.
  (2009) "Meleager's sweet tears. Observations on weeping and pleasure," in Fögen (ed.) (2009) 311–34.
  (2011) "Epicurus on the gods," in J. Fish and K. R. Sanders (eds.) *Epicurus and the Epicurean Tradition*. Cambridge: 53–71.
  (2014) "The joy of giving: Seneca *De beneficiis* 1.6.1," in E. Emilsson, A. Maravela, and M. Skoie (eds.) *Paradeigmata: Studies in Honor of Øivind Andersen*. Athens: 171–76.
Kühn, W. (2011) "L'attachement au soi et aux autres," in M.-O. Goulet-Cazé (eds.) *Études sur la théorie stoïcienne de l'action*. Paris: 237–366.
L'Hoir, F. S. (1992) *The Rhetoric of Gender Terms*. Leiden.
Laín Entralgo, P. (1970) *The Therapy of the Word in Classical Antiquity*. New Haven.
Lana, I. (1991) "Le 'Lettere a Lucilio' nella letteratura epistolare", in P. Grimal (ed.) *Sénèque et la prose Latine*. Geneva: 253–89.
Laurand, V., Malaspina, E., and Prost, F. (eds.) (2021) *Lectures plurielles du De ira de Sénèque: Interprétations, contextes, enjeux*. Berlin.
Laurenti, R. (1979) "Aristotele e il *De ira* di Seneca." *Studi Filosofici* 2: 61–91.
Leeman, A. D. (1953) "Seneca's plans for a work 'Moralis Philosophia' and their influence on his later epistles." *Mnemosyne* 6.1: 307–13.
  (1954) "Posidonius the dialectician in Seneca's letters." *Mnemosyne* 7.3: 233–40.
  (1965) *Orationis Ratio*. 2 vols. Amsterdam.
Lentano, M. (2009) "La gratitudine e la memoria: Una lettura del *De Beneficiis*." *Bollettino di Studi Latini* 39.1: 1–28.
  (2014) "*De Beneficiis*," in Damschen and Heil (eds.) (2014) 200–6.
Liddell, H. J., Scott, R., and Jones, H. S.; (eds.) (1940) *A Greek–English Lexicon*, 9th edition. Oxford.
Lindheim, S. (2003) *Mail and Female: Epistolary Narrative and Desire in Ovid's Heroides*. Madison, Wisconsin.
Lipsius, J. (ed.) (1632) *L. Annaei Seneca Philosophi Opera Quae Exstant Omnia*. Antwerp.
Lloyd, G. E. R. (1979) *Magic, Reason and Experience*. Cambridge.

Long, A. A. (1971 "Freedom and determinism in the Stoic theory of human action," in A.A. Long (ed.) *Problems in Stoicism*. London: 173–99.
  (1986) *Hellenistic Philosophy*. Berkeley and Los Angeles.
  (1996) *Stoic Studies*. Cambridge.
  (1999) "Stoic psychology," in Algra et. al. (eds.) (1999) 560–84.
  (2002) *Epictetus: A Stoic and Socratic Guide to Life*. Oxford.
  (2006) *From Epicurus to Epictetus: Studies in Hellenistic and Roman Philosophy*. Oxford.
  (2009) "Seneca on the self: Why now?" in Bartsch and Wray (eds.) (2009) 20–37.
Long, A. A., and D. N. Sedley (eds.) (1987) *The Hellenistic Philosophers*. 2 vols. Cambridge.
Lowenstam, S. (1998) "Seneca's 'Epistle Sixty-Five'", *Memoirs of the American Academy in Rome* 43: 63–78.
MacKendrick, P. (1989) *The Philosophical Books of Cicero*. London.
Malaspina, E. (2020) "Se soigner soi-même et vaincre la colère. Une nouvelle exégèse de Sen., *De ira* 3,13,1." *Museum Helveticum* 77.1: 59–73.
  (2021) "*De ira* 3,10–24 Une transition faible: De la prophylaxie au traitement et des *precepts* aux *exempla,*" in Laurand, Malaspina, and Prost (eds.) (2021) 173–200.
Malchow, R. (1986) *Kommentar zum zweiten und dritten Buch von Senecas Schrift "de ira" (= dial. 4 und 5) I–II*. Diss. Erlangen-Nürnberg.
Malherbe, A. (1988) *Ancient Epistolary Theorists*. Atlanta.
Manning, C. E. (1974) "The consolatory tradition and Seneca's attitude to the emotions." *Greece & Rome* 21.1: 71–81.
  (1981) *On Seneca's "Ad Marciam"*. Leiden.
Maso, S. (1999) *Lo sguardo della verità: Cinque studi su Seneca*. Padua.
Maurach, G. (1970) *Der Bau von Senecas Epistulae Morales*. Heidelberg.
  (2000) *Seneca: Leben und Werk*. Darmstadt.
Mazzoli, G. (1989) "Le 'Epistulae morales ad Lucilium' di Seneca: Valore letterario e filosofico." *Aufstieg und Niedergang der Römischen Welt* 2.36.3: 1923–77.
Menn, S. (1999) "The Stoic theory of categories." *Oxford Studies in Ancient Philosophy* 17: 215–47.
Merrill, A. D. (ed.) (1893) *Catullus*. London.
Moraux, P. (1973) *Der Aristotelismus bei den Griechen: von Andronikos bis Alexander von Aphrodisias*. Berlin.
Motto, A. L. (1970) *Seneca Sourcebook: Guide to the Thought of Lucius Annaeus Seneca*. Amsterdam.
  (1985) *Seneca, Moral Epistles*. Chico.
Motto, A. L., and J. Clark. (1968) "Paradoxum Senecae: The Epicurean Stoic." *Classical World* 62.2: 37–42.
Mutschmann, H. (1915) "Seneca und Epikur." *Hermes* 50.3: 321–56.
Nussbaum, M. C. (1994) *Therapy of Desire: Theory and Practice in Hellenistic Ethics*. Princeton.

(2004) "Emotions as judgments of value and importance," in R.C. Solomon (ed.) *Thinking About Feeling: Contemporary Philosophers on Emotions.* Oxford: 183–99.
(2009) "Stoic laughter: A reading of Seneca's *Apocolocyntosis*," in Bartsch and Wray (eds.) (2009) 84–112.
Obbink, D. (1989) "The atheism of Epicurus." *Greek, Roman, and Byzantine Studies* 30.2: 187–223.
Oliensis, E. (1998) *Horace and the Rhetoric of Authority.* Cambridge.
Plaza, M. (2006) *The Function of Humour in Roman Verse Satire: Laughing and Lying.* New York.
Pohlenz, M. (1948–1949) *Die Stoa: Geschichte einer geistigen Bewegung.* Göttingen.
Poster. C. (2007) "A conversation halved: Epistolary theory and Greco-Roman antiquity," in Poster and Mitchell (eds.) (2007) 21–51.
Poster. C., and L. Mitchell (eds.) (2007) *Letter-writing Manuals and Instruction from Antiquity to the Present: Historical and Bibliographic Studies.* Columbia.
Poulakos, J. (1983) "Gorgias' Encomium to Helen and the defense of rhetoric." *Rhetorica* 1.2: 1–16.
Pratt, J. (2015) "On the threshold of rhetoric: Gorgias' Encomium of Helen." *Classical Antiquity* 34.1: 163–82.
Préchac, F. (ed.) (1945–64) *Sénèque: Lettres à Lucilius*, 5 vols. Paris.
Price, A. (2005) "Were Zeno and Chrysippus at odds in analyzing emotion?" in Salles (ed.) (2005) 471–88.
Rabbow, P. (1914) *Antike Schriften über Seelenheilung und Seelenleitung auf ihre Quellen untersucht.* Leipzig.
Raccanelli, R. (2010) *Esercizi di dono: pragmatica e paradossi delle relazioni nel "de beneficiis" di Seneca.* Palermo.
Ramondetti, P. (1996) *Struttura di Seneca, De Ira, II–III: Una proposta d'interpretazione.* Bologna.
Reydams-Schils, G. (2005) *The Roman Stoics. Self, Responsibility, and Affection.* Chicago.
(2011) "Authority and agency in Stoicism." *Greek, Roman and Byzantine Studies* 51.2: 296–322.
(2017) "'Becoming like God' in Platonism and Stoicism," in T. Engberg-Pedersen (ed.) *From Stoicism to Platonism: The Development of Philosophy, 100 BCE–100 CE.* Cambridge: 142–58.
(2019) "How to Become Like God and Remain Oneself," in M. Niehoff and J. Levinson (eds.) *Self, Self-Fashioning and Individuality in Late Antiquity.* Tübingen: 89–104.
Reynolds, L. D. (ed.) (1977) *Seneca: Dialogi.* Oxford.
(ed.) (1965) *L. Annaei Senecae Ad Lucilium epistulae morales.* 2 vols. Oxford.
Richardson-Hay, C. (2006) *First Lessons: Book 1 of Seneca's Epistulae Morales – A Commentary.* Bern.
Richlin, A. (1992) *The Garden of Priapus: Sexuality and Aggression in Roman Humor.* New York.

(1996) "Producing manhood in the schools," in W. Dominik (ed.) *Roman Eloquence: Rhetoric in Society and Literature.* London: 90–110.
Rist, J. (1969) *Stoic Philosophy.* Cambridge.
(1989) "Seneca and Stoic orthodoxy." *Aufstieg und Niedergang der römischen Welt* 2.36.3: 1993–2012.
Roller, M. (2015) "The dialogue in Seneca's *Dialogues* (and other Moral Essays)" in Bartsch and Schiesaro (eds.) (2015) 62–75.
Rosati, G. (1981) "Seneca sulla lettera filosofica: Un genere letterario nel cammino verso la saggenze." *Maia* 33: 3–15.
Rosenmeyer, P. A. (2001) *Ancient Epistolary Fictions: The Letter in Greek Literature.* Cambridge.
Rosenmeyer, T. G. (1989) *Senecan Drama and Cosmology.* Berkeley.
Röttig, S. (2022) *Affekt und Wille: Senecas Ethik und ihre handlungspsychologische Fundierung.* Heidelberg.
Runia, D. (2008) "Philo and Hellenistic doxography," in Alesse (ed.) (2008) 13–54.
Russell, D. C. (2004) "Virtue as 'likeness to god' in Plato and Seneca." *Journal of the History of Philosophy* 42.3: 241–60.
Salles, R. (2005) *The Stoics on Determinism and Compatibilism.* Aldershot, UK.
(ed.) (2005) *Metaphysics, Soul and Ethics. Themes from the Work of Richard Sorabji.* Oxford.
Sampino, F. (2008) "'Beneficium', società e potere: Una lettura del *De Beneficiis* di Seneca," in G. Picone (ed.) *Clementia Caesaris: modelli etici, parenesi e retorica dell'esilio.* Palermo: 281–300.
Scarpat, G. (1965) *La Lettera 65 di Seneca.* Brescia.
Schafer, J. (2009) *Ars didactica: Seneca's 94th and 95th letters.* Göttingen.
(2011) "Seneca's *Epistulae Morales* as dramatized education." *Classical Philology* 106.1: 32–52.
Schiesaro, A. (2015) "Seneca and Epicurus: The allure of the other," in Bartsch and Schiesaro (eds.) (2015) 239–51.
Schmid, W. (1984) "Eine falsche Epikurdeutung Senecas und seine Praxis der erbauenden Lesung (Epic. Gnom. Vat. 60)" in *Ausgewählte philologische Schriften*, ed. H. Erbse and J. Küppers. Berlin: 151–266.
Schofield, M. (1983) "The syllogisms of Zeno of Citium." *Phronesis* 23.1: 31–58.
(1991) *The Stoic Idea of the City.* Cambridge.
Schönegg, B. (1999) *Senecas* Epistulae morales *als philosophisches Kunstwerk.* Bern.
Schoonhoven, H. (1980) *Elegiae in Maecenatem: Prolegomena, Text, and Commentary.* Groningen.
Schöpsdau, K. (2005) "Seneca über den rechten Umgang mit Büchern." *Rheinisches Museum für Philologie* 148.1: 94–102.
Schorn, S. (2009) "Tears of the bereaved: Plutarch's *Consolatio ad uxorem* in context," in Fögen (ed.) (2009) 335–65.
Schottländer, R. (1955) "Epikureisches bei Seneca." *Philologus* 99: 133–48.
Scourfield, J. H. D. (1993) *Consoling Heliodorus: A Commentary on Jerome, Letter 60.* Oxford.

Seal, C. (2021) *Philosophy and Community in Seneca's Prose*. Oxford.
Sedley, D. N. (1989) "Philosophical allegiance in the Greco-Roman world," in M. Griffin and J. Barnes (eds.) *Philosophia Togata: Essays on Philosophy and Roman Society*. Oxford: 97–119.
  (1998) *Lucretius and the Transformation of Greek Wisdom*. Cambridge.
  (1999) "Hellenistic physics and metaphysics," in Algra et. al. (eds.) (1999) 355–411.
  (2005) "Stoic metaphysics at Rome," in Salles (ed.) (2005) 117–42.
Segal, C. P. (1962) "Gorgias and the psychology of the logos." *Harvard Studies in Classical Philology* 66: 99–155.
Setaioli, A. (1988) *Seneca e i greci: Citazioni e traduzioni nelle opere filosofiche*. Bologna.
  (2000) *Facundus Seneca. Aspetti della lingua e dell'ideologia senecana*. Bologna.
  (2003) "Seneca e Cicerone," in E. Narducci (ed.) *Aspetti della fortuna di Cicerone nella cultura latina. Atti del III Symposium Ciceronianum Arpinas*. Florence: 55–77.
  (2007) "Seneca and the divine: Stoic tradition and personal developments." *International Journal of the Classical Tradition* 13.3: 333–68.
  (2009) "A recent book on Seneca and his conception of the self," *Ancient History Bulletin* 23: 70–84.
  (2014a) *"Epistulae Morales"* in Damschen and Heil (eds.) (2014) 191–200.
  (2014b) "Ethics I: Therapy, self-transformation, 'Lebensform'," in Damschen and Heil (eds.) (2014) 239–56.
  (2014b) "Ethics III: Free will and autonomy" in Damschen and Heil (eds.) (2014) 277–99.
  (2021) *"De ira* 2,18–36 De la prophylaxie au contrôle de la colère," in Laurand, Malaspina, and Prost (eds.) (2021) 119–49.
Sharples, R. W. (2007) "Peripatetics on happiness," in Sorabji and Sharples (eds.) (2007) 627–37.
  (2010) *Peripatetic Philosophy, 200 BC to AD 200: An Introduction and Collection of Sources in Translation*. Cambridge.
Sihvola, J., and T. Engberg-Pedersen (eds.) (1998) *The Emotions in Hellenistic Philosophy*. Dordrecht.
Smith, R. S. (2004) 'Review of *Die Vorstellung vom Willen in der Morallehre Senecas* by Rainer Zöller. *Bryn Mawr Classical Reviews*.
  (2014a) *"De Otio,"* in Damschen and Heil (eds.) (2014) 147–52.
  (2014b) "Physics I: Body and soul," in Damschen and Heil (eds.) (2014) 343–62.
  (2020) "Myth, poetry and Homer in Seneca *Philosophus,"* in Garani, Michalopoulos, and Papaioannou (eds.) (2020) 50–80.
Sorabji, R. (2000) *Emotion and Peace of Mind: From Stoic Agitation to Christian Temptation*. Oxford.
Sorabji, R., and R. W. Sharples (eds.) (2007) *Greek and Roman Philosophy, 100 BC – 200 AD (BICS suppl. 94)*. London.

Stevens, J. (2000) "Preliminary impulse in Stoic psychology." *Ancient Philosophy* 20.1: 139–68.
Striker, G. (1991) "Following nature: A study in Stoic ethics." *Oxford Studies in Ancient Philosophy* 9: 1–73.
Strozier, R. (2002) *Foucault, Subjectivity, and Identity: Historical Constructions of Subject and Self.* Detroit.
Sullivan, R. G. (2007) "Classical epistolary theory and the letters of Isocrates," in Poster and Mitchell (eds.) (2007) 7–20.
Summers, W. C. (ed.) (1910) *Select Letters of Seneca: Edited with Introduction and Explanatory Notes.* London.
Sykutris, J. (1931) "Epistolographie," in A. Pauly, G. Wissowa, and W. Kroll (eds.) *Paulys Realencyclopädie der classischen Altertumswissenschaft*, Suppl. 5. Stuttgart: 185–220.
Takaki, K. (2014) "Benefits and communication: Semiotics in Seneca's *De beneficiis.*" *History of Philosophy Quarterly* 31.4: 293–316.
Thraede, K. (1970) *Grundzüge griechisch-römischer Brieftopik.* Munich.
Tieleman, T. (2003) *Chrysippus' On Affections: Reconstruction and interpretation.* Leiden.
  (2007) "Onomastic reference in Seneca: The case of Plato and the Platonists," in Bonazzi and Helmig (eds.) (2007) 133–48.
  (2021) "Sénèque et les pré-passions," in Laurand, Malaspina, and Prost (eds.) (2021) 266–76.
Traina, A. (1974) *Lo stile drammatico del filosofo Seneca.* Bologna.
Trapp, M. (2007) *Philosophy in the Roman Empire.* Aldershot, UK.
Tsouna, V. (2009) "Epicurean therapeutic strategies," in J. Warren (ed.) *Cambridge Companion to Epicureanism.* Cambridge: 249–65.
Tsouni, G. (2017) "Didymus' epitome of Peripatetic ethics, household management, and politics: An edition with translation," in W. Fortenbaugh (ed.) *Arius Didymus on Peripatetic Ethics, Household Management, and Politics.* New York: 1–68
Usener, H. (1887) *Epicurea.* Leipzig.
Van Wassenhove, B. (2021) "Moral sententiae and progressor emotions in Seneca's philosophical works" *Classical Philology* 116.4: 613–23.
Veillard, C. (2022) (ed.) *Hécaton de Rhodes et la transformation de l'éthique stoïcienne: Les fragments.* Paris.
Veyne, P. (1993) "The final Foucault and his ethics," trans. C. Porter and A. Davidson. *Critical Inquiry* 20: 1–9 Reprinted in A. Davidson (ed.) *Foucault and His Interlocutors.* Chicago, 1997: 225–33.
Voelke, A.-J. (1973) *L'idée de volonté dans le Stoicisme.* Paris.
Vogt, K. (2006) "Anger, present injustice and future revenge in Seneca's *De Ira,*" in Volk and Williams (eds.) (2006) 57–74.
  (2020) "Seneca," in E. N. Zalta (ed.) *Stanford Encyclopedia of Philosophy* (Spring 2020 Edition), https://plato.stanford.edu/archives/spr2020/entries/seneca/.

Volk, K., and G. Williams (eds.) (2006) *Seeing Seneca Whole: Perspectives on Philosophy, Poetry and Politics*. Leiden.
von Arnim, H. (ed.) (1921–24) *Stoicorum Veterum Fragmenta*. 4 vols. Leipzig.
Vottero, D. (ed.) (1998) *Lucio Anneo Seneca: I frammenti*. Bologna.
Wachsmuth, C. (ed.) (1884–1912) *Ioannis Stobaei Anthologium*. 4 vols. Berlin.
Wagoner, R. (2014) "Seneca on moral theory and moral improvement." *Classical Philology* 109.3: 241–62.
Wardy, R. (1996) *The Birth of Rhetoric: Gorgias, Plato, and Their Successors*. London.
Warren, J. (2004) *Facing Death: Epicurus and His Critics*. Oxford.
Watson, P., and L. Watson (2009) "Seneca and Felicio: Imagery and purpose." *Classical Quarterly* 59.1: 212–25.
White, S. (2002) "Happiness in the Hellenistic Lyceum." *Apeiron Supplement* 35, 69–93.
  (2004) "Lyco and Hieronymus on the good life," in W. Fortenbaugh and S. White (eds.) *Lyco of Troas and Hieronymus of Rhodes*. New Brunswick: 389–409.
Wilcox, A. (2012) *The Gift of Correspondence in Classical Rome: Friendship in Cicero's Ad Familiares and Seneca's Moral Epistles*. Madison.
  (2020) "Seneca on Augustus and Roman fatherhood," in Garani, Michalopoulos, and Papaioannou (eds.) (2020) 23–49.
Wildberger, J. (2005) "Seneca and the Stoic theory of cognition: Some preliminary remarks," in Volk and Williams (eds.) (2006) 75–102.
  (2006) *Seneca und die Stoa: der Platz des Menschen in der Welt*. 2 vols. Berlin.
  (2014) "The Epicurus trope and the construction of a 'letter writer' in Seneca's *Epistulae Morales*," in Wildberger and Colish (eds.) (2014) 431–65.
  (2017) "Amicitia and Eros: Seneca's adaptation of a Stoic concept of friendship for Roman men in progress," in F. Zini and G. Müller (eds.) *Philosophie in Rom - Römische Philosophie?: Kultur-, Literatur- und Philosophiegeschichtliche Perspektiven*. Berlin: 387–425.
  (2021) "*De ira* 1,5–21 La raison et la colère: La réfutation de la métriopathie dans le *De ira*," in Laurand, Malaspina, and Prost (eds.) (2021) 56–82.
  (ed./trans.) (2007) *Seneca, De ira—Über die Wut: Lateinisch/Deutsch*. Stuttgart.
Wildberger, J., and M. L. Colish (eds.) (2014) *Seneca Philosophus*. Berlin.
Williams, G. D. (2012) *The Cosmic Viewpoint: A Study of Seneca's Natural Questions*. Oxford.
  (2014) "Double vision and cross-reading in Seneca's *Epistulae Morales* and *Naturales Quaestiones*," in Wildberger and Colish (eds.) (2014) 135–66.
Williams, G. D. (ed.) (2003) *Seneca: De Otio; De Brevitate Vitae*. Cambridge.
Williams, G. D., and K. Volk (eds.) (2015) *Roman Reflections: Essays on Latin Philosophy*. Oxford.
Willis, J. (ed.) (1970) *Macrobius: Saturnalia*. Leipzig.
Wilson, M. (1987) "Seneca's epistles to Lucilius: A revaluation." *Ramus* 16: 102–21.

(1997) "The subjugation of grief in Seneca's 'Epistles'," in S. Braund and C. Gill (eds.) *The Passions in Roman Thought and Literature*. Cambridge: 48–67.

(2001). "Seneca's *Epistles* reclassified," in S. J. Harrison (ed.) *Texts, Ideas, and the Classics*. Oxford: 164–87.

Winston, D. (2008) "Philo of Alexandria on the rational and irrational emotions," in Alesse (ed.) (2008) 201–20.

Wolkenhauer, J. (2014) *Senecas Schrift "De beneficiis" und der Wandel im römischen Benefizienwesen*. Göttingen.

Wray, D. (2009) "Seneca and tragedy's reason," in Bartsch and Wray (eds.) (2009) 237–54.

Zöller, R. (2003) *Die Vorstellung vom Willen in der Morallehre Senecas*. Munich.

Passages Treated

Aristotle, *Nicomachean Ethics*
  1.10: 113, 119
  10.7: 22
Arius Didymus ("Doxography C"), *by section and Wachsmuth page*
  1 (117.4–118.4]): 122
  8 (126.12–24): 122
  12 (129.19–130.12): 123
  13 (131.19–132.8): 123
  13–14 (132.8–12): 128
  14 (132.19–21): 123
  14 (132.21–133.2): 123
  14 (133.6–11): 123
  15 (137.4–5): 122
Arrian of Nicomedia, *Preface to the Discourses of Epictetus*
  5–8: 198

Callimachus, *Hymn to Apollo*
  110–12: 277
Chrysippus, *by SVF number*
  3.471 (Galen, *PHP* 5.2.22): 4
  3.697 (Diog. Laert. 7.121): 21
  3.702 (Plutarch, *Stoic Self-Contradictions* 1033d): 22
Cicero, *De Finibus*
  3.17–18: 22
Cicero, *Tusculan Disputations*
  2.17: 106
  3.12: 163
  3.32–33: 105
  3.83: 47, 166

Epictetus, *Discourses*
  1.4.31: 197
  1.26.16: 197
Epicurus, *Key Doctrines*
  4: 104, 105
  5: 94–5
  31: 95
Epicurus, *Letter to Menoeceus*
  125: 105
  135: 101

Macrobius, *Saturnalia*
  2.4.12: 259–61

Philo of Alexandria, *On the Migration of Abraham*
  156–57: 170–1
Plato, *Phaedrus*
  274e–277a: 199–202
Plato, *Republic*
  6.496cd: 23–4
  6.487cd: 24
Plutarch, *On Moral Virtue*
  449a: 165

Quintilian, *Institutio Oratoria*
  9.2.9: 13

Seneca, *On Anger*
  1.3.7–8: 48
  1.7.4: 138
  1.8.2–3: 139
  2.1.1: 140
  2.1.3–4: 140–1
  2.1.4: 141
  2.3.4: 157
  2.3.5: 141
  2.4.1: 142
  2.5.1–2: 143–4
  2.18.1: 147–8
  3.1.1: 150–1
  3.3.2: 152
  3.5.2: 153
  3.10.1: 154
  3.12.1–13.2: 156
  3.39–40: 158
Seneca, *On Benefits*
  1.1.9: 74, 77
  1.5.2–6.1: 59
  1.6.1: 68–9

2.31.1: 63
2.31.2: 69
2.32.3–4: 64
2.33.1: 65
2.35.1: 64–5
3.17.3–4: 69
4.2.1: 93
4.19.1–3: 92–3
4.26.1: 73
5.13.1: 112
5.20.1–2: 68
6.20.1–6.21.4: 77–9
6.23.1–2: 79
7.32: 75
Seneca, *On Clemency*
2.4: 152–3
Seneca, *On Happiness*
4.2–5: 54
4.5: 190
7.1: 95
9.1–3: 95
12.5: 94
13.2: 94
13.2–3: 227–8
15.2: 184
Seneca, *On Leisure*
1.1–8.3: 18–21
5.2: 22
5.4: 24
5.6: 23
6.1: 23
7.1: 98
7.2: 23
Seneca, *Letters on Ethics*
2.5–6: 99
6.5–6: 203–4
8.1–2: 28–9
8.2: 208
9.10: 96
12.3: 226
13.17: 90
16.1: 272
17.10: 10
19.1: 215
20.9: 100
21.2–5: 10
21.5–6: 279–80
21.10: 94
22.2: 207–8
23.2–3: 180
23.5–6: 180
23.9: 100
24.2: 106
24.18: 104
27.3: 183

29.10–11: 232
30.14: 104
33.1–2: 256–7
33.5: 258
34.1: 215
36.3: 273
38: 210–12
40.1: 205
45.2: 204
46.1: 90
46.1–3: 215–16, 249–50
47.21: 11
48.3: 96
48.5–7: 229
49.8: 228
50.6: 49
54.4–5: 105
56.1–3: 223–4
58.20: 31
58.25: 30
59.1–2: 179–80, 219–20
59.16: 183
63.1: 162
63.4–7: 173–4, 189
64.2–5: 216–17
64.6–8: 33
65.15–18: 33–4
66.1–6: 34–5
66.45–46: 96–7
67.2: 36, 39
68.1–2: 37
68.10: 37
71.17: 117–18
71.18: 118–19
71.24: 48
71.27: 53, 54
71.32: 49–50
71.36: 50
72.2–3: 272
73.5–8: 74
74.22: 120
75.3: 248
76.28–29: 182
78.18: 105
80.3–4: 50
81.3–7: 67–8
82.8–10: 231
84.1–2: 269–71
84.5–7: 275–6
84.8: 276–7
84.9–10: 280–1
84.11: 281–2
85.3: 114
85.24: 116–17
85.30–31: 113

Seneca, *Letters on Ethics* (cont.)
87.12: 112
87.38: 114
88.2: 273
88.5: 112
89.10: 115
92.1: 125–7
92.6: 129
92.6–10: 123
92.8: 52–125
92.14: 121, 127
92.16–17: 130
92.25: 122, 123–4
92.35: 251–2
94.41: 203
97.16: 103
99.2: 161
99.14: 162
99.15: 163
99.18–19: 164–5, 167–9
99.25–26: 107, 172–3
99.32: 162
100.8: 255
105.7–8: 103
109.4–5: 185
113.1: 31, 234
113.18: 49

113.20–22: 235–6
113.23: 62
113.25–26: 236
114.1: 241
114.3: 243–5
114.4: 242
114.5: 251
114.6–7: 242
114.14: 247
114.22: 246, 254
115.1–2: 247
116.1: 114
117.11: 115
118.13: 120
122.3–16: 224

Seneca, *Natural Questions*
1 *praef.* 3: 80
1 *praef.* 15: 92
2.6–7: 91
6.20.5–7: 90

Seneca, *On Tranquility of Mind*
2.4–5: 183, 208
3.1–8: 25
12.5: 48

Tacitus, *Annals*
14.53–56: 3

Index

Academy: New or skeptical, 24, 112
　Old, 118–19, 127
anger, 53, 135–59, 171, 214
animals, 43, 48, 78, 137, 234
Annaeus Serenus, 2, 14, 18, 89
Antiochus of Ascalon, 119
Antipater of Tarsus, 114, 120, 150, 192
aochlēsia (ἀοχλησία). *See* pain: absence of
apatheia (ἀπάθεια). *See* impassivity
Aristotle, 40, 57, 111–14, 118, 130, 137
Arius Didymus, 110
assent, 42, 47, 49, 79, 141, 146–47
Athenodorus of Tarsus, 25, 29
Augustine of Hippo, 195
Augustus, 259–61

benefits, 57–59, 184–86
　defined, 59
　in early Stoicism, 58
　in Epicureanism, 58, 96
breath (*pneuma*), 42, 49, 92

cavillatio, 229
children, 43, 71, 137, 148, 163
Chrysippus, 20, 62, 76, 253
　on benefits, 58, 60
　on emotions, 4, 47, 138, 165, 171
Cicero, 9, 100, 111, 195, 230, 255
Cleanthes, 58, 62, 245
consolation, 107
consolations, 8, 146, 160
contemplative life, 17–39, 97, 190
Crantor of Soli, 163
crudelitas, 152
Cynicism, 54, 164

death, 104–5, 163, 231, 278–80
determinism, 44, 50, 76
Diodorus of Tyre, 131
diseases of mind (νοσήματα), 46, 52
drunkenness, 246, 253

eclecticism, 87
emotions
　compete with reason, 45, 52, 125
　in Stoicism, 44–47, 137, 178–79, 218
　while reading, 199, 214
Empedocles, 196
Epictetus, 197–98, 230
Epicureanism
　ethics, 93–97, 227
　life of study, 19, 97–98
　physics, 91–92
　Seneca's knowledge of, 87–91, 101
　theology, 91–93
　use of maxims, 101, 233
Epicurus
　life, 88–89, 122
　style of writing, 256
　treatise on benefits, 58
eupatheiai, 46, 54, 168–72, 179

fate. *See* determinism
fear, 45, 117, 155, 165, 214
　in Epicureanism, 92, 102–6
　remedies for, 104–5
feritas, 143, 152
Foucault, Michel, 262, 265–69
freedom, 79–80
friendship, 55, 57, 68–69, 162, 168, 184–86
　in Epicureanism, 96
　in Stoicism, 47, 69, 217
function argument, 40

gods, 71–75, 80, 91–93
Gorgias of Leontini, 195
gratitude, 63–68, 72
grief, 107, 146, 162–64

Hadot, Pierre, 197, 265, 268
Hecaton of Rhodes, 58, 70, 192
Hieronymus of Rhodes (Peripatetic philosopher), 123, 131

Horace, 225, 278
humor
　incongruity, 223–24
　invective, 224–26
　logic puzzles, 228–31
　puns, 223–24
　satire, 223–24

illness, 24, 32, 34, 36
impassivity *(apatheia)*, 46, 54–55, 107, 114, 163
impressions, 42, 47–50, 140–41
impulse (ὁρμή), 43, 49, 141
ingenium, 243–45, 274–75
insanity, 143–44, 149, 152–53
Isocrates, 196, 210

joy, 46, 54, 68–69, 169, 176–92, 217
justice, 95, 103, 139

letters, 204–7, 213
Letters on Ethics, 9–11, 18, 27–38, 57, 98–102, 111, 160, 202–21, 223, 231–37, 279–80
logic, sophistical, 228–31
Lucilius Junior, Gaius, 2, 32, 161
　as addressee, 9, 210, 213, 279
　as author, 215, 249, 278, 280
　philosophical allegiance, 99, 233
Lucilius, Gaius (satirist), 225
Lucretius, 23, 91, 196, 278

Macrobius, 259
Maecenas, Gaius Cilnius, 3, 239, 241–43, 250–52, 259–61, 278
memory, 67, 105, 189, 199, 205
　in Epicureanism, 95, 173
　of the departed, 168, 173
Metrodorus, 58, 89–90, 106–7
　on grief, 173
mind
　of animals, 43, 48, 137
　directive faculty, 42, 62, 252
　material nature, 42, 46, 48, 171
　parts of, 124–27
mollitia, 242

Natural Questions, 80, 90–92, 111
Nero, 3, 57

On Anger, 51, 111, 135–59, 167, 214
On Benefits, 57–83, 93, 184, 231
On Happiness, 93–95, 189–90, 227
On Leisure, 17–27, 97–98
On Tranquility of Mind, 199, 208
otium, 17

pain
　absence of, 121, 123
　from torture, 106–7, 117–18
　in Epicureanism, 104–5
Papirius Fabianus, 255
Peripatetics, 7, 51, 58, 109–32, 137
Philo of Alexandria, 166, 171
Pindar, 277
Plato, 23–24, 34, 40, 44
　on writing, 196, 199–203, 278
pleasure, 121
　in contemplation, 22
　in Epicureanism, 94
　versus joy, 180, 220, 255
pneuma (πνεῦμα). *See* breath
political participation. *See* contemplative life
Posidonius, 24, 91, 114, 150
pre-emotions, 47, 52–53, 141–42, 164–67
pre-rehearsal of future ills, 105

Quintilian, 13

reading
　emotions in, 199, 214
　self-creation through, 264–66
　therapeutic, 195–96, 209–10, 233

satire, 223–26
selection, 22, 121
Seneca, Lucius Annaeus
　life, 2–3, 32, 36
　philosophical stance, 6–7, 87–88
　plays, 13–14
　poetry, 13–14
　therapeutic aims, 3–5, 27–30
　use of maxims, 98–102
　use of sources, 9, 110–11, 176–77, 191–92
　works, see *Letters on Ethics, Natural Questions, On Anger*, etc.
Seneca, Lucius Annaeus the Elder, 2, 13, 240, 248
Sextius, Quintus (Roman philosopher), 33, 216
slavery, 10, 70–71
soul. *See* mind
Stoicism
　determinism, 44
　emotions in, 44–47, 191
　ethics, 46, 121
　life of study, 19, 21–25
　metaphysics, 234
　paradoxes, 61, 63, 236
　theology, 71, 80, 92–93
　theory of action, 42, 62

studium, 269, 271–73
subtilitas, 31

tension, 252
Theophrastus, 58, 111
theōria (θεωρία). *See* contemplative life

verecundia, 248
Vergil, 279
vice. *See* diseases of mind (νοσήματα)
virtue, 49, 93, 95, 240, 252
    sufficiency of, 112, 115–16

virtus, 239
voluntas. *See* will

will, 44, 50, 60, 62, 75–76
    divine, 76–79
writing
    self-creation through, 262–63, 265–68, 275–77
    survival through, 278–80
    versus orality, 196–204, 210

Zeno of Citium, 20, 139, 197, 204, 231

For EU product safety concerns, contact us at Calle de José Abascal, 56–1°, 28003 Madrid, Spain or eugpsr@cambridge.org.